THE KAISER'S U-BOAT
ASSAULT ON AMERICA

Should there ever be a history of this U-boat war, this monstrous lie, it must reveal the lack of education and the stupidity of the militarists, and the rottenness of the entire chauvinist ruling class in Germany.

Diary of Kurt Riezler, Private Counsellor to the German
Reichskanzler, April 11, 1917.

THE KAISER'S U-BOAT
ASSAULT ON AMERICA

GERMANY'S GREAT WAR GAMBLE
IN THE FIRST WORLD WAR

HANS JOACHIM KOERVER

Pen & Sword
MILITARY

AN IMPRINT OF PEN & SWORD BOOKS LTD.
YORKSHIRE – PHILADELPHIA

First published in Great Britain in 2020 by
PEN & SWORD MILITARY
An imprint of
Pen & Sword Books Ltd
Yorkshire - Philadelphia

ISBN 978 1 52677 386 9

Typeset in Ehrhardt MT & 11/13
by Aura Technology and Software Services, India.
Printed and bound in the UK by TJ International Ltd.

Pen & Sword Books Ltd incorporates the Imprints of Pen & Sword Archaeology,
Atlas, Aviation, Battleground, Discovery, Family History, History, Maritime,
Military, Naval, Politics, Railways, Select, Transport, True Crime, Fiction,
Frontline Books, Leo Cooper, Praetorian Press, Seaforth Publishing, Wharncliffe
and White Owl.

For a complete list of Pen & Sword titles please contact

PEN & SWORD BOOKS LIMITED
47 Church Street, Barnsley, South Yorkshire, S70 2AS, England
E-mail: enquiries@pen-and-sword.co.uk
Website: www.pen-and-sword.co.uk

Or

PEN AND SWORD BOOKS
1950 Lawrence Rd, Havertown, PA 19083, USA
E-mail: uspen-and-sword@casematepublishers.com
Website: www.penandswordbooks.com

Contents

4 1916 – All Options on the Table

5 1917 – All-out Uboat Offensive and War with America

Appendix

Preface

There is more agreement among international historians on the assessment of the Second World War or the Napoleonic era than on the interpretation of the First World War. Even after 100 years, writing about the First World War remains an extremely challenging task.

I use broad strokes. My intended audience is the ordinary reader, who pursues the study of history to better understand the context of the present.

The Imperial Navy conducted indiscriminate submarine warfare in 1915 and 1916, often in direct opposition to orders from the Emperor or his Chancellor. The Imperial Navy's spiritual founder, Grand Admiral Alfred von Tirpitz, personally had a hand in the sinking of the *Lusitania* on May 7, 1915, and later of the *Arabic* and the *Sussex*. All of these were avoidable disasters for Germany's image and reputation, and did nothing to further an effective prosecution of the war. They occurred expressly against the wishes of Germany's Supreme Commander, Emperor Wilhelm II and his Chancellor, Theobald von Bethmann Hollweg.

These highly publicized incidents at sea pushed the German Empire to edge ever closer to war with the United States. Only energetic diplomatic intervention by President Woodrow Wilson in 1915 and 1916 prevented hostilities from breaking out at that time.

German Navy and Army blunderings deliberately provoked the April 6, 1917 entry of the United States into the First World War. Their intent was to rule out any possibility of a negotiated peace and to set the German Reich on a course for definitive victory or defeat. Defeat is what they got.

The militarism of Kaiser Wilhelm's Germany, and the refusal of his admirals and generals to submit to the primacy of politics, is a recurring theme throughout this history of German submarine warfare.

I have written this book for readers interested in a general history of the Uboat war, but it also offers professional historians an opportunity to explore the wealth of sources provided to further investigate my assertions.

For ease of readability, where quotations are not cited in their entirety, I have not used brackets ([...]) to indicate the omissions, but have instead compiled the quotations in a way that I hope is meaningful.

Acknowledgments

I wish to thank Mr and Mrs Bredow of the Uboat Archive in Cuxhaven, for their exceptionally warm and unbureaucratic assistance, also Monika and Franz Reinisch, Ronald Hopp, and Christoph Kehrig for their assistance and constructive criticism.

I would also like to express my gratitude to my history professor Prof. Dr. Klaus Schwabe, for his encouragement on my work and to Dr. Werner Rahn for all of his sound advice regarding literature and sources.

A further word goes to my friend Erik Juergen-Karl Dietrich, who untiringly stood ready to provide active support and advice, even at the most challenging moments.

About Me

I earned an MA in History in 1986 from the University of Aachen, Germany. Since 1989, I have worked as an IT Consultant. Previous books include:
Room 40, 2 vols.
German Submarine Warfare in the Eyes of British Intelligence

Hans Joachim Koerver, December 2018

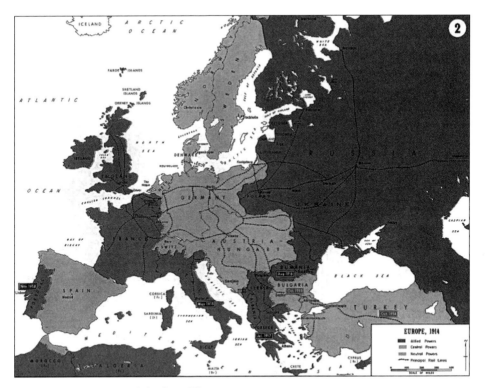

Europe at the Beginning of the Great War.

Allies / Entente: Great Britain, France, Russia, Italy (1915)

Central Powers: Imperial Germany, Austria-Hungary, the Ottoman Empire, Bulgaria (1915).

Neutrals: Sweden, Norway, Denmark, the Netherlands, Switzerland and Spain.

Primary Personnel

Woodrow Wilson (1856–1924), President of the United States 1913–21.

Edward Mandell 'Colonel' House (1858-1938), Wilson's closest advisor.

Kaiser Wilhelm II (1859–1941), German Emperor 1888–1918.

Theobald von Bethmann Hollweg (1856–1921), Imperial Chancellor 1909–17.

Grand Admiral Alfred von Tirpitz (1849–1930), Secretary of State of the Imperial Naval Office (RMA) 1897–1916.

Grand Admiral Henning von Holtzendorff (1853–1919), head of the Imperial Admiralty Staff 1915–18.

Erich von Falkenhayn (1861–1922), Chief of the Army General Staff 1914–16.

Paul von Hindenburg (1847–1934) Chief of the Army General Staff 1916–19.

Erich Ludendorff (1865–1937), Quartermaster general of the Army General Staff 1916–18.

Edward Grey, (1862-1933), British Foreign Secretary 1905-16.

David Lloyd George (1863–1945), British Prime Minister 1916–22.

Timeline

1914	4th Aug.	Outbreak of war between Germany, Russia, France, and Great Britain.
	5th Aug.	British blockade: all German ships are seized.
	20th Aug.	The Royal Navy stops neutral ships on the high sea.
	21st Dec.	Tirpitz interview about a German submarine blockade of the British Isles published.
1915	4th Feb.	Declaration of unrestricted submarine war to commence February 18th.
	7th May	Sinking of the *Lusitania*.
	19th Aug.	Sinking of the *Arabic*.
	19th Sep.	Complete suspension of German Uboat merchant war.
1916	26th Feb.	Unrestricted Uboat war.
	24th Mar.	*Sussex* torpedoed without warning
	20th Apr.	*Sussex* Note: Wilson insists on a complete halt to unrestricted submarine warfare.
	27th Apr.	Cancellation of the Uboat merchant war in the Atlantic.
	Sep.	Bethmann's peace feelers to Wilson.
	9th Oct.	Restricted Uboat war.
	12th Dec.	Bethmann proposes a peace conference.
	18th Dec.	Wilson's proposal for a negotiated peace.
	19th Dec.	Prime Minister Lloyd George refuses Wilson's proposal.
1917	9th Jan.	German decision for all-out Uboat war to begin on February 1st.
	22nd Jan.	Wilson's speech: 'Peace without Victory'.
	1st Feb.	Unrestricted Uboat war begins.
	3rd Feb.	Wilson breaks off diplomatic relations with Germany.
	1st Mar.	Zimmermann telegram published in the American press.
	16th Mar.	U-70 torpedoes the American freighter *Vigilancia* without warning.
	21st Mar.	Wilson's decision for war – a special session of Congress is convened.
	6th Apr.	American declaration of war on Germany.

Measures and Abbreviations

1 GRT (Gross Registered Ton) = 100 cubic feet (2.83 cubic meters space available for carrying cargo (freighters)

1 ton = total internal volume (warships)

1 kn = 1 knot = 1 nautical mile/h
1 nm = 1 nautical mile

RM = Reichsmark (1 RM 1914 corresponds 20 EUR 2018)
USD = US Dollar (1 USD 1914 corresponds 100 USD 2018)
GBP = Great Britain Pound (1 GBP 1914 corresponds 400 GBP 2018)
Currency conversion 1914: 1 GBP = 5 USD = 20 RM

Coastal Uboat – short-range submarine used in the coastal waters of the North Sea, the British Channel and the Adriatic.
Uboat – ocean-going submarines with a range of 5-10.000 nautical miles: All Uboats from U-19, UB-18 and UC-16 on.

1
PRE-WAR

Chapter 1

World Economy

In the decade before 1914, foreign-policy tensions and crises multiplied. The major European powers began to consider the question of the role of their national economies in a future war. The main question was how to maintain food supply and industrial production, if – as some pessimists expected – a modern mechanized war were to last not just a few months, but years.

For Great Britain's forty-six million residents imports came exclusively from overseas rather than over land. The value of these goods (15.7 billion RM) amounted to one third of the national income (46 billion RM).

The United States was an economic giant at this time on account of its large population and high productivity. It accounted for over fifty per cent of the global economic output. The American domestic markets of food, commodities and energy were self-sufficient and only depended on imports for special products. The export of surplus food and commodities financed these imports.

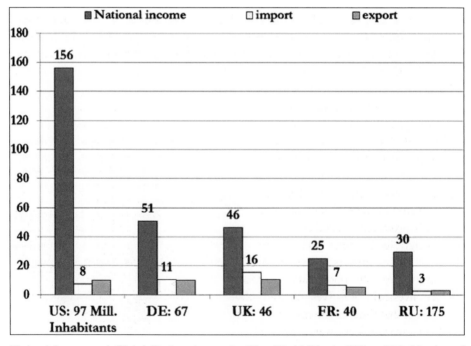

National Income and Global Trade prior to the First World War in Billion RM, Number of Inhabitants in Million.[1]

The national economies of the United States and Germany grew twice as fast as all others. In both nations, one-third each of the population was occupied in agriculture and in industry, the rest in trade, transportation, finance, administration, and other services. Germany, with its sixty-seven million people had overtaken England in industrial output. Seventy per cent of German imports came from overseas; it imported about twenty per cent of its food requirements, and most raw materials for its industry.

The German Empire produced one quarter of the worldwide demand for steel, while the United States accounted for half. Steel was the basis of transportation: railroad tracks, steam engines, locomotives, carriages, bridges, and ships. Machines, factories, and towering office buildings all required steel, as did warships, guns, and shells for munitions.

France and Russia ranked second to the major economic powers. Japan and Italy were developing countries that together produced only half of the 2.6 million tons of steel in Franz Josef's Austro-Hungarian Empire.

The numbers are staggering because they are so lop-sided. In 1913, world merchant fleets moved 335 million GRT in goods. Nearly one quarter of worldwide goods were shipped to England. Within the lifetimes of many of her inhabitants, Great Britain had changed into a highly industrialized country. From about 1850 on, farmers and agricultural workers became dock hands, sailors, miners, and factory workers. Food production had been 'outsourced' to overseas for the most part.

The country depended on imports. Loss of dominion over sea lanes meant famine. Admiral Lord Fisher described the situation as early as 1903: 'In the month of May, England has three days food in the country – in the month of September [after the harvest] there is three weeks food. Stop incoming food for a week or two, and the country must capitulate!'[2] More than one-third of all British imports were shipped under flags other than British.[3]

In 1914, Germany was self-sufficient in the production of carbohydrates and fat. But the cultivation of grains for bread, potatoes, and sugar depended on imported fertilizer. Stock breeding and milk production relied completely on foreign feed grains such as rye. Loss of these imports would, in the mid-term, lead to poor harvests and reduce livestock. Reserves of food did not exist at that time. In the case of disrupted trade in any significant way, famine in Germany was a real possibility, as well.

Steel Production in 1913, Million Tons.[4]

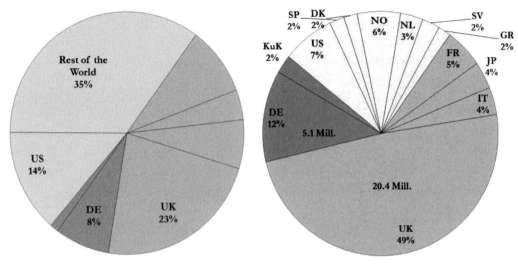

Above left: Oversea Imports in 1913: 335 Million GRT.[5]

Above right: World Merchant Fleet in 1913: 41.8 Million GRT.[6]

Industrial production, by contrast, had a reserve of materials to last several months. A war that lasted years, not just months, would rapidly lead to industrial standstill. Only in coal production, the primary energy source at that time, Germany and England were not only self-sufficient, but even exported.

The world's merchant fleet had more than 22,000 ships that exceeded 100 GRT by 1913. In all, tonnage amounted to 41.8 million GRT. Germany's commercial fleet of 5.1 million GRT was the second largest, lagging considerably behind Great Britain's 10,000 ships with 20.4 million GRT.[7]

Germany's merchantmen transported sixteen per cent of the global traffic – twice the amount of the country's own imports and exports. Small states (Belgium, Holland, Denmark, Norway, Sweden, and Spain) were collectively well-positioned, transporting together about one-third of the world's goods. The United States only possessed a relatively small merchant fleet of less than 3 million. GRT.[8]

Eight thousand large vessels of more than 1,600 GRT transported goods across the oceans, while the remaining 14,000 ships engaged in trade along the coasts. Sailing vessels still accounted for twenty per cent of the fleet and approximately ten per cent of the total tonnage. They found steady work in inter-coastal trade, as well as in the transportation of goods that were not constrained by timely deliveries, for example, wheat from Australia or nitrates from Chile. In contrast to the coal-fired steamboats, sail ships did not rely on the global British-French coal bunker network.

Ships and the seas were England's lifeblood. Britain transported nearly forty per cent of all goods worldwide. In 1912, her shipyards produced 1.9 million GRT

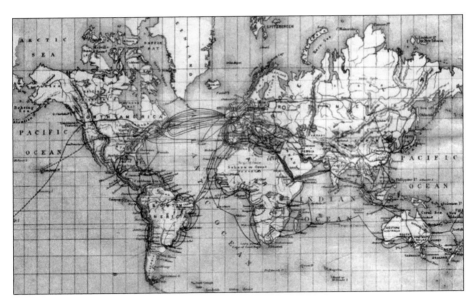

Submarine cable system in 1913.

in new construction of a worldwide 3.3 million GRT.[9] Profits on shipbuilding were high, British ship owners cashed in on valuable cargoes, British marine insurance, the monopoly of Lloyd's of London took in fat premiums, and British banks booked hefty profits on many levels.

Three quarters of the all transportation took place between northern Europe and North America. We can compare the transportation density of the time by analogy, using this map of the then-existing submarine cables:

Structure of the World Merchant Exchange

US historian Jonathan Clay Randel remarks about the communication system at that time: 'A trader without the telegraph was as helpless as a blind man.'[10] In 1914, the 'Victorian Internet' consisted of over 60,000 miles of seabed and land cables. This system connected all major cities on the globe with one another. Cables efficiently and quickly carried purchase and sales orders, news, and correspondence between private individuals, companies, banks, and governments.[11] Virtually all of these cables ran through London and were in the possession of British companies. International information exchange was a British monopoly.

There were only five independent German cable lines in 1914. Like all modern countries of the time, the German Empire increasingly relied on radio communications. It established the first radio transmission stations in 1913, to enable communications with remote receivers in America, Africa and Asia.

All warships and the most modern merchant ships had wireless transmission (W/T) apparatus onboard by 1914.

The Gold standard was the international monetary system at this time. Every unit of paper money corresponded to a firm, guaranteed exchange rate in gold that was on deposit at national central banks. If, for example, a European company wanted to purchase cotton in the United States, it had to pay on-site in USD. To obtain USD, they had to import another product, or even gold, to America, and convert the value into USD. This tangible barter of goods, or gold, automatically balanced trade. In the long run, no nation could export more than it could import, and vice-versa. Persistent high import deficits in a foreign currency had to be counter-financed by short-term foreign credits, and foreign currency credits were scarce and expensive in times of physically existing and limited currency and high interest. Consequently, a constant exchange rate was usual in the pre-war decades: 1 pound sterling (GBP) = 5 US dollars (USD) = 20 German Reichsmark (RM).

Global financial institutions enabled international trade. They bought up the debts of trading partners and settled them mutually, even in foreign currencies. The center of this business was London, where the banks effected daily transactions valuing several billion dollars. Key to this highly complex international commerce interchange was the worldwide telegram system.[12] Ownership of cargo could change hands several times during transit. For instance, ships could leave North American harbors with steel, wheat and cotton, without knowing whether they would call at Rotterdam, London or Hamburg, or to whom they would deliver the goods once there. Thousands of ships with millions of cargo loads crossed the oceans on a daily basis. It had become difficult to precisely determine the destination of specific cargo, or even its owner.[13]

The German Empire could not hope to protect its sea trade by military means. The Imperial Navy, the second largest fleet in the world, possessed no worldwide network of bases and coaling stations. England and France did. Its effective reach was essentially restricted to the North and Baltic seas. Even an overwhelming German North Sea fleet could never have prevented foreign cruisers from raiding commerce – a 'guerre de course' – intended to destroy German maritime commerce.

Chapter 2

Anglo-German Naval Arms Race[1]

Emperor Wilhelm II (1859-1941), in his craving for admiration, could change his opinion on a subject several times a day, depending on whomever had last spoken with him. The only – contradictory – constants during his reign were, in spite of his rumbling appearances on the world stage, his personal fear of a European war, and his wish for a 'large' fleet.[2]

Admiral of the Fleet Alfred von Tirpitz (1849-1930) was the polar opposite of the Emperor. Once a plan was developed, he carried it out in the face of any and all objections or facts. And he had but a single vision: the expansion of the Imperial Navy to become at least the second largest in the world, later referred to as the 'Tirpitz Plan' (Volker Berghahn).

There had been no humiliation or provocation by another power, no logical need, other than the combined will of these so radically different Siamese twins: from 1900 to 1914, Tirpitz quadrupled the German fleet from 256,000 to almost 1,000,000 tons.

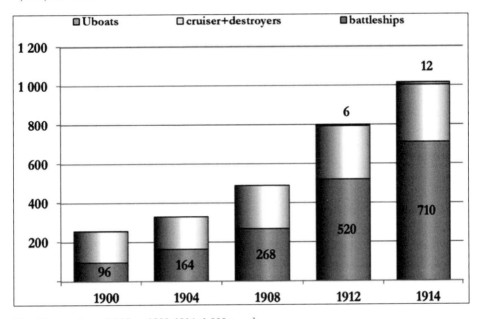

The German Imperial Navy 1900-1914: 1 000 tons.[3]

Germany's neighbors were alarmed, especially Great Britain. Winston S. Churchill, in his post-war history of World War I, wrote: 'All sorts of sober-minded people in England began to be profoundly disquieted. What did Germany want this great Navy for? Against whom, except ours, could she measure it, match it, or use it?'[4] For a war against France and Russia in the North Sea and in the Baltic, a German fleet with less than half of this strength would have been more than sufficient. Churchill observed: 'The British Navy is to us a necessity and, from some points of view, the German Navy is to them more in the nature of a luxury. Our naval power involves British existence. It is existence to us; it is expansion to them …'[5]

A German-British naval arms race commenced. Technical developments favored Germany in the beginning. Naval gunnery range and fire power increased steadily, and in 1905, the introduction of the steam turbine unleashed a new 'speed' revolution in warship propulsion.

Suddenly, it was possible to build bigger, faster, and better-armored warships. The HMS *Dreadnought* of 1906 was the first British battleship to incorporate revolutionary technical innovations. With a top speed of twenty-one knots, she had twice the fire power of any previously-built ships, now marginalized as 'pre-dreadnoughts'. The concurrent introduction of the *Invincible* class battlecruiser was equally important. It had overwhelming fire power and a twenty-four knot flank speed that was capable of out-running any other existing warship.

Speed was an extra form of life insurance. Speed determined whether a ship should engage with a weaker or distance itself from a superior opponent. The combination of speed with an increased gun range is like a boxing match between a heavyweight and a lightweight. The heavyweight holds the lightweight at a distance with his longer arms and can deliver more, and heavier blows than he has to absorb.

The 'Dreadnought revolution' made all other battle fleets in the world obsolete. These radical changes also compromised the heretofore unchallenged superiority of the British Navy. The naval armament's clock was set back to zero.

Tirpitz was quick to react: The first German dreadnoughts were put to sea in 1907. By 1909, twelve British and ten German dreadnoughts were either under construction or already in service. For one brief moment in history, it looked as though the Imperial Navy would be able to manage the establishment of a fleet equal to the Royal Navy.

Britain was abashed. The situation was not tenable. The Royal Navy doubled its construction program in 1909: It laid eight new dreadnought keels, rather than the four previously planned. The British Empire determined to keep a one-third superiority in battleship strength over the Imperial Navy – at any price.

It was a rule of thumb in maritime warfare that a fleet that was one-third stronger would be able to annihilate the enemy. Before the invention and deployment of radar and spotter aircraft, naval warfare had a duel-like quality to it.

There was no cover, there could be no true ambushes. Surprises were rare or happenstance. Ships sighted each other at about the same time on the open sea and opened fire at great distance with heavy artillery. To obtain the upper hand, England needed to build more ships than Germany. 'Two keels for one' became the slogan of Britain's naval building program – for each German dreadnought, two British would be built.

Tirpitz had to have recognized that England would never give in. In Jesuitical astuteness, he bent the following rule of thumb to continue German naval armament: As long as the Imperial Navy could count on maintaining at least two-thirds of the number of dreadnoughts the Royal Navy had, it would be too 'risky' for England to wage a war at sea with Germany; England would 'yield' and make 'concessions', and would even seek out an alliance with Germany.

Besides, other nations also had large fleets. Should Great Britain become involved in conflict with another maritime power, Germany would, as the not so innocent bystander, be able to throw its weight into the conflict.

The British countered this simple-minded Tirpitzian reasoning and approached France and Russia. Before Great Britain would allow itself to be virtually blackmailed by Germany in its own backyard, it preferred to make concessions to France and Russia in its colonial empire. The alliances of the First World War began to take form.

Great Britain, stressed by the financial burden of the armament, made diplomatic overtures to Imperial Germany in 1912. It sought to end the arms race. Under pressure from Tirpitz, the Emperor rejected the proposal. The entire German-British naval armament race was a sort of a 'Cuban crisis' in slow motion. If either of the main players blinked, a collision was inevitable.

Dreadnought fever spread worldwide. The fast-growing US navy threatened to relegate Germany to third place. France also began building a dreadnought class, Russia built battleships in their Baltic yards to fight against Germany, and in the Black Sea ports to fight against Turkey. Turkey ordered its own dreadnoughts from British shipyards, and Italy, as well as the Austro-Hungarian Empire, began to arm itself in earnest.

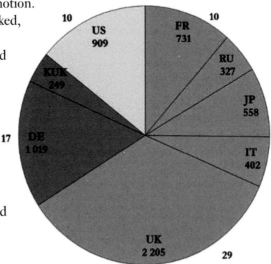

The War Fleets in summer 1914 (1,000 tons) and the Numbers of Dreadnoughts.[6] NB KUK is the Austro-Hungarian Empire

Even some German naval experts questioned the naval program with a priority for capital ships.[7] Long-range, fast-moving cruisers could damage an enemy's merchant ships on the high seas. Aircraft and Zeppelins were promising new reconnaissance weapons and could one day control the air. A single mine or torpedo could send the biggest ship to the bottom of the sea within minutes. Minelayers, torpedo boats and submarines became effective weapons.

Submarine technology developed rapidly at the beginning of the 20th century. Great Britain had sped up the submarine development as a cost effective defensive weapon to protect domestic coast lines and harbors. The construction costs of one battleship corresponded to that of twenty submarines. The highly competitive Diesel engine replaced the petroleum engine in 1909, and transformed the existing coastal submarine into an offensive weapon with oceanic range. In August 1914, Great Britain possessed seventy-two submarines, seventeen of which were high-sea Diesel-powered boats. Germany had fourteen coastal Uboats and fourteen modern Diesel boats in service.[8]

England consistently built more, and also stronger battleships than Germany, and had taken a new leap forward with the *Queen Elizabeth* class in 1912: these ships had double the firepower of the first dreadnoughts and, at twenty-four knots, nearly the same speed capability as traditional battle cruisers.

Tirpitz planned to surpass this accomplishment: fast-moving battleships, traveling at between twenty-seven to twenty-eight knots, would lead Germany out of the armament dead-end. At least until the next round in the armament race – the English commissioned ships in 1914 that carried seaplanes – the first 'aircraft carriers'.

But whatever the obstacle, Tirpitz would continue to build battleships until the end of his service as head of the Imperial Navy. We will see in the following chapters what consequences Tirpitz's priority for capital ships had on the submarine war.

In the summer of 1914, the German Chancellor and the Foreign Office began to fear the plan was leading Germany into a checkmate, or at least very close to it. Billions of RM had flowed into a naval fleet strategically to England, while the army, urgently in need of armaments against Russia and France, had its budgets slashed. No one dared to openly admit the truth about what was so patently clear to even the most casual observer: that Britain could not be beaten in the naval arms race.

Naval propaganda had oversold itself in the years leading up to the war. Consequently, most conservatives in the German parliament rallied behind Tirpitz, who had unleashed an unparalleled propaganda campaign using his Naval Press Office.[9] Battleship construction had become a matter of national prestige. A close confidant of the Imperial Chancellor, Kurt Riezler (1882-1955),[10] noted in his diary that any critic of the boundless and pointless battle fleet construction who dared to express himself publicly would be torn apart 'by the Navy's press mob'. Furthermore, he would incur the 'opposition of the Emperor and the parliament, as well as public opinion'.[11]

Theobald von Bethmann Hollweg (1856-1921), Imperial Chancellor from 1909 to 1917, tried in vain to come to terms with England. Riezler reported on the situation during the July 1914 crisis, just days before the outbreak of war: 'Did it have to come to this? The Chancellor, with his conscientious self-martyrdom, is considering his own possible mistakes. Whether, in 1912, he should have insisted on his resignation, submitted but rejected after the Emperor had decided in favor of Tirpitz [rejecting the English proposal on arms limitations]. Then Tirpitz, or some other politician of this sort, would have become Chancellor. Many say that Tirpitz is hindering any agreement with England only because he wants to enact it himself, as the new Chancellor. But he will not be able to accomplish this, because no one [outside the country] trusts him. The man is generally a puzzlement – he knows precisely that with all his dreadnought construction, our relative strength to England will not change at all, because the English can and will always build twice as much. An eminent organizational talent, a dyed-in-the-wool politician, however, very cunning in his methods and completely without integrity. For Tirpitz, the Navy is an end in itself.'[12]

Naval Merchant Blockades

In contrast to naval military discussions, based on simple algebra – numbers, guns, speed and range of warships –, the debate over maritime trade rules during hostilities was judicial and diplomatic. International powers modified long-established maritime law at the International Naval Law Conference in London in 1908.

A hostile state could be cut off from sea trade through an internationally-declared blockade. For such a blockade to be effective, all harbors and all coastlines had to be blocked continually and completely.

Enemy merchant ships were allowed to be engaged anywhere on the ocean, but neutral vessels were only allowed to be stopped within the declared blockade zone.

Cargos of neutral ships seized in this zone were to be divided into:

a) absolute contraband: products with exclusively military use, such as weapons and ammunition
b) conditional contraband: goods with military as well as civilian use, e.g., commodities such as copper, which was utilized in both the civilian and military areas
c) goods on the 'free list', which listed everything else, e.g., food.

Neutral ships with cargo contained on the free list (grain, for instance) were permitted to pass through the blockade zone to reach a hostile destination. Cargo that included weapons or ammunition was considered contraband, and would be confiscated. The ship was then labeled a 'blockade-runner' and seized. With conditional contraband (such as potassium nitrate, which could be processed into fertilizer as well as explosives), the neutral ship was seized, and the cargo declared a 'prize of war' by a court specifically empowered to decide whether or not cargo should be seized or released. No matter what the decision, the neutral vessels themselves remained free after conclusion of the procedure.

Heated discussions broke out over the question of contraband. Germany wanted to see raw materials on the free list. Great Britain was opposed, asking: 'what then can we seize?'[13] The question remained unresolved. A high-ranking English naval officer put the matter succinctly: 'I suppose contraband of war is whatever the strongest party chooses to make it.'[14]

The procedure for seizing a merchant ship was unequivocal: The naval vessel hoisted flag signals to demand the other ship to stop. If the vessel did not stop or delayed, the man-of-war had the option of lobbing warning shots across the bow. The naval ship had to provide safety of the crew and passengers. It could take them on board or put them in lifeboats and assist in reaching the nearest shore. Cargo was the object: the goods, not the ship or the human beings aboard. Spilling the blood of sailors or passengers, especially women and children, would have been considered unthinkably barbaric and was absolutely forbidden

Interestingly, none of the major powers ratified the 'Declaration of London'. They did not want their hands tied in the future. A basic consensus existed in August 1914 regarding central issues, such as the seizing of ships under cruiser warfare rules, also called 'prize law'. There was, however, significant room for interpretation of individual definitions, such as 'contraband'. In the event of a war, all of these undecided details would inevitably lead to serious conflicts between combatants and neutral countries.

War Planning – Great Britain

Great Britain started to work out detailed plans for war with Germany in 1906. The British naval command decided that a sea blockade could force Germany to its knees.[15] The German armament industry had sufficient supplies of domestic coal or iron, but food production depended heavily on imports. The British naval attaché in Berlin summarized his country's strategy in January 1907 as 'starving Germany into submission by destroying her sea-borne trade'.[16]

A 'continental' strategy – an intervention that supported France with British troops – complemented the 'Atlantic' one in 1908. British statesmen feared that Germany could overrun France, as it had in 1870. Such a development would render the long-term 'Atlantic strategy' ineffective, since it forced Britain to deal with a Germany in possession of French resources and coastlines.[17] Hence, Great Britain was determined to use its small army on the continent as early as possible in a looming conflict in order to prevent the defeat of France.

Simulated German Uboat Blockade around the British Isles.[18]

In view of the increasingly powerful defense weapons in coastal waters (mines, torpedoes and, at least initially, submarines), the British Admiralty did not want to risk its capital ships in a dangerous close blockade, but decided on a less costly distant blockade. The British navy planned to close the English Channel as well as the North Sea between Scotland and Norway with minefields and naval vessels to block German access to global trade. Even if this distant 'blockade' was undefined by international law, it fulfilled the same purpose as a coastal blockade as defined by the London Declaration: to cut off Germany from international trade.

The most serious problem with this plan was the fact that Britain could not legally seize ships flying neutral flags in international waters. British Admiral 'Jackie' Fisher thundered in December 1908: 'MIGHT IS RIGHT and when war comes we shall do just as we jolly well like. No matter what your laws are! We've got to win and we ain't going to be such idiots as to keep one fist tied behind our back! There's a law against sinking neutral merchant ships but we should sink them – every one! We can pay two or three millions indemnity afterwards if willing but we shall have saved about 800 millions in getting victory and getting it *speedily*.'[19]

Submarines presented a promising new blockade weapon. England and Germany both envisaged deploying submarines in close coastal and harbor blockades. The Royal Navy planned to deploy thirty-six Diesel submarines for blocking the German North Sea harbors,[20] and, on the German side, a naval study from May 1914 calculated that the German navy needed 222 submarines to cut off sea trade to the British Isles.[21]

This internal staff study turned out to be purely a game on paper: The Imperial Navy possessed only a handful of modern long-range, but largely untested, Diesel submarines at that time.

War Planning – Imperial Germany

If the German Empire wanted to wage war, whether offensively or defensively, it would have to be a very short war. A long war meant starvation. Victory at sea against the Royal Navy was improbable and quick success against the vast Russian Empire equally unlikely. In view of German dependence on food imports, and faced with a menacing merchant sea blockade by the Royal Navy, a quick, decisive war was the best – perhaps the only – option. The Army Chief of Staff, Count Alfred von Schlieffen, had already prepared for such an eventuality in 1905.

Schlieffen had worked out a solution: the so-called 'Schlieffen Plan', that involved a rapid campaign against France. The Russian-French stranglehold would be broken, and Germany would have free access to the 'world oceans' through its control of the French coastlines.

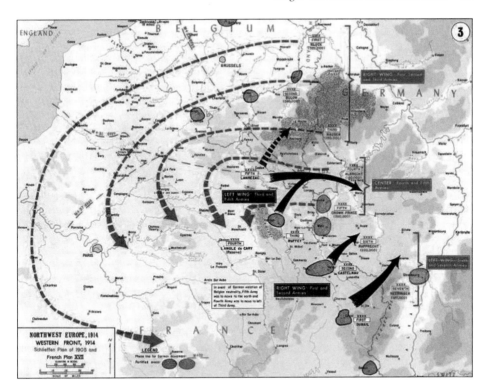

The Schlieffen Plan.[22]

Tirpitz biographer Raffael Scheck explains the situation for the German Imperial Navy: A victory over France would ensure bases in the Atlantic and the French colonial empire. And, just as in 1871, Germany could extort enormous financial reparations from France, which it could use for further naval armaments. Thus strengthened, Germany could then defeat England one day, in a 'Second Punic War'.[23]

The Army was so certain of victory that it even refused operational support from submarines in the English Channel to disrupt British troop transports bound for France. In the view of the Chief of Staff, firmly convinced of victory, the more British soldiers came across, the better. Riezler tells of Moltke's answer to Bethmann Hollweg's question, at the beginning of July 1914, regarding the chances of a war: 'He said yes! We will be successful.'[24]

The real problem with the 'Schlieffen Plan' was that it was no 'plan', based on existing numbers of troops, operable at the touch of a button, but only a 'simulation'. Schlieffen had calculated the number of German divisions necessary to be able to conclusively defeat France in 1905. His computational superiority existed only on paper. In terms of numbers, the German Army never achieved superiority over the French Army.[25] Responsibility for this lay squarely at the feet of Tirpitz, with his insatiable naval ambitions. It was the Navy that received the biggest share of budget resources. It was a risky gamble – if the Schlieffen Plan was to succeed, and victory was to be gained, the Army would need to pull off a miracle.

And America?

Woodrow Wilson (1856-1924) became American president in 1913. In the first two years of his presidency he concentrated mainly on internal reform programs. His closest advisor Edward Mandell 'Colonel' House (1858-1938), took care of American foreign policy.

House was Wilson's political alter ego. He never held an official function, but acted solely in his capacity of a private person and confidant of the President, the only individual who had the complete trust of the President. Wilson said about House: 'Mr. House is my second personality. He is my independent self. His thoughts and mine are one. If any one thinks he is reflecting my opinion by whatever action he takes, they are welcome to the conclusion.'[26]

House developed a direct personal diplomacy especially with British diplomats and politicians which helped in 1913 to defuse potential conflicts between the two powers in the western hemisphere. He corresponded directly with US ambassadors in London and Berlin.

House regarded the situation in Europe with sorrow, especially the conflict between England and Germany as manifested in the Naval Arms race. His idea was a general disarmament in Europe. In May, 1914 he visited London and Berlin trying to bring about an understanding with a view to peace.

On May 27, 1914 he met Admiral Trirpitz for a private hour. 'Von Tirpitz and I talked largely of armaments, I pleading for a limitation in the interest of international peace and he stating vigorously the necessity of Germany's maintaining the highest possible order of military and naval organization. He disclaimed any desire for conquest and insisted it was peace that Germany wanted, but the way to maintain it was to put fear into the hearts of her enemies.'[27]

On June 1, House met the Kaiser: 'I found him much less prejudiced and much less belligerent than von Tirpitz. He declared he wanted peace because it seemed in Germany's interest. 'She was menaced on every side. The bayonets of Europe were directed at her', and much more of this he gave me. I told him that the English were very much concerned over his ever-growing navy, which taken together with his enormous army constituted a menace; I told him that the President and I thought perhaps an American might be able to better compose the difficulties here and bring about an understanding with a view to peace than any European, because of their distrust and dislike for one another. He agreed to this suggestion.'[28]

Nothing came out of the idea when House visited Paris and London. His impression of the situation in Europe as described to the President: 'The situation is extraordinary. It is militarism run stark mad. There is too much hatred, too many jealousies. Whenever England consents, France and Russia will close in on Germany and Austria. England does not want Germany wholly crushed, for she would then have to reckon alone with her ancient enemy, Russia; but if Germany insists upon an ever-increasing navy, then England will have no choice. The best chance for peace is an understanding between England and Germany in regard to naval armament, and yet there is some disadvantage to us by these two getting too close.'[29]

The editor of the House Papers, Charles Seymour: 'What Colonel House soon realized was that in Germany there was a sense of fear as well as aggressiveness, the fear of the man tortured by uncertainty and ready to jump at the throat of the first who seemed to move. Conscious of the enmity which it had aroused, Germany kept its revolver cocked and would let it off at the least whisper.'[30]

At a dinner with the British Foreign Secretary, Sir Edward Grey, on June 17, 1914 House eaborated on his impressions of Germany: 'I told of the militant war spirit in Germany and of the high tension of the people, and I feared some spark might be fanned into a blaze. I thought Germany would strike quickly when she moved; that there would be no parley or discussion; that when she felt that a difficulty could not be overcome by peaceful negotiation, she would take no chances but would strike. I thought the Kaiser himself and most of his immediate advisers did not want war, because they wished Germany to expand commercially and grow in wealth, but the army was militaristic and aggressive and ready for war at any time.'[31]

When he finally sailed back to America in mid-July, the crisis leading to the outbreak of the Great War had already been set in motion.

The risky Schlieffen plan finally failed. In the First Battle of the Marne in September, 1914, the German offensive ground to a halt. Military planning proved to be a house of cards and the long-awaited war had arrived.

2
AUGUST 1914 – MELTDOWN

Chapter 3
Great Britain

Pre-war conservatives believed that interlocking royal family relationships among the ruling monarchies in Europe would prevent any war. Equally delusional, socialists thought that the international solidarity of the working class would make war impossible. Ever-clever economists were no less deluded in their belief that world economic integration and dependence would make a great war inconceivable. They were all mistaken.

According to historian Nicholas Lambert, the economic 'meltdown' in England began when Austria handed an ultimatum to Serbia on July 23, 1914.[1] Industry immediately feared war between Austria and Russia. Stock traders expected that Germany would intervene, which made an entry into the conflict by France and Great Britain likely.

Sales orders flooded the financial markets. Everyone wanted liquidity in the case of a global war, and that in gold. Bankruptcy not only threatened private banks, but the central banks of the nation states also experienced a global bank run. Within days, stock exchanges and financial institutions in London, Paris and New York closed. Currency exchanges, gold transfers and all international financial dealings came to a halt. And this happened before the first shot had been fired or war had even been declared.

Businesses could no longer afford to finance exports and imports. Factories closed, goods piled up in ports and ships lay idle. Winston Churchill, First Lord of the British Admiralty and eyewitness to the economic chaos, noted on July 31, 1914: 'The city has simply broken into chaos. The world's credit system is virtually suspended. You cannot sell stocks and shares. You cannot borrow. Quite soon it will not perhaps be possible to cash in checks. Prices of goods are rising to panic level.'[2]

Just before the war started, the risk of interrupted critical food imports threatened England. Leading British politicians feared famine, recession, unemployment, social unrest, even revolution. On August 3, Cabinet Minister Lord Esher stated: 'The chief fear that haunts ministers appears to be not the naval or the military situation, but the inevitable pressure of want of employment and starvation upon the operatives; this may lead to a highly dangerous condition of affairs.'[3]

War with Germany began the next day. The fear of riots forced the cabinet to keep two of the planned six divisions scheduled for deployment in France on the home front.[4]

The Grand Fleet concentrated in the Scottish harbor of Scapa Flow. England unquestionably ruled the Sea but it recognized that even if the Royal Navy destroyed the German High Seas fleet, the war might still not be decided. French Prime Minister Georges Clemenceau once remarked that the annihilation of the Imperial Navy would leave a nice whirl in the North Sea, but it would not win the war.[5]

Churchill remarked that the Grand Fleet could lose the war on one fateful afternoon. He deemed risky excursions into the mine-infested waters off the German coast too dangerous. In return, the Royal Navy would attack the German fleet as soon as it ventured into the North Sea. It waited two years for this to happen, but at the battle of Jutland in May 1916, the only engagement of the two opposing capital fleets, the outcome was not decisive.

From August 5, 1914 on, British cruisers patrolled the English Channel and the waters to the north of Scotland and seized German merchant ships. On August 20, the British government published the first blockade regulations. The Royal Navy began to confiscate contraband on neutral ships bound for Germany. Only neutral vessels with goods specified on the free list were permitted to reach German harbors. Stopping and boarding neutral ships in international waters and accompanying them to British harbors for search and seizure was not in compliance with the Declaration of London. The British also kept ships with foodstuffs until the freight was spoiled or the shippers agreed to sell it. This procedure was more than just illegal on the level of the Declaration of London, but defied all maritime law. Only the superior strength of the Royal Navy made the enforcement of the blockade possible.

A British Cabinet minister summarized the British strategy at the end of August 1914: 'We decided that we could win through by holding the sea, maintaining our credit, keeping our people employed and our industry going – by economic pressure, destroying Germany's trade, cutting off her supplies.'[6] Britain's economy recovered quickly and production soon exceeded pre-war levels.

Great Britain also needed to address the possibility of Germany purchasing conditional contraband, for example copper, oil and cotton, from neutral agents in neutral countries such as the United States, and shipping the cargo on neutral ships to Europe's neutral harbors. German agents then could buy and transport the shipments by rail or ship to the Fatherland. This concept was called 'continuous voyage' and pointed at the final destination of the goods. It was not included in the regulations of the London Declaration and thus became an important topic for discussion in the British Cabinet.

The British blockade policy at the beginning of the war was anything but logical. For instance, in August 1914, large amounts of wheat departed New York for Holland on neutral ships. How was a 'free list' product on a neutral ship bound for a neutral harbor, but which might ultimately find its way to the enemy, to be treated? Seize the neutral ships? Mine neutral Dutch or Swedish harbors? Some ships had their cargos confiscated, while others reached their neutral destinations.[7] Procedures varied. In the Holland example, Britain accepted the formal guarantee of the Dutch government to prevent the resale of imported goods to Germany.[8]

Chapter 4
Imperial Germany

On July 31, the Imperial War Department placed the navy on alert. More than 250 units readied themselves for war: Thirty-eight battleships, forty cruisers, and more than 170 destroyers, torpedo boats, and other vehicles. The twenty-four submarines represented but a small fraction of this fleet.[1] The Imperial Navy's main combat strength lay in its capital ships of the High Seas Fleet in Wilhelmshaven, might dreadnoughts, cruisers and destroyers.

But by Imperial order, this High Seas Fleet was to remain passive. There would be no sorties in search of battle. Submarines, minelayers and torpedo boats were the weapons of choice. Their task was to generate enemy losses until reaching a balance of power with the Royal Navy.[2] The German battle fleet stayed moored. Thus, the German government tacitly acknowledged the inferiority of the High Seas Fleet and the failure of Tirpitz's strategy.

The declaration of war against Russia came in the late afternoon of August 1, 1914. That same evening, Emperor Wilhelm believed that he recognized signs that England would remain neutral during a purely German-Russian conflict. To the horror of Army Chief of Staff Count Helmuth von Moltke the Emperor halted the Army's build-up in the west. Moltke left the meeting in a fit of rage, 'blue and red in the face', and broke out in sobs – 'fickle William' had 'cancelled' the Schlieffen Plan: World War I had been aborted!

Kaiser Wilhelm II.

Hours later news from London shattered the Emperor's hope, and the westward march of the Army for the attack on France began as originally planned.[3] The First World War commenced! The mood among the generals lifted, and champagne corks popped. Prussian Minister of War Erich von Falkenhayn (1861-1922) told the Chancellor on this occasion: 'Even if we should perish – what joy we have experienced!'[4]

Kaiser Wilhelm II was Commander of both the Army and Navy, but there was little strategic cooperation between them. Historian Christopher Clark described: 'Even during the first years before outbreak of war virtually no arrangements had been made for coordinated operations of the army and the navy, and no attempt was undertaken to synchronize strategies carefully to the options which were pursued by the German diplomacy. Germany remained strategically driverless in this regard.'[5]

The Army Chief of Staff von Moltke (1848-1916) tried to shield the troops from the Emperor's incalculable interventions as best he could. The Prussian aristocrats, the noblemen, ran the Army in reality.

However, with the Navy, things were substantially different. Emperor Wilhelm II had, at Tirpitz's request, dissolved the Navy's supreme command in 1899.[6] This shift subordinated a dozen naval institutions directly to the Emperor. According to Clark this deliberate strategy created a direct and unchecked command structure for the Kaiser.[7]

But the Kaiser was unable to lead. Wilhelm's daily routine vacillated around the navy, world power politics, domestic policy, travel, historical paintings, and card games. Whoever was able to gain the Emperor's ear usually got what they wanted. One day, he commanded the navy to build more Uboats, the next day, to construct new battleships. He intervened sporadically down to the lowest level in every naval affair. As naval historian Granier wrote:

'Weak nerves and hysteria, an inability to perform serious and disciplined work, and a notorious reluctance to make difficult decisions hindered the monarch from effective leadership of his Navy.'[8] Further: 'With this polycracy [*sic*], even in peace time, tensions and strategic chaos in the country's leadership were inevitable. During a war, this could only have catastrophic results.'[9] After the war, historians wrote articles with titles like 'L'anarchie navale Allemande',[10] or spoke of 'improvisation',[11] or even of a 'bureaucratic balkanization'[12] of the German Imperial Navy.

The Naval Cabinet under Admiral Georg Alexander von Müller (1854-1940), was responsible for human resource affairs of the navy. Because of his permanent presence at the Imperial Court and direct

Admiral Georg Alexander von Müller.

personal access to the Emperor, von Müller played an important role in all naval questions. He was in fact something like the ambassador of the navy at the Imperial Court.

The Naval Admiral's Staff under Hugo von Pohl (1855-1916), and later Gustav Bachmann (1860-1943) and Henning von Holtzendorff (1853-1919), was responsible for the operational planning.

The High Seas Fleet Command under Friedrich von Ingenohl (1857-1933) and later Hugo von Pohl and Reinhard Scheer (1863-1928), commanded the main armed forces of the navy, including the bulk of the submarine force.

The Imperial Navy Office (Reichsmarineamt – RMA) under Assistant Secretary Admiral of the Fleet Alfred von Tirpitz and his successor Eduard von Capelle (1855-1931), was responsible for construction, liaison with the parliament, financing, and long-term planning of the navy. He was formally subordinate to the Chancellor of the Reich; however, in truth, it was the most powerful and autonomous of all naval institutions under the Kaiser.[13]

The Imperial Chancellor, Theobald von Bethmann Hollweg, head of the government and the Foreign Office, generally exerted a tempering influence on Wilhelm's naval policy – to the major annoyance of the naval departments. He had to try to coordinate all the divergent wishes of navy, army, Ministry of Finance,

Above left: Admiral Alfred von Tirpitz.

Above right: Chancellor Theobald von Bethmann Hollweg.

and the Foreign Office, and to keep control over each of these more or less uncoordinated branches of government. It was the permanent squaring of the circle.

High above the fray floated Tirpitz. He had direct access to the Emperor at all times. The public considered him the 'father' of the German Navy, which he had expanded during the last sixteen years from a modest coastal navy to the second-largest fleet in the world. He was the spider in the web, holding all the threads, and the unofficial Supreme Commander of the fleet. In the political circles of Berlin, Tirpitz's ambitions for the position of Imperial Chancellor were an open secret. To his great disappointment, the Kaiser did not nominate him Supreme Commander of the navy at the outbreak of war. Wilhelm named him only 'Adviser' to the Admiral's Staff. He became a 'consultant to the consultant' to the Emperor in naval questions.

It was evident at the beginning of the war that Emperor Wilhelm lacked power as Chief of Fleet. He had planned to use the fleet in the Baltic against Russia, but his admirals had refused.[14] Riezler wrote: 'The Navy will wage war only against England, and has refused every operation in the Baltic Sea.'[15] Against the will of his admirals, Wilhelm could accomplish nothing. With regard to the Emperor's fickleness, evidenced in the near-cancellation of the Schlieffen Plan, the Admirals decided, with resolute independence, to move forward.

At 8 a.m. on August 2, the Chief of the Admiral's Staff, von Pohl, arbitrarily ordered the opening of hostilities against Russia in the Baltic Sea.[16] 'The SMS *Augsburg* and SMS *Magdeburg* left on August 2 just before 9:40 a.m., with three cheers for His Majesty the Emperor, and steamed away at high speed. They bombed the [Russian] naval port of Libau from 7:51 to 8:12 p.m.'[17]

When the Navy took action, the question of a declaration of war against France was still undecided and England's position uncertain. Had the Imperial Navy fired the first shots of the Great War with the twenty-one-minute bombardment of Libau in the evening of August 2? Kaiser Wilhelm was informed of the sortie only after it happened.[18]

Ten thousand kilometers to the east of Berlin, in the German naval base of Tsingtao on the eastern Chinese coast, the small cruiser *Emden* opened hostilities against Russia in the Far East on August 3 with the seizure of a Russian steamer. Immediately following the declaration of war against France on August 3, two German cruisers in the Mediterranean shelled French harbors in North Africa.

The Navy attacked vigorously, and acting on personal initiative. From a military perspective, these attacks were bee stings, but in the still open and undecided diplomatic situation during those first days of August, they were for other nations unmistakable signals of the Navy's – and Germany's – lust for war. In creating a fait accompli, the Navy had effectively excluded another 'mood swing' of Emperor Wilhelm. Was this the intention of the fleet commanders?

The English declaration of war followed on August 4, 1914. The Great War had begun.

The first submarine campaign against the Grand Fleet in the North Sea in August 1914 was unsuccessful and caused heavy losses: 'The failure of the submarines was a disappointment [for the Kaiser].'[19] The navy mined the German Bight. A maritime trench war began, in which German and British minelayers and minesweepers, destroyers, and cruisers clashed sporadically. At the first engagement between British and German scouting units at the end of August, three German cruisers sank near Heligoland.

The war of attrition turned out to be a failure. The British Grand Fleet had no intention whatsoever of satisfying Germany and venturing into the mine-infested waters off the German North Sea coast.

Germany's economy

By the end of July, more than 1,000 large German merchant vessels with 3.9 million GRT were at sea.[20] During the following weeks, the Entente captured 900,000 GRT. Some 1.4 million GRT evaded marauding British navy cruisers and sought safe haven in North and South American parts and another 1.3 million GRT in Asian ports. Germany retained a home fleet of 1.6 million GRT for trade in the Baltic and the North Sea. Thus, the second largest merchant fleet in the world disappeared from the oceans. Within weeks, the capacities of worldwide ocean-borne trade decreased by over ten per cent.

German banking and financial sectors were less dependent on foreign capital than Great Britain, and survived the first weeks of the war comparatively unharmed. However, the mobilization of the army reduced the workforce drastically. German economic performance decreased about twenty-five to thirty per cent and remained mired at this level for the entire war.

The Kaiser and his court meanwhile welcomed early reports of the army's advances. The military dominated, and political objections had to step back. Riezler reports typical statements from army staff officers at this time: 'Anything is possible with, or by, force.'[21] And: 'An orgiastic militaristic esprit generally prevails here.'[22] With the hurried advance of the army came massacres of the civilian population in Belgium and northern France. People as far up as the Chancellor's office knew about the atrocities, but accepted them tacitly. Riezler noted: 'Executions in small towns, all men from 16 to 60 years old, thousands shot on the meadows, every tenth corpse lay a step ahead. The women had to bury them. No one dares to say anything against military necessity.'[23]

By the middle of September, the Blitzkrieg in France had failed. In the Imperial Headquarters, a 'very low-spirited' mood suddenly reigned. Chief of Staff Moltke had collapsed with a nervous breakdown, and evenings with the Emperor became 'very subdued.'[24]

A 'great hangover' began. Months later, Riezler noted in his diary: 'All of the original planning was undone by the Battle of the Marne.'[25] And: 'Everything hinged on the Battle of the Marne. If we had won there, everything would have been fine.'[26] The Army had miscalculated the war plan: von Falkenhayn replaced von Moltke.

The front lines bogged down in trench warfare, the High Seas Fleet lay idly in harbor, Germany was cut off from international cable communication, the Allies would soon sack her colonies, her merchant fleet had disappeared from the oceans, and badly needed imports were not forthcoming.

Tirpitz came under pressure to justify himself. He first hid behind the Emperor's order issued at the beginning of the war not to use the battle fleet. However, as time passed, he began to let on more and more loudly that this happened against his will and that an immediate deployment would have held more promise of success. He then cemented the typical Tirpitzian post war legend that the government had kept the fleet in harbor against his will.

Riezler noted in his diary at the beginning of October 1914: 'Tirpitz (the father of the lie) and the Uboats. This disastrous person with his battle fleet! Today, rather than his useless huge ships, we should have small cruisers, etc.!'[27] Moreover: 'The father of the lie is making sure that he is not blamed for the idiotic battle fleet politics. He seemingly apologizes, but continues, however, with his bald-faced lies. Tirpitz shields himself behind the Chancellor because at first he had wanted to save the fleet. If the Chancellor were to say, "deploy", he would backtrack at once.'[28]

In his post-war memoirs, Tirpitz maintained that holding back the fleet had happened against his demands. There is enough evidence in the navy files to prove that no one ever considered what would have been a suicidal attack on the Grand Fleet. The figures were unequivocal.[29] Tirpitz biographer Raffael Scheck writes: 'The picture emerging from the wartime documents and the postwar polemics shows a nervous Tirpitz, who feared that his life's work would be destroyed either through battle or through avoidance of battle. With his back to the wall, he gave contradictory messages.'[30]

For the Imperial Navy a first bright spot in the horizon came on September 22, 1914. Submarine U-9, under Lieutenant-Commander Otto Weddigen, sank three British cruisers within one hour off the Dutch coast. Admiral Müller reported from the Imperial Court: '... the first news of the smashing success of U-9 against three English armored cruisers. We are thrilled, and the Emperor is blissfully happy.'[31]

A technically outdated submarine with a crew of thirty-five had sunk three cruisers with more than 2,000 men on board: 1,400 of them drowned. The German propaganda hailed Weddigen as the new 'Achilles'.

The German fleet was in dire need of heroes. Could the submarines represent a new opportunity for the Imperial Navy?

Chapter 5

Communication

On August 5, 1914, British ships cut the German overseas cables in the North Sea and evicted Germany from the international telegraph cable system. Sending of encoded telegrams from Germany was still possible by Wireless/Telegram, but only non-coded telegrams could be sent from neutral countries, as, for example, from the German embassy in Washington via American radio transmitters.

Sweden came to Germany's assistance in August 1914, and secretly made the Swedish Foreign Ministry's telegraph cable system available to the German Foreign Office. Daily, several dozen coded telegrams went out from Berlin to the German Embassy in Stockholm and from there, via the Swedish diplomatic cable network, to the German Embassy in Washington and back again. Diplomatic communication with other neutral states worked the same way.[1]

It took the British until May 1915 to catch wind of this 'Swedish detour', since all Swedish telegrams ran through London. However, they did not exert pressure on Sweden to give up this truly 'non-neutral' assistance until the fall of 1917. In the meantime, they profited from the decoding of these telegrams.

No one in Berlin knew that the British had come into the possession of the most important German code books and could thus decipher most German messages. The story of the secret code originates in 1914, when on August 28 the German cruiser *Magdeburg* ran aground in bad weather off the Russian coast in the Baltic Sea. In the wreck of the *Magdeburg*, the Russians discovered two German code books. Russian naval officers handed one of the codes directly to the British First Sea Lord Winston Churchill.[2]

Code is a fixed combination of figures and letters that precisely define a certain word. Cypher (or also written cipher) is a mathematical 'translation' of the code, which occurs at particular time intervals, in accordance with previously-established mathematical algorithms. The weakness of this procedure is that certain words appear over and over with a statistical likelihood, e.g., 'ship, route, north, south, stormy west winds, 7 knots' etc. Any talented crypto-analyst could decipher such an encrypted message after a time. But if he was in possession of the code books with the keywords, he would be able to decode in real time.

Churchill immediately recognized the value of the abandoned code books. On November 8, he formed the British Admiralty's cryptology department, 'Room 40', a team of mathematicians, philologists, crossword puzzle lovers, and naval officers who possessed a working knowledge of the German language.

From the end of 1914 until the end of the war, they deciphered almost the entire German naval W/T, in total more than 200,000 messages.

The German Foreign Office and its embassies in neutral countries also used the cyphering method of the '*Magdeburg* codebook' to exchange diplomatic and other messages. The exposure of Mata Hari and the discovery of the Zimmermann telegram in 1917 represented merely two isolated results of the deciphering of German diplomatic messages.

The British side was also able to decode German commercial telegrams concerning purchases in neutral countries. This advantage became apparent in mid-1915, when the British 'intelligence community' systematically checked up to 50,000 telegrams per day for suspicious companies, dealers, goods and financial transactions. They began to decipher and analyze obviously suspicious messages.[3]

In 1915 and 1916, this intelligence analysis substantially contributed to unmasking the network of German cover companies and agents in neutral countries. Britain now could determine the true 'final destination' of goods and their financing, solving the 'continuous voyage' dilemma.

However, the most important immediate effect of the deciphering was the work of Room 40 with respect to anti-submarine warfare: 'As soon as a Uboat began to operate in our waters, her presence and her position were known, as a rule, first vaguely by wireless or other information, and then in some detail a day or two later when attacks were reported or when survivors from sunk ships had been landed and questioned.'[4]

A chain of wireless receiving stations along the British coastline could determine the transmission site of a W/T message within approximately fifty miles and allowed rough positioning. 'Other information' referred to the deciphered radio messages of the Uboats, which sent out their positions by wireless every four hours on their journey through the North Sea. When they re-entered the North Sea from an operation in the Atlantic, submarine commanders filed detailed reports with the home station on the sunken tonnage and special incidents.

At first, all that information rarely had a direct tactical effect on fighting hostile submarines. Only a handful of the approximately 170 German Uboats lost in combat during the war resulted from the efforts in Room 40.

It often took half a day before a destroyer arrived at the last known Uboat position. By that time, the submarine was already 100 sea miles away, perhaps submerged somewhere in a circle of 30,000 square sea miles.[5] The airplane played no role in the naval sea war at this time: there was still no radar, and, instead of the active sonar (ASDIC) used in the Second World War, only passive, short-ranged hydrophones were available. Depth charges were not invented until 1916. The only anti-submarine weapons available in the first years of the war were mine barriers, artillery, and rams. Admiral Beatty, commander of the British battle cruisers and, later, of the entire Grand Fleet, summarized the initial helplessness in anti–submarine war: 'It is a prodigious job, as it is like looking for a needle in a bundle of hay, and, when you have found it, trying to strike it with another needle.'[6]

Still, the British Admiralty stayed informed about the number of available German submarines throughout the entire war, their cruises and the Uboat armament program. Not without justification Room 40 thus summarized its significance in 1920: 'It must be borne in mind that in this, as in every other aspect of the naval war, the British had an advantage over the Germans due to a circumstance which it is highly improbable could ever occur again in any future war.'[7]

Chapter 6
Neutral Countries

Europe

The neutral European states were from the beginning of the war involved in the re-export of goods of all kinds to Germany. Individual countries sold their entire domestic food and raw material production at top prices, only to cover their own needs at world market prices with oversea imports.[1] The profit from trade with Germany was simply too tempting – food sold for double the world market price, aluminum for triple the value, and copper, quadruple.[2]

At the end of September 1914, four times the typical annual Dutch copper imports were shipped from the US to Rotterdam. Denmark, Norway, and Sweden tripled their general imports.[3]

United States of America

At the end of July 1914, Europeans sold their investments on the US stock exchange on a massive scale. Everyone was in need of dollars or, better yet, gold. The British pound and the French franc were exchanged for US dollars by

US President Woodrow Wilson.

the millions; on July 31 their exchange rates fell by thirty per cent. On the same day, Wall Street shut its doors for months, and the US government outlawed the exportation of gold. A three-month economic recession followed in the United States. Wall Street did not reopen until November of 1914.[4]

The recession triggered a transportation crisis. The German merchant fleet had accounted for sixteen per cent of the total world transportation. When it disappeared from the oceans within days after the beginning of hostilities, the world's transportation capacity decreased by roughly ten per cent. The relatively small US merchant fleet of three million GRT could not compensate for the missing capacities. American President Woodrow Wilson feared on July 31 that grain and cotton, the main exports of the American economy, would rot in the warehouses or even on the fields, as no one would be able to get them to European markets.

The Wilson administration evaluated the possibility of buying the German ships interned in America and operating them under the Stars and Stripes. But Great Britain opposed the plan, citing a regulation under the London Declaration: combatants did not have to recognize a flag change after the commencement of a war. The Royal Navy treated every German ship seized after August 4, 1914, even if sailing under another flag, as a hostile ship subject to confiscation. An enlargement of the 'neutral' merchant fleets using formerly enemy ships to facilitate German indirect imports did not, of course, suit Britain.

The US government succeeded in taking over about 372,000 GRT of interned German ships in North and South America, mainly oil tankers, which it used exclusively in the western hemisphere under the tacit tolerance of the Royal Navy.[5] Only if it was to their advantage did Britain exploit ambiguities in London Declaration regulations.

Cotton accounted for one quarter of American exports. Germany had purchased approximately twenty per cent of the entire harvest in 1913. The 1914 harvest in October and November 1914 was a bumper crop. By the end of 1914 cotton bales had piled up in US ports. Prices dropped by half, far below production costs. Four million workers in the American South were directly affected.[6]

Great Britain had major doubts about allowing cotton to get through to Germany. The Germans had to provide clothing for millions of soldiers. Without cotton, there would be no uniforms, and a by-product of cotton processing was gun cotton, an important ingredient in the production of explosives.

The tensions brought on by the blockade grew. At the end of September Colonel House discussed with the President the seizure of American vessels by Great Britain: 'Wilson read a page from his [book] 'History of the American People', telling how during Madison's Administration the [British-American] War of 1812 was started in exactly the same way as this controversy is opening up. The passage said that Madison was compelled to go to war despite the fact that he was a peace-loving man and desired to do everything in his power to prevent it, but popular feeling made it impossible. The President said: "The circumstances of the War of 1812 and now run parallel. I sincerely hope they will not go further." I told the British Ambassador about this conversation. He was greatly impressed.'[7]

Great Britain let Wilson know by mid-October, 1914 that England would rather risk war with the United States than give in on the general blockade question. On the cotton situation, however, it was prepared to soften. In the US no one wanted war, and cotton was the most pressing problem. The two countries compromised.[8] Twenty American cotton freighters should pass the British blockade during March 1915 to call on Bremerhaven. Directly or indirectly, the German Empire obtained approximately seventy-five per cent of its pre-war cotton imports from the United States.[9]

Prior to the war, the German chemical industry was a worldwide leader. In the area of dyes for the textile industries six large German companies formed the 'dye trust', responsible for 70% of global production. The United States produced only 10% of the world's manufactured dyes via American subsidiaries of the dye trust, and was dependent on large imports of German primary products. At the outbreak of the Great War, the German government issued an export ban on these products to ensure that the war economies of the Allies would not profit.

American ambassador James W. Gerard reported from Berlin in November, 1914: 'We still have lots of work. I have been especially engaged in getting cotton in and chemicals and dyestuffs out. We have to have [German] cyanide to keep our mines going and dyestuffs to keep endless industries, and the Germans know this and want to use this as a club to force us to send cotton and wool in. So they only let us have about a month's supply at a time.'[10] It would take years to increase American dye production to overcome the dependency on German imports.

Even if the important transportation crisis had been eased and the cotton and dye problem seemed to be solved for the moment, the basic problems caused by the British blockade intensified further. On October 20 the British government published new blockade regulations (Order of Council): The Order declared all raw materials and industrial commodities absolute contraband.

Wilson did not yet lodge a formal protest. His biographer, Arthur S. Link, wrote: 'In those troubled times, Britain was mistress of the seas in fact as well as in name; with one arm of her fleet she could keep the Imperial Navy at bay and with another exercise a watchful control over the sea lanes from the New World to western Europe.'[11]

British maritime power was a fact. The Royal Navy's actions to stop neutral ships in international waters was as illegal as the blockade of food imports to Germany, but the blockade methods the navy used – flag signals, warning shots, research and seizure – corresponded at least in form with traditional maritime law. The President of the United States, in view of a public supporting strict neutrality, did not risk any conflict with Great Britain in favor of Germany. With the British, Wilson hoped for compromise on individual issues, even if it took harsh diplomatic protest to reach it.

After the war, the British Foreign Minister, Edward Grey, described the Cabinet's line of thinking: Since Germany was far less dependent on imports than Great Britain, it was better for England itself to continue the war without the blockade than to break with the United States, and to deprive itself of all access to American resources. 'The object of diplomacy, therefore, was to secure a maximum of blockade that could be enforced without a rupture with the United States.'[12]

Finally, toward the end of 1914, large orders for ammunition and other military goods started coming in from the Allies, reversing the recession of the American economy. American Secretary of State William Jennings Bryan had maintained in August 1914, 'Money is the worst of all contrabands.'[13] Now, private banks could extend credit to the European powers, the lion's share of which, due to their appetites for supplies and transportation possibilities, benefited the Allies.[14]

Link wrote: 'The President and his advisers were simply learning to accept the most important economic consequence of neutrality, which was the development of a large war trade between the United States and the Allied countries.'[15]

US exports rose four-fold until the end of 1914.[16]

Ménage à trois – Triangular Relations

For both war camps the neutrals posed special problems; they always had to keep in mind their important role in trade, transportation, and production.

And America was in a class of its own. Its economic power had exploded in the last decades. No reasonable statesman could neglect their overwhelming importance in the world economy.

Since the outbreak of the war, Wilson viewed a negotiated peace between the Europeans as the ideal solution. The US President had no interest in the complete victory of one of the two blocks, the Entente or the Central Powers under German leadership, whose new, unrivaled power position in Europe would only release energy for overseas expansion, perhaps, for instance, in the South American backyard of the United States.[17]

The US President had already brought up the idea of an 'association of nations' in August 1914. A League of Nations seemed to him the best guarantee for a future peaceful world order.[18]

Mediation of a negotiated peace as an 'honest broker' was one of the major themes of his foreign policy in the coming years, but from the beginning it was regarded with mistrust on the European end.

The Allies asked themselves about the price to pay for this 'help' and what peace it would be – some kind of a *Pax Americana*, with an 'Open Door' for competing

American goods and capital imported into their Empires?[19] In Britain, America was not regarded as a friend – it was a rival. The US Navy had just overtaken the German Fleet in size, and was still growing. But the Allies had become increasingly dependent on US-sourced war materials and Wilson's goodwill. Allied leaders never forgot 'that Wilson had it in his power, by a stroke of the pen, to hamper seriously the Allied war effort.'[20] They were in a dilemma.

German leadership on the Western Front complained that American-manufactured munitions had intensified Allied fire power. Moreover, imported war materials made factory workers in Britain and France available for conscription. Everybody in Germany who wanted to discredit Wilson's peace ideas only needed to point to this, implying that the US was abetting her enemies.

American ambassador James W. Gerard reported from Berlin in January, 1915 to the President: 'I do not think that the people in America realize how excited the Germans have become on the question of selling munitions of war by Americans to the Allies. A veritable campaign of hate has been commenced against America and Americans. [Foreign Under Secretary] Zimmermann showed me a long list of orders placed with American concerns by the Allies.'[21]

At this time there were 5 million German-Americans living in the United States who openly supported pro-German war propaganda, and the large Irish community could be counted on in their anti-British feelings. Zimmermann continued, so said, 'that in case of trouble there were five hundred thousand [military] trained Germans in America who would join the Irish and start a revolution. I thought at first he was joking, but he was actually serious.'[22]

US industries and exports were troubled. European immigrants were split in their sympathies for the Allies or the German camp. By 1915 America had become a distant, largely invisible, participant on the European battlefieds. Wilson had to act carefully.

Chapter 7

British Blockade and German Uboats

The British Cabinet began to diversify its naval strategy at the end of 1914. The Admiralty tried to establish a strict blockade. The Foreign Office raised objections against it for fear of conflicts, especially with the United States. The Trade and Agriculture ministries tried to promote as many exports as possible, so as to be able to pay for imports with the income, even at the risk of indirect trade with the enemy through re-exports by neutrals.[1] From a financial perspective, it made more sense to accept the re-exportations to Germany rather than risk a trade deficit, which would have destabilized the exchange rate of the pound and raised the price of imports from foreign-exchange countries.[2]

The blockade was extremely porous. Products from the free list were allowed to pass. To deal with Germany's indirect contraband trade with neutral countries, Great Britain could only attempt to exert diplomatic pressure on the neutral European states to limit re-exportation to Germany; it possessed, however, no method of overseeing or preventing this. British Admiral Jackie Fisher confessed: 'We really are stupid in our funk of neutrals.'[3]

The Admiralty admitted this feeling internally: 'In effect, therefore, we had waived a part of our undoubted rights as regards conditional contraband in exchange for the possibility of inducing the neutral governments to prohibit the export of all contraband articles to which we attached importance.'[4] This policy had been designed as a concession to the United States.[5]

Action against the indirect trade of neutral governments with Germany was also unsystematic. British blockade cruisers confiscated every load of copper, so that by the end of December 1914, nearly all of its exporters had come to an arrangement with England. The worldwide copper trade now took place under British control; its export to Germany, directly or indirectly, came to a virtual standstill.[6]

Even the definition of contraband among the Allies caused enormous difficulties. France refused to put its aluminum on the list, Canada its nickel, England its tin, and the Foreign Office wanted to exclude nitrates (used in fertilizer and production of explosives), so as not to annoy Chile. The Allies did not want to weaken their exports, even with the risk that these resources indirectly reached Germany via the neutrals.

On November 5, 1914, Great Britain declared the entire North Sea a 'war zone', i.e. a military restricted area; in December the Royal Navy removed all buoys and navigational markers, and in January, vast minefields were laid. Now, to ensure safe passage through the North Sea, ships from neutral governments had to call at English harbors and take pilots aboard.[7]

The domestic pressure in England was even greater than the problem to prevent indirect trade from the neutral countries to Germany: 'This government has more protests from its own shippers and merchants than it has from all neutrals combined.'[8] The monopolist Lloyd's of London insured the entire neutral trade, while British banks financed it.

The historian Nicolas A. Lambert wrote in 2012: 'One might well argue that the greatest untold scandal of the First World War – though admittedly the case is largely circumstantial – was the degree to which contraband trade through neutral countries was financed by the City of London and carried across the Atlantic in British ships.'[9] For the duration of the entire war, it was impossible for the British government to mend these holes in the British financial system: the resistance of the banks was simply too strong.[10] In the beginning of January 1915, a British banker confidentially admitted in a letter to a friend: 'If the financing of contraband trade via Scandinavia by certain financial houses in London were discontinued, the contraband trade would collapse. It is perfectly sickening to think that these banks are making profits at the expense of our soldier's lives.'[11]

Great Britain prepared for a long war in the beginning of 1915. In order to finance imports, England had to export. However, millions of men served in the armed forces, diminishing the domestic work force. Exports decreased as a result. Due to the mounting trade deficit, the exchange rate for the pound collapsed, while cargo rates and food prices rose, threatening to affect Britain's social structure.[12]

On January 22, 1915, Prime Minister H. H. Asquith stated: 'There is no doubt that we are at least beginning to feel the pinch of war, mainly because all the German ships which used to carry food are captured or interned, and the Admiralty has commanded for transport etc. over 1,000 of our own. Further, the Australian crop has failed & the Russian (which is a very good one) is shut up, until we can get hold of Constantinople & open the Black Sea.'[13] The Prime Minister explained that it was cheaper to storm the Dardanelles than to organize and subsidize a state-supported grain program.[14]

German Path to the Uboat War

The submarines of the High Seas Fleet came under the command of the 'Leader of the Uboats', Commander Hermann Bauer on August 30, 1914.[15] Due to their limited range, the outdated Koerting Uboats U-5 to U-18 could operate only in the North Sea. In the first two years of the war, less than two dozen modern Atlantic submarines (U-19 upward) were available. Due to their limited range of only two to three days at sea, the thirty-two coastal submarines in the UB-I and UC-I classes played only a marginal role in the trade war taking place in the waters between Holland and England. The German navy had ordered these subs in August 1914. Beginning in spring 1915, they patrolled the coastlines from stations in Flanders.[16]

German naval leaders regarded the declaration of the British blockade on October 20 and the war zone declaration on November 5, 1914, as the opening of an outright economic war.[17] This generated lively discussions over countermeasures. The Chief of the Admiral's Staff, von Pohl, believed that seven submarines would be sufficient for a blockade of England, even if they were not constantly on blockade service: 'Just the enforcement of the blockade for a few days will achieve the desired success.'[18] Now the discussion pivoted – as in England – on the question: declare a blockade or a war zone?

Within a blockade zone, naval warfare would have to be conducted according to the Prize Rules of the London Declaration. Then, every neutral ship within the blockade zone might be stopped and examined, and, in case of a 'blockade break', the cargo could be confiscated. But a handful of submarines operating part-time could not be regarded as an 'effective' blockade according to London Declaration. The Admiral's Staff assumed that even 'our own Prize Courts would judge this blockade to be ineffective.'[19]

The only alternative was the declaration of a 'war zone', but the question of the treatment of neutral ships in a war zone was completely undefined.

Discussions among political leaders, the navy and the army were on-going, when, on December 21, 1914, Tirpitz, in a newspaper interview with an American journalist, floated the up-to-then incomplete plan for a submarine commerce war with the international public: 'What will America say if Germany declares a submarine war against all hostile merchant ships? England wants to starve us: we can play the same game. Surround England, torpedo every English ship or those of its allies that approaches any harbor in England or Scotland, and thereby cut off the majority of the food supply.'[20] Tirpitz used the expression 'iron curtain of submarines', which the German propaganda took up enthusiastically.

The most popular admiral of the Imperial Navy explained his plans in front of the world. This, to say the least, unusual action engendered serious criticism from the German leadership.

Admiral von Müller told of the reaction in the Imperial Headquarters: 'Big excitement about an interview released in the American newspapers that Tirpitz had given, primarily about submarine trade war against England.'[21]

And from von Pohl: 'Extremely unfortunate, that our military plans have been disclosed,'[22] and: 'The publication in the press is, for military reasons, also very concerning. Now, the English can prepare countermeasures well in advance. Moreover, it is wrong to already draw the attention of the public to our intentions, without having any certainty that our military means will be sufficient to carry out a Uboat war against England.'[23]

Riezler stated: 'Tirpitz has given an interview to the United Press, where he anticipates the idea of a blockade of England, and tries to cover up the collapse of his battle fleet politics by proposing a Uboat war; von Pohl is furious about this. Moreover, Tirpitz is allowing himself to be celebrated as the future Chancellor.'[24]

Tirpitz biographer Scheck writes: 'Tirpitz, however, believed [the submarines] should be deployed as effectively as possible, and he decided to reveal its potential to the press. He wanted to test American reactions to the prospect of unrestricted submarine warfare, distract domestic attention from the inactivity of the battle fleet, and arouse popular pressure against the reticence of the Chancellor. Depicted as the strongman in the German government and as Bethmann's probable successor, Tirpitz again found a naval issue that could mobilize a broad spectrum of the German public. Even newspapers usually siding with Bethmann put high hopes in them [Tirpitz's proposals]. Under Tirpitz's influence, the Naval Office provided the press and right-wing politicians with biased information about the potential of the submarines and helped unleash a public campaign for unrestricted use of the Uboats and against Bethmann.'[25]

In his post-war memoirs, Bethmann Hollweg added: 'Publicly, the enemies were advised to prepare for a Uboat blockade; publicly, the German people were made aware of their possession of an infallible weapon. From this point on, it was impossible to tear submarine warfare from the heart of the nation.'[26]

England and her allies were warned; the neutral countries became aware of a submarine merchant war and began to have concerns. In Germany, Tirpitz's interview unleashed a publicity storm. The Pan-German and rightist newspapers, fed by Tirpitz's Naval Press Office, began to propagate the idea that there was a means to conclude the war triumphantly, but that the Emperor and his Chancellor stood in the way. Tirpitz had come back to his old form.

The overriding open question was: how could a handful of submarines, operating on a part-time basis, convince the British Empire to yield, or perhaps even force it to a peaceful resolution?

3
1915 – TRIAL AND ERROR

Chapter 8

Step by Step to the Uboat War

At the end of 1914, the Imperial Navy knew that they did not have enough submarines to 'cut off supply to England, so that a famine would ensue.'[1]

Bethmann Hollweg was against a submarine blockade. On January 9, the Chancellor reported to the Emperor 'that the current general political situation permitted neither a commercial submarine blockade nor aerial bombardment against civil London. The Chancellor proved to be correct,' as Müller noted.[2] The Emperor decided on a postponement of the submarine war against commerce. The navy was not satisfied with the Emperor's decision of January 9. It insisted upon a war of deterrence, as Pohl expressed: 'The heavy material losses of ships and goods, as well as the loss of numerous sailors and passengers [sic!] will thus have such an effect on the leadership [in England] that they will call for peace.'[3] In a blatant act of countermanding official orders, the Chief of the Admiral's Staff, von Pohl, ordered the High Seas Fleet to prepare the submarines for commercial warfare on January 11.[4]

The admirals recommended a war of deterrence, the only feasible tactic taking into account the small number of submarines: all merchant ships around England, whether hostile or neutral, were subject to sinking by torpedo, without warning. This would deter the neutral states from trade with England, and the losses of British ships would achieve a 'moral' effect. The concepts of deterrence, and achieving 'moral' effects, were, and remain, the 'ultima ratio', the last arrow left in the quiver of a desperate warrior.

Tirpitz reported the navy's demands for air raids against London and a submarine and mine war against England to the popular press.[5] Riezler opined, 'Tirpitz is only creating public propaganda for a Uboat war so that he will, in the end, be able to say that the Foreign Office under Bethmann has rejected it.'[6]

Navy officials discussed intensifying a war of terror. The Commander of the High Seas Fleet, Friedrich von Ingenohl, suggested on January 22, 1915 the sinking English hospital ships – in spite of The Hague agreement of 1907. Under the agreement these ships remained under the protection of the Red Cross and international law prohibited any attack on them.[7]

But to instigate a real submarine war, the Imperial Navy had to create a fait accompli. A step by step deployment of the submarines had to subsequently force the government and the Emperor to justify the war effort.

From January 17 to 22, U-19 cruised in the waters between Holland and England. While there it sank a British merchant ship in compliance with maritime prize rules.[8]

U-21 set out on January 23 from Emden with the order 'to inflict damage to the hostile trade in the Irish Sea,'[9] and, on January 30, near Liverpool, it sank three British merchant steamers in accordance with cruiser warfare rules.[10]

On January 26, 1915, Pohl suggested sinking merchant ships off the French channel coast without warning.[11] On February 1, the Imperial Navy autonomously declared these waters a 'war zone', in which every troop transport would be sunk without warning.[12] The British Admiralty reacted and ordered merchant ships to hoist either no flag at all, or a neutral flag. The Imperial Navy soon became aware of the deceptive use of flags.

U-20, under Lieutenant-Commander Walther Schwieger, had left port on January 25 from Wilhelmshaven with orders to sink any ships at daylight without warning, 'if certain observations point to their use for military transport purposes', and to sink every ship sailing in by night to Calais or Le Havre.[13] Schwieger, without warning, sank three Allied merchant ships by torpedo on January 30, killing twenty-one sailors. These were the first civilians killed in submarine warfare, and the first merchant ships torpedoed without warning.

Schwieger sighted a ship off Le Havre at dawn on February 1: 'Ship identified clearly as a hospital ship. Attacked it because my order was to sink any ship running in at night to French ports.'[14] Schwieger fired a torpedo, but it missed.

The British hospital ship *Asturias* later documented the torpedo attack. A diplomatic back and forth ensued. The Imperial Navy at first essentially denied the presence of a German submarine, then retreated and stated that the commander had identified the ship as a hospital ship only after the torpedo had been fired.[15] Spindler, in his books on the German navy, stuck to this obviously falsified version: 'In the belief that he had sighted a military transport, Schwieger attacked the ship by torpedo without warning.'[16]

Until the beginning of February 1915, a total of seven merchant ships

Lieutenant Commander Walther Schwieger.

had been sunk within two weeks, three of them without warning. Spindler, in his 'official' German history of the Uboat war, tried to create the impression that the Imperial Navy exclusively directed all submarine activities prior to the 'official' declaration of the submarine commerce war against Allied troop transports. The Imperial Navy had already instigated an unrestricted commerce war by January 1915, without any orders from the Supreme Command. The Navy was waging its own, separate war.

In the following chapters, we will repeatedly see these kinds of autonomous operations on the part of the Imperial Navy, especially from the trigger-happy Lieutenant-Commander Schwieger. Rear Admiral Spindler, a Uboat staff officer during World War I, wrote the 'official' post-war history. In a massive white-washing of the Navy's role in World War I, he intended to create the false impression that the Imperial Navy had been a simple 'political object' of the Government, and that it had been under political control. Spindler suppressed or twisted any irritating or disturbing facts that contradicted this. Facts that clearly indicated that Tirpitz's Navy acted autonomously with its own strategy, in opposition to the government and even to the Army, had to fit into the Navy version: 'The Navy with its Uboats could have won the war, if it hadn't been crippled by the political authorities.'

Meanwhile, in Berlin, further discussions continued. Pohl assured Bethmann Hollweg that he should not expect any serious repercussions from the neutral governments. On February 1, 1915, the Chancellor and the Army Chief of Staff, Falkenhayn, agreed to a Uboat campaign. Pohl used a chance opportunity for reaching the Emperor in private, and got his approval for the submarine war on February 4.[17] Admiral von Müller observed: 'Pohl has gotten the approval of the Chancellor, who was not very well-informed about naval affairs at that moment, and who now deeply regrets this; on the 4th of February, Pohl caught the Emperor completely off guard.'[18] Bethmann later reported to Admiral Müller 'that he agreed to the Uboat commerce war only under the public pressure of the gang led by Tirpitz. Bitter words about the "special politics" of the Navy – meaning Tirpitz.'[19]

On February 4, Germany declared the waters around the British Isles a 'war zone'. All hostile ships would be destroyed without warning starting on February 18. The German government warned neutral governments that because of the deceptive practices of the British regarding flags, errors were likely to occur.[20]

For Great Britain the announced unrestricted Uboat war was a gift from heaven: In the face of the German action, the Cabinet could finally institute stricter measures toward the neutral governments.[21] The British Foreign Secretary, Edward Grey, confided to a friend on February 6: 'The contraband difficulty was greatly relieved by Germany's having announced a blockade of England and that she will sink ships trying to run it, drowning the crews. This will enable England to do ditto to Germany but to guarantee not to murder the crews.'[22]

The United States protested vehemently against the planned commerce war on February 10. The Wilson administration announced that it would hold the German government responsible for the loss of any American ship or citizen, and reserved the right to any and every measure necessary to protect American citizens and possessions on the high seas.[23]

The American protest startled Bethmann. He wanted to avoid difficulties with America at all costs. On February 15, with the approval of Falkenhayn, the Chancellor was able to obtain an injunction against the sinking of neutral ships from the Kaiser: 'Falkenhayn saw a threat of war in the American announcement, and believed that that would be the end of us economically; he was in favor of giving in at any price. The polite, but firm request from the Chancellor was finally approved by the Kaiser.'[24] Müller described the result: 'No submarine warfare against the neutral states.'[25] Two radio messages went out to the submarines at sea on February 15 with instructions not to attack neutral ships.[26]

Bethmann assured Wilson on the next day that American ships were not to be attacked. At the recommendation of the American Naval Attaché in Berlin, the navy committed to station 'civilian pilots' on board the submarines to avoid mistaking American ships for those of the enemy.[27] American cotton steamers were still in the Channel en route to Bremerhaven.[28]

The new Chief of Admiral's Staff, Gustav Bachmann (von Pohl had become Commander of the High Seas Fleet), reported on the preparations for submarine war to the Emperor on February 17. Admiral Müller assessed: 'Unpreparedness of the submarines for the blockade, the announcement of which increasingly proves to have been extremely clumsy.'[29] The same day, the Kaiser, the Chancellor, the Army, and the Navy agreed on the conditions of the commerce war: Submarines could sink hostile merchant ships in the war zone without warning, hospital ships and neutral ships were to be spared. There was still no word about passenger liners.[30]

The navy had already discussed this latter point internally. On February 12, Bachmann, the new Chief of Admiral's Staff, wrote to Pohl, Commander in Chief of the High Seas Fleet: 'It is in the military interest to make submarine warfare as effective as possible. Do not shy away from sinking enemy passenger liners. Their loss will cause the greatest impact.'[31]

Due to their mix of civilian passengers and freight, Allied passenger liners posed a special problem. Their speed of up to twenty-five knots made them ideal auxiliary cruisers. In Great Britain – as in Germany – at the time of their construction, they had already been prepared, with the support of the government, for the onboard installation of guns. At the beginning of the war, the British had taken many of them into service as auxiliary cruisers or troop transports. However, their enormous coal consumption quickly turned out to be a handicap, so that most of the liners were taken out of military service by the end of 1914.

At the beginning of 1915, the British Cunard Line resumed traditional transatlantic passenger service between Liverpool and New York with four ships: the *Orduña*, *Lusitania*, *Cameronia* and *Transylvania*; the White Star Line did the same with the *Adriatic*, *Baltic*, *Arabic* and others. These steamships, with up to 30,000 GRT, could carry several thousand passengers and crew, and required seven to eight days for an Atlantic crossing. After one week in port, they would head out to sea again. Each ocean liner made monthly round-trips from Liverpool to New York and back. Weekly, two passenger steamships departed Liverpool and two others arrived from America. The departure times were set weeks or even months ahead. Any German consular official or shipping company agent in Holland or Scandinavia only needed to take a look at 'Lloyd's List', a daily shipping newspaper of fifteen to twenty large-format pages, to see what the timetable was and to inform Berlin. Not only were the passenger liners listed, but the arrivals and the intended departure times of all merchant ships were published long in advance.

The Germans needed no spy ring to gain detailed insight into British trade: a daily glance at 'Lloyd's List' was sufficient. The publication was finally stopped in April 1917, when the Uboat war became a deadly menace.

After the German announcement of unrestricted submarine warfare, House discussed with Foreign Secretary Grey mid February, 1915 Grey's idea to lift the food blockade in the event the Germans cancelled unrestricted warfare and continued to follow international cruiser rules. The editor of the House papers: 'The conversations were significant, for this is the germ of the idea soon to be developed by House, which he later termed the "Freedom of the Seas". As Grey realized, the practical application of the idea would be of immense value to Great Britain, an island depending for its life upon the continuity of its merchant trade.

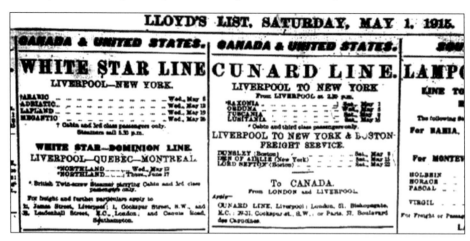

Lloyd's List for Saturday, May 1, 1915.

But House saw that the Germans, blockaded as they were and also largely dependent upon overseas trade, would be attracted by it. It might serve as the beginning of negotiations. The fact which must touch the sense of humor of the historian is that the "Freedom of the Seas", later so bitterly opposed by the British and regarded generally as a German trick, was first suggested by the British Foreign Office as a means of furthering British interests.'[32]

This idea found approval with Secretary of State William Jennings Bryan and President Wilson.[33] An official American proposal of this concept went to London and Berlin on February 20.

Bethmann and the Foreign Office welcomed it, and on February 28, the Chancellor, the Emperor and Tirpitz discussed the American foray.[34] Admiral Müller reported: 'Tirpitz raised his opposition to the Chancellor in an indelicate way, while, in the interest of German prestige, he demanded from England not only the release of grain and raw material supplies, but also the release of the interned German merchant ships. An absolutely senseless demand, which would only cause Germany to heap the ignominy of the refusal of American mediation completely on itself.'[35] Tirpitz decided to use the only effective and popular weapon the Navy possessed – Uboats – without any restriction.

Chapter 9

First Submarine War

The first-ever submarine war 'officially' began on February 18, 1915. U–18 was the only boat at sea. Room 40 deciphered a radio message on February 19 with instructions to spare two American passenger liners, the *West Haverford* and the *Philadelphia*.[1]

The German naval radio station in Norddeich broadcast on February 21 that the *Arabia* would leave Liverpool on February 24.[2] The *Arabia* was a 7,900 GRT British passenger ship. This was the first German wireless message regarding a British passenger liner. The instruction 'to spare' the ship was missing. Was this a request to the Uboat-Commander to attack the passenger liner?

U–30 operated with moderate success in Liverpool Bay during this week, where it sank two freighters, one without warning.

The next submarines west of England were U–20, with Schwieger as commander, and U–27, under the command of Lieutenant-Commander Bernhard Wegener. The Supreme Commander of the submarine fleet, Hermann Bauer, ordered them to a distant operation in the Irish Sea on February 23.[3] Room 40 deciphered this order on the same day,[4] and two days later observed the departure of U–27 on a northerly course in the direction of Scotland, and of U–20, on a westerly course through the Channel.[5]

This allowed the Royal Navy ample time to carry out defensive maneuvers. Every available craft, from unarmed fishing boats to armored cruisers, was sent out to patrol the seas, hoping to force the submarines to dive and exhaust their batteries, or to surprise a Uboat, ram it or sink it with artillery. A radio message informed the submarine captains on February 27 that all merchant traffic bound for Liverpool was being directed through the North Channel.[6]

Lusitania

U–27 arrived there on March 1 and cruised for four and a half days, but refrained from attacking any ships, not even a steamer anchored close by. In his deck log, Wegener entered: 'Steamers were not attacked because according to [Bauer's order] K.d.U.Nr. 28, the *Lusitania* is expected in English home waters on March 4, and I believe that my current position is the most favorable one for an attack on her.'[7]

'K.d.U.Nr. 28' was Bauer's operational order for U–27, which has disappeared without a trace from the German naval archives. Wegener's plan was to attack

SS *Lusitania*.

the *Lusitania*, therefore he behaved discreetly, so as not to betray his presence. Over the next four days, he repeated his intention to wait for the *Lusitania* in his war diary, before giving up his waiting position on the morning of March 5 and departing for another operational area.

The *Lusitania* was one of the largest ships in the world, at over twenty-six knots faster than any warship. She was the pride of the British ship-building industry. Indeed, her sinking would truly have made 'a great impression' on England, comparable only to the shock of the *Titanic* disaster three years earlier. The British Admiralty registered the presence of U-27 with precision and sent out two destroyers to escort the *Lusitania* to Liverpool. The next night, she sailed through the North Channel and remained in Liverpool for two weeks because of the 'Uboat danger'.[8]

U-20 arrived in the Irish Sea on March 7. The next day, Norddeich signaled: 'Steamship *Baltic* of the White Star Line with 18,000 tons of war material for Liverpool left New York on 3 March.'[9] Schwieger calculated that the *Baltic*, a passenger liner of 28,000 GRT, would have to pass through the North Channel a week later, around March 10 or 11. He proceeded to the North Channel, right into the operational area of U-27. His reason for doing so, Schwieger noted in his logbook, was 'to destroy a fat steamer in the northern part of the Irish Sea.'[10] On March 11 around 02:30 a.m., floating in the dark night on the smooth seas of the North Channel, he made out a ship: 'A very large passenger liner with her lights darkened passed by at highest speed. Attack in the dark of night and on this fast moving target impossible.'[11] Schwieger had missed his 'fat steamer' from a distance of 2,000 meters. It was not an easy task for an Uboat with torpedoes that had a 1000-meter range to target an object running at higher speed and perhaps also on a divergent course.

The next 'Uboat wave' in the Irish Sea in March consisted of U-29, under Lieutenant-Commander Otto Weddigen and U-28, under Lieutenant-Commander Georg-Günther von Forstner. This submarine commerce war to the west of England was actually a rather loose series of combat patrols. The 'strangulation of England' had more the character of a part-time blockade, since for days or even weeks, submarines did not even man the two planned 'blockade stations'.

On March 4, Weddigen left Emden on the U-29's first cruise, in the direction of the English Channel. Even this brand-spanking new submarine did not yet sport a deck gun, the traditional weapon to stop and sink merchant ships. On March 10, Norddeich announced the departures of two British passenger liners from London on March 12, and the departure of the *Lusitania* from Liverpool on March 13.[12]

On the morning of March 12, U-29 surfaced off the coast of Cornwall, and before noon, Weddigen had stopped four steamers, using flag signals or shots from his flare pistols. He gave the crews ten minutes to disembark, and then proceeded to sink them, either by opening the seacocks, using explosives or a torpedo. He dragged the lifeboats towards the coast until he met another ship, which took on the crew. According to one of the English captains: 'He then came and took my two boats in tow and invited me to come aboard the Submarine. He asked me to have a glass of wine, which I accepted. The men on deck that I saw could all speak good English. They were all well, fit, happy and appeared to be enjoying themselves the same as if they were on a picnic.'[13] Even without a deck gun Weddigen stopped and sank one unarmed merchant ship after another in British coastal waters at daylight, without any risk for his boat or for the crews of the British vessels (Weddigen stopped all ships by warning). Restricted submarine commerce war seemed to be a picnic in those days.

The next day, Norddeich repeated the radio message concerning the departure of the *Lusitania* from Liverpool.[14] Weddigen was already on his way north. The Royal Navy spotted U-29 off the Hebrides on the 15th. The next sighting of the submarine came on March 18 from on board the HMS *Dreadnought*, which led a squadron of battleships along the eastern coast of Scotland. U-29 had fired a torpedo on one of the warships, and at 12:28 p.m., a periscope came in sight dangerously close to HMS *Dreadnought*. The ship immediately changed course and rammed the submarine. The British sailors saw part of the rising Uboat tower with the number 29 before the submarine sank. Weddigen had worked his way through the protective shield of destroyers to the front of the battleship column, had released his first torpedo and had then prepared for another attack.

On this, his last journey, he had seemingly ignored all requests to attack passenger liners; he had sunk merchant ships only according to prize rules, and had saved his torpedoes for warships. No Uboat in the First World War ever got as close to the British Grand Fleet as Weddigen's.

The German Admiral's Staff criticized the towing of lifeboats and sinking according to cruiser rules: 'The deterring effect of the submarine war will be lost if it is felt that passing the blockade zone is no longer a serious risk to the lives of the crews.'[15]

One week later, U-28, under the command of Freiherr Georg von Forstner, became the next submarine to join the 'war zone' in the Irish Sea. It stopped the liner *Falaba* on March 28 with several hundred passengers and crew aboard. Forstner gave them ten minutes to abandon the ship. Panic broke out, lifeboats capsized. Forstner waited a total of twenty-three minutes and then, as clouds of smoke announced approaching vessels, fired a torpedo.[16] It turned out to be impossible to evacuate hundreds of people quickly and securely in such a situation.

The torpedoing of the *Falaba* killed 104 people, among them a US citizen. An outcry swept through the American press, but Wilson considered this to be an isolated incident and did not react.[17]

Altogether, between February 18 and the end of March, German submarines sank 90,000 GRT, and in April, another 40,000 GRT, primarily to the west of England. Two-thirds of all these ships, in the majority less than 1,000 GRT, not worthy of a torpedo, the submarines sank according to cruiser rules. Even with experienced commanders, only half of the torpedoes hit their marks. With six to eight torpedoes aboard, on average three to four ships per patrol could be sunk without warning.

The torpedoes were a mix of the (for the most part outdated and unreliable) 'bronze torpedoes', with a range of few hundred meters, and modern 'G torpedoes', with a 1,000 m range; the latter were scarce, however, and reserved for the High Seas Fleet.[18]

In spite of the two-month preparation period, most submarines were not yet equipped with a deck gun, forcing the commanders to stop ships with flag signals and flares, to bring a machine gun on deck, or simply shoot with rifles in order to lend urgency to the demand to stop. From the outbreak of the war the German navy had requisitioned and armed hundreds of auxiliary ships. The submarines only received deck guns after urgent demands from the commanders in April and May 1915. The submarines generally remained in their operational areas no longer than eight to ten days, although they could survive up to six weeks at sea.

The outdated petroleum boats, U-5 to U-18, used in the North Sea and the Channel, were internally nicknamed 'suicide boats'. By the end of 1915, they had either been lost or decommissioned to the submarine school for training purposes. The Navy did not even commit all available modern boats from U-19 upwards to the west of England during the commerce war; many of them stayed in the North Sea, where the Imperial Navy hoped to attack units of the Grand Fleet.

A maximum sinking quota obviously held no priority in the first submarine war on commerce. Deterrence was the aim.

The loss of ships was damaging to the British. However, it was not a real threat: losses still remained well below the rate of new ship construction. The deciphered radio messages forewarned the Royal Navy of the presence of submarines in the Atlantic supply lines. When this occurred, the British Admiralty sent out every vessel that could float, from old cruisers right down to unarmed fishing trawlers, in the hopes of surprising a hostile submarine and ramming or shelling it. In the event of a 'submarine threat', the British navy held back merchant ships in the harbor or diverted them. What remained disconcerting for the British was the German interest in passenger liners, which garnered such high attention in their wireless.

In other respects the German submarine war even proved to be an advantage – Great Britain could now enforce stricter blockade measures on the neutral states as a reprisal against the illegal German actions.

Chapter 10
British Blockade in Spring

The British government declared 'its intention to isolate Germany completely from the international trading system by imposing a complete interdiction, inbound and out, over all German overseas trade' on March 11, 1915.[1] This was no longer a blockade measure, legal or not, but a justified 'retaliatory measure'. Prime Minister Asquith publicly stated that same month: 'If, as a consequence, neutrals suffer inconvenience and loss of trade, we regret it, but we beg them to remember that this phase of the War was not initiated by us.'[2]

An internal report on the blockade revealed the view of the British Admiralty: 'The great race of starvation began. The realist may point to those naval factors which probably made it inevitable that Germany's reply to our blockade measures should be the submarine. Whether it be regarded as a legitimate gambler's throw which failed, or as an unparalleled series of terrorist crimes, there can be no doubt that it rallied neutral and Allied opinion against Germany as nothing else could have done.'[3] It was the opportunity 'to cut our way with comparative ease out of the legal tangle in which we had become involved. The order of March 11, 1915, enabled us to stop all goods of enemy destination, origin, or ownership. Furthermore, we could now take the vitally important step of cutting off the enemy's export trade to countries overseas. Thus, the order of March 11 may be said to have marked the beginning of a comprehensive blockade.'[4]

The prevention of German exports made the counter-financing of its indirect imports via the neutrals impossible. By the end of 1915, German overseas exports had essentially ground to a halt. England permitted exports of miniscule amounts via the neutral countries to the United States only for 'political reasons'.[5]

Though Wilson had accepted the British cutting off all neutral trade with Germany, he nonetheless protested sharply against the legal hardening of inter-neutral trade.[6] Wilson wrote to Lansing on March 30, 1915: 'Together England and Germany are likely to drive us crazy, because it looks oftentimes as if they were crazy themselves, the unnecessary provocations they invent.'[7]

But it was far from a 'watertight' blockade. Among the European neutrals, Holland, Denmark and Norway cooperated with the objectives of the British, but the openly pro-German Sweden stubbornly refused any concession to English demands.

England did not opt for harsher measures against Sweden, because, like Germany, it depended on Swedish iron ore. The route via Norway and Sweden represented the only possibility of transit to Russia via Finland. Just like Imperial Germany, the war cut Russia off from world trade. Germany blocked routes through the Baltic Sea, and Turkey controlled those leading through the Dardanelles. Sweden handled huge commercial contracts for the German Empire under its protective mantle of neutrality. It reacted to the British blockade with the demand to have the right to trade the same amount of goods to Germany as to Russia.

Goods destined for Russia were diverted to Germany. Russia itself bought German products from Sweden in exchange for grain, and English companies also actively participated in indirect trade with Germany.[8] The convoluted trade situation forced London to admit in May 1915 that 'the whole policy of cutting off German supplies by means of the blockade is being practically frustrated by the failure to prevent the export of certain important classes of goods, notably foodstuff, from this country.'[9]

Chapter 11
Kaiser, Reich and Tirpitz

Grand Admiral Alfred von Tirpitz had been 'Assistant Secretary of the Imperial Navy Office' since 1898, the German Secretary of the Navy. In all these years, Emperor Wilhelm II had been like putty in his hands, and had enthusiastically supported his naval armament. The outbreak of war had affected their relationship negatively. Riezler described the Chancellor's view: 'For the Kaiser, Tirpitz is finished. He is fed up with his lies. Tirpitz has been pushed aside in the naval management by the vain Pohl; now he does nothing but talk big and stir up trouble. His dismissal is impossible, though, because of his popularity with the simple people.'[1]

Bethmann Hollweg had been Imperial Chancellor since 1909. Although Tirpitz was formally subordinated to him, the Emperor had the power to dismiss or appoint any secretary, as well as the Chancellor. The Kaiser was by nature indecisive. He anxiously paid attention to the mood of public opinion, which the political parties in the Reichstag, the German Parliament, represented. The Conservatives and the National Liberals formed the political 'Right;' the left-wing Liberals and the Social Democrats formed the 'Left'. The Catholic Center Party maintained a delicate balance in between. During the war the Center party shifted from the right camp to the left. The Reichstag approved budgets, but could not appoint the government. That was Kaiser Wilhelm's domain.

If a minister had fallen out of favor with his Imperial Majesty, he was made aware discreetly. The unwritten byzantine court laws expected him to insist upon his resignation in this situation, to which the Emperor then leniently agreed. If a minister decided that he could no longer work for the Emperor, he submitted his resignation. The Emperor then decided whether to accept it or not.

Before the war, the indispensable Tirpitz had played this little post-feudalistic game half-a-dozen times when differences over naval armament arose, only to be retained in office each time with new concessions from the Emperor. Wilhelm was exceedingly indisposed to personnel changes within his circle. He held on tightly to his political staff, which had to maneuver through the frequent occasions of seemingly irreconcilable conflict between the departments.

Bethmann Hollweg was in a difficult situation. The Right virtually despised him, because they suspected him of resolving long pent-up internal conflicts with political reforms. Riezler wrote in October 1914: 'Spoke with Chancellor about these attacks from the Right, said that the Conservatives were worried about their future political influence. However, he is resolved under no circumstances to pursue conservative politics after the war. He agreed that I had been right in saying that the government up until now had formally ruled conservatively, but had acted liberally, and that in the future it would have to be the other way around.'[2] The Left viewed Bethmann with distrust and suspected him to be a conservative Prussian aristocrat.

Bethmann Hollweg characterized his governing methods as 'diagonal politics'. This was not a politics of ever-changing majorities, but an attempt to maneuver through the insurmountable opposition on the domestic front.

The Rightist parties in parliament demanded that the government state their war objectives. Since the disastrous execution of the Schlieffen Plan in September 1914, Bethmann had suppressed all discussion of this topic in the press. Neither he nor Chief of Staff Falkenhayn still believed in the possibility of a decisive victory against France and Russia on land. The Chancellor hoped to either break-up the Entente coalition through a separate peace with one of the partners, or to negotiate peace. To define final war objectives was illusory and counter-productive in this fluctuating situation. It would only serve to endanger the required cooperation between the government and the central-left parties in parliament during the war. The center-left also leaned toward favoring a negotiated peace.[3]

The Right wanted to achieve vast annexation of land both in the west and the east of Germany, as well as further unrestricted naval armament. The German Empire was to rise from a respectable continental power to a new super-power, based on absolute European hegemony. The only imaginable end to the war was a *Siegfrieden*, a 'peace by victory', meaning the subjugation of all enemies. Heavy industry and the mighty coal and steel barons supported these rightist parties, as well as the 'Pan-Germans'.

The 'Pan-German League' consisted of 20,000 members who came from the higher levels of the state bureaucracy, the military and the bourgeoisie. With sectarian zeal, they elevated nation and race to a religion. Even in the pre-war peace time, the chairperson of the Pan-Germans, Heinrich Class, promulgated an offensive war and limitless annexation in the west and east, including the forced emigration and expulsion of the inhabitants of the new lands, an ethnic 'purification' of Europe. He had described his agenda already in 1912 in his popular book *If I Were the Emperor*. The Pan-Germans were also anti-Semitic and demanded the expulsion of German Jews, or at least their legal degradation to a medieval non-citizen status without any rights. They envisioned a hierarchically structured state, ruled by a self-appointed elite. Instead of the 'weak' Emperor, a vigorous 'Führer' (leader) ruled. Their intolerance and recklessness turned to outright rage.[4] The Pan-Germans agitated as an extra-parliamentary opposition at the time. Sympathizers among the right-wing Reichstag representatives represented them indirectly in national politics.

With populist slogans for a peace through victory, annexation, and a reckless submarine war they demanded the impossible from the Chancellor. They wanted to publicly shame Bethmann for not reaching unattainable goals – a classic populist strategy. The Pan-Germans thus attacked the Chancellor and weakened him, which also indirectly affected the 'weak' Emperor. With chauvinistic slogans, the Pan-Germans tried to destabilize the government in the eyes of the public. The leader of the Catholic Center Party, Matthias Erzberger, noted once that it would be less expensive to lock up all the Pan-Germans in lunatic asylums than to continue the war under the banner of their unlimited demands.

Emperor Wilhelm's son, Crown Prince Wilhelm had demonstrated his Pan-German sympathies before the war. Could he possibly have believed that when he looked in the mirror he saw a 'vigorous leader'? Riezler described a scene between Bethmann and the Crown Prince shortly before the outbreak of the war: 'Correspondence between the Chancellor and the Crown Prince. Surrounded entirely by Pan-German and completely uneducated officers, he has again shot off some belligerent telegrams to Pan-German speakers and authors. The Crown Prince has written a long letter, demanding war and anti-socialist laws, external aggression and internal use of force. Silly expressions. Where have all the educated officers gone, who once made Prussia a great power?'[5]

For the coalition of Pan-Germans, conservatives, major industrialists, and the military, the ideal candidate for the post of the Chancellor was either Tirpitz or Hindenburg. Only a popular general or admiral could enforce a strictly 'patriotic' course and push the Emperor into the background, as was the case in the times of Otto von Bismarck.[6] Tirpitz's biographer, Scheck, wrote: 'This circle worked to replace Bethmann with a hard-liner, preferably Tirpitz, who would strive for a *Siegfrieden*, a German dictate guaranteeing vast expansion of German power through annexations and indirect control over neighboring states. Bethmann's right-wing opponents also believed that only a victory triggering a wave of nationalist passion would safeguard Germany's authoritarian political structures. They conversely expected a compromise peace to lead to the democratization of the Reich or, in the worst case, revolution.'[7]

The government held an even more pessimistic view, as Riezler stated at that time: 'The path leads to a socialist state. The more moderate the end of the war is, the faster it will arrive. The huge challenges that will need to be faced after the war can only be conquered through state socialism.'[8]

Tirpitz schemed at the Imperial Headquarters in spring of 1915. He discussed with generals, naval officers and industrialists whether the Crown Prince could neutralize the Emperor and replace him, and whether Hindenburg or himself could do the same with Chancellor Bethmann. Tirpitz wrote in a letter to his wife on March 27: 'I see only one way out: the Emperor has to claim he is sick for 8 or more weeks, Hindenburg must take Bethmann's place and army and navy be led by him and the Emperor.'[9]

Long before the war, the elites speculated in hushed voices about the mental condition of the Emperor, and now they feared that his health had deteriorated further.[10] The Pan-Germans had already suggested the idea of replacing the Kaiser with the Crown Prince before the war in 1913. Tirpitz decided to contact the Emperor's personal physician.[11]

Tirpitz's intrigue to overthrow the Kaiser came to the attention of Admiral Müller, who noted in mid-April, 'the Emperor's personal physician's serious concern about an intrigue playing out in the headquarters to declare the Emperor temporarily unfit to rule, and to create a regency under the Crown Prince.'[12]

By neutralizing the Emperor, Tirpitz hoped that the Crown Prince entrusted him with the Naval High Command, or perhaps even appointed him Imperial Chancellor.

To what extent the Emperor knew about this intrigue remains unclear. In the end, nothing came of it. At any rate, he did not dare to dismiss Tirpitz, who was unassailable on account of his popularity and the support of the Right.

And his popularity was yet to rise, through the further events of the submarine war. After a gap of several weeks, in mid-April Britain again intercepted German radio messages concerning British passenger liners.[13]

Chapter 12

Lusitania

In April, only three Uboats operated west of England: U-24 for eleven days, U-32 for two days, and U-22 for one day.[1] Storms, technical problems, and the massive deployment of English patrol vessels and warships led to the meager result of only four sunk ships, with less than 5,000 GRT. Room 40 carefully monitored these activities.

U-30 under Lieutenant Rosenberg passed by Scotland at the end of April, and set course for the southern coast of Ireland, where it sank seven ships totaling 18,434 GRT. Rosenberg noted in his logbook the strong presence of patrol vessels on the southern Irish coast, which forced him to frequently submerge.[2] Room 40 had followed all of this in detail.[3]

On May 1, the American press published an advance notice from the German Embassy warning all American travelers not to proceed into the declared 'war zone' around the British Isles on ships under the British flag, because a 'definite' danger of destruction existed.

The warning appeared right below an announcement by the Cunard-Line of the departure of the *Lusitania* from New York to Liverpool on this date, as well as the upcoming departures of the *Transylvania*, *Orduña*, *Tuscania* and *Lusitania* through June.

The German 'warning' was not about a trip on a specific British liner on a particular date, but about travel in general on British ships. There was no message that Germany would possibly detain or even attack a passenger liner on account of the cargo or on account of their former use as auxiliary cruisers. The American newspaper reader might have asked himself whether this was merely a German propaganda coup intended to inflict damage to the British passenger lines.

The official warning issued by the Imperial German Embassy about travelling on *Lusitania*.

The day before the *Lusitania*'s departure from New York on the morning of April 30, Captain Schwieger left Emden aboard U-20 and took a northerly course. The operational order in his war diary no longer exists in the archives of the Imperial Navy.[4] Schwieger knew that the merchant ship traffic had been routed to the southern Irish coast; he also knew that the *Lusitania* had set out on April 17 from Liverpool,[5] and that another liner, the *Adriatic*, had arrived at Liverpool on April 29.[6] He could calculate that the *Adriatic* would leave Liverpool around May 6, and that the *Lusitania* would arrive off the southern Irish coast around May 7.

During his journey through the North Sea in the direction of Scotland, Schwieger announced his position every four hours by wireless. Room 40 deciphered his transmissions.[7] A war pilot, Lanz, 'who knows all the English ships', was aboard. The submarine commander sighted a Danish passenger ship on the night of May 3: 'An attack on her not possible, because she is running at least 12 kn and is on an unfavorable course.'[8] Schwieger clearly intended to attack a neutral passenger liner, and only the unfavorable circumstances prevented this action. At noon on May 5, U-20 lurked off the western Irish coast at Fastnet Rock. That afternoon, Schwieger sank a small English sailing vessel with his new 8.8 cm deck gun, in compliance with prize rules. The survivors reached the coast in the evening and reported the presence of a German submarine.

Schwieger reported his position via wireless to Norddeich in the evening: '51.32 N 8.22 W.'[9] This was off the Old Head of Kinsale, a traditional landfall for transatlantic traffic after a long overseas oceanic voyage with its inherent displacements due to wind, currents and waves. Here, ships corrected their navigational coordinates for the rest of the trip.

Schwieger fired a torpedo at a Norwegian merchant ship that night, but missed.[10] Room 40 noted a sighting of U-20 around 21:30 at Daunts Rock.[11] By the end of the day, the Royal Navy had clearly observed several unequivocal signs of the presence of a Uboat off the coast of southern Ireland. At this time, the *Lusitania* was still 750 nautical miles to the west, another one-and-a-half days of journey: plenty of time for a warning.

U-20 steered eastward. Schwieger pursued and shelled a British ship at the southern entrance of the Irish Sea in the morning of May 6. The ship eventually struck its flag and a torpedo from U-20 sank it. The crew escaped into lifeboats and reported the presence of U-20 in the evening.[12]

Around 11:40 a.m., a large steamer came into view, but disappeared shortly thereafter in a fog bank. Schwieger steamed full speed ahead in the direction of the presumed heading of the ship. And suddenly: 'Crash dive, because the steamer emerged out of the fog abeam. Ordered full speed to get into a favorable attack position.' And around 12:30: 'Attack cancelled, as the vessel passed by at 3,000 m distance and high speed on a divergent course. It was a passenger ship of the White Star Line, approx. 14,000 tons, no flag flying.'[13] In fact, it had been the *Arabic*, which had left Liverpool the day before, and which narrowly escaped sinking on this day. Schwieger seemed to have no luck when it came to liners. In the afternoon he added another merchant ship to his prizes.

Schwieger received the following radio message from Norddeich in the evening of May 6: 'S.S. *Lusitania* leaves Liverpool for New York on May 15th.'[14] This was confirmation that the *Lusitania* was on schedule and could be expected the next day at the Old Head of Kinsale. U-20 immediately turned around and steered on westward course.

The submarine passed the English naval base at Queenstown/Cork on the morning of May 7. Around 13:15, U-20 dived when it sighted a British warship, the only one it had encountered during this time in its area of operations. It was the old cruiser *Juno*, sent out to escort the *Lusitania*.[15] The Royal Navy called her back to her base in the morning on account of 'Uboat danger'. In the safety of the harbor, she met up with the other patrol vessels that had made life difficult for U-30 a week earlier.

Fifteen minutes later, Schwieger gave the order to surface. The weather was sunny and clear with excellent visibility.[16] Here is Schwieger's own account:

7 May 15   North Atlantic

2:05 pm.   Ahead, 4 funnels and 2 masts of a steamer have appeared, with a course set directly at us (coming from the SSW, it is steering toward Golley Head). Ship identified as a large passenger steamer.

2:25 pm.   Went to 11 m and proceeded at high speed on a converging course with the steamer, hoping that along the Irish Coast it will change its course to starboard.

2:50 pm.   The steamer turned to starboard, in the direction of Queenstown, and has enabled an approach for finding a firing position. Until 3 pm, full-speed ahead to get in front of it.

3:10 pm.   Clear bow shot at 700 m (G-Torpedo at 3 m depth), angle 90°, estimated speed 22 sm. Torpedo struck starboard side close behind the bridge.
             There followed an extraordinarily heavy detonation, with a very large cloud of smoke (far above the front funnel). After the explosion of the torpedo, there must have been a second one (boiler or coal or powder?) The superstructure above the point of impact and the bridge has been torn apart, fire has broken out, and the smoke

is covering the upper bridge. The ship stopped immediately and quickly listed sharply to starboard, at the same time, the bow is sinking. It appears as though it will capsize soon. On board the ship there is great confusion; the lifeboats have been swung clear and some have been lowered into the water. Complete panic must be reigning: some boats, full of people, rushed downward, struck the water with the bow or stern first and filled with water at once. On the port side, because of the slope, fewer boats have been swung clear than on the starboard side. The ship is blowing off steam. On the bow, the name *LUSITANIA* in golden letters has become visible. The funnels were painted black, the stern flag had not been hoisted. It was running at 20 nm.

3:25 pm.   Since it seems as though the steamer will only remain above water for a short remaining time, went to 24 m and steered toward the sea. Also, I couldn't have fired a second torpedo into that swarm of people, who were only trying to save themselves.

Schwieger left the scene on a northerly course. Room 40 deciphered a radio message from U-20 on the morning of May 12: 'Has sunk 1 sailing vessel, 2 steamers and *Lusitania*.'[17] At the naval headquarters in Wilhelmshaven, no one seemed paralyzed with shock: less than six hours later, a personal response from the Commander in Chief of the High Seas Fleet, Admiral von Pohl, went out to the commander of the submarine: 'C-in-C to Norddeich for U-20. To Captain and crew my warmest appreciation of success achieved of which H.S.F. [High Seas Fleet] is proud and my best wishes for return.'[18]

Summary

From a long distance away, Schwieger had already made out the *Lusitania* as a passenger liner. It was unmistakably one of the largest vessels in the world. Aboard U-20, Pilot Lanz had served for years with the White Star Line as a merchant marine officer, and must also have identified it. Over the course of forty minutes, under ideal visibility, the *Lusitania* approached to 700 m distance from U-20. Through his periscope, Schwieger must have seen the faces of the men, women, and children on deck. At the moment he ordered fire, he knew that he was attacking an unarmed passenger liner, the *Lusitania*, with thousands of civilians aboard.

Could a small Lieutenant-Commander like Schwieger have acted on his own initiative, without instructions? Bauer's order from March authorizing to sink the *Lusitania*, which U-27's deck log mentioned several times, as well as the constant

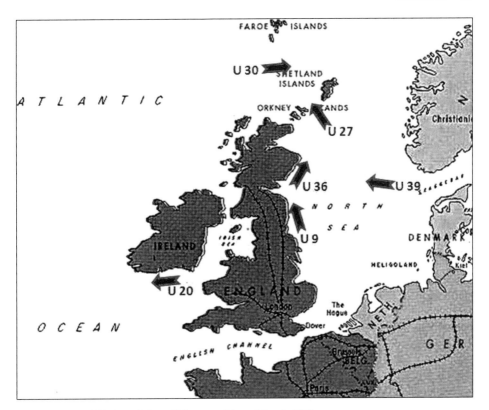

German and British knowledge of Uboat positions, May 7, 1915.

barrage of radio messages concerning British passenger liners, contradicts this possibility. German prisoner of war, Uboat Commander Kurt Tebbenjohanns of the UC-44, stated in 1917, while English interrogators questioned him about the sinking of the *Lusitania*: 'The officer concerned had received positive orders to sink the ship, as definite information had reached Germany that she was carrying munitions of war. The officer was placed in a very difficult position, and I myself would probably have acted in the same way under the circumstances, but I should have been very sorry indeed to do so.'[19] And, finally, the operational orders of the submarines that are normally attached to the war diaries 'vanished'. After the defeat in November 1918 the Imperial Navy had ample time and a motivation to destroy compromising documents regarding the attacks on passenger liners in the archives.

No written order authorizing Schwieger to sink the *Lusitania* is left in the German Navy Archives, but all facts presented here cannot doubt its existence.

The submarine commanders truly were in a difficult situation. The Kaiser had personally admonished them in February 'to let the crew disembark before sinking if possible,'[20] but Admiral Tirpitz had asked them at a social occasion at this time to 'unofficially' ignore any restricting orders from the government.[21]

It was up to every submarine officer personally to decide how to react in each encounter. Commanders such as Schwieger systematically hunted down liners and neutral ships. Most of the officers may have tried to avoid situations which could bring them in moral conflict: for instance, in March 1915, Captain Wegener, ordered to sink the *Lusitania*, took his U-27 on the ocean floor every night – the best time to take out a passenger liner – to 'give his crew rest'. Schwieger never did such a thing. Only commanders of Weddigen's standing dared to openly ignore the orders and to act according to the traditional rules of all sailors at seas.

Who could have ordered the sinking of the *Lusitania*? Would Captain Bauer or the Admirals Bachmann and Pohl have arbitrarily undertaken to arrange such an infamous deed? The only person in the Imperial Navy who could dare to challenge the Chancellor and international law, to act against the Emperor's will, and to sit in the background and order the sinking of liners, was Tirpitz.

And the British? Through their radio deciphering they had known about the interest of the Germans in the passenger liners for months. Until the beginning of May, they had done everything in their power to protect them from the submarines; then, however, they recalled warships back to the harbors because of the 'Uboat danger'. In the first week of May 1915, the liners ran in and out of the war zone, unprotected and unwarned. It was like allowing a friend to enter a minefield without a warning.

In the 1980s, Patrick Beesley, a member of the anti-submarine division in Bletchley Park during the Second World War, was the first to lay eyes on the 'top secret' classified documents of the British Admiralty from the First World War. He published his book *Room 40* based on them in 1984. He promulgated the view that the Winston Churchill Admiralty purposely 'sacrificed' the *Lusitania* to provoke a German-American conflict.[22]

Colonel House had travelled to Europe on the *Lusitania* at the end of January 1915 to explore the chances of a negotiated peace through American mediation. On May 7, the day of the *Lusitania* sinking, he had a meeting with British Foreign Secretary Sir Edward Grey. House reported: 'We spoke of the probability of an ocean liner being sunk, and I told him if this were done, a flame of indignation would sweep across America, which would in itself probably carry us into the war.'[23] Later, House was with King George in Buckingham Palace: 'We fell to talking, strangely enough, of the probability of Germany sinking a trans-Atlantic liner. King George said: 'Suppose they should sink the *Lusitania* with American passengers on board...'[24]

Was Tirpitz a betrayed betrayer? Riezler characterized the prevailing course of the war at the end of 1915: 'A mixture of crime and idiocy on all sides.'[25]

Chapter 13

War of Words

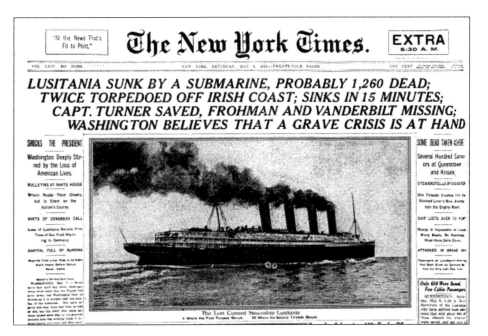

Breaking News, *The New York Times*.

Washington

Wilson received the first news about the sinking of the *Lusitania* on the evening of May 7, 1915, Eastern Standard Time. He called off all public events and meetings with politicians or his advisers, and withdrew for three and a half days.[1]

The *Lusitania* was not a warship, she was not armed, and she was not under the command of the Royal Navy. She was a civilian passenger liner in the service of the Cunard Line, with more than 2,000 passengers and crew members aboard. She carried cargo, and the German Navy had a strong suspicion that it might include absolute contraband. To confirm this suspicion, a German submarine could have made the *Lusitania* stop and searched her. The torpedoing of a non-warship, neutral or hostile, without warning, whether in a blockade zone in accordance with the London Declaration, or in a self-declared 'war zone', was an offense against international law. And when it concerned one of the largest passenger vessels in the world, with 1,209 civilian victims, it caused a shock similar to that felt at the sinking of the Titanic in 1912. The collision with an iceberg may have made humanity doubt the feasibility of the dream of controlling nature through technology, however, the sinking of the *Lusitania* by a warship seemed to ring in a new dark age for the world's civilization. Wilson sat at his typewriter and began to draft a diplomatic note to Germany.[2]

Berlin

In Berlin, the news about *Lusitania* arrived on May 8. Admiral von Müller wondered: 'War with America? Telegrams from Tirpitz and Bachmann have been sent for the purpose of establishing a firm position toward America.'[3]

Tirpitz had already pieced together the Navy's version, even before he could have 'officially' known that a German Uboat sunk the *Lusitania*: 'In the interest of the state, it is of absolute necessity to now stand firm against the neutrals, and especially against the United States. Our legal position must be that the *Lusitania* was an auxiliary cruiser and had a cargo of ammunition aboard.'[4] The ammunition aboard the *Lusitania* was only suspected. It turned out to be fact later, but the assertion that she was an armed auxiliary cruiser was preposterous. Auxiliary cruisers were not in the habit of transporting paying passengers across the oceans, or announcing their departure and arrival times in the newspapers weeks in advance. Even an unarmed passenger liner with contraband aboard was still a passenger liner, not an auxiliary cruiser.

Tirpitz's denial strategy: 'potential auxiliary cruiser + maybe ammunition aboard = auxiliary cruiser = warship' made its way so deeply into the German psyche that the 'auxiliary cruiser' thesis still finds advocates in the 'serious' German press 100 years later.[5]

In any case, the Imperial Navy did not feel compelled to change its course, and on May 12 and 16 continued to send radio messages to the submarines containing journey times of passenger vessels.[6]

Washington

Wilson convened his cabinet on May 11. Everyone at this meeting agreed that the US did not want to enter into a war, but that the sinking of the *Lusitania* was unacceptable. It must, so was the consensus, be answered with a strict protest, even at the risk of a serious diplomatic crisis with Germany.[7] Assistant Secretary of State Robert Lansing favored a single sharply worded note to Germany, while Secretary of State Bryan wanted to deal with the *Lusitania* incident through an international arbitration board. He also proposed a concurrent note to Great Britain protesting the blockade. Bryan did not want to be involved in the Uboat war because he feared that the United States would thereby be ever more entangled in the European conflict and eventually be forced to take sides. The *Lusitania* was a British ship, not an American, and international law only dealt with compensation for the US citizens aboard the vessel who had died.

Wilson decided to proceed with Lansing's proposal rather than Bryan's: One terse note of protest to Germany, in which the American government demanded the abandonment of unrestricted submarine warfare. This note was sent out on May 13.[8]

The British cleverly avoided the danger of an American protest note about the blockade and the transportation of ammunition aboard the *Lusitania*. Grey signaled to Washington on May 14 that he was 'considering' an abolition of the food embargo – meaning a partial lifting of the blockade – in return for the complete cessation of submarine warfare by the Germans. Wilson's biographer, Link, wrote: 'It was the first ray of hope from Europe in many months; such an Anglo-German agreement would at once end all American tension with Germany and might even be the means of ending all trouble with the British.'[9]

At just the right moment, Grey flattered Wilson in his role as a mediator and returned to the President's old proposal from February. England signaled that it was ready to negotiate, and with this cheap trick prevented an American diplomatic protest against the transport of explosives aboard passenger liners at the same time. Wilson only needed to demand a complete cessation of submarine warfare from Germany to get back to his original concept of trading an end of submarine warfare for the abolition of the food blockade. Thus he kept America out of the European conflict. It was an idea too simple and tempting. All quarrels with Germany over Uboats and with Great Britain over the blockade would have ended with one stroke.

The US government passed the proposal to Berlin on May 19.[10] Gerard reported to House on 25 May, 1915: 'I gave your suggestion to [the Foreign Ministry] this morning. This proposition of permitting the passage of food in return for the cessation of submarine methods has already been made and declined. If raw materials are added, the matter can perhaps be arranged. Germany is in no need of food. Of course the conditions they make are impossible. This does away with their contention that the starving of Germany justifies their submarine policy. I think this strengthens your already unassailable position.'[11]

House responded the same day: 'The Allies would never agree to allow raw materials to go through; therefore I can do nothing further. I am terribly sorry, because the consequences may be very grave.'[12]

Seymour concluded, 'Thus ended the most favorable opportunity for settling the controversy that later was to exercise momentous effect upon the course of the war and the fate of Germany. Had Berlin accepted the compromise, not merely would Germany have obtained the food of which, as she complained, her starving civilian population was deprived by an illegal blockade, but she might have avoided the quarrel with the United States that brought America into the war. Whom the Gods would destroy…'[13]

Grey may have been satisfied. The German government did not cooperate with Wilson; the President would have to increase the pressure.

The First *Lusitania* Note

Wilson's first *Lusitania* note arrived in Berlin on May 15. Bethmann could not react immediately because of the opposition within the Navy and the heated mood of public opinion toward Wilson's demand for cessation of unrestricted submarine warfare. To gradually smooth the crisis he could only apply delaying tactics.

German submarines sank three neutral ships in May without warning. Events started to escalate. First and foremost Bethmann had to prevent a worsening of the *Lusitania* crisis. Riezler wrote: 'Uboat warfare. The repeated sinking of neutral ships has begun to enrage the Chancellor; he finally has gone to the Emperor to get clear instructions to the Navy prohibiting this. The Emperor permitted Tirpitz and Bachmann to be present [in the meeting] – of course, they say that such orders would render Uboat warfare ineffective, etc.'[14] Bethmann pushed Bachmann on May 27, 'that until the resolution of the differences with America [*Lusitania* note], the neutrals are be treated with special protection.'[15] He sent a message to Wilson on May 28, in which he regretted the human loss as a result of the sinking of the *Lusitania*, but pointed to the ship's role as an ammunition transport. The next day, Wilson submitted a terse answer over a – albeit fruitless – submarine attack on an American ship on May 25 south of Ireland.

At a discussion under the chairmanship of the Emperor on June 1, Bachmann voiced the opinion that the ban on sinking neutral ships would make the submarine war ineffective. In that case it would even be better to suspend it completely. Tirpitz agreed with him. However, for domestic and political reasons, he judged the cancellation of the submarine war to be unfeasible. He indirectly supported the continued sinking of neutral ships.[16] The Chancellor found an ally in Falkenhayn, as Bachmann noted in his diary: 'Falkenhayn rejected the sinking of neutral ships, because the entry of the United States into the war had to be expected as a result, which would have an unfavorable influence on the European neutrals. Under such circumstances, he would no longer be able to bear the responsibility for conducting the overall war; it is not the armed power of the United States, but the moral impact of her opposition on the remaining neutral states that would be disastrous.'[17] And, 'since the Uboat war has not shown an appreciable effect at all,' Falkenhayn had doubts about a significant increase by the sinking of neutral vessels.[18]

Emperor Wilhelm elected to continue the submarine war, but without attacks on neutral ships. The day after the Emperor's decision, Bachmann summarized the Imperial order as follows: 'In dubious cases, it is preferable to allow a hostile merchant ship to pass rather than to sink a neutral ship.'[19] The following radio message went out to the submarines on June 1: 'Merchant ships only to be attacked if quite convinced that they are hostile.'[20] Bethmann was satisfied: 'Torpedoing neutral ships will no longer occur, except through error. I have no objection to a Uboat war that will be carried out according to this order.'[21] Bethmann had enforced a firm cessation of attacks on neutral ships as a first step.

Bethmann's next step was to deal with the question of enemy passenger liners. He obtained an order from the Kaiser to the Navy on June 2, 1915, which prohibited the sinking of passenger liners, but this order was not allowed be disseminated outside the navy. This caused an uproar with Bachmann and Tirpitz, who argued that in practice this restriction meant the complete renunciation of the submarine war. Their argument clearly shows that the torpedoing of passenger liners was a key element of their submarine war of deterrence. Once only hostile merchant vessels were left to sink, the small numbers of available submarines were not able to achieve a significant result.

Bethmann was unable to get a confirmation from Bachmann 'that the Uboats had been instructed not to attack passenger liners anymore.'[22] Bachmann and Tirpitz submitted their resignations on June 6 in protest against this order, but the Kaiser rejected them.[23]

Riezler wrote: 'The Chancellor had demanded that the submarines spare passenger ships during the negotiations with America, and after the usual blubbering from the Navy, which always maintains that nothing is technically feasible, the Kaiser sided with the Chancellor. Therefore, Tirpitz und Bachmann announced their resignations. The Kaiser, in consultation with Müller, rejected these very energetically.'[24]

Tirpitz was ironclad in his popularity, but Bachmann had fallen out of favor with the Kaiser: 'I need a loyal person on the Admiral's Staff, not someone who merely follows Tirpitz blindly.'[25]

Wilhelm ordered the Admiral's Staff on June 6 to inform the submarine force that attacks on passenger ships were henceforth forbidden.[26] The Imperial Navy refused, because 'the submarines at the western British coast are out of range of our wireless transmitters.'[27] Von Pohl proclaimed to Bachmann on June 7 that it was impossible to inform the boats at sea.[28]

In fact, the submarines never received this Imperial order because it was simply never sent out. Room 40's documents include a gapless inventory of all of the approximately one hundred intercepted and deciphered German radio messages to the Uboats from the beginning of June through the end of August 1915, and there is no message concerning the sparing of passenger liners.[29] The Admiral's

Staff noted – cynically – on July 30, 1915: 'The secrecy expressly ordered by his Majesty concerning his order to spare passenger liners has been carried out by the Navy with the most assiduous conscientiousness.'[30]

Could anyone characterize this episode with words other than a 'boycott' on the part of the admirals, or better, 'insubordination'?

The Second *Lusitania* Note

In a conversation with the German Ambassador in the United States, Count Bernstorff, on June 2, Wilson demanded the 'total abolition of the submarine war on moral grounds.'[31] Grey may have been satisfied even more: Wilson had switched roles from mediator to referee and was thus on a collision course with Germany. Wilson's next note demanding a total cancelation of the submarine war went out to Berlin on June 9. Secretary of State Bryan, fearing that Wilson's course would lead to an uncontrollable involvement in European affairs, protested and refused to sign the note. He resigned in protest. Robert Lansing became his successor.[32]

Through various warnings from Bernstorff, Bethmann knew that a break with America was inevitable if Germany did not give in. Riezler wrote on June 10: 'So, the Navy must give in. German public opinion in this case [abandoning Uboat war] is very negative. Now the American note has arrived, moreover, Bryan has resigned – no further details are known here because of the bad connections.'[33]

The strategy of the Chancellor and the Kaiser remained 'no break with America. We will have to promise to spare American ships and British passenger liners.'[34] The Emperor decided that Bethmann and the navy should jointly formulate a note in response to Wilson.

The propaganda of the Imperial Navy against any form of concession inflamed German public opinion. Above all, American ammunition deliveries to the Allies had led to a bitter mood in Germany toward the United States, which the navy thoroughly exploited. Admiral Müller reported on June 23, 'public opinion in Berlin is growing more and more agitated against the Chancellor and more and more pro Tirpitz. This will unequivocally lead to a catastrophe – at least in the press – if the American note is not completely rejected.'[35] An exemplary headline in the German press: 'Torpedoing will go on.'[36]

House was pessimistic. On June 16 he wrote in his diary: 'The difficulty is not with the German civil authorities, but with the military and naval as represented by von Tirpitz and Falkenhayn. The feeling is not good between the Foreign Office and von Tirpitz, for their differences are irreconcilable. In my opinion, von Tirpitz will continue his submarine policy, leaving the Foreign Office to make explanations for any 'unfortunate incidents' as best they may. I think we shall find ourselves drifting into war with Germany, for there is a large element in the

German naval and military factions that consider it would be a good, rather than a bad, thing for Germany.'[37]

Riezler wrote on June 23: 'Intrigues. The Navy mobilizes the opponents of the Chancellor against him with their propaganda for an unrestricted Uboat war, to which he is commonly known to be opposed. The Chancellor is losing his connection to the Right ever more. The Right is quite senseless, completely addicted to the hyperbole of violence.'[38]

The Kaiser held a conference with Tirpitz, Bachmann and Müller on June 25, 1915. Tirpitz and Bachmann offered the cessation of the submarine war in return for the complete lifting of the British blockade, 'an illusionary proposal' in Müller's judgment.[39] Tirpitz opposed giving in to the United States, as Müller reported: 'In answering the American note [Tirpitz argued], one must take into consideration not only the effect on the American public, but also the reaction of our own people. Here, His Majesty interrupted the Secretary of the Navy to say that it didn't matter to him what the people thought. The people understood nothing about the matter and they were being misled. Any sensible person here would feel duty-bound to help educate the public and to stand up against the indoctrination of hate. One must really doubt the clarity of mind in certain circles. Following these at times very impassioned statements from His Majesty, Tirpitz felt as though he had been slapped in the face.'[40]

The days between June 12 and July 4 passed with a chaotic back and forth between Bethmann, Tirpitz, Bachmann, Müller, and others over the content of the answer to the American note – they could not overcome their incompatible, contradictory positions.[41] When the group presented a first draft to James Gerard, the American Ambassador to Berlin, on July 4, he reacted in a harsh tone: 'That's absolute idiocy, and will only provoke a war with the United States.'[42] Now Gerard clearly overstepped his authority, he personally had to lend a hand to rescue the peace. In cooperation with the Foreign Office, and without informing his superiors in Washington, he began to compose several handwritten drafts of an answer note.[43] Müller reported: 'Eventually, American Ambassador Gerard himself had to formulate the note to his own government, an awful indication of the poverty of our political leadership.'[44] He added, 'The note of response is like a suit upon which three different tailors have worked.'[45]

The note was presented to the Emperor on July 6. Müller noted: 'He was totally uninterested in its content and was only satisfied by the fact that it had finally been created without objections from the Navy.'[46]

Gerard was also satisfied – 'his' *Lusitania* note was sent on July 8 to Washington. In it, the German government offered assurances that it would undertake all measures possible not to endanger the lives of American passengers, which meant putting a stop not to the overall, but rather only to the unrestricted submarine warfare. Wilson received this message on June 12. He retired to his rooms and sat down alone at his typewriter to begin to work out an answer.

Orduña

The indefatigable commander of U-20, Walter Schwieger, meanwhile set out on his fourth submarine mission since the beginning of the year. He went on a northerly course from Emden on July 3, 1915. U-20 passed Scotland on July 6 and ventured into the Atlantic, in the direction of southern Ireland. Schwieger sighted neutral ships by the dozen and left them unharmed. In the morning of July 9, he again found himself in his old hunting grounds south of Queenstown/Cork, not far away from the wreck of the *Lusitania*, where, in clear weather, he sighted a 'large steamer.'[47] Schwieger dove and fired a torpedo at the ship from a distance of 1,000 m: 'Missed. Torpedo passed just behind the stern. I underestimated the speed.'[48] U-20 surfaced and from a 4,000 m distance fired with its deck gun at the vessel, which was sailing off at maximum speed.[49]

Schwieger had not only misjudged the speed, but had also, despite the clear weather and short distance of 1,000 m, shown himself to be completely wrong about the size of the ship: It was not a '6,000-8,000 ton freighter', but the 15,499 GRT British passenger liner *Orduña*. Even once surfaced, Schwieger obviously failed to notice his 'mistake', and continued to fire shells into an obvious passenger ship with several hundred people on board, including twenty-seven Americans.

From any other German submarine commander, a single case like this could have been – maybe – excused as a one-time 'mistake' – but not from the professional passenger liner hunter Walther Schwieger. A submarine had again deliberately torpedoed and attacked a passenger liner.

The Third *Lusitania* Note

News of the torpedoing and shelling of another English passenger liner by a German submarine arrived just as Wilson drafted his next note. The American press expressed outrage about this new incident, but Wilson knew that the public and Congress wanted to avoid conflict with Germany. He retracted his demand for a complete cessation of the submarine war. In his third *Lusitania* note, he concentrated only on the rights of neutrals, which he wanted Germany to respect. He insisted that the submarine war be conducted according to cruiser rules, and that the German government issue an official apology. Additionally, it should pay for damages arising from the *Lusitania* incident. In reaction to the *Orduña* affair, he threatened to break off diplomatic relations if there were further incidents with passenger liners.[50] But he also promised joint action when it came to the question of the freedom of the seas, in other words, against the British blockade.

The new note arrived in Germany on July 21. Riezler documented the negative public reception: 'Among the people and also at court, there is considerable fury at America, which, of course, also works against the Chancellor.'[51]

Bethmann noticed, however, that Wilson was backing off, along with new overtones in this note. Wilson now accepted restricted German submarine warfare. And since, with the Imperial order dated June 2, the possibility of the sinking of passenger liners seemed to be excluded, Bethmann Hollweg felt that he had gotten over the hump. He merely had to apologize and negotiate the reparations to be paid in the *Lusitania* affair. And America did not exactly exert any pressure on this issue. Washington sent out signals via Bernstorff and Gerard not to react to Wilson's note for the time being, and to let the whole matter cool down.[52]

While all of this was playing out, the Imperial Navy continued her opposition to every moderation in the liner question. Müller wrote on July 19, 1915: 'The Navy wants to continue to sink all enemy liners, while the Chancellor wants to postpone this until the negotiations with America are completed.'[53]

Only one day later it seemed as though the navy finally relented: 'In the morning, conference with Tirpitz and Bachmann. Everything harmonious, even the rejection of a reinforced form of the Uboat war (torpedoing of passenger liners without warning) found quiet approval.'[54]

This 'quiet approval' by the navy, however, actually represented instead the ignorance of the political leadership. A statement from the Admiral's Staff described the mood in the Navy: 'With respect to the attempt of the Foreign Office to pacify America through compliance, the Navy is obliged to resist, and to fight against any restriction on the Uboat war with all its energy and with all available, even extreme, means. If the Foreign Office and the Chancellor do not see that our vital interests as well as our dignity require vigorously rejecting American pressure, it must be made clear to them that a public debate on the subject will leave them no choice. It is the people's right that all available weapons be used with the utmost efficiency.'[55]

The Navy's 'extreme means' was the sinking of passenger liners. After a two-month break, radio messages to submarines concerning passenger liners began again on July 21: 'English S.S. *Arabia* of P & O Line, 8 000 tons is sailing 24th July of London for Asia.'[56] An announcement followed on July 24, reporting the departure of the *Cymric* from New York to Liverpool, and on August 2: 'In the next few days the following English steamers will probably arrive at Liverpool from New York: S. S. *Arabic*, 10,600 tons White Star Line. S. S. *Saxonia* 10,400 tons.'[57] Only through fortuitous circumstances the *Arabic* had escaped sinking on May 6.

Chapter 14

Arabic

On the morning of August 19, U-24, under Lieutenant-Commander Rudolf Schneider, marauded the sea off the south Irish coast. Around 07:00 it commenced artillery fire on a British ship, the *Dunsley*, which sank slowly. At about 07:45, 'a large steamer' came into view. It was the British passenger liner *Arabic*, 15,801 GRT, which had cast off the day before from Liverpool. Aboard were 423 passengers and crew. At 05:00 in the morning, the *Arabic* had received a submarine warning and had swung out eight lifeboats on both sides. At around 09:00, patrol boats briefly escorted her. However, they soon left. About 11:00, the captain of the *Arabic* sighted the sinking *Dunsley*, and headed straight in its direction to assist the ship.[1] Around 11:30, Schneider fired a torpedo: 'After 40 sec., a hit on the ship, the steamer starts to sink immediately. People leave the ship in lifeboats. After 7 minutes the steamer has disappeared. Name could not be made out, no flag was hoisted, seems to have been a 5000 ton freighter and passenger ship.'[2] Forty-four people died, including two Americans.

Schneider's entry in his war diary leaves the impression of a mistake, as if once again an experienced submarine commander had, for hours, observed in his periscope a large passenger liner coming directly at him. Once again, with normal visibility and less than 1,000 yards distance, he had incorrectly estimated the size of the ship, and not noticed the swung-out lifeboats that were a typical indication for a passenger ship. To be able to hit a vessel with a torpedo, knowledge about its course, speed and distance were necessary, and from these parameters, the size could be determined with mathematical precision. Schneider had simulated a mistake in his deck log. Later, he was forced to admit having noticed 'many life boats' on this 'fat goose'.[3]

SS *Arabic*.

Washington

Wilson learned about the sinking of the *Arabic* that same day. He remained passive the entire week, waiting for more detailed information and gauging the public reaction. In keeping with the last *Lusitania* note, he was now forced to break off diplomatic relations with Germany, which almost certainly led to war. US public opinion at that time was strictly against an American entry into the war.[4] Wilson confided to House on August 21: 'The people of this country count on me to keep them out of the war. It would be a calamity to the world at large if we should be drawn actively into the conflict and so deprived of all disinterested influence over the settlement.'[5] But Germany had to grasp the gravity of the situation. A newspaper article on August 22, which was widely known to have been influenced by the White House, threatened the break-off of diplomatic relations.[6]

Link writes: 'Much depended upon his success in managing the negotiations so as to strengthen the Imperial German Chancellor in his struggle with the navy, about which Wilson already knew a good deal from press dispatches, Gerard's reports, and other sources.'[7]

Berlin

The news of the *Arabic* sinking reached Berlin on August 21. Bethmann immediately recognized the danger of a break with America. Had the Kaiser 'given in' again? Bethmann sent a telegram to the Imperial Headquarters on the same day: 'Please confirm whether the Imperial order to spare the large liners was recently lifted.' The answer was negative. Suddenly Bethmann understood that the Navy had simply refused to obey the Imperial order.

A thunderstorm loomed. Müller wrote on August 24: 'In the Imperial Headquarters, great concern about threatening voices from America regarding the torpedoing of the *Arabic*.'[8] The same day, Bethmann initiated the sending of the following radio message to the Uboats: 'Remember the limitations ordered by the All Highest [the Kaiser].'[9]

If the order from June 2 had never reached the commanders, then this wireless must have been quite confusing. At the same time, radio messages with the journey times of passenger liners continued.[10]

Bethmann demanded a new Imperial order on August 25: 'Unfortunately, the behavior of one single Uboat Lieutenant-Commander will determine whether America declares war on us or not. The Uboat war against passenger liners must be conducted according to cruiser rules. Washington must be informed about this order.'[11]

He sent Bernstorff a message for Wilson and the American press that same day, begging for time to clarify the circumstances. He explained that, in the event that American lives had been lost, this happened against the intentions of the government, and that Germany would offer complete clarification and compensation.[12]

Washington understood the message: Germany was giving in, the danger of a conflict had passed. Link writes: 'Even so, as Wilson and Lansing knew, the task ahead would not be easy. There was, first of all, the necessity of forcing the issue to a conclusion without, however, driving the Germans into desperate resistance and thereby tipping the scales against the Chancellor and the Foreign Office in the struggle of control of the German foreign policy.'[13] But now the United States would once and for all insist on a restricted submarine war and the inviolability of passenger liners.

Another conference took place between the Chancellor, Tirpitz, Bachmann, and Falkenhayn, under the chairmanship of the Kaiser on August 26. Müller recalled: 'When, at about 1 o'clock, they were called before the Emperor, conflicting opinions exploded once again, and the management of the discussion was again a disaster.'[14] Riezler wrote about this meeting: 'Big fight with the Navy about the *Arabic*. Falkenhayn on the Chancellor's side. The Emperor ruled against Tirpitz. It will be ordered that we not sink liners without warning.'[15]

Bethmann overruled the navy, and on August 27 obtained approval from the Emperor that Washington was to be officially informed about the prohibition of sinking passenger vessels.[16] As a result, Tirpitz once again submitted his resignation on the same day. The next day in the morning, the Emperor summoned Müller: 'The Emperor, who had received the letter of resignation from Tirpitz was beside himself about it.'[17] Only after the Emperor conceded that Tirpitz be consulted in the 'formulation of the war aims and peace conditions' did the latter rescind his letter of resignation.[18]

Bethmann informed Wilson about the new instructions for sparing passenger liners on August 28. To speed up communication, Wilson had offered the Germans to use the American diplomatic cable line from Berlin via the Netherlands (and London) to Washington.[19]

The following radio message went out to the submarine force on August 30: 'Henceforth, passenger steamers may only be sunk after warning has been given and the passengers and crew have been saved.'[20] From the point of view of the Chancellor, he had defused the *Arabic* crisis, and the danger of war seemed averted.

Lieutenant-Commander Schneider arrived in Emden on August 26. Bachmann tried to 'convince' him on August 31 to depict the sinking of the *Arabic* in his report to the Kaiser as an act of self-defense against the *Arabic* as it attempted to ram his Uboat. To Tirpitz's outrage, Schneider refused this act of falsification 'with tears in his eyes'.[21] In the end, whether Schneider gave in or the admirals fudged the facts, the 'ramming-version' became basis of the report to the Kaiser and, consequently, part of Spindler's 'official' history of the submarine war.[22]

The Kaiser relieved Bachmann of his post as Chief of the Admiral's Staff on September 4; his successor was Admiral Henning von Holtzendorff, an opponent of Tirpitz. Riezler wrote: 'Bachmann replaced by Holtzendorff. Everyone knows that Tirpitz had requested his resignation and that Holtzendorff's appointment is a victory for the Chancellor over him.'[23]

An Imperial decision, that had been overdue for many years, decided the struggle between the navy and the Chancellor, and in line with Bethmann Hollweg's objectives.

Colonel House noted in his diary: 'Germany thus yielded on the main issue, and it may fairly be said that Mr. Wilson had won a great diplomatic victory. The President had been working to safeguard a principle by compelling from Germany a written acknowledgment of its validity: the principle that if submarines were used, they must observe the established rules of warning, visit, and search, and also provide for the safety of non-combatants. Henceforth attacks such as those upon the *Lusitania* and *Arabic* could not be made except in violation of the promise given by the Germans. So much had the President won, and without the exercise of force. But the victory was not clean-cut. No formal disavowal was made of the sinking of the *Lusitania* or the *Arabic*. Furthermore, the German promise was implied rather than explicit. They had given orders to the submarine commanders to abide by Wilson's demands, but they evidently reserved the right to change those orders whenever conditions suited them.'[24]

And the Imperial Navy was unwilling to even follow the orders of the Kaiser. Müller wrote: 'Fighting mood in Berlin. [Tirpitz] is seething with rage and wants to submit a new letter of resignation.'[25] Navy censors allowed newspaper articles critical of the moderate government line and demanding further unrestricted submarine warfare to slip through to publication. Müller reported: 'The Kaiser is absolutely furious with Tirpitz, whom he declared to be the instigator of the whole intrigue.'[26]

Müller wrote again on September 13: 'Tirpitz full of wounded vanity and rage at Bethmann and Holtzendorff. Contempt towards everyone other than himself.'[27] An infuriated Tirpitz could simply not accept his defeat.

Hesperian

On the evening of September 4, Schwieger in command of U-20 was the only German submarine lurking to the west of England, off the southern Irish coast near Fastnet Rock. Room 40 had carefully monitored his movements.[28] Before heading out on August 29, he must have been aware of the violent discussions concerning the future course of submarine warfare. This could possibly be his last cruise in the current hunting season, his last opportunity to 'blow up' a fat vessel. By this time, Schwieger had sunk 73,000 GRT worth of ships, and he was 'top-gun No. 2' of the Uboat captains, just 5,000 GRT, a single ship, behind Max Valentiner.

In his war diary, Schwieger stated that his wireless was out of order since his departure due to 'technical problems'.[29] Thus, 'officially', he had never received the Imperial order of August 30, strictly prohibiting the sinking of passenger vessels. But oddly enough, he was still capable of sending out his position by wireless on August 31 and on September 3.[30] That day he torpedoed a steamer identified 'by his little red stern flag' as British.[31] Unfortunately the color red was not only reserved for the British mercantile navy – he had sunk the neutral Danish vessel *Frode* without warning. Schwieger's apparently increasing ineptitude in identifying ships, coupled with his exuberant joy of shooting, had claimed a new victim.

On September 4, under a star-studded sky, Schwieger noted a vessel closing in at around 20:50: 'Through the periscope, recognizable only as big dim shadow.' At 21:25, Schwieger fired from a distance of 300 m: 'Torpedo hit the forecastle in front of the bridge. It was a large 10,000 t auxiliary cruiser, 1 funnel, 2 masts. Speed around 14 sm. After the impact, many lights became visible.'[32]

The 'auxiliary cruiser' was in fact the British passenger ship *Hesperian*, 10,920 GRT, with 650 passengers on board. Eight people died in the explosion of the torpedo, others drowned later during the evacuation of the vessel. No Americans were among the victims.

As previously mentioned, Schwieger was capable of identifying a passenger liner on a dark night from a distance of 2,000 m in March. On this clear night, and at a distance of 300 m, he could only make out a 'big dim shadow'. Schwieger obviously manipulated his deck log to create the impression of an error.

Ambassador Gerard reported from Berlin on September 7: 'The navy people frankly announce that they will not stop submarining, no matter what concessions are made by the Chancellor and Foreign Office, and now the torpedoing of the *Hesperian* proves it.'[33] House: 'The letters of Ambassador Gerard gave an extraordinary picture of the political confusion there, which contrasted forcibly with the efficiency of German military organization.'[34]

Berlin and Washington

Bethmann Hollweg learned of Schwieger's latest deed on September 5. Following Müller the Chancellor was 'horrified that once again a large English liner – the *Hesperian* – has been torpedoed.'[35] For Bethmann it was clear that Schwieger did not act individually – the Imperial Navy had openly opposed the Kaiser's order! Bethmann's only option was to repudiate everything. He ordered the Foreign Office to deny that any German submarine had been in the surroundings, and to state that a mine must have caused the sinking of the *Hesperian*. Link writes: 'Officials in Washington apparently still (and rightly) thought otherwise, but the State Department did not have enough evidence to challenge the German denial.'[36]

In the *Arabic* incident, the Imperial Navy produced an oath from Lieutenant-Commander Schneider that the *Arabic* had tried to ram his boat. Bethmann Hollweg was incapable of doubting an officer's word of honor. Therefore he responded to Lansing on September 7 that reparations in the *Arabic* case would be impossible and that this controversy must be brought before the international court of law in The Hague. The publication of this answer, in combination with the smoldering *Hesperian* affair, unleashed a wave of outrage in the US press.[37]

Wilson and Lansing were shocked and disappointed. Wilson asked House on September 7: 'Shall we ever get out of the labyrinth made for us all by this German frightfulness?'[38] Lansing lost his patience: 'The whole tenor of the note [September 7] is a cold and uncompromising declaration, that the commanders of submarines have practically a free hand though bound, technically, by some general form of instructions and that if they make mistakes, however unwarranted, their Government will support them.'[39]

Lansing turned the question of the punishment of Lieutenant-Commander Schneider into a litmus test. This demand contained a certain logic – if there had been a ban on the sinking of liners, then, consequently, Schneider had to be punished for the sinking of the *Arabic*. If he was not punished, it would be an admission that no such order had existed. Lansing explained to Bernstorff on September 12 that the United States expected punishment, otherwise it would consider breaking off diplomatic relations.

Berlin

Berlin capitulated. The Foreign Office sent a message to Bernstorff on September 17 signaling its willingness to punish Schneider in case he acted contrary to his orders.

Bethmann still had to rein in the unruly navy. If it acted contrary to the absolutely explicit Imperial order dated August 30, then the only way out was a complete abandonment of submarine warfare. Holtzendorff broadcast an Imperial Order to cease all submarine activities to the west of England and in the Channel on September 19.[40] In view of the evident refusal of the navy to conduct a restricted Uboat war, this was the only option left to stop a submarine war that respected no limitations. It was not the navy which called a halt to the submarine war as Spindler's post-war whitewashed, 'official history' of the submarine war made it appear. According to the 'official' account the war had become 'senseless' and the navy 'protested' the continual 'restrictions' from the political leadership. As a matter of fact, the political leadership made the call in reaction to a navy run amok.

In Washington, Ambassador Bernstorff finally cut the Gordian knot in the *Arabic* case. He arbitrarily gave an assurance on October 5: 'The Imperial Government regrets (and disavows this act) and has notified Commander Schneider accordingly.'[41] The text of this message had been dictated to him by Lansing. Once again an American diplomat intervened and saved peace for the moment.

Bethmann learned of this 'solution' to the *Arabic* question from foreign newspapers and at first was outraged over his ambassador's insubordination. However, at least the *Arabic* crisis was resolved.

In Washington, the crises of the previous months had led Wilson to a change of heart, as he explained to House on September 22: 'Much to my surprise he said he had never been sure that we ought not to take part in the conflict and if it seemed evident that Germany and her militarist ideas were to win, the obligation upon us was greater than ever.'[42]

Wilson had to recognize that the military leaders in Germany acted beyond the control of the political leadership. Should the former continue to maintain the upper hand, then sooner or later a critical confrontation was inevitable, along with all the consequences that arose from it, up to and including war with Germany. For the first time, Wilson confronted the option that was being forced upon him: giving up American neutrality.

Chapter 15
Tirpitz's Uboat War

From January 21 to September 30, 1915, German submarines sank 267 merchant ships with 671,000 GRT in the North Sea and the Atlantic, including twenty-one neutral ships without warning. This resulted in an average monthly sinking rate of approximately 80,000 GRT. With an average of four submarines at sea at any given time, this meant a daily sinking rate of around 600 GRT per Uboat and day at sea.[1]

Worldwide, new construction of merchant ships in 1915 amounted to 1.2 million GRT; Great Britain produced half of that amount.[2] German submarine operations merely halved the increase of the world merchant fleet. These losses were heavy, but did not cut England off from its Atlantic transport lanes.

The Uboat offensive began with twenty-four ocean-going submarines. From the middle of January until the end of September 1915, the Imperial Navy lost eleven of these boats while ten new ones came into service. At the end of September 1915, twenty-three submarines were available. From a purely military perspective, the inflicted damage was minimal, but the losses were catastrophic. To destroy 1.5% of the world merchant fleet, Germany lost one third of its submarine fleet.

In terms of foreign policy, Germany created several fierce confrontations with the United States. Falkenhayn and Bethmann now had to incorporate a US war against the German Empire in their calculations. German-American relations at the end of 1915 were enormously strained.

Compounding the military failures in 1915 with the foreign-policy damage, Tirpitz's strategy can only be described as desperado politics.

The Imperial Navy was a 'closed shop'. It refused to obey the direct orders of the Emperor, would not cooperate even with the army, and it ignored Falkenhayn's negative opinion of the submarine war. Tirpitz waged his own war. The Imperial Navy resembled a medieval order of knights, not unlike the Templars or the Knights of St. John in the days of the crusades, who, without regard for any other authorities in the feudal hodge-podge, operated and existed only for themselves. This was a typical reflection of the kind of post-medieval chaos that existed in 'modern' Wilhelminian Germany at the beginning of the twentieth century.

Kaiser William, as Emperor and Supreme Commander of the Navy, still was unable to dismiss even a low-ranking lieutenant such as Walther Schwieger, who had been directly involved in three of the four passenger liner incidents (*Lusitania*, *Orduña*, *Hesperian*) and was quite obviously a vassal of Tirpitz and not the Kaiser. Of course, Schneider was also never punished, but was instead decorated at the end of 1915 with the second-highest order of the Empire. Schwieger even received the 'Pour le Mérite' medal in 1917 for sinking 175,000 GRT of ships, including the 30,000 GRT of the *Lusitania* and the 10,000 GRT of the *Hesperian*.

In 1915, Kaiser William found himself caught between the Scylla of an extreme right-wing opposition headed by Tirpitz, and the Charybdis of a war with the United States. Both threatened his throne and his central role in the Empire. Tirpitz's putsch plan in the spring of 1915 would have relegated the Kaiser into the background. Eventually this happened with the establishment of a military regime under Generals Hindenburg and Ludendorff in 1916/17. Following the entry of the United States in 1917, the war was lost in 1918, revolution broke out, and forced Wilhelm to abdicate. In the precarious environment of 1915 and 1916, the Kaiser did not dare to act decisively, but tried to steer a middle course.

It is hardly surprising that Wilson began to reconsider. The British blockade had created a new economic reality, including new trade flows. The economic interests of the United States moved ever closer to the Allies. Germany as an economic factor had ceased to exist. Additionally, it was no longer the predictable Bethmann who determined the course in Berlin, but the reckless military leaders. Wilson's diplomatic weapons were threatening to become blunt.

And Tirpitz – what were the gains of his policies after the first twelve months of war? He had covered up the strategic failure of his naval armaments through submarine propaganda and had rallied the right wing behind him. As in the tale of the hare and the tortoise, he kept up the pressure on the government, never giving it a moment's peace, while weakening Bethmann and the Kaiser with his radical, yet very popular, proposals. Behind the scenes, he quietly continued the construction of his battle fleet. Was this perhaps the true purpose of his Uboat propaganda?

Chapter 16

British Blockade in Autumn

To cut Germany off from world trade, three separate commodity flows had to be brought under control. The first was the export from America to Europe, through which goods reached the Allies and the European neutrals. Second, Great Britain had to control its own exports to the European neutrals. England's role in intermediary trade was important. British Fleet Commander Admiral John Jellicoe wrote on September 1, 1915: 'Great Britain has become a base for the supply of Germany via the neutral countries of certain goods.'[1]

The final and decisive element in the chain was the export from European neutrals to Germany. It would have been best to have put them on a 'diet', allowing them to import only enough for their own consumption. But how could these quantities be determined? Where were the international numbers and statistics? At the time, at best, only national statistics existed. Pro-German Sweden, for example, published no figures about exports and imports until 1917.

The British government created a central 'War Trade Department' (WTD) in May 1915, to collect, compile and analyze international trade information. The success or failure of the blockade depended on the precision of this work. As a result, a reliable statistical foundation existed by the end of 1915.

A WTD subsection, the 'War Trade Intelligence Department' (WTID), had some one hundred staff members at the end of 1915. It systematically evaluated all companies and merchants involved in international trade. The basis for this work was the deciphering of commercial telegrams by the cable censors. As mentioned earlier, the British had not only captured the German Naval code book, but also several merchant codebooks. In March 1915, 150 co-workers at the cable censorship office checked and identified suspicious telegrams and translated them. By the end of the war, this institution grew to 800 staff members, who inspected eighty million cable messages during the war, ten million of which were followed up on in detail, close to 5,000 per day. Postal letters were treated in the same way.

Starting in the middle of March, 1915, the War Trade Department published a 'Who's Who in War Trade', updated monthly, for all institutions involved in the British blockade. Firms and persons who were particularly suspicious were put on a 'blacklist'. At the end of 1916, the 'data base' of the WTID, its card index, included 250,000 entries.

Another WTD subsection, the 'War Trade Statistics Department' (WTSD) generated statistics for the first time in 1915 about the imports of neutral states.

Reasonably reliable numbers became available in September for the first half of the year 1915. This work became the basis for the 'diet' enforced on the neutral states later in the war: the rationing of their imports.[2]

All 190 British banks cooperated on a voluntary basis with the 'Finance Section' of the WTD. As always in the case of 'spontaneous cooperation' between private enterprises and state institutions, government control was extremely lenient. For the duration of the war, the financial blockade never became watertight. Money always found its way in those days, just as it does today. Maybe this explains why historians cannot find any more compromising documents from the Finance Section ('Cornhill Committee') in the British archives.[3]

The WTID analyzed all available intelligence, no matter how reliable. From there, a flow of instructions made its way to all concerned departments. British customs and tax offices harassed suspicious firms and merchants. British banks refused to extend credit, and cable companies stopped delivering telegrams to them. The Royal Navy's cruisers at sea had precise information about the cargos of ships and their final destinations. The patrolling warships could identify and easily seize contraband for Germany; and the British prize courts had enough evidence to justify the capture of neutral vessels and their cargos.

With the suppression of all necessary telegram communication, Germany's indirect export trade via the neutrals became impossible, and, with the deciphering of all related messages, German imports from neutral states could be seized. In many ways, this new British system served to obstruct German access to foreign goods, money and credit.[4]

Landing on the British black list could mean ruin for a company. This economic pressure gave Britain a great global punch, especially for individual economic stake holders outside Great Britain. One example from the summer of 1915 was the American Irving National Bank in New York: it financed a significant portion of the indirect trade with Germany. The British government blocked its entire telegraph communication with the outside world in July. It took until October, after long and tough negotiations with the British Foreign Office and a commitment to no longer finance German or Austrian trade, that the British government lifted the telegram blockade, and the bank could resume correspondence with her global partners and clients.[5]

This mechanism brought the main flow of world trade under British control. However, there were still enough small estuaries and creeks to accommodate contraband traffic. On this level a prolonged cat-and-mouse game between the British and German or neutral traders took place.

A certain restricted cooperation between US companies and Great Britain developed, using the 'Navicert' system. American shipping companies transmitted freight documents in advance to London. Only after the cargo had received British permission to pass the blockade unmolested by the Royal Navy and the

British customs offices – 'Navicert clearing' – did the ships leave their American ports for the voyage to Europe.[6]

But the general situation was unsatisfactory. As House wrote, 'The tightening of the British blockade in the early summer had evoked a storm of complaints from American shippers, who insisted that Wilson and the State Department were truckling to the British and were careless of American interests. They demanded retaliation.'[7]

The only available weapon – a stop of the munition deliveries to the Allies – was blunt. House on July 24, 1915 to the President: 'If we placed an embargo upon munitions of war and foodstuffs our whole industrial and agricultural machinery would cry out against it.'[8]

The result was endless and fruitless diplomatic quarrels between Washington and London that were slowly poisoning their relationship. House: 'The British and French were in no mood to analyze [Wilson's] policy objectively nor to make allowance for conditions in the United States which they did not understand. They regarded themselves as the defenders of civilization and they believed that they were fighting the battles of America, which either from cowardice or greed remained aloof and gathered a golden harvest from its sale of munitions.'[9] And: 'The richer we grow through the acceptance of their insistence that we sell them munitions of war, the more unpopular we become. They cannot look at the situation fairly, and perhaps we could not under like circumstances. I loathe the idea of our making money out of their misfortune, but nevertheless it is inevitable; and if we refused to give economic aid in this way, our name would have been anathema just the same.'[10]

But Grey insisted on the British blockade, as he explained to House on November 11, 1915: 'The friction and trouble that we have over this matter are so great that I have often wished, in despair, to give it up; but that would go near to abdicating all chance of preventing Germany from being successful. I am convinced that the real question is not one of legal niceties about contraband and other things, but whether we are to do what we are doing, or nothing at all. The contentions of your Government would restrict our operations in such a way that Germany could evade them wholesale, and they would be mere paper rights, quite useless in practice. As it is, it looks as if the United States might now strike the weapon of sea power out of our hands, and thereby ensure a German victory.'[11]

And that was the last thing Wilson wanted.

Chapter 17

America and Germany

Once the waters had calmed regarding the *Lusitania* and *Arabic* incidents, the American public became more and more resentful at increasing German intervention in domestic politics. Pacifist organizations, bribed politicians, journalists, and newspapers (Hearst), anti-British Irish organizations (IRA), and the well-organized German minority in the United States vehemently demanded to stop American munitions exports to the Allies and called for Wilson's energetic action against the British blockade.

It was no secret that the German Embassy in Washington orchestrated most of this campaign.[1] A German spy ring under Navy officer Franz von Rintelen, which attacked international shipping with firebombs from American ports, was dismantled in August 1915.[2] Wilson stated on August 4: 'I am sure that the country is honeycombed with German intrigue and infested with German spies. The evidence of these things is multiplying every day.'[3] Lansing suspected the involvement of Ambassador Bernstorff, trying to stir up trouble between the United States, Mexico and Japan, and inciting pro-German voters against Wilson. 'Taken all together Count Bernstorff was a dangerous man and required constant watching.'[4]

IRA members were involved in acts of sabotage and explosions in ammunition factories. Wilson and Lansing received information, that the German Military Attaché, Franz von Papen, and Naval Attaché, Karl Boy-Ed, masterminded the effort. The US government declared Boy-Ed and Papen personae non gratae at end of 1915 and forced them to leave the country.

Wilson expressed in December 1915 his anger over German-Americans who 'had poured the poison of disloyalty into the very arteries of our national life. Such creatures of passion, disloyalty, and anarchy must be crushed out.'[5]

From the American point of view, relations with Germany at the end of 1915 were no longer 'friendly'. And they were not about to improve.

House wrote on November 28, 1915 to Secretary of State Lansing: 'The necessity of the United States making it clear to the Allies that we considered their cause our cause, and that we had no intention of permitting a military autocracy to dominate the world, if our strength could prevent it. We believed this was a fight between democracy and autocracy and we would stand with democracy. [It is] impossible to maintain cordial relations with Germany, not only for the reason that her system of government was different in its conception from ours, but also because so much hate against us had been engendered.'[6]

Colonel House stated: 'We are much nearer a break with the Central Powers [Germany and Austria-Hungary] than any time before.'[7]

Wilson demonstratively began to upgrade the navy and army through a 'preparedness-program',[8] and brought up the *Lusitania* incident again. A letter from Lansing arrived in Berlin on December 17, with the request for reparations. The Chancellor hastened to confirm Lansing's demand two days later. The *Lusitania* case was still open.[9]

Seymour: 'The United States was caught between the belligerents, her neutral rights threatened by the war methods of each side. Colonel House believed it possible to worry along, but he was convinced that in the process the moral credit of the United States with the world would disappear and at the end of the war we should find ourselves without friends. This would be bad enough in case of an Allied victory. It might be fatal if the Allies failed. The United States could not risk a German victory, House insisted, nor could our Government look forward to an indefinite quarrel with both belligerent groups: with the Germans over submarine 'accidents'; with the Allies over their restrictions upon trade. 'Shall we ever get out of this labyrinth?' Wilson asked of House.'[10]

4

1916 – ALL OPTIONS ON THE TABLE

Chapter 18

Storm Warning

Chief of Staff Falkenhayn assured the Chancellor in November 1915 that Germany's material resources were sufficient for another three years of war, but warned that the British blockade would undermine the support of the public to continue the war. He tersely rejected Bethmann's proposal for a negotiated peace: 'It is no longer a traditional war, but a battle for sheer survival.'[1] Falkenhayn changed his stance on the submarine war and, in December 1915, told the Foreign Office: 'So, I am very sorry, but I have to distance myself from you on the question of the Uboat war.'[2]

His opinion now was that Germany had nothing to lose by leading an unrestricted submarine war.[3] He planned a new offensive for 1916, as described by his biographer, Holger Afflerbach: 'The Navy would undermine England with an unrestricted submarine war, while the Army, for the first time since November 1914, would once again attack on the western front.'[4] And: 'Both actions – weakening the French on land and conducting a submarine war at sea – were, according to Falkenhayn, the best options for making Germany's principle enemies ready to discuss peace.'[5] He began to plan for his 'Battle of Verdun'.

Erich von Falkenhayn.

The heads of the Army and the Navy met on December 30, 1915. Holtzendorff and Falkenhayn agreed that a conflict with America would not be detrimental to Germany, because a 'submarine war with no restrictions will, by the end of 1916, be so severely damaging to England that it will sue for peace. A powerful and decisive Uboat offensive can be unleashed by the end of March.'[6]

In a memorandum dated January 4, 1916, Holtzendorff declared that 'enough submarines are available for a submarine campaign against Great Britain which, if conducted without restrictions, would, within four months, induce the British to make peace.'[7] Even Müller was now quite optimistic about a renewed submarine war, because 'we now have more and better-equipped Uboats than we did in the premature and hastily-prepared campaign of February 1915.'[8]

In fact, by January 1916, the Uboat division had in total twenty-one ocean-going and twenty coastal submarines, all modern Diesel-powered units.[9]

In the Mediterranean, six coastal and seven long-range submarines operated out of the Austro-Hungarian bases of Cattaro/Kotor and Pola/Pula in the Adriatic Sea. They reported to the Admiral Staff command in Berlin, and operated in accordance with cruiser rules, as well as with spectacular efficiency.

The Mediterranean Uboat Flotilla developed tactics of its own: the submarine commander fired a surface warning shot from a great distance at the still unidentified vessel, and then had the cargo papers brought on board. That way, the submarine avoided the dangerous approach to the freighters, which were armed with deck guns with increasing frequency or, worse, were disguised submarine traps. By examining the papers onboard the submarine, the commander determined nationality and cargo of the steamer without risk. Sinking armed merchantmen without warning was in compliance with cruiser rules, but even in this case, most commanders preferred 'working' with the deck gun: the artillery duel between the warship and the merchant vessel nearly always ended with the latter lowering its flag.

The most 'effective' Mediterranean submarine commander on record was Lothar von Arnauld de la Perière, who sank during the war over 200 ships, comprising around 450,000 GRT – all in accordance with prize rules. He only attacked armed vessels or ships in a convoy without warning.

The 'Flanders Corps' in Belgium was a navy presence of heavy coastal batteries, torpedo boat flotillas, marines, aircraft fighters and Uboats, all under the command of Tirpitz's RMA in Berlin. At the beginning of 1916, sixteen small coastal submarines of the UB-I und UC-I classes, based in the Flemish ports of Ostend und Zeebrugge since April 1915, operated in the waters between Flanders and England. These small boats went out to sea weekly, usually for two or three days. The UC-I class were minelayers; the UB-I boats had two torpedoes; neither class had deck guns. They had sunk a total of 40,000 GRT of merchant ships in 1915, most of which were small British fishing vessels. Their main task was the protection of the Flemish coastline against British heavy units that were shelling German coastal fortifications. Towards the end of 1915, a UB-I submarine operated for the first time in the English Channel off Calais.[10]

This coastal submarine flotilla grew in February 1916 with the reinforcement of four new UB-II class Uboats, which had six torpedoes on board, an 8.8 cm deck gun and the capability of remaining at sea for ten to fourteen days. For the first time, the submarines of Flanders could operate in the English Channel as far as the southern coast of Ireland.

Overall, the combat strength of the ocean-going submarines had grown: all now had deck guns. Starting in spring 1916, some eight to ten new submarines per month would arrive from the yards.

Only one submarine of the High Seas Fleet had operated on a cruise to the west of England since September 1915. The stubborn refusal of the German High Seas Fleet to conduct restricted submarine war had granted Great Britain five months of rest and preparation of the Atlantic sea lanes.

Riezler described the Chancellor's view in January 1916: 'Falkenhayn had declared two weeks earlier that the war would have to be brought to an end by the onset of winter, but that there was no certainty that this could be brought about, and no military means to ensure it – a breakthrough on the western front was unlikely and, even should this prove possible, it was unclear whether it would be enough to defeat France. The Chancellor called for Tirpitz and Holtzendorff, to question them regarding the potential effectiveness of a Uboat war. Tirpitz's response was immediate – commence war on the morrow and he was certain that within only a few months, England would be forced to her knees. Holtzendorff replied that the political aspect was not his concern – the war could not be started until March, but then, with the power of the current technology, the destruction and terror [sic!] that could be wrought upon England would, within four to eight months, make her beg for peace. The Chancellor had voiced his thoughts, but had not yet taken a firm position. He saw in Falkenhayn's assertion that the military means had been exhausted in a 'coup de désespoir' [an act of desperation]. He held that if we proceeded thusly, the English could only yield once their backs were to the wall, since any concession would be an admission that they had lost control of the seas and had abdicated all political power: it would mean a breach with America and the alienation of the neutral states. Were we to be the losers, we would be beaten to death like a mad dog.'[11]

Bethmann Hollweg explained his position on January 8 during another conference with the navy: '[I don't] shy away from Uboat warfare as a last resort [ultima ratio], but every person involved must be clear about its impact on the neutrals. This would accordingly force America and all other neutrals, mostly undecided as of yet, to take sides with the Allies. If – in this situation – we could not ensure a direct and complete victory, then this would inevitably lead to utter defeat for Germany [finis Germaniae].'[12]

Tirpitz argued that the entry of the United States into the war was unlikely. The navy now had the ability to sink many more times the number of ships as it had in 1915. He assured the leader of the Center Party, Matthias Erzberger, on January 10, 1916, 'a ruthless Uboat war would force England to its knees within six weeks.'[13]

Müller wrote on January 11: 'Invited to spend the evening with the Chancellor. After dinner, he spoke very earnestly about the difficult decision regarding the escalation of Uboat warfare, which he feared could lead to denunciation by the entire civilized world and a crusade against Germany. It seemed to him like a renewed resolution to wage war. And we were not in such a hopeless position as to stoop to an act of desperation. Strong disapproval of the 'gambler', Falkenhayn.'[14] Bethmann confided to Müller on January 12 that there were not sufficient numbers of submarines available. 'He was considering advising the Kaiser to select another Chancellor, one who could unswervingly enter into a ruthless Uboat war.'[15]

Holtzendorff worked out another memorandum on January 13, 1916, which 'statistically' proved that within a very short time period, a Uboat campaign would be overwhelmingly successful. The submarines – according to his calculations – would be able to sink 600,000 GRT of merchant vessels monthly, perhaps even more. Consequently, after four million GRT of the world's merchant fleet had sunk to the bottom of the sea, England would, within six to eight months, be forced to sue for peace.[16]

Another Imperial conference under the chairmanship of Kaiser Wilhelm took place on January 15, involving Bethmann, Falkenhayn, Müller and Holtzendorff. Wilhelm initially expressed his horror that 'the torpedoing of large passenger liners with women and children aboard was unprecedented barbarian cruelty, bringing only the hatred and toxic wrath of the rest of the world upon us.'[17] Müller wrote: '[Emperor Wilhelm] faced the most serious decision of his life. The Kaiser asked me to demand that the Chancellor prepare all diplomatic measures for the commencement of a submarine war on March 1.'[18]

Once again, another indecisive delaying tactic by the Emperor. How was Bethmann to ever obtain Wilson's consent to the sinking of neutral ships without warning? It was a mission impossible.

The Chancellor used the interim to draft a memorandum against unrestricted submarine warfare. Riezler wrote on January 18, 1916: 'Spent last evening with the Chancellor. He read aloud his excellent calm and deliberate exposé regarding the Uboat question. In his thoughtful manner, he lists all

Henning von Holtzendorff.

counterarguments; fundamentally, that the projected Allied loss of four million GRT would presumably be counterbalanced by the confiscation of the 3.5 million GRT of German vessels interned abroad. The decision will be very difficult for His Majesty. He feels incapable of rejecting the demands of the military leaders, who are convinced that they will deliver a decisive stroke. But he has become very critical; I feel that His Majesty will side with the Chancellor. In spite of everything – in this matter, he is cautious and responsible; his restraint must be appreciated.'[19]

American Intervention

Wilson kept up the pressure on Germany, but also looked for alternative ways to stay clear of an armed conflict with the German Empire.

In a note to the Allies dated January 18 Wilson and Lansing proposed the disarmament of their merchant vessels. In return, Germany would conduct submarine warfare in compliance with cruiser rules. The intention of their 'modus vivendi' proposal was to defuse the submarine matter. Disarmament of the merchant vessels would remove any military pretext for an unrestricted submarine campaign by Germany.[20] In reality, the number of merchant ships that were equipped with artillery was relatively small; and the military efficiency of this armament was quite poor.

Wilson had waited for an answer from the German government in the *Lusitania* case since the middle of December. Lansing demanded a German admission that the sinking had been an illegal act on January 15.[21] He expressed his discontent with the status of the negotiations on January 28, and would not exclude a possible break in diplomatic relations. A 'last chance' note was sent out to Berlin on January 29.

Müller wrote on January 31: 'Impertinent demand by the American government has arrived in Berlin. We are to admit that the sinking of the *Lusitania* was an illegal act. With this, in the future, our hands would be tied – that's the crux of the matter. The Emperor, as he told me, was shocked; by now, he had totally forgotten that the *Lusitania* affair was still up in the air.'[22] And the next day: '[The Kaiser was] sleepless half the night over the idea of bearing the responsibility for another war. His poor German people have already made so many sacrifices. It is so terribly difficult for him.'[23]

Bethmann was in an impossible situation: while he struggled with the military over the issue of unrestricted submarine warfare, Wilson now demanded that he kowtow in the *Lusitania* case. Giving in would lead his numerous opponents on the Right to overthrow him. Any concession was political suicide.

Wilson's special envoy and confidante, Colonel Edward House, came to Berlin at the end of January 1916 to assess the situation. In a telegram to Wilson dated February 2, he observed: '[Navy and Army] think war with us would not be so disastrous as Great Britain's blockade. The civil Government believes that if the blockade continues, they may be forced to yield to the navy; consequently they are unwilling to admit illegality of their undersea warfare. They will yield anything but this. If you insist upon that point, I believe war will follow.'[24] Wilson recognized that proceeding too aggressively could tip the scales to the disadvantage of the Chancellor. He retreated and no longer insisted upon the 'illegal act' clause, merely upon compensation. By the beginning of February, the rehashed *Lusitania* crisis was over. Arthur Link noted: 'The truth was that Wilson and Lansing had retreated from a very advanced position both because Wilson did not want a break and because they both had suddenly realized that congressional opinion would not tolerate a rupture over this particular issue.'[25]

The Allies unanimously rejected the disarmament of their cargo ships. Lansing informed the German government on January 26 that the US government considered the torpedoing of armed merchant vessels without warning to be legitimate. His intention was to mount pressure on the Allies. The Secretary of State advised Germany to wait another month before starting their submarine campaign, giving the Allies time to make further concessions in the disarmament question.[26]

For Bethmann, the American decision was an important asset in his negotiations with the military: He could offer a concession in this case. The navy accepted immediately and worked out new orders for the sinking of armed merchant ships.[27] Bethmann informed Wilson confidentially on February 6 that from February 29 armed merchant vessels would be treated as auxiliary cruisers.[28] He approved the navy's new orders on February 11.[29]

The British government was outraged. It condemned these developments as collusion between the United States and the German Empire. Foreign Secretary Grey wrote on February 14: 'The proposal of the United States is an attempt to re-adjust the balance of sea power in favor of our enemies.'[30]

Wilson had to realize that his proposal, intended to de-escalate the situation, had the opposite effect. Grey was right, the entire armed vessels initiative had developed to the advantage of Germany, which interpreted it as a broadening of restricted submarine warfare, and that with the express consent of the US government. It had been an error.

Wilson tried to reopen the discussion with Great Britain by introducing a differentiation between 'offensively' and 'defensively' armed steamers.[31] Lansing advised Bernstorff on February 16 to hold off for another month with the submarine campaign, to buy time for the American government to follow up on these questions with the Allies. He also expressly insisted that no passenger liners be attacked.[32]

Müller wrote on February 19: 'Bad news from America. They want us to delay the war of destruction against armed merchant ships until the United States has reached an agreement with the other powers.'[33]

Another conference, held on January 26, under the chairmanship of the Kaiser, produced no results. There was no rapprochement between the contradictory positions of the Chancellor and the military.

Riezler summarized the situation at the end of January: 'To and fro over the Uboat war. The Chancellor hasn't yet decided. Dangerous risks, but impossible to deny a certain chance of success. The question is, do we want to take the enormous risk of alienating the neutrals at this still undecided stage of the war? Evaluation of the general war situation terribly difficult. Military successes still possible, but no decisive ones. Our Allies will collapse by the end of the year. So, success is needed now. We can only win the war if England is beaten to the point of making concessions to us. Even without the submarine issue, the situation is gloomy.'[34]

War of Memoranda

Holtzendorff's '600,000-ton memorandum' was leaked to the public at the beginning of February 1916, with discreet assistance from the navy.[35] It became the 'Bible' for all supporters of unrestricted submarine war. According to Riezler: 'The Naval Office has again prematurely passed on to the press a position paper against England (threatening to torpedo every ship, because the merchant steamers were armed). Great agitation; the rabble-rousing begins again.'[36] Bethmann ordered Tirpitz on February 9 in vain to stop the press campaign.[37]

What was the basis for Holtzendorff's numbers? How had his calculations resulted in 600,000 GRT of monthly sinking: seven or eight times more than in 1915, with the same number of available submarines?

Holtzendorff estimated on March 1, 1916, that 'perhaps fourteen' and on April 1 'possibly seventeen' ocean-going submarines of the High Seas Fleet would be available for service. He excluded the small coastal submarines in his calculations. Based on 'experience from February to the end of October 1915', he estimated a daily sinking rate per boat at sea of 4,085 GRT. Assuming four boats at sea per day in the North Sea and the Atlantic, this would result in 480,000 GRT per month in the north. In the Mediterranean, he calculated a very optimistic 120,000 GRT monthly, and in the mine war, 'more than 26,640 GRT'. In total, a monthly sinking quota of 'at least 631,640 t' could be expected, which by the end of 1916 would accumulate to '3,789,840 tons' of Allied ships destroyed.

His fundamental miscalculation was the daily sinking rate. To compare it with the reality of 1915: in all theatres of war combined, 1,044,205 GRT had been sunk that year. An average of 3.82 Uboats had been at sea daily. This made an average daily sinking quota of around 760 GRT per boat. Holtzendorff had simply multiplied this by between five to six. Had his 'experiences' deluded him, or could this have been accounting fraud?

To reflect reality: in March and April 1916, an average of 9.29 Uboats were at sea daily, each of which sunk approximately 531 GRT per day. The total for these two months was 296,961 GRT, equaling a monthly sinking quota of 148,031 GRT.

All this was far removed from Holtzendorff's chimerical numbers. The Uboats only twice during the war sank more than 600,000 GRT monthly. In April 1917 forty-one boats at sea daily (the average daily sinking quota per boat was 642 GRT) sank 797.503 GRT, and in June 1917 forty-seven submarines (432 GRT) sank 614,057 GRT during that month.

Due to enhanced anti-submarine measures, the daily sinking rate per Uboat decreased from 760 GRT in 1915 to below 250 in 1918. In the Second World War, the best daily submarine sinking rate on the German side was approximately 400 GRT in 1940, and on the American side, in the Pacific war against Japan, some 231 GRT per day per submarine during 1944.

Holtzendorff's 600,000 GRT per month was doubted even by 'master of lies' Tirpitz, who publicly estimated at the end of January 1915 that about '300,000' tons was more realistic.[38]

Nevertheless, the Navy's public propaganda campaign worked. Riezler noted on February 11: 'Enormous hullabaloo about the Uboats. Great hate-mongering against the Chancellor as a consequence of the Navy propaganda, which whispers in the ear of each of the Chancellor's enemies that we could destroy England, if we only wished. Manipulated numbers try to show that six weeks of Uboat warfare would be sufficient for this, etc. etc.'[39] And, according to Scheck: '[The rightists] pushed the government into accepting unrestricted submarine warfare and replacing Bethmann with Tirpitz. Unrestricted submarine warfare should achieve what Tirpitz's fleet building had failed to do: stabilize the political system and, eventually, strengthen its authoritarian component.'[40]

Bethmann remained skeptical. Müller wrote on February 11: 'The Imperial Chancellor strongly distrusts the Navy's numbers, pointing only to the discrepancies between Tirpitz's and Holtzendorff's numbers. With the expected entry of America into the war, the destruction of England within six to eight months is a pipe dream.'[41]

Falkenhayn pressed for the start of the submarine campaign: 'Uboat war must begin on March 10, and diplomatic preparations must be initiated immediately.'[42] Holtzendorff reassured the Kaiser on February 16, 'I repeat again, that with a brutal submarine war, England will be defeated within six to eight months.'[43]

Holtzendorff prepared the operational order to the Uboats on February 19, which prohibited attacks on neutral ships and permitted the sinking of armed merchant vessels.[44] The order did not mention passenger liners with one word. Two days later, the Kaiser received information about these instructions: 'Holtzendorff presented the order for the Uboats; the start date for the campaign was still left open. His Majesty agreed completely.'[45]

The tactical framework for a restricted submarine war had been laid, but the start date was still undecided. Bethmann communicated to Lansing on February 18 that the new orders to the Uboat commanders were in compliance with the American proposal.[46]

The battle of Verdun opened with a nine-hour artillery barrage on February 21. After several days, however, the attack came to a standstill, with heavy losses. Falkenhayn had opened the gates to the 'Hell of Verdun.'[47]

On February 22 Holtzendorff fixed the start date for the submarine campaign on March 1, 1916.[48] Admiral Reinhard Scheer, Commander in Chief of the High Seas Fleet, included in his February 23 order to the commander of the Uboat forces, Hermann Bauer, that passenger liners were not, under any circumstances, to be attacked.[49]

Riezler wrote on February 22: 'Uboat war, again and again. What will the Kaiser decide? Should Bethmann resign? The press and the people seem to be completely deranged in their support for unrestricted Uboat warfare. Hatred for the Chancellor. Consequently, he will have to – and is ready to – resign. The nation is willing to plunge itself into ruin. Unrestricted submarine warfare is for them an intoxicating orgy of violence. Like a bunch of drunken idiots. Perhaps the English were right when they argued that the Germans had gone mad. A rage of violence. There are limits to the use of violence: it makes sense only if it pays off. All intermediate forms of Uboat war – exempting the passenger liners, the neutrals – are refused by the Navy, which always finds pretexts. Unscrupulous rabble-rousing: the people believe that we have 60 to 200 Uboats; in fact, only fifteen ocean-going submarines are available for the Atlantic.'[50]

Müller described a meeting with Bethmann and Holtzendorff on February 22: 'The Chancellor appeared desperate. I warned Holtzendorff that Bethmann would insist upon guarantees from the Navy not to create a new *Lusitania* affair.'[51] This meeting ended with no consensus; at a conference on March 4, under chairmanship of the Kaiser, a decision would have to be reached.

Müller noted on February 24: 'It seems that the Kaiser has firmly decided not to wage unrestricted war against the neutrals. This could explain his current disinterest in the affair.'[52]

Bethmann Hollweg's Memorandum[53]

The Chancellor had prepared a memorandum for the Kaiser. It was 'without doubt one of the most significant documents dealing with German policy during the First World War,' according to historian Karl Birnbaum.[54]

To begin with Bethmann questioned the numbers that the navy had given, underlining the very different calculations provided by Holtzendorff and Tirpitz. Even if the navy would indeed be able to sink four million GRT, would this be sufficient to force England to sue for peace? New construction, along with the 1.7 million GRT in interned German ships abroad – confiscated in the event of a war with the United States – would offset the losses. And: 'With the tiny number of our Uboats and their ineffectiveness at night, a watertight blockade of England is not feasible. With or without a convoy, England will always be able to push a certain number of ships through the blockade. A Uboat war would surely mean a break with America and lead to a coalition of all the remaining neutrals against us; this would then bring about the revitalization of the military, economic and financial positions of our opponents. The question is, whether we are in such a desperate situation that we feel forced to take such a risk-fraught gamble, placing our existence as a great power in danger, while the chances of winning – in other words, of defeating England by Autumn – are very uncertain. I have to respond in the negative.'

To avoid a break with the United States, the Chancellor proposed conducting only restricted submarine warfare on the oceans.

Bethmann announced to the Chief of the Admiral Staff on February 29 that in the event of an Imperial decision for ruthless submarine warfare he would submit his resignation.[55]

The Kaiser had defined and authorized the tactical approach to a restricted Uboat war by the end of February 1916, but a start date was still undetermined. The navy continued to demand unrestricted submarine warfare.

Chapter 19

Conflicting Decisions

Riezler noted on February 29: 'It is all about the Uboat question now. To and fro of memoranda. Looking at the number of available Uboats, the answer is simply clear. Nothing that would provoke a war with America may be undertaken.'[1]

Müller wrote on March 2, concerning the Kaiser: 'His Majesty obviously very uncomfortable at the thought that he has to decide once and for all about Uboat war. [Bethmann very critical of] the Navy's optimism (beating down England in six to eight months); he foresees a certain war with America, the Netherlands, Denmark and Rumania, and the presumable secession of our allies. Negotiations today with Falkenhayn to avoid confronting the Kaiser with a decision between "Chancellor vs. Falkenhayn and Holtzendorff."'[2]

Müller continued: '[Bethmann Hollweg] very nervous, chain-smoking cigarettes, moving from one chair to another. He was resolved to avoid a break with America, and likewise resolved to resign, should the decision go against him.'[3]

Müller had already prepared a solution for the Emperor: 'Wait and observe first the effectiveness of attacks without warning on armed steamers. The Kaiser was visibly relieved, and retired to his bomb-proof bedroom.'[4]

Riezler wrote: 'The Emperor said the next day that he was in favor of [Bethmann's] memorandum, and that he didn't want to risk war with America – the Chancellor need not worry, he would tell this to the two others [Falkenhayn and Holtzendorff].'[5] Kaiser Wilhelm assured the Chancellor 'that we had far too few boats to bring England to her knees, and that he wouldn't be so foolish as to provoke a war with America.'[6] Bethmann reported to Müller the next day: 'The Kaiser is in complete agreement with my memorandum.'[7]

March 4 1916 marked the day of the decisive Imperial Council meeting. Present were the Emperor, the Imperial Chancellor, Chief of Staff Falkenhayn, and Chief of the Admiral Staff, Holtzendorff. At the Kaiser's wish, Tirpitz had not been invited, and even his 'ally' Falkenhayn, who had found fault with 'Tirpitz's ineffective manner' in discussions, had not objected.[8]

Müller wrote on March 4: 'His Majesty opened the meeting quite reasonably. First, Holtzendorff reported about the number of available forces, then the Imperial Chancellor argued spiritedly against the war.'[9] Bethmann followed the line of reasoning he had set out in his memorandum. Successful diplomatic preparation for a submarine war could not be concluded before April 1. 'At this point, the Kaiser said: Well, today is the 4th of March, let us set the 4th of April for the start.'[10]

All in all, it was a clear victory for the Chancellor: 'The next day, Sunday, after church [the Kaiser sought out] the Chancellor to expressly thank him for his firm position, which had enormously relieved his own difficult position. The Chancellor had managed to enforce his will in unanimity with the Kaiser, and without a clash. The Kaiser, when things become serious, is always wise. Good handling of the situation by the Chancellor, clear superiority in character and intellectual greatness over the others.'[11]

The Kaiser clearly didn't want to snub both the navy and army through the rejection of unrestricted submarine war, so he 'postponed' the decision. The same day, Bethmann wrote: 'Dilatory form of the decree in deference to Falkenhayn.'[12]

The Imperial 'decision' caused a certain amount of confusion among the participants.[13] Müller wrote: 'What was the result of this meeting? In my opinion – unfortunately no formal résumé was provided – it is the following: The Kaiser wants to wait for a month and observe the result of submarine warfare against armed merchant vessels. In the meantime, the Foreign Office is to prepare for intensified warfare, blocking England completely. The Kaiser will decide when this next step is to commence.'[14]

Riezler noted: 'The Kaiser decided upon a postponement until the 1st of April, in an attempt to elude America – but there is no doubt that on April 1 he will once again come to the same decision that he did today – in other words, to prohibit unrestricted Uboat warfare, so long as the Chancellor isn't willing to take that risk. [With the postponement] he had wanted to appease Holtzendorff and Falkenhayn.'[15]

It was left unclear, however, whether unrestricted submarine warfare would begin automatically on April 1, or if the Kaiser would again have to approve it. The Chancellor inquired of Admiral Müller, via Riezler on March 5, 'whether unrestricted Uboat warfare had only been delayed for a month, or if the Emperor had left the decision open, waiting to see what the situation would be at that time?'[16]

Holtzendorff's interpretation was: 'Unrestricted submarine warfare against England will commence on the 1st of April. Until then, submarine warfare is to comply with the orders dated the 1st of March.'[17] Müller disagreed with Holtzendorff: 'In my opinion, His Majesty has not approved unrestricted Uboat warfare to begin in one month.'[18]

It was clear to Bethmann that there would never be American acquiescence to unrestricted submarine warfare. He told the Kaiser on March 17: 'Convincing America to accept [unrestricted] Uboat warfare by the 1st of April is completely hopeless.'[19]

A 'heated controversy' broke out between Falkenhayn and the Kaiser over the Imperial decision.[20] The Kaiser proved to Falkenhayn 'that there was not anywhere near the necessary number of Uboats available as Falkenhayn and the public had demanded for unrestricted Uboat warfare. He kept calm in this discussion, but [Falkenhayn's] opposition wasn't overcome. His Majesty eventually agreed to have more submarines built and to accelerate their construction.'[21]

Would the navy accept this defeat, or did Tirpitz have another poison arrow in his quiver?

Exit Tirpitz

Even before the decisive meeting on March 4, to which Tirpitz had not been invited, there was general indignation about the press campaign he had mounted. '[Holtzendorff] shared the disgust of the Chancellor over the pro-Uboat warfare and contra-government agitation in the press, and the Naval Office's dubious role in it.'[22] Müller wrote about the meeting on March 4: '[The Emperor] condemned the failure of the Naval censorship department and ordered it to be moved [from Tirpitz's Naval Office] under the direction of the Admiral Staff.'[23]

Riezler wrote: 'Idiotic incitement by the press. The Kaiser is furious about it – now everyone condemns it, including Holtzendorff and Falkenhayn. Strictest orders to Tirpitz to turn this department over to Holtzendorff. The incitement is simply incredible. Naval officers visit the local newspapers and, by offering them tempting publication offers, try to influence them to see things their way.'[24] And: 'Now we are waiting to see if Tirpitz will resign, or if he will act in such a manner that he can be forced to resign. If not, then he must be immediately dismissed. It was a blunder on Bethmann's part not to have already enforced this years ago. Now, the final member of the group responsible for the failed pseudo power politics of the first decade of the 20th century will fall.'[25]

A representative of Tirpitz's Naval Office responded to an inquiry from the second Chamber of the Parliament on March 3, stating that the navy possessed a total of 203 submarines that were at the ready, or under construction, or in a trial phase, fifty-four of which were active.[26] Tirpitz had added up all units that in mid-February 1916 were on order only (27), still in the yard (108), or being used as training units (26), plus the small coastal subs (22). In fact, only twenty ocean-going Uboats were available for merchant war, seven in the Mediterranean and thirteen in the North Sea.[27]

Riezler wrote: 'Tirpitz has provided the Parliament with an absolutely misleading report about the number of available Uboats; his calculations even include boats that do not yet exist. 203. But he says nothing about the completion time.'[28]

Müller reported that on March 5 Bethmann complained 'bitterly about Tirpitz, who provided Parliament with a very misleading statement about our Uboat division (54 Uboats now on the frontline, 203 ready or under construction); misleading, because no word is mentioned about the completion time, only the creation of the appearance that these numbers of boats are available for submarine warfare over the next six to eight months. The Imperial Chancellor is now firmly committed to eliminating Tirpitz.'[29]

Falkenhayn wrote about Tirpitz: '[Tirpitz] was constantly lying. As soon as someone tried to pin him down, he would evade. What I was told about the number of available submarines changed by the minute.'[30]

To the outrage of the Kaiser, Tirpitz refused to give up oversight of the naval censorship department, and then reported himself ill. Müller wrote on March 9: 'His Majesty, in disgust, showed me Tirpitz's letter, which he correctly interpreted to be a resignation. I calmed him, and immediately gained his approval to let Tirpitz go now.'[31] The Kaiser decided to dismiss Tirpitz and to purge the Naval Office of all 'toxic elements'. Tirpitz was requested to submit his resignation on March 12.[32] Müller noted: 'Wrote the response to Tirpitz's report of illness; answered him with a request for his resignation.'[33] According to Riezler: 'Tirpitz was sent an expression of regret about his illness and a demand for his resignation. The internal shock will pass.'[34]

Müller on March 13: '[The Kaiser] received Tirpitz's letter of resignation, brimming over with arrogance. His Majesty very indignant, felt offended in his Imperial grandeur, spoke again about the Uboat war, saying that he had decided against unrestricted warfare only because we still didn't have sufficient resources. He had been shamelessly duped by Tirpitz and the Navy in the numbers they had given him.'[35] The Kaiser formally accepted Tirpitz's resignation on March 15. His successor was Admiral Eduard von Capelle.

Riezler's assessment of his arch-enemy was almost mild: 'Strange. Tirpitz au fond a charlatan – all of his notions were false. The people worshiped his will of iron, which they found lacking in Bethmann. He has created a fleet – untimely and inadequate – but at any rate, he has created something and lived out his ideal.'[36]

Admiral Müller wrote: 'The Tirpitz-Chancellor conflict has been continuous throughout recent years, yes, throughout the Chancellor's entire tenure. It became extreme when Tirpitz, in discussions regarding Uboat warfare, arrogantly rejected any compromise with America, and the Kaiser had to make a decision. In the meantime, the Pan-German press has, in a way that is criminal, incited the people. A wink of the eye from Tirpitz could have stopped this. But to the contrary, press articles have been published, more and more impertinent in tone, favoring unrestricted submarine warfare and demanding the sinking of neutral ships. Finally, the last straw was the erroneous number of boats given to Parliament.'[37]

One hundred years later, to the contemporary observer these proceedings appear to be scenes from a madhouse. Why had these conflicts not been resolved much earlier? During peacetime, Tirpitz armed against England, while Bethmann tried to ease Anglo-German relations. In wartime, Tirpitz wanted a peace through victory, by way of submarine warfare and confrontation with the neutral states, while Bethmann attempted to reach a peace of understanding and to avoid any conflicts between Germany and the United States.

The Navy and the Foreign Office followed contradictory strategies, and the Kaiser supported each of them intermittently. Bismarck had created a stable political system, which in order to function required a strong Chancellor and a weak Kaiser. The strong Chancellor was the exception, a weak Kaiser the rule. Wilhelminian Germany tore itself apart in explosive internal conflicts, and the political authorities, who had already lost their legitimacy with the Socialists and the Liberals, were now also losing it with the right. Scheck wrote: 'Tirpitz's dismissal was a milestone in the disaffection of the German right, both old and new, with the Kaiser and – though less conspicuously – the monarchic system. In the eyes of most conservatives, the constitutional order of the Bismarckian state had allowed a weak and incapable regime to survive and expel Tirpitz, its only energetic minister. Many of them began to consider changing the political system instead of solely demanding different policies.'[38]

But Tirpitz had left a ticking time bomb, which, within weeks, would lead Germany in the direction of the abyss – a war with the United States.

Chapter 20

Hurricane

The cryptologists in Room 40 deciphered the following radio message to the Uboats on February 6: 'To all ships. Warning of storm.'[1] The officer on watch may have been perplexed: this was the first wireless to the submarines with weather news since the beginning of the war. And the most remarkable aspect: there was no German submarine at sea this day.

Another weather message followed on February 23: 'Storm warning. Hurricane, snow squalls from the east to be expected immediately and till the evening.'[2] Now U-70 was on patrol, as were some of the smaller Flanders submarines. Why this effort? In Room 40, they may have asked themselves if perhaps this was some kind of a coded message. Hadn't a new German offensive started a few days earlier in France, at a place called Verdun?

The New York Evening Sun 1916: Chorus: 'Majesty, We Never Sink Neutral Vessels!' Kaiser: 'Bless You, My Lambs!'.[3]

The crew in Room 40 had more than enough to do to decipher, translate and analyze hundreds of German naval wireless messages daily around the clock. Since these remained the only 'weather' radio messages intercepted during the war, this episode would be quickly forgotten.

On the following day, UB-18 put out to sea from Ostend, and on the 25th, UB-2, another submarine from the Flanders flotilla, followed. UB-2, without warning, sank an unarmed British freighter by torpedo on February 26, and the following day UB-18 sank an armed French ship in the same manner.

These were the first sinkings without warning in British home waters since September 1915. By March 24, the day the *Sussex* was attacked, twenty large vessels had been sunk, the Flanders boats had sunk twelve of them, and *all* by torpedo without warning, including seven unarmed and four neutral vessels.

The most spectacular case was undoubtedly the sinking of the Dutch passenger liner *Tubantia*, 13,911 GRT, on March 16 by UB-13. The ship had left Amsterdam the day before on a course to South America. To avoid dangerous passage of the British Channel at night, the *Tubantia* anchored at 2 am off the Channel entrance, in the waters between the Netherlands and England, under full illumination. According to the war diary of UB-13, its commander had – once again – erred in assessing the size of the ship: he took it for a 2,000 to 3,000 GRT unidentifiable steamer, and fired his torpedo around 03:35.[4]

Spindler accepted this 'mistaken' version in his work: '16 March, unidentified steamer of around 2000 t [was sunk].'[5] The name of the *Tubantia*, the largest neutral vessel ever sunk during the war, does not appear in his 'history.'[6]

The Imperial Navy first suggested that the *Tubantia* had hit a floating mine. When the rescue teams found remnants of a German torpedo in the wreck, the navy further denied all responsibility: the torpedo had got lost a month before as a stray; the British must have captured and fired it from one of their submarines on the *Tubantia*.

In the war diaries of UB-18 and UB-19, which put out on March 6 and 9, the following identical order with the signature of Karl Bartenbach, the commander of the Flanders flotilla, can be found: 'All steamers running between England and France – with the exception of hospital ships – are to be attacked by torpedo.'[7] To torpedo all vessels except hospital ships meant to sink all vessels without warning, whether hostile or neutral, armed or unarmed, including channel ferries and passenger liners. And this was exactly what the Flanders submarines had been doing since the end of February 1916.

The official post-war 'history' erroneously claims: 'The virtual start of the merchant war by the [Flanders-]boats came following the order March 11, 1916.'[8] But in fact, it had already begun two weeks earlier, and was being conducted as unrestricted, not limited, submarine warfare, as the March 11 orders demanded. While the Chancellor, Kaiser, navy and army still conferred, the Flanders submarines had acted: in their war theatre, they ruthlessly sank – before the eyes of the world's public – anything that floated.

Ship	Date	Nat.	sunk	BRT	U
Arbonne	26/02/16	UK	w/o warning	672	UB 2
Au Revoir	27/02/16	FR	w/o warning	1 058	UB 18
Teutonian	04/03/16	UK		4 824	U 32
Rothesay	05/03/16	UK		2 007	U 32
Trois Freres	06/03/16	FR		106	U 32
Ville du Havre	07/03/16	FR		3 100	U 32
Harmatris	08/03/16	UK	w/o warning	6 387	UB 18
Louisane	09/03/16	FR	w/o warning	5 109	UB 18
Silius	09/03/16	NO	w/o warning	1 551	UB 18
Tubantia	16/03/16	NL	w/o warning	13 911	UB 13
Willie	16/03/16	UK		185	U 70
Lindfjeld	17/03/16	NO		2 276	U 70
Port Dalhousie	19/03/16	UK	w/o warning	1 744	UB 10
Skodsborg	20/03/16	DK	w/o warning	1 697	UB 29
Nominoe	20/03/16	FR	w/o warning	3 155	UB 29
Langeli	20/03/16	NO	w/o warning	1 565	UB 29
Aranmore	21/03/16	UK		1 050	U 43
Kelvinbank	22/03/16	UK	w/o warning	4 209	UB 18
Bougainville	22/03/16	FR		2 248	U 70
Kannik	23/03/16	NO	w/o warning	2 397	UB 18
Salybia	24/03/16	UK	w/o warning	3 352	UB 29

Ships sunk in February and March 1916, Flanders UB-boats highlighted (dark grey=allied, light grey=neutral).[9]

The submarines of the High Seas Fleet had received an order from the new Commander in Chief Reinhard Scheer on February 28: 'Submarine commerce war is to begin at the west coast of England.'[10] This was to be a Uboat war within the limitations established by the Kaiser.

In fact, Imperial Germany was now conducting two different submarine wars – an unrestricted one in the waters of the Channel, and a restricted one in the North Sea and the Atlantic.

Would a Bartenbach or a Holtzendorff ever have ventured to act autonomously, against the orders of the Kaiser? There existed but one Naval officer who did not shy away from a coup d'état or from insubordination: Tirpitz. It will be recalled that the Flanders Corps reported directly to his Naval Office: it was Tirpitz's private fleet. It can only have been Tirpitz who, at the end of February, had ordered unrestricted submarine warfare for the Flanders boats, triggered by the wireless codeword 'Hurricane' on February 23, two days after Falkenhayn's Verdun offensive had begun.

Was Tirpitz convinced at this time that he could win the duel against Bethmann? The army and public opinion backed him. Once it began, would the Kaiser risk abandoning an unrestricted submarine war, and had Bethmann not declared that he would resign in this case? Ruthless submarine warfare was the mechanism that could cause Bethmann to fall, and then a new Chancellor Tirpitz could erase all traces.

Bethmann was very busy in Berlin during these weeks, attempting to appease the public uproar over Tirpitz's dismissal. He was completely oblivious to what was happening on the high seas.

The cartoon at the beginning of this chapter from the contemporary US press could have expressed Wilson's feelings during these days: Imperial Germany had assured him that the Uboat commanders would act like lambs and abide by the American restrictions, while actually they were wolves and would indiscriminately torpedo hostile vessels and neutral passenger liners alike. Was Germany playing a duplicitous game with him? At the least provocation, he would have to react forcefully.

Domestic Shock

Following Tirpitz's dismissal and the Imperial decision against unrestricted submarine warfare, emotions ran high in Germany. Riezler wrote on March 15, 1916: 'Tumultuous times here. People are livid because of Tirpitz and the failed hopes for the submarines. The enormous support for the Uboat campaign had arisen from their yearning for peace – the propaganda had convinced them that England would crack within only a few weeks. Vain hopes; now they mourn in despair. Increasing economic distress, no end of the war in sight. Strange, most people are quite naive about peace; the worst crises are yet to come.'[11] And on March 22: 'Still wild times. Petitions about the submarine war are being distributed to Reichstag representatives (750,000 copies,) declaring that war with America is better than starvation.'[12]

Bethmann forced Tirpitz's successor, Admiral von Capelle, to retract the propaganda and, in a Reichstag inquiry, tell the truth. Riezler wrote on March 26: 'Capelle's detailed information is so horrifying that we can only be glad to have averted this calamity. With the present resources, nothing could have been achieved.'[13]

The Reichstag leadership held a closed meeting on March 28 to debate the Uboat war in private.[14] Capelle gave the facts: To the west of England and in the Channel, three Uboats per day were available on average. Capelle declared: 'It is impossible for this small number of Uboats to be able to establish an iron curtain around England's west coast and effectively cut off British supply.'[15]

To continuously man the three stations in the Atlantic, a minimum of fifteen submarines were required, since the journey to and from these stations took two weeks, and the usual stay there was another two weeks. After a one-month cruise, the submarines had to spend several months in the yard to be overhauled. At the moment, twenty submarines were available. Each submarine had enough torpedoes on board to sink four to five ships; to sink more than these, artillery also had to be available. For Capelle, these numbers proved 'that unrestricted Uboat warfare as it has been conceived – sinking *all* vessels without warning – is simply impossible.'[16]

One hundred Uboats were under construction. 'Our Uboat division will not reach maximum strength this summer, but rather next winter or, more likely, in the spring.'[17]

He concluded: 'Despite best efforts to induce me, I remain unconvinced that six months of Uboat warfare in the summer, with a potentially adequate but in no way overwhelming number of forces available, will be sufficient to force England to surrender and to hand over the control of the seas to us. For this, rather more would be necessary.'[18]

'Rather more' than twenty submarines were suddenly needed. Like an ice-cold shower, this information from the top abruptly silenced all right-leaning 'Uboat-warriors', and generated outrage at the deceptiveness of the navy in the center-left camp.

Tirpitz's navy propaganda had pushed the government to the forefront of public opinion, using fantastical demands and numbers. Tirpitz's opponents never had the chance to respond openly to the facts without revealing the military situation to the enemy. This was exactly what now took place in the 'confidential' parliamentary session – weeks later, the details of Capelle's 'confession' leaked to the world press.

Riezler noted on April 15: 'The Uboat question is dead at the moment – but under the surface, it continues. At any time, the situation with America could resurface again. Falkenhayn persists on and on. Recently, he came back to this question, arguing that through brutal warfare, results to the eight- or tenfold could be achieved. This is total rubbish – but the Chief of Staff insisted on his 'feeling'.'[19]

The navy and the public now kept silent on the submarine question. Falkenhayn remained the last 'Uboat-warrior'. After several days, his Verdun offensive had ended in the usual western front butchery; both sides continued for months to throw battalion after battalion into the artillery barrage.[20] After the failed Schlieffen plan, the Kaiser had hastily nominated Falkenhayn as a surrogate for Chief of Staff Moltke, who had completely failed. His colleagues in the army and General Staff nicknamed Falkenhayn 'the gambler' because of his strong inclination to take risks; at any rate, he kept out of politics, so Kaiser Wilhelm stood up for him against massive criticism. The only alternative replacement would have been the more popular generals Hindenburg and Ludendorff, the magnificent victors against the Russians on the eastern front. But Ludendorff, the 'mastermind' behind the dull Hindenburg, was a 'political' general with strong supporters on the right, tremendously ambitious, and willing to go to extremes. Wilhelm had no need for another strong militarist at his court, who – like Tirpitz – would only try to push him into the background.

The isolated Falkenhayn was in search of an excuse: should his risky strategy at Verdun fail, it was because the Uboats had not stopped the ammunition transports in the English Channel.

Chapter 21

Sussex

Wilson's biographer, Arthur Link, noted: 'Ironically, the dire German-American crisis was touched off, not by a long-range U-boat of the High Seas Fleet operating in British waters, but by one of the small UB submarines of the Navy Corps Flanders Flotilla, that sailed in the Hoofden [waters between England and Holland], the English Channel, and off the eastern English coast.'[1]

In the afternoon of March 24, 1916, Lieutenant-Commander Herbert Pustkuchen, captain of UB-29, torpedoed the French channel ferry *Sussex*, 1,353 GRT, with a clear view and from a distance of 1,300 meters. According to his war diary – and Spindler – he had 'mistaken' her for a mine layer.[2] 325 passengers were on board, including twenty-five Americans. The torpedo tore off the ship's bow, but the vessel was able to reach Boulogne under its own steam. The attack cost eighty victims, including four injured Americans.[3]

Sussex after the torpedoing in Boulogne.

Washington

Lansing and House pressed Wilson to act immediately and to threaten the break-off of diplomatic relations, but Wilson, faced with the confused situation in Germany, decided to await clearer information.

Link writes: 'The trouble, he probably thought, was that no one really knew what the Germans were doing. Had they in fact begun the unlimited submarine campaign?'[4] And: 'No one at the State Department understood the new submarine campaign. Submarines had apparently sunk some ships without warning, others after warning. And none of the ships thus far destroyed had been armed.'[5]

Wilson had enough details to substantiate the sinking of the *Sussex* by a German Uboat without warning on April 5, 1916. Additionally, new facts had come to light about the sinking of the *Tubantia* and others. He began to work on a new note to Germany. House informed British Foreign Secretary Grey in a letter dated April 7: 'Our relations with Germany now seem to be going steadily to the breaking point and we are making all our preparations to that end.'[6]

Berlin

In Berlin, the angry storm clouds caused alarm, but the Admiral Staff reassured the Foreign Office on April 8 that submarine commanders executed a sinking only following a warning.[7] Bethmann had to trust this information, and on April 11 he sent a message to Lansing: 'Germany willing to conduct submarine warfare with due regard to neutral rights. We naturally stand by our assurances to America and have issued such precise instructions in this line that according human foresight errors can be excluded.'[8] And on the same day, he wrote to Colonel House: 'If President Wilson wishes peace this is in full agreement with Germany's wishes. Germany hopes that the development of German-American relations will make possible cooperation to bring about peace.'[9] How must these messages have sounded to President Wilson's ears?

Washington

Link writes: 'Never before, not even during the *Lusitania* crisis, had such awful responsibility been his to carry alone.'[10] Wilson would no longer enter into discussions about armed merchantmen or other details. In the face of the obvious German game of deception, this would have only meant lost time. 'There was nothing to debate; the evidence was conclusive. He would express his abhorrence of submarine warfare and present an ultimatum threatening a break in diplomatic relations. At the same time, he would make it possible for Germany to accept *because acceptance would not mean yielding effective use of submarines as commerce destroyers* [italics in original].'[11]

The gravity of the situation was clear to every responsible politician in the United States: War with Germany was imminent, and it was up to Berlin to start or avoid it.

The US government sent the note on April 18 and it arrived at the Foreign Office in Berlin two days later: 'Unless the Imperial Government should now immediately declare and effect an abandonment of its present methods of submarine warfare against passenger and freight-carrying vessels, the Government of the United States can have no other choice but to sever diplomatic relations with the German Empire altogether.'[12]

Berlin

Müller wrote on April 21: 'Arrival of the American note, better characterized as an ultimatum.'[13] Since the leading political circles in Germany were still not aware of the 'two submarine wars', the expression 'the abandonment of its *present* methods' led to confusion. Was Wilson demanding a complete halt to the submarine war?

The next day, Müller wrote: 'In the evening, the Chancellor informed His Majesty about the note. The Kaiser appeared to be unperturbed, and continued to play cards, speaking calmly about the note.'[14]

Falkenhayn, in discussion with the Chancellor on April 22, stated that he would not consider unilateral concessions towards the United States if Great Britain did not relent on the issue of the blockade.[15]

Wilson informed the German ambassador on April 23 that a complete hiatus of the submarine war during the negotiations would be taken as an initial positive sign.[16] Bethmann remarked to the Austro-Hungarian Ambassador on April 24 his intention to 'use all means to prevent a break with America.'[17]

The same day, in a meeting between the Chancellor and the navy, Capelle gave in for the first time, that a submarine war conducted in accordance with cruiser rules, using the deck guns, could be successful. A new order to the submarines, directing them to conduct warfare according to prize rules, was prepared.[18]

Riezler's entry dated April 24: 'Nerve-wracking days. Bad news from America. American note very displeasing. Consultations. Situation is quite simple: England will not conclude peace as long as it holds out hope on America. Two different strategies possible: 1.) To frustrate this hope by no longer provoking America, which means leaving the Uboats in port. 2.) War with America and sinking at least triple the number of vessels that are currently being sunk. The first method more practical, as the prerequisites for the second do not yet exist. Additionally, Wilson has signaled that if we will yield, he will enforce peace on the Allies. A lot of bluff [on the American side], but better not to take any risk, and to make an affirmative gesture, so that international law will have been restored on our part, and then it is up to the United States to restore it on the other side [British blockade].'[19]

Holtzendorff as well now took a surprisingly mild stance in a discussion with the Chancellor and von Capelle on April 26: submarine war against England would be senseless, should America take sides with the Allies.[20]

The Kaiser assured Bethmann on April 26 that 'he wants to avoid a break with America under any circumstances.'[21]

Müller noted on April 27: 'Negotiating with Imperial Chancellor and Holtzendorff. Much difficulty in confessing to the unwarned torpedoing of the *Sussex* and in promising submarine commerce warfare that is in accordance with cruiser rules.'[22]

Reinhard Scheer, Supreme Commander of the submarines in the High Seas Fleet, opposed any retreat. He claimed that, in view of the heavy losses that would thereby be inflicted, submarine warfare conducted in compliance with prize rules was impossible. He ordered the withdrawal of all submarines on April 27, in effect aborting the submarine war.[23]

Riezler wrote on April 28: 'No doubt, cruiser warfare more difficult and dangerous. But the German Empire cannot risk collapse on account of the interests of the submarine commanders. The press clamors. Aggrandizing by the Chancellor, who, if anyone mentions the domestic problems or recommends taking them into account in the formulation of the answer note, merely scoffs.'[24]

Wilson sent notice to Berlin on April 28 that he insisted only upon the abandonment of the 'illegal' submarine war, and that he would tolerate a restricted one.[25]

Internal discussions in Germany about how to react to Wilson's note became more and more confused. Müller noted on April 28: 'Note to America again uncertain, mostly due to the resistance of General Falkenhayn.'[26] Riezler wrote on April 29: 'The Chief of Staff completely intransigent. Insists upon relentless Uboat warfare; if not [conducted], no chance of victory, instead, defeat due to exhaustion. He credits the Navy's arguments. No one knows if perhaps he isn't only looking for a pretext to justify a change of [the Army's] strategy to the defensive.'[27]

And, on April 30: 'I fear the American Ambassador deems us half-crazed. He doesn't understand why we can't come to a clear decision; he is completely right in saying, "You will win the war anyway." He constantly reiterates that Wilson, once this question is resolved, will be forced to take action against England. He is completely right. Increasing anger of the neutrals toward England. Very unpleasant for England, and important for the constellation at a peace conference. Renewed submarine war a sword of Damocles for Wilson; he must at least attempt to mediate peace. Whatever does Falkenhayn want? Passing off the responsibility for Verdun, or overthrowing the Chancellor, and then conducting relentless Uboat warfare? If that gamble were to work, then he would be the savior who led Germany to world domination; if not, then it's the Navy who is to blame. The Kaiser is wavering.'[28]

Müller's entry on April 30: 'Falkenhayn justifies his opposition: since the Verdun offensive was begun on condition of a parallel Uboat campaign, he would be forced to halt operations in Verdun if the Uboat war were to be abandoned. A stunning juxtaposition. The Kaiser has fallen into line with Falkenhayn and has told the Chancellor: 'you now have to decide about the Uboat war and Verdun.' The Chancellor was outraged, as were Holtzendorff, Capelle and I.'[29]

Bethmann was stricken. Riezler noted: 'Chancellor upset by the effort to make him responsible for a halt to the Verdun battle.'[30] Müller remarked on May 1: 'In view of his differences with Falkenhayn, and the animosity of the agitated public opinion, the Chancellor regards his position as indefensible; in the interest of the Fatherland, it would be better to give up his position to Falkenhayn.'[31]

On the evening of May 1, Bethmann reported to the Kaiser explaining that the German response was a political concession, that America would accept a submarine war conducted in accordance with the cruiser rules, and that the Uboat war need not be abandoned. The note from the Foreign Office admitted the erroneous torpedoing of the *Sussex* and offered compensation. Submarine warfare would be conducted in compliance with prize rules; in return, Germany expected Wilson's commitment to the restoration of international law in the issue of the British blockade. Should this not succeed, the German government left open the possibility of a renewed unrestricted submarine war.[32]

After days of wavering between Falkenhayn and the Chancellor, Kaiser Wilhelm decided in favor of Bethmann and agreed to the note. Müller wrote on May 1: 'When we arrived in the evening, the Chancellor, following his decisive conference, was just leaving. The Kaiser approached and told us that he had agreed to the note: it was excellent. In awareness of the opposition of Army and Navy, he had excluded them from the discussion.'[33] Bernstorff delivered the German note to Wilson on May 5, 1916.[34]

Finally, with this clear decision, the Kaiser had cut the Gordian knot. Falkenhayn resigned the following day, and only after violent discussions rescinded his resignation. Müller observed: 'Falkenhayn acquiesced. We all suppose that his resignation was meant as a protest against the mild reaction to the American note, and as a means of documenting his opposition to the exclusion of escalated Uboat warfare. Should he not obtain a sweeping victory at Verdun, then he can blame it on the lethargic Uboat war. But it will certainly be difficult for him to establish a relationship between these two things.'[35]

Bethmann communicated his evaluation of the situation to the German Ambassador in Sweden on May 5: 'Our note of response will oblige [Wilson] to act against England, in view of its violation of international law. It is not expected that England will abandon its economic war against us under this pressure. Wilson, therefore, who is in the middle of his presidential candidacy, will be in a situation in which he can augment the pressure on England for a peace of understanding.'[36]

He added, 'On our side, the desire for peace is very intense, and should the harvest fail, our economic difficulties will develop into a catastrophe. Should we become convinced that a Uboat war cannot bring England down, we will have to grasp at any opportunity to come to peace.'[37]

Riezler noted on May 7: 'My God, what confusion about such a simple, rational affair, so crystal clear that any wise person cannot dither about it – the current economic misery, the imponderability of the [Uboat] weapon. Public opinion quite subdued. Most of those who earlier were screaming for unrestricted submarine warfare have recently become frightened. As to the whole matter – pure idiocy. Originally an idea of Tirpitz's, to throw blame on the Foreign Office, but he never intended to implement it. Criminal.'[38]

Müller noted on May 9: '[The Kaiser] told us about a telegram from Count Bernstorff (our Ambassador in Washington), according to which Wilson had accepted the German note.'[39]

But Wilson made it clear that Germany's respect for the rights of neutral states could not depend on the actions of other governments, and that he expected Germany's strict adherence to this in the future.[40] Müller: '[The Kaiser] explained immediately, that the tone certainly seemed abrupt, but in reality, was the style of a know-it-all who was backing down. In any case, the conflict had been overcome.'[41]

Conclusion

What was at the core of the *Sussex* affair, the most severe clash between Imperial Germany and the United States since the outbreak of the war? Wilson had expanded the prize rules to Germany's advantage, conceding the right to torpedo armed merchantmen. In return, in compliance with American wishes, the Imperial government had repeatedly postponed the start of the Uboat campaign. However, unknown to the political leadership, the Flanders Uboats had, at the end of February, commenced unrestricted Uboat warfare. Wilson felt duped, and reacted with a strict ultimatum, just short of war. Bethmann's extremely risky task was to constrain the Navy to obey the Kaiser's order. Holtzendorff and Capelle finally conceded, with the surprising admission that a submarine war in accordance to cruiser rules was indeed feasible. However, Commander in Chief Scheer disagreed, and abruptly broke off the Uboat war which the High Sea Fleet's submarines carried out to the west of England. He had intended the Uboats to be used for military purposes, acting as scouts, and to prepare for a sea battle [Jutland – Skagerrak, at the end of May]. The Flanders submarine flotilla stopped its Uboat merchant war at the end of April, and was once again restricted to purely coastal defense missions. The Navy, now rid of their demon, Tirpitz, had conceded. For the moment. The sinking statistics, some 100,000 GRT in March and April each, were insignificant, as in the campaign a year earlier.

The only resistance had come from Chief of Staff Falkenhayn. Whatever his personal or strategic reasons, he acted according to Tirpitz's intentions: to obtain *a posteriori* legitimization for a ruthless submarine war, which would consequently lead to Bethmann's resignation. The Chancellor had been about to capitulate. The Kaiser, after typical indecisiveness, ruled at the last moment in favor of the civil leadership. Ordinarily, reason and common sense came to Wilhelm only when he had his back to the wall, when he was *forced* to choose between two alternatives. But the imminent conflict between the military and the civil leadership in Wilhelminian Germany, however, continued to smolder.

Bethmann had gained a temporary victory and had, for the moment, avoided a US-German war. Additionally, he must have felt that he had won Wilson's support in the blockade question and for a negotiated peace.

Chapter 22

British Blockade in Spring

Great Britain created its own Blockade Ministry for the centralized supervision and coordination of all necessary measures in January 1916. In the spring, all neutral imports were restricted in accordance with the statistics that had been worked out, and were frozen at pre-war levels.[1]

All US exports were now subject to the 'Navicert' system. England negotiated or enforced limitations on exports to Germany from Switzerland,

'Collect nettles, the German cotton. Bavarian Nettle Department, Munich'.

Holland and Denmark. Resistant neutrals, such as Norway or the especially recalcitrant Sweden, became victims of an import embargo by the Allies. However, enough loopholes still remained.[2]

'While naval vessels patrolled, stopped ships and seized cargoes, the real picket line was in the offices of Whitehall, at port stations in Liverpool, Portsmouth and around the globe. It was more a diplomatic blockade, but no less choking, and it was intelligence that made it possible.'[3]

Companies that on the basis of deciphered cable messages came under suspicion, experienced global pressure. Neutral shipping lines were threatened with exclusion from the worldwide Allied coal bunker network. If a company complied, it was placed on the 'White List', and could carry on global shipping services with British and French coal, but if there was resistance, it had to accept that its future operations would be restricted to the North Sea and the Baltic.[4]

Thus, the response of an American cotton dealer to a potential German buyer in November 1916: 'We desire to call your attention to the necessity of not allowing our name to appear in any communications you may send to our friends in Germany. We cannot take chances of the British authorities seeing our names in connection with German business at the present time, all of which you will understand and appreciate.'[5]

And the rejection of a Swedish bank to the request of a US trading company at around the same time: 'We do not at all like to stand as assistants to Germany in any case whatever. We have had much trouble in our business on account of such matters. You will therefore kindly use another firm for the purpose. You will understand that we do not wish to run any risk of getting our business broken by England.'[6]

By the end of 1916, all neutral banks had caved in under the British pressure.[7]

Germany drastically felt the consequences of the British blockade in 1916. Her industry still maintained up to eighty per cent of pre-war production levels, but food became the chink in the German armor.

In the winter of 1915/16 the German government rationed fat, sugar, and bread. By the end of the winter, months before the next harvest, potato stocks had already been exhausted and bread was scarce. The import of fattening feed for animals had already collapsed in 1914, leading to the 'great swine massacre' in April 1915 – one third of the swine inventory was slaughtered, and, consequently, in 1916, fat and meat were scarce.

One third of the pre-war workforce had been engaged in farming, but many men and horses were in military service now, thereby drastically reducing the workforce. Before the war, one of the most important goods for agriculture was nitrogen fertilizers imported from overseas. Only a recently-invented industrial process (Haber-Bosch) saved Germany from the worst – nitrates could now be extracted from the atmosphere. But the major portion of this nitrogen was reserved for the production of explosives; the use of fertilizers in agriculture decreased dramatically.

Domestic food production collapsed in 1916. Globally the harvest was bad overall, but in Germany the consequences were catastrophic. Farmers only harvested half of the pre-war potato crop. In the fall of 1916, the population's potato rations declined by fifty per cent. German farmers had to plant turnips, a fast growing fall vegetable normally used as pig feed. This crop somehow was to quell the escalating menace of starvation in the winter of 1916/17.

The agrarian population was at the source of food production. The Army and Navy somehow supplied the soldiers and sailors with food. The wealthy could provide for themselves from the flourishing black market, where about one-third of the rarely available domestic food production was sold at horrific prices. Inhabitants of metropolitan areas, however, and workers in the industrialized areas – a quarter of the population – were cut off from extra supplies; with the meager rations available, they suffered hunger. Between the fall of 1916 and the summer of 1917, this segment of the population lost twenty to thirty per cent of their bodyweight.[8]

The inequitable distribution of food and the lamentable inability of the bureaucracy to get a grip on the black market caused further ill feelings toward the state's authorities.[9]

Chapter 23

Peace Wanted?

America

In the spring of 1916, following the *Sussex* crisis, America's attention was again redirected to the British blockade, which was being rapidly expanded beyond Germany's borders to include Europe's neutral countries. To prevent trade between the neutrals and Germany, Great Britain had decided to allow these countries to import only what was necessary for their own needs, thereby cutting Germany off from the world market through indirect trade with the neutrals.

This violation of the international trade rights of the neutral countries and the refusal of Britain to allow even medical products or baby food to be delivered to Germany met with outrage in the United States.[1]

The Irish Easter Uprising in April 1916 and its abrupt suppression by the British Army struck a catastrophic blow to Great Britain's reputation in the United States. Officially, England had gone to war to avenge Germany's aggression against neutral Belgium, but in its treatment of Ireland, as well as of certain other European neutrals, Britain was behaving no better than the Germans. Wilson's biographer, Arthur S. Link, wrote: 'Certainly, everything for which British Liberalism has stood, as contrasted to Prussian Junkerism [German militarism], has been brushed away.'[2]

This had no impact, however, on the American supply of food and weapons to the Allies. The United States of America was an economic superpower that produced half of the world's economic output. Monthly Allied orders valued at 300 million dollars (comparable to approx. 30 billion dollars 2018 value) went out to the United States, leading to an economic boom and full employment. Link states: 'As one member of the [British] Cabinet wrote, Americans would never sacrifice their pockets to their politics.'[3]

The vast majority of Americans wanted no involvement in the European war, and presidential elections were coming up in late 1916.[4] Link: 'A peace move would be enormously popular in any event; a successful peace move would make him irresistible in the presidential campaign.'[5]

Great Britain

In defiance, Britain rejected Wilson's initial peace feelers in early May 1916. London hoped for a crushing success via a series of simultaneous Allied summer offensives on the Eastern and Western fronts.

Colonel Edward M. House, Wilson's chief political advisor, complained about British Foreign Minister Edward Grey on May 10: 'The impression grows that the Allies are more determined upon the punishment of Germany than upon exacting terms that neutral opinions would consider just. This feeling will increase if Germany discontinues her illegal submarine activities.'[6] House was disappointed: 'We have given them [the British] everything and they ever demand more.'[7]

On May 13 he noted in his diary: 'For two years, Grey has been telling me that the solution to the problem of international well-being depended upon the United States being willing to take her part in world affairs. Now that we indicate a willingness to do so, he halts, stammers and questions. I am distinctly disappointed. I can see, too, a distinct feeling of cock-sureness in the Allies since [their defensive success at] Verdun. This will grow in the event that they have any [offensive] success themselves, and I can foresee trouble with them.'[8]

Wilson was undaunted. On May 27, 1916, he publicly announced that the US government was ready 'to suggest or initiate a movement for peace among the nations now at war, at these lines: first, such a settlement with regard to their own immediate interest as the belligerents may agree upon. Secondly, a universal association of the nations to maintain the inviolate security of the highways of the seas, and to prevent any war – a virtual guarantee of territorial integrity and political independence.'[9]

Wilson was no naive idealist. His concern, first and foremost, was America's interests and his highest priority was to preserve the neutrality of the United States. The overriding theme of his re-election campaign was to keep the United States out of the war in Europe. Wilson hoped to mediate for peace, or at least for a cessation of the fighting and, through the founding of a 'world community of nations', to be able to bring about a new, stable postwar order.

The American newspaper *The New Republic* commented: 'Mr. Wilson has broken with the tradition of American isolation in the only way which offers any hope to men.'[10]

With pronounced cynicism, French Prime Minister Georges Clemenceau remarked: 'If the creator needed seven days to organize a couple of creatures of which the first born instinctively tore each other apart, Mr. Wilson, in one sovereign word, is going to create men such as have never been seen, whose first need will be love and universal harmony.'[11]

British Foreign Minister Grey feared American mediation. In the eyes of the Cabinet an undecided peace, a Germany left undefeated, would have meant the strengthening of the German Reich. There was insistence on a 'fight to the finish', the defeat of the enemy, the elimination of Germany as a major European power.[12]

Seymour: 'Colonel House was naturally and bitterly disappointed. Apparently [the Allies] wanted American assistance without any conditions, not so much to secure a permanent and a just peace as to crush Germany.'[13]

British historian David French consigns the motivation to raw imperialism: 'The British did not fight the First World War simply to safeguard their security in Europe, nor did they fight it simply to safeguard their possessions in the Middle East and India. The war was a struggle for the division of world power. The Germans sought to supplant Britain as a world power by creating a middle-European empire stretching from Hamburg and Belgium to the head of the Persian Gulf. It was a war in which British policy-makers measured victory or defeat by the extent to which they were able to frustrate German ambitions and to maintain Britain's security in both Europe and in the Middle East and India.'[14]

As long as either of the two warring camps in Europe held out hope for survival, negotiations for peace were futile. Wilson's initiative came to nothing.

Germany: Peace by Victory or a Negotiated Peace?

In Germany, the Chancellor and his Chief of Staff Erich von Falkenhayn were already convinced that it was no longer possible to win the land war.

In a diary entry in February 1916, the Flag Lieutenant of the High Seas Fleet staff, Ernst von Weizsäcker, described the Imperial Navy's disappointment: 'Army leadership is also at a loss. The war will lead to mutual exhaustion, ending in a stalemate. That would be very regrettable. The Army's view of the general military situation is extremely disheartening. The only truly effective means available to the Navy is [unrestricted] Uboat warfare, which, however, America will not tolerate.'[15]

Internally, a major battle brewed over the use of the only available offensive weapon: Uboats.

The Navy promised that England would be defeated within six months by means of an all-out submarine campaign and the sinking, without warning, of every vessel afloat in a declared war zone around the British Isles, whether hostile or neutral. A peace by victory.

Bethmann Hollweg argued against this, saying that it would provoke the United States, with its enormous resources, to enter the war leading almost certainly to Germany's defeat. The alternative he proposed was Uboat cruiser warfare to gradually bring about a reduction of the world's merchant fleet, which consisted of over 20,000 ships with 43 million GRT, half of which were British. This would put the Allies under economic pressure and gradually lead to a willingness to negotiate. In addition, there was Wilson's economic power position to consider, through which he could exert pressure on the Entente for peace.

Restricted Uboat warfare would result in a negotiated peace; unrestricted Uboat warfare seemed to promise victory.

Propaganda from Germany's political right, especially from the Pan-Germans, called for total, unrestricted Uboat war. At that time, the 'Pan-German League' consisted of 20,000 members who came from the higher ranks of the government, the military and the bourgeoisie. The League represented the old Prussian aristocratic and landed classes who, with sectarian zeal, elevated nation and race to the status of a religion. Pan-Germans demanded peace by victory, with Germany's elevation to a world power through annexations in Europe and in the colonial empires of its enemies. They preached violence from within and without – an energetic 'Führer', supported by a self-proclaimed elite, should be in charge, instead of the 'weak' Emperor and his 'feeble' Chancellor.

Why was this propaganda so successful within the middle classes of the Wilhelminian society? Why was a negotiated peace so unpopular?

The Middle Classes

A negotiated peace meant, first of all, that there would be no war indemnities as there had been in the Franco-German war of 1871. War costs were around two billion Reichsmark per month and, in May 1916, the war debt already amounted to 45 billion RM (equivalent to 900 billion USD in 2018). This corresponded to the gross national product for the peace year 1913, or about a sixth of the nation's wealth, which had now literally been dissolved into the smoke of gunpowder. With no reparations from foreign powers, Germany would have to absorb these costs alone.

The war was financed by the sale of bonds: the dutiful citizen emptied his savings account, took out a loan on his life insurance, and mortgaged his home. The patriotic middle class citizenry converted their assets into war bonds at – at this time a very moderate – five per cent interest. Personal jewelry was offered up by patriotic citizens who exchanged wedding bands for iron rings with an enameled likeness of the Kaiser. The population was asked to dig ever deeper into personal wealth and goods to support the state's dwindling resources.

Repaying a huge debt in the event of an indecisive end to the war would only be possible by means of inflation and/or higher taxes. There was nothing to be had from laborers who already could barely scrape by on their meager wages; the situation was the same with the small number of aristocrats, who generally were moderate gentleman farmers. Big industry knew how to defend itself. That left the middle class which would largely be stuck with the bill.

In the eyes of the Wilhelminian bourgeoisie, a negotiated peace would bring with it threats of onerous taxes and onerous social reforms, of property loss, social discontent and revolution.

The Army

The Prussian nobility, the so-called 'Junkers', held leading positions in the army and in the higher offices of the government. Politically, the nobility in Prussia was privileged by a special census suffrage, which always provided the necessary conservative majority in the Prussian Parliament and allowed the prevention of any reforms in the Reich that would be to their detriment.

Before the war, by protracted obstructionism they had successfully prevented any changes to the socio-political status quo that threatened to make them losers. Bethmann, suspected of supporting reform, was regarded as the embodiment of the devil himself. An indecisive conclusion to the war would usher in negative socio-political upheaval quite possibly leading to the economic end of their national status. In fact, loss of the ancient social caste system in Germany followed the Armistice of 1918 and, with no small dash of irony – but at a slower pace – in Britain where upper class society also began a slow but permanent slide into irrelevance following the Great War.

The Imperial Navy

For the German Fleet, a negotiated peace threatened its very existence. Attempts at further expansion before 1914 had already bumped up against financial limitations.

One of Wilson's central demands for an enduring peace was disarmament and the restoration of military balance. Along with financial hardships following the war, the size of the Imperial Navy would have been greatly reduced. The dream of the High Seas Fleet – elevation to world power status – was doomed and proud naval officers would be set adrift ashore.

The naval historian Holger Herwig wrote: 'Only a "peace of victory" could preserve the Prussian-German sovereign state and its constituent elements. Only within this Wilhelminian, class-conscious society could naval officers hope to maintain their privileged positions as 'first-ranked in the state', since only a victorious Germany would be able to conduct world politics on such a grand scale that an enormous battle fleet would be required.'[16]

Uboat Propaganda

Propaganda is, by nature, required to be primitive. The Imperial Navy simply maintained the unproven assertion that unrestricted Uboat warfare yielded far more sinkings than conventional maritime war prosecuted with cruiser rules. Therefore, unleashing the full force of its undersea stealth weapon was the surest route to an overwhelming victory.

At the beginning of 1916, the Chief of the Admiralty Staff Admiral Henning von Holtzendorff had 'calculated' that in this scenario Uboats would sink 600,000 GRT monthly, thus forcing England's capitulation within half a year.

What was the effect of all this on ordinary citizens of the Wilhelminian Empire who believed the official government position that out of envy of Germany's growing international trade, her enemies had first surrounded and then attacked the country? Should all the deaths and personal sacrifice have been in vain? There was some satisfaction, at least, in the fact that German armies stood deep in enemy territory. Mostly, they reasoned, the war was justified and seen as a sacred crusade to defend German culture and customs, most especially from darkly threatening foreigners. And if the admirals, those indisputable experts, made assurances that a means existed with which the war could be won within only a few months, my God! – why weren't the Kaiser and the Chancellor choosing that path? Propaganda and reality were worlds apart.

Even within the Kaiser's Navy there was much controversy over the potential effectiveness of unrestricted submarine warfare. Lieutenant Weizsäcker stated: 'We cannot actually give a *guarantee* that an end to the war with England can be accomplished within six months. Neither the figures on the tonnage to be sunk nor those on the presumed residual effects are certain. I have no confidence in the promises of the Admiralty Staff and the Imperial Navy that, with the Uboats, they will, in six months' time, be able to bring England to its knees. All of the naval experts that have been consulted agree that this timeframe is too optimistic. How should a government react, when it is provided with false information? How can it accept proposals, whose mendacity cannot be hidden?'[17]

The Government

Theobald von Bethmann Hollweg came from a conservative-liberal aristocratic family. At the young age of 29 he became a district chief executive, and for decades he lived through the rapid changes in Prussian society that were brought about by the turbulences of industrialization.

Early on, he witnessed the stubborn anti-reform stance of the Junker classes fighting for their economic survival and remained deeply skeptical of his egoistic, elitist peers. At the age of 49 he was appointed Prussian Minister of the Interior and four years later, in 1909, he became Imperial Chancellor.

Bethmann's war policy was, in large part, based upon collaboration with political centrists, the liberal left, the socialists, and the trade unions – not out of sympathy for their ideals – but because of the right's reform blockade. Riezler believed that 'truly decisive government, including a reasonable foreign policy, is only feasible with the left. However, the Kaiser, the Prussian officialdom, the military, and the Navy, make this impossible.'[18]

Even the government itself was not at ease with its chosen course, but there was no alternative to the attempt to work with social realities as they existed. And these concessions, borne out of necessity, could not be rolled back once peace was achieved. It was the beginning of a continually accelerating process that the war had set in motion. Riezler observed: 'What will become of Germany internally? Without major concessions to the left, it will be almost impossible to restrain the trade unions. The socialist SPD is a major radical party, steeped in pacifism, and if the government behaves stupidly, there is potential for revolution.'[19] And, 'The Chancellor spoke of the post-war nightmare that is troubling him, of revolution in the wake of the war. The immense needs of the simple soldiers who would be returning home, and the general disappointment with an undecided outcome to the war. The uselessness of the bourgeoisie, who can only stand up to the left when their chauvinistic passions have been incited. Since it is not possible to breach the supremacy of the Prussian nobles, the Junkers, they must simply disappear as a political class.'[20]

Such thinking led to even more hatred of Bethmann by conservatives. In the summer of 1916, Riezler noted: 'How odd, that people still do not understand that, internally, we are probably facing revolution of the highest degree, whether it be quiet or loud, which will make the entire existing spirit of official Germany – its chauvinism, its blustering Kaiser, its militarism, its aggressive fleet build-up, etc., untenable. In the political upper classes, there is with rare exception, a complete lack of reason.'[21]

The right-wing opposition fought against this perspective with all means at its disposal. Uboat propaganda became a weapon against the reform-friendly Chancellor and the possibility of peace negotiations. For those inside these circles, no compromise existed. In the war against Britain, there could be only victory or defeat, and within Germany, either democratization or a military dictatorship.

Conclusion

In the eyes of Germany's political right, a negotiated peace threatened upheaval to the existing social order, either through reforms issued from above and/or a revolution rising up from below. Only a 'peace of victory' could guarantee the survival of the existing social order and the continued domination of the old elite classes.

Unrestricted Uboat warfare became the opposition program of the right. In turn, Wilson would react by breaking off relations so that no further American peace initiatives were to be expected, Bethmann Hollweg resign, and the topic of internal reform was tabled.

During the second half of 1916, Bethmann fought to prevent unrestricted Uboat warfare and to negotiate a peace settlement. Perhaps with an end to the war politicians and diplomats would be able to remove the military from power and regain their freedom to act.

Chapter 24

Uboat Warfare

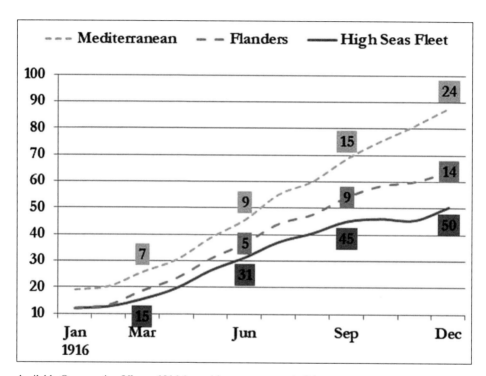

Available Ocean-going Uboats 1916 (monthly average, rounded).[1]

Uboat Forces

Over the course of 1916, Germany's Uboat fleet grew from two dozen hulls to a fleet of nearly one hundred boats. However, even in terms of crew and tonnage, the force still represented less than ten per cent of the total fleet.

About two-thirds of the boats belonged to the High Seas Fleet and its major naval units in Wilhelmshaven, operating out of the German North Sea ports in the Atlantic under the command of Admiral Reinhard Scheer.

Ocean-going Uboats stationed in Bruges, in occupied Flanders, were deployed in the English Channel, the Irish Sea, and the Bay of Biscay and reported to the Imperial Naval Office in Berlin.

Uboats of the Mediterranean flotilla, based with the Austrian-Hungarian Adriatic fleet stations, were commanded by the Admiralty Staff.

The High Seas Fleet under Admiral Scheer, the Imperial Naval Office under Admiral Edward von Capelle, and the Admiralty Staff of the Imperial Navy under Admiral Henning von Holtzendorff comprised three independent naval authorities directly subordinate to the Kaiser. With their individual Uboat forces, they pursued very different deployment strategies.

In protest of concessions made by the Kaiser and Chancellor during the *Sussex* crisis, at the end of April 1916 Admiral Scheer had redeployed his Uboats to waters in the west of England. He categorically refused to conduct merchant warfare under prize rules. In 1916, Uboats of the High Seas Fleet were used sparingly. Consequently, submarine warfare on Atlantic routes to England was completely suspended for six months, from May to mid-October 1916.

Available Ocean-going Uboats end of 1916.[2]

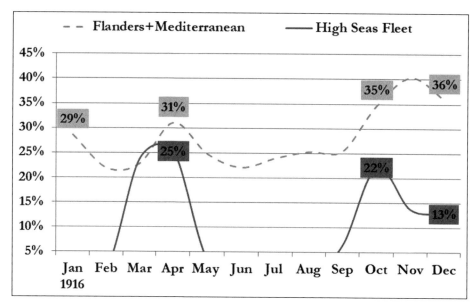

Percentage of Available Ocean-going Uboats deployed in Merchant War.[3]

Beginning in July 1916, the Flanders Uboats returned to the English Channel to conduct war in accordance with prize rules.

Only the Uboats in the Mediterranean were used throughout 1916 for permanent merchant warfare.

The Mediterranean – A Story of Aces[4]

As early as September 1915, a handful of Uboats had already been relocated to prosecute the merchant war in the Mediterranean. These Uboats were based in the Austrian-Hungarian naval base of Cattaro (now Kotor, Montenegro), close to where the Adriatic and the Mediterranean connect. From here they could reach their operational areas within 24 hours. During the pre-war period, all German warships stationed outside home waters reported to the Admiralty Staff. This policy continued with Mediterranean-based fleet assets.

In May 1915, Italy declared war on Austria-Hungary, but not on the German Reich. Italy declared war with Germany more than a year later, in August 1916. Uboats in the Mediterranean were deployed as Austrian-Hungarian warships under the Austrian war flag. They also participated in attacks on Italian commercial shipping.

On her transit to the Mediterranean in November 1915, U-38 under the command of Lieutenant Max Valentiner destroyed fourteen ships, comprising 45,000 GRT. On November 8, Valentiner sank the Italian passenger steamer *Ancona* without warning, resulting in the deaths of 208 passengers, including eight citizens of the United States.

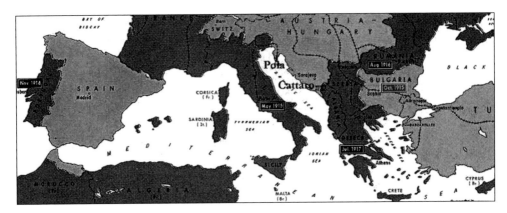

Uboat Bases Pola and Cattaro in the Adriatic.

US President Wilson had already reacted sharply to the sinking of *Lusitania* in May and *Arabic* in August 1915. He now renewed his protests. Austria-Hungary had to take the blame, apologize to the United States and promise to punish the 'Austrian' commander.

Vienna intervened with the German authorities insisting that Uboat war must be conducted in compliance with cruiser warfare rules. On December 4, 1915, Admiral Holtzendorff established rules for submarine warfare in the Mediterranean: neutral freighters and unarmed enemy ships could only be captured strictly under prize rules.[5]

However, on December 30 when Max Valentiner torpedoed the British passenger liner *Persia* without warning causing 334 casualties, Austria refused to play the part of the scapegoat again. They admitted to the US that German boats were operating in the Mediterranean and demanded that the German Admiral Staff rein in its Uboats and cease any further attacks on passenger liners. The Admiral Staff acquiesced.

From that point, merchant warfare in the Mediterranean was conducted according to the regulations governing prize rules. Chief Admiral Holtzendorff, the strongest proponent of radical Uboat war, found himself compelled to bow to foreign policy considerations.

The War Theater

Successes by submarines in the Mediterranean were largely a result of the proximity of the bases to operational areas. This allowed Uboats to deploy for longer periods than was possible in the north, where the boats lost eight to ten travel days per cruise from their North Sea bases into the Atlantic. In addition, weather conditions in the Mediterranean were far more favorable. Largely absent were the kind of raging North Atlantic storms that for days or weeks rendered weapons inoperable. Also, the enemy's defenses were weak and split between Italian, French, and British command posts.

Berlin's Admiralty Staff was far away, and the young Uboat officers were largely on their own, away from politicizing admirals or inflamed public opinion. It was a lieutenant's war.

Six of the ten most successful German submarine commanders in the First World War came from the Mediterranean flotilla. These half-dozen men alone accounted for 675 ships destroyed with 1.7 million GRT of tonnage: that is, 50% of all ships sunk in the Mediterranean (3.4 million GRT) and approximately 15% of the total German sinkings (around 11 million GRT).[6] All six commanders survived the war.

In the Mediterranean, Uboat warfare was never concentrated in any one particular area, for example, at the exit of the Suez Canal or in the Straits of Gibraltar. Instead it was widespread, thus contributing markedly to the wholesale decimation of tonnage. The enemy was attacked not near his well-defended naval bases but at his weakest position on the long, poorly-defended shipping routes that crisscrossed the Mediterranean Sea.

British naval intelligence, 'Room 40', correctly characterized the history of the Mediterranean merchant war as a 'story of aces'. The young commanders' great successes, combined with lax supervision, allowed them an unprecedented degree of freedom in the execution of their orders.

'Top gun' was 30-year-old Lothar von Arnauld de la Perière of U-35. His wartime success rate was more than 200 ships, comprising 450,000 GRT and all in accordance with prize rules. The only vessels he attacked without warning were troop ships, armed merchant freighters, and convoyed vessels. He refrained from attacking passenger liners and hospital ships.

Room 40, the Royal Navy's deciphering department, described him thus: 'He developed tactics of his own, in which he shewed consummate skill. He practically abandoned the use of torpedoes, except when attacking warships or transports, preferring to rely on gun-fire. He soon had his two 22 pdr. guns replaced by a single 4.1", manned by a picked up gun-layer from the Fleet Sea Fleet. His usual practice was to open fire at about 6,000 yards, and gradually close to 3,000, but not nearer, until the crew had abandoned ship. He then fired three shots into her at close range, one forward, one amidships and one aft, which usually sufficed to sink her. Throughout his career, he shewed great consideration for the lives of crews of sunken ships, generally giving them time to take to their boats, even after the declaration of unrestricted warfare. His behavior was in this respect in marked contrast to that of Valentiner, who shares with him the reputation of being the most successful commander in the service.'[7]

Von Arnauld's most brilliant cruise was from July to August 1916 after eight operational deployments in the Mediterranean and a bag of fifty-eight enemy ships already destroyed (amounting to 153,000 GRT).

Lieutenant Lothar von Arnauld de la Perière, U–35, and his Deck Gun.

U-35[8]

Late on July 26, 1916, U–35, flying the Austrian war flag, embarked from the Bay of Cattaro shortly before midnight. The boat displaced almost 900 tons submerged with a crew of thirty-five. She could remain at sea for up to six weeks. Diesel engines permitted a surface top speed of sixteen knots. Submerged, she could cover up to 80 nm before the batteries used to power the electric motor were exhausted, and needed to be recharged by returning to the surface. Armament was a 10.5 cm (4.1 inch) deck gun and eight to ten torpedoes.

Following his first cruise in late 1915, Arnauld – now a fledgling Uboat commander – had perfected the use of his weapons system's strengths and weaknesses and honed his attack tactics. The long-range deck gun was effective within a radius of six kilometers (3.73 miles), thereby dominating an area of over 100 square kilometers (64 square miles). With its superior above-water speed, the submarine could overtake any fleeing steamer and, by engaging his artillery, force his prey to strike its colors. Should the adversary prove too strong, or hostile warships appeared on the horizon, U-35 simply abandoned the engagement and quickly submerged.

A torpedo launch is inefficient at slow underwater speed and Arnauld needed to approach his moving target at a range of at least 1,000 meters. With his limited arsenal of torpedoes (and a statistical miss rate of 50%), this tactic, even for an experienced Uboat commander, would have resulted in the sinking of only a handful of vessels per cruise. For at-sea engagements of merchantmen, the deck gun was the most effective weapon.

Lookout on U-35.

Speed and firepower of hostile warships were superior to Uboats. A single, well-landed shot to the submarine's pressure hull generally rendered a submarine incapable of diving, thus robbing it of its most effective defense measures. Arnauld's insurance was to maintain an appropriate distance, whether from enemy warships, submarine traps, or armed merchant ships. This allowed a few minutes time to decide between retreat or attack.

On the evening of July 28, off the coast of Malta, Arnauld stopped his first steamer and sank it with his deck gun. For the next three weeks captain and crew worked unceasingly from sunrise to sunset, with and without success, to pursue, stop, and inspect all manner of vessels, from small fishing boats to sailing ships to large steamers. At night, Arnauld allowed the crew to rest as they proceeded to new operational areas.

To confound anyone trying to pin-point his location, U–35 constantly changed position. Arnauld commented: 'The increased surveillance has become particularly noticeable. It is my opinion, that in the face of such strong defense measures, the prospect of success exists only if, whenever possible, our location is changed daily, before any counteraction can be undertaken.'[9]

Von Arnauld, Studying the Map while Smoking a Cigar

After Malta, U–35 ran along the Tunisian coast, then headed towards Sardinia and Marseille, circled around to the Balearic Islands, returned to the French Riviera, steamed in the direction of Genoa, and from there past the eastern coast of Corsica on a southerly course back in the direction of Malta, before heading into the Otranto Strait. On the evening of August 20, following a 25-day journey, U–35 arrived back in Cattaro. During the entire trip, the weather remained stable: the winds were minimal, the sea was calm, and visibility was excellent.

Arnauld's mission tactics were characterized by caution. He began his attacks from a great distance, firing warning shots. If resistance from an armed steamer was too fierce, he quickly abandoned the battle.

Once he had forced a vessel to strike its flag, he gave a signal that the ship's

Pursuit of a Sailing Vessel.

papers were to be brought by lifeboat to the submarine. Arnauld took the time to review in private the captured documents and identify the vessel and its cargo. Meanwhile, he held the freighter at a distance, with a warning shot if necessary, so as not to become the victim of a ramming attempt.

Allied vessels were categorically sunk. With neutral ships, he acted simultaneously as prosecutor and judge. If, for instance, a cargo intended for delivery to the enemy consisted of lumber, he had to decide whether it was made up of tree trunks (not contraband) or ready-cut pit props (contraband) or boards to be used for the manufacture of boxes that might have been intended to store ammunition.

If Arnauld decided to sink a neutral vessel because it was transporting contraband, he then gave the captain of the merchant ship a 'certificate of sinking', which explained the circumstances and the justification. With this 'certificate', the owners of the ship and the cargo could go before the 'Prisengericht', the German prize court, to appeal the decision and sue for damages; often they were successful. As long as the matter concerned the ownership rights of neutrals, everything followed a legal capitalistic course during the war.

Before sinking any freighter, Arnauld gave the ship's crew about twenty minutes to collect their belongings and get into lifeboats. Then, with the deck gun, he shot 'air holes' beneath the waterline, or sent a command on board to scuttle the vessel by opening the bottom valves, or by explosive charges, or, in the case of a wooden sailing ship, simply by setting it on fire.

Boarding the ship to be sunk had another special purpose: Uboat crews, touted by German propaganda as the 'Knights of the Deep' had to sustain themselves on a meager diet of bread, tea, jam, and canned meat. Room 40 recorded crew statements by prisoners of war: 'They had three meals per day: Morning – coffee, marmalade. Noon – soup, roast meat or bacon, preserved food or vegetables, potatoes. Evening – tea, marmalade.'[10] To raise spirits at the start of a mission, many captains sent a plundering party aboard one of the vessels to be sunk to replenish the scant galley pantry and raise morale. Also according to Room 40, captured German Uboat sailors 'admitted… that they were glad of the supplementary provisions which they could get from the ships which they sank.'[11] Plundering neutral ships often resulted in diplomatic skirmishes but did not prevent the continuation of the practice throughout the entire war.

Crew of U–35.

Uboat defense

On this 25-day voyage there were dozens of sightings of enemy warships, but each time Arnauld was able to elude them on the surface. Twice, aircraft forced him to submerge and on three occasions his boat was pursued by enemy warships and attacked with artillery and depth charges.

The most dangerous situation came in the early morning hours of August 15, when a stopped steamer unexpectedly opened fire at a range of 6,000 meters with hidden guns. Arnauld immediately dove. 'During the dive maneuver I could watch through the tower windows as the impacts came closer and closer, to within 50 meters. Just as the boat fully submerged, I could hear the impacts right on the tower. Fortunately, the U-35 submerged safely and was not damaged.'[12]

When it came to traps, extreme caution and maintaining a great distance were the only tactics.

Conclusion

Arnauld steamed 4,407 nm above water and 241 nm submerged, fired five torpedoes (two of which missed), expended 389 artillery shots and three signal cartridges, and sunk fifty-four ships (over 90,000 GRT).

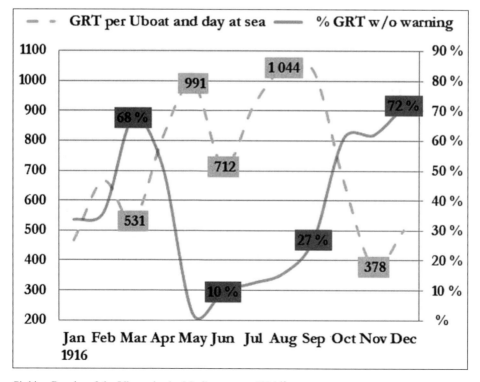

Sinking Results of the Uboats in the Mediterranean 1916.[13]

U–35 itself suffered no damage or loss of crew. The ship's engines and guns worked reliably. Only the W/T and the gyro compass occasionally failed. On the enemy side, there had been only one death – in an artillery duel with an armed English steamer.

Arnauld's 'Mediterranean tactic' was successful and in full accord with cruiser warfare rules. Arming of merchant ships was beyond applicable maritime law and Wilson silently tolerated the warningless torpedo attacks on armed cargo vessels.

The success of the Mediterranean boats was the result of the right mix of caution and aggression on the part of the commander, a reliable boat with an experienced crew, good weather, the ability to stay out for long periods in the operational area, and a weak and fragmented enemy defense.

The more intense the use of torpedoes and the higher the proportion of the tonnage sunk without warning, the lower became the sinking average per Uboat per day at sea, as is clearly demonstrated by the above graph for March and November 1916.

Rear Admiral Arno Spindler, publisher of the official post-war history of the Uboat merchant war, who during the first year of the war served as an officer in the First Uboat Flotilla, confirmed that 'More could be accomplished with 200-300 grenades than with seven to ten torpedoes, half of which, on average, missed their marks. In open waters by daylight, enemy defenses posed no significant danger.'[14] Furthermore, 'A type of cruiser warfare had developed, the so-called "Uboat warfare following prize rules", because commanders on their own initiative had found this to be the most effective tactic.'[15]

Throughout 1916, Uboats in the Mediterranean sank over 380 ships, comprising 923,000 GRT. For the eighty-four Uboat cruises of that year, three boats were lost to mines but not a single boat was destroyed by enemy warships. Each Uboat sunk counted for over 300,000 GRT of merchant tonnage destroyed.

While the Mediterranean proved to be an ideal hunting ground for Uboats during the first war years, it was quite a different story in the heavily guarded, shallow waters of the English Channel.

Flanders and the English Channel – Mission Impossible[16]

In the spring of 1915, two dozen UB-I and UC-I class Uboats were stationed in the Belgian ports of Bruges, Zeebrugge, and Ostende.

These 200-ton boats with a fifteen-man crew did not carry guns but were instead equipped with torpedoes or mines. They remained at sea for two to three days per week and operated in coastal defense missions in the waters between the Netherlands and England. In the merchant war, they did not play a significant role.

The Imperial Navy greatly expanded its presence on the coast of occupied Belgium in 1916. Reinforced positions included heavy coastal artillery, naval infantry, reconnaissance and fighter aircrafts, torpedo boats, destroyers as well as submarines. The aptly named 'Flanders Naval Corps' was commanded by

Flanders Bases: Ostende, Zeebrugge, Bruges.

UC-I Mine-laying Uboat.

Admiral Ludwig von Schröder and reported to the Imperial Naval Office under Grand Admiral of the Fleet von Tirpitz (until March 1916), and later to his successor Admiral von Capelle.

The submarine base was the picturesque, remote town of Bruges (popularly, 'the Venice of the North'), from which the boats could transit to the ports of Ostend and Zeebrugge via inland canals. Due to frequent bombardment by the Royal Navy, the first submarine bunkers were built there.

Above and below: German Uboat Shelters in Bruges, Occupied Belgium.

The following spring (1916) introduced the first ocean-going boats of the new UC-II and UB-II classes to Flanders. These boats were capable of remaining at sea for several weeks, making it possible to operate in the Channel as far as the south coast of Ireland and south to the Bay of Biscay.

Their strategic mission was the disruption of Allied troop and ammunition transports in the English Channel. However, intensive Allied defense measures made this utterly impossible.

Troop and supply ships were being escorted by torpedo boats and destroyers, and patrolling warships constantly forced Uboats into emergency dives. In addition, submarines confronted frequent periods of bad weather and experienced difficulties in navigating shallow coastal waters with their strong tidal currents.

These setbacks resulted in high losses. Of seventy-seven Atlantic Uboats of the UC-II, UB-II, and UB-III classes sent to Flanders during the war, sixty were lost.[17] The life expectancy of a Flanders boat was ten months (corresponding to conditions experienced in 1943 during the Second World War). Among Uboat captains, the Flanders flotilla earned the nickname 'drowning command'.

In 1916, losses to Flanders Uboats were already four times greater than losses in the Mediterranean, and in 1917 the factor would rise to nineteen. The English Channel was the area of the world with the strongest anti-submarine defenses.

The Uboat weapon system was asymmetrical – it had a devastating effect when used against the slower merchant vessels on the open sea, but was extremely vulnerable when it came to hostile warships and mines. An attack on heavily-armed enemy fleets or strongly defended naval bases would be suicidal. Numerous surface patrol boats and strategically-placed minefields rendered the blockade of enemy trading ports impossible. Only in the most remote and least protected war theaters – like the Mediterranean or the open Atlantic – was it possible to achieve success with few losses.

UB-II Type Ocean-going Uboat running into Ostend, Occupied Belgium.

The Baltic – British Submarines and German Convoys[18]

The Baltic Sea was a secondary war theater for the Imperial Navy. The Russian fleet had retreated behind a vast minefield in the Gulf of Finland and only occasionally ventured into the open, breaking out with light surface vessels.

Room 40 described the Baltic Sea battlefield as the 'junk yard of the German fleet'. In truth, Germany's Baltic fleet consisted of obsolete cruisers and torpedo boats along with a handful of submarines.

In August 1915, half-a-dozen modern British E-Class submarines broke through the German barriers at the entrance to the Baltic Sea and took positions at Russian bases in the Gulf of Finland. In the ensuing months, following prize rules, they sank several German freighters carrying Swedish iron ore.

In the winter of 1915/16, when the Baltic froze, Germans had time to reorganize their defenses. Patrols were reinforced to prevent the entry of any more British submarines. Hundreds of smaller auxiliary vessels worked in submarine search flotillas, extensive net and mine barriers were laid, zeppelins and aircraft were sent on patrol, and a handful of ships were converted into decoys to trap submarines.

In a further measure, in March 1916, the Imperial Navy organized an 'Escort Service for the Protection of Merchant Ships in the Baltic Sea'. 'Three times per week, merchant steamers will have the opportunity to travel the routes indicated under the escort of warships.'[19] Thus the Imperial Navy was the first during the the war to introduce the convoy system for merchant ships.

The change in tactics was a resounding success and owners of German shipping companies immediately urged that this service be expanded to include all routes, with more frequent trips and with an increased number of escorts.[20]

German convoys rendered British submarines ineffective in the merchant war, and were soon limited in Baltic operations against German warships.

England had forbidden its submarines to attack the mostly neutral ship traffic in the Baltic Sea without warning. Britain was dependent upon the Danish, Norwegian, and Swedish freighters of the world trade fleet, as well as the resources of these countries, and did nothing to provoke conflict with the Scandinavians. On the opposite side of the Atlantic, Wilson watched, vehemently demanding from all belligerents adherence to maritime war rules – and not only for the Germans. An *unrestricted* British submarine war against the neutral freighters in the Baltic supplying Germany with vital Swedish iron ore was therefore out of question.

The Germans thereby got a taste of their own medicine. A handful of British submarines tied up hundreds of ships and thousands of men. The value of the convoy in merchant warfare could hardly have escaped them.

Uboats Strike at the High Seas Fleet

Scheer ignored a directive to deploy his Uboats according to prize rules, as had already been successfully adopted in the Mediterranean. On April 27, Admiral Müller, naval representative at the Imperial Court, noted, 'In the Mediterranean, a tactical procedure is employed that helps to avoid Uboat losses in prize rules warfare. I shared this information with Scheer but he ignored it.'[21]

The High Seas Fleet also rejected the tactic on the grounds that 'This procedure is by no means quite safe, since the submarine is also still at risk.'[22] It is ironic that Scheer refused to deploy his weapons because of the potential risk of losses.

In a meeting with the Admiralty Staff on May 7, 1916, Scheer's Chief of Staff, Trotha, disputed the possibility of conducting restricted Uboat merchant warfare in the north. The High Seas Fleet regarded this 'type of warfare as hopeless. With heavy losses to the Uboats it would deliver only a minimal gain.'[23]

Even the Admiralty Staff's demand was rejected. And Holtzendorff's warning that 'His Majesty will require the Uboat merchant war to be continued in some form'[24] also failed to make an impression.

On May 16, Admiral Müller protested to Admiral Holtzendorff: 'As I write, the Uboat war is at a standstill in the North Sea. That is more than a reproach, it is a serious mistake on the part of the war leaders.'[25]

In a letter to Holtzendorff on May 17, 1916, Scheer reiterated the impossibility of using High Seas Fleet Uboats in accordance with prize rules. 'It is my conviction that the use of submarines to conduct merchant warfare in accordance with the proposed method is militarily unjustifiably disproportionate to the success that can be expected.'[26] He suggested that the enhanced armament of merchant ships would lead to heavy losses in the north. Here, Uboat war could only be conducted by torpedoing without warning.

On May 21, 1916, in a letter to the High Seas Fleet, Müller criticized Scheer's insistence on ruthless Uboat warfare. 'In my opinion, the Navy's expectations regarding the effects of the Uboat blockade are just as exaggerated as their underestimation of the effect that a break with America will have.'[27]

The author of the official German history of Uboats in the 1914–18 war, Arno Spindler, criticized the admirals' lack of competence in judging the usefulness of submarines[28] and concluded, 'Without taking into account the effectiveness and political advantage of cruiser warfare using Uboats, they declared that giving in to Wilson's wishes [Uboat warfare following prize rules] would be equivalent to a complete ban on using the Uboat weapon.'[29]

Chapter 25

Krupp and the Uboats

Guns and butter

The name *Krupp* is synonymous with Germany's rise to an industrial world power at the end of the nineteenth century, the emergence of international armaments manufacturers, and the arms race that preceded the First World War.

The Krupp firm's rapid growth in the decades before the war was a reflection of Germany's industrialization. At the time of its founding, following victory over France in 1871, the German Reich was still a largely rural, non-industrial country, but in the twenty-five years leading up to the First World War the country developed rapidly and with great effect, and by 1913 produced half of Europe's steel.

The number of employees at the 'Friedrich Krupp in Essen' company rose from 12,000 in 1874, to 25,000 in 1899, and to 83,000 by the outbreak of the Great War.[1] According to company historian Harold James, weapons manufacturing in peace time made up approximately half of total revenue and total profits.[2] Krupp was, by far, the most important German armaments manufacturer.

As was the case with other industries of the kind – Schneider-Creusot in France, Vickers and Armstrong-Whitworth in England, and Skoda in Austria-Hungary – Krupp primarily served the national weapons market. If a modern industrial state did not wish to become dependent on foreign armament suppliers, then reliance on foreign arms purchases was out of the question. The national armaments companies, shielded from competition, demanded inflated prices. If the state wanted to create and maintain a national arms industry it had to accept this as an indirect subsidy to its national weapons suppliers.[3]

The Krupp Company also became a synonym for advancements in weapons technology. In-house research facilities developed guns that were capable of ever greater range and possessed ever more power. At the same time, Krupp built increasingly solid armored plates that could protect against these weapons. Moreover, the family-run firm had a monopoly in the production of armored gun turrets and artillery for the Imperial Navy.[4]

The expanding process of industrialization created a growing working-class, resulting in the 'social question'. In the 1880s Bismarck's social reforms – the creation of health, accident, and pension insurance – had curtailed the effects of the worst excesses of 'Manchester capitalism' on this new class. For decades, Germany's social system continued to be viewed from the outside as one of the most harmonious in the world.

What did not change were the twelve-hour work days, the six-day week with no annual paid leave, the hard physical labor and the often unhealthy working conditions, the cramped quarters in dark tenement houses in which large families lived, and the meager income that allowed for only the absolute necessities. Industrial workers generally led monotonous lives that lacked opportunity for advancement for themselves or their children.

This 'fourth estate' distanced itself from traditional values and authority, and embraced a new religion: socialism. The redistribution of property from the hands of the few into communal property would supposedly relieve the economic distress of the workers and lead to a new and better form of social order. This alternative to misery and insecurity became the main theme in the minds of socialists and their representatives in the factories, the trade unions.

In contrast, the basic attitude of the political right was to refuse any concession or reform. The contradictions inherent in this looming domestic political conflict, the 'social question', prevailed through Wilhelm II's entire reign, and deepened. The conservative 'reform blockade' rejected every solution proposed, while, with economic progress, industrial workers continued to expand, and its political power – through the deputies of the Social Democratic Party (SPD) in the Reichstag – grew stronger. In 1912, the SPD became the most powerful group in the German Parliament. From a conservative perspective, revolution seemed to be at the doorstep.

The Krupp Company differentiated itself from other capitalist firms by providing paternalistic social benefits to their workers. It built company-owned employee housing, organized food and medical care, and offered educational and cultural services thus creating social calm in its factories – trade unions excepted.

In keeping with this 'lord of the manor' approach, Krupp provided misery-relieving benefits from its unassailable position of power, financed by richly profitable government contracts. Krupp's paternalistic model was: weapons for the world and social peace in Essen.[5]

There were attempts to address the 'social question'. A welfare state could bring social equilibrium, it was believed. But only with taxpayer money from the middle class and the elite. Understandably, this solution met with vehement opposition. As long as the reins of government, education, justice, police, the army, and manufacturing remained in ruling establishment hands, socialism could be fought off. Concessions of any sort would – in their view – open the floodgates.

As he stated to the Kaiser, Gustav von Krupp zu Bohlen und Halbach, chairman of the board of Krupp Works, also feared 'that the country would be facing serious domestic difficulties. The workers would well understand that they already had all the power in their hands.'[6] And in a letter to a friend he wrote, 'For a long time, I have been deeply troubled by the downward path of our monarchical and state authority on the slippery slope to democracy.'[7]

Financially powerful industrialists generally supported the conservatives. More than a few also supported the Pan-Germans whose expansion and annexation programs promised direct access to new raw material resources. Arming the fleet would be the catalyst to Germany's rise to world-class status.

The Germania Yard

To expand its armament empire, in 1902 Krupp acquired the Germania Yard in Kiel which saw its revenues and number of workers multiply from prewar years.[8] Along with the construction of merchant ships, the Yard primarily built warships for German and foreign navies.

Overall, Germania Yard's financial success remained problematic. Under Grand Admiral Tirpitz's command the Imperial Navy kept its pencils sharpened to examine costs for war fleet construction. The Reich operated three state-owned naval shipyards, in Danzig (Gdansk, Poland), Kiel, and Wilhelmshaven, which allowed them to compare building costs between state and private shipyards, and to control them.

The manufacture of fleet armaments never generated excessive profits, and there was not even a glimmer of the emergence of a military-industrial complex[9] which might have kindled further upgrades to maritime defenses. Arming the fleet was solely the idea of Grand Admiral von Tirpitz and the Kaiser.

Krupp, on its own initiative, also invested in technological advancements for warships. One new weapon system particularly attracted its attention, the submarine.

Uboats

France was a military force, both on land and at sea. It maintained a large army to protect its land borders with Germany, Italy, and Spain and a naval force to protect its worldwide colonial empire. France could not afford to concentrate the bulk of its resources in its navy, as England had done. Only with new, higher-quality weapons systems could the French fleet hope to compensate for its inferiority in numbers. Thus, at the end of the nineteenth century France invested in the development of new naval technologies.

French long-range armed cruisers were designed to conduct merchant warfare in all ocean waters. Torpedo boats and mine barriers barred enemy access to its coasts and ports. In 1888, the first submarine was put into service, and ten years later an obsolete French warship was successfully sunk for the first time by a torpedo fired from a submerged submarine. The Royal Navy paid attention.

In 1900, the USA sought to expand its maritime power and commissioned its first submarine, the USS *Holland*. The Royal Navy acquired a license for replication and in 1901, HMS *Holland* entered into service.[10] The Russian navy also placed orders for *Holland*-type submarines.

The Germania Yard, now part of the Krupp empire, enticed a leading French submarine engineer to work for them. In 1903 he built a prototype. Kaiser Wilhelm came to look, and high-ranking German naval officers took part in dive tests.[11]

However, no orders for Uboats from the Imperial Navy were to be expected. Krupp's leading naval engineer at the time, Hans Techel, wrote, 'The German Navy was still taking a wait-and-see attitude towards the building of submarines, so that Krupp was able to take credit for the development of this new weapon, even though no orders from the German Navy were to be imminently expected.'[12]

In fact, the Imperial Navy ignored the new weapon and its promising potential. In contrast to the French Navy which went about energetically equipping itself with new weapon systems, Tirpitz remained stubbornly committed to the construction of battleships. For him, Uboats were, and remained, an 'undesirable stepchild'. In 1904 Krupp received its first order for the construction of Uboats – from Russia.[13]

U-1 – Germany's First Submarine

Looking back at the Imperial Navy's attitude in 1904 towards technical innovations, Techel remarked, 'It has always been characteristic of the German Navy that they have introduced innovations only after these have already reached a certain, somewhat advanced state of development. This is the reason that U-1 came along relatively late (on December 3, 1904) at a time when other countries already had a large number of submarines.'[14]

U-1.

When it came to submarines, the German Navy was far behind other European fleets. Battleship construction was the exception. In October 1905, only twelve months after the revolutionary British HMS *Dreadnought*'s keel was laid (outclassing all previous capital ships and triggering an arms race), did the Imperial Navy follow suit with SMS *Nassau*.[15] In 1907 France introduced this new class, followed in 1909 by Italy, Russia, and Austria-Hungary. Tirpitz's reaction reveals that the Imperial Navy's fixation on the battle fleet was focused on England.

On December 14, 1906, two months after construction of SMS *Nassau* began, U-1 was commissioned.[16] The next seventeen orders for Uboats, submitted up until 1910, were divided between Krupp's Germania Yard and the Imperial shipyard in Danzig. The boats' displacement increased to about 500 tons and with their petroleum engines the surface range widened to approximately 1,000/1,500 nautical miles.

The Diesel Motor

Diesel fuel and engines got the name from their inventor, Otto Diesel, in 1897. Technology historian Lyle Cummins noted that 'Between its 1903 debut in submarines and 1918, Diesel propulsive power doubled every three years'[17] and Germany became a leading manufacturer of Diesel engines. MAN Machinery Works dominated this industry branch worldwide, later to be joined by AEG, Siemens-Schuckert and Germania Yard.

In 1904, French engineers installed the first MAN Diesel motors in their submarines.[18] The decision paid off.[19] And from 1907 onwards, the Royal Navy used Diesel motors in their D-class submarines. Towards the end of 1909, for export submarines, Germania Yard also made the switch to Diesel.

Diesel changed the importance of submarines by transforming them from a tactical weapon used to defend ports, coasts and naval bases into a strategic offensive weapon. Now, they could be deployed on the broad oceans to destroy hostile economies in a classic war of commerce against enemy trade fleets.

Seven years after the French and four years after Britain, the Imperial Navy had abandoned its reservations about the Diesels. In 1911, Krupp and MAN developed an 880 hp engine weighing 20 tons, two of which were installed in the four newest boats, hull numbers U-19 to U-21.[20] The range of this new 800-ton submarine class, each loaded with six torpedoes, was 7,600 nm with a 35-man crew and a surface speed of 15 knots.

At the outbreak of the war in August 1914, there were 400 submarines in service worldwide, most of them obsolete coastal boats. Great Britain had seventy-two, including seventeen Diesel-powered ocean-going boats. Germany possessed twenty-eight, fourteen of which were modern Diesels. All this despite Tirpitz's obsession with capital ships. Without Krupp, there would never have been any German ocean-going submarines when war began.

In the decade leading up to hostilities, engineers at Krupp's Germania Yard had caught up with technological lags in Uboat construction. Until the end of the war, Germania Yard remained by far the foremost builder of German submarines. By 1918, the Yard had built a third of all the Kaiser's submarines. With its ever-innovative designs and modifications, the company had positioned itself at the forefront of submarine development.[21]

Chapter 26

Merchant Submarines

As a result of the British blockade, within a matter of months German industry began to experience a critical shortage of important precious metals. Almost all pre-war strategic raw materials were imported.

Nickel and other precious metals used to harden steel were in short supply. Gun barrels wore out fast, sending their shots off-target, sometimes landing on their own storm troops rather than on the enemy's front line. The saying in the German trenches became, 'The infantry's worst enemy is its own artillery.'

Even such an 'innocent' product as natural rubber became critical to the war effort. Lack of this resource meant that German gas masks had to be made from leather and leaked after several hours. On the other side, Allied gas masks made from rubber kept out deadly gases for days. The rubber shortage also meant that the wheels of many German trucks had to be made of iron. Cobblestone roads could thus be navigated only slowly and unpaved roads not at all.

Krupp possessed large stores of nickel in its warehouses in the United States and was the owner of a leading submarine shipyard. In May 1915, Germania Yard engineers began with blueprints for a submarine freighter, and in October Gustav Krupp personally placed an order for two over-sized merchant Uboats.

To emphasize the civilian character of these 'commercial' submarines, an independent cover-company, the German Ocean Rhederei, was founded to serve as owner and operator. As the boats were being built the company assembled the crews, all of whom were former members of the Imperial Navy who had been released specifically for this purpose.[1]

Dye

Merchant Uboats could be used not only to import goods, they could also get past the British export blockade of German products.

The lack of German dyes still continued and led to a crisis in the US textile industry, threatening 400,000 jobs. German historian Jan Heitmann writes that in the autumn of 1915, leading American textile industrialists turned 'to the country's political leaders and called on them to exert all of the American government's influence to both convince the German government to ease the export ban on dyes, as well as convince the British to issue transit permits for dye transports.'[2]

Freepost Plus RTKE-RGRJ-KTTX
Pen & Sword Books Ltd
47 Church Street
BARNSLEY
S70 2AS

DISCOVER MORE ABOUT PEN & SWORD BOOKS

Pen & Sword Books have over 4000 books currently available, our imprints include: Aviation, Naval, Military, Archaeology, Transport, Frontline, Seaforth and the Battleground series, and we cover all periods of history on land, sea and air.

Can we stay in touch? From time to time we'd like to send you our latest catalogues, promotions and special offers by post. If you would prefer not to receive these, please tick this box. ❑

We also think you'd enjoy some of the latest products and offers by post from our trusted partners: companies operating in the clothing, collectables, food & wine, gardening, gadgets & entertainment, health & beauty, household goods, and home interiors categories. If you would like to receive these by post, please tick this box. ❑

We respect your privacy. We use personal information you provide us with to send you information about our products, maintain records and for marketing purposes. For more information explaining how we use your information please see our privacy policy at www.pen-and-sword.co.uk/privacy. You can opt out of our mailing list at any time via our website or by calling 01226 734222.

Mr/Mrs/Ms ....

Address..

Postcode...................................... Email address...

Website: www.pen-and-sword.co.uk Email: enquiries@pen-and-sword.co.uk
Telephone: 01226 734555 Fax: 01226 734438
Stay in touch: facebook.com/penandswordbooks or follow us on Twitter @penswordbooks

Merchant Submarine *U-Deutschland*.

In December 1915, the US ambassadors in Berlin and London worked to develop guidelines to solve the problem for America. Germany willingly cooperated and, in January 1916, under American pressure, the British government agreed 'to guarantee the safe passage of two shiploads of dye, with a maximum total value of five million dollars – two-fifths of the pre-war imports'.[3]

At this point, Ocean Rhederei entered the picture. The company suggested that, with the new cargo submarine *U-Deutschland*, the German government could transport the dyes directly to America as freight. The American government had no objections to this short-cutting of the process or of circumventing Britain.[4]

Accordingly, on March 28, 1916, after five months under construction *U-Deutschland*, the world's first merchant submarine, was launched, and commissioned on April 16.

At 1,575 tons displacement and a cargo capacity of nearly 800 GRT, the vessel was the world's largest submarine. Two 380 hp Diesel engines gave her a surface speed of 9.5 kn and 215 tons of stored fuel oil allowed a range of 14,000 nm. This made it possible to sail to ports in the United States without having to refuel for the return journey. The boat was manned by two officers and twenty-six crew. To boost morale and prevent boredom there was an on-board library, a gramophone and a harmonium. Construction costs came to approximately four million Reichsmark.[5]

In early May 1916, with the help of German-Americans, a dock with a warehouse was rented in Baltimore, Maryland. Everything was prepared for the arrival of the *U-Deutschland*.[6]

The Voyage

Secret departure of *U-Deutschland* from Heligoland on June 23, 1916, with 163 tons of dyes on board was made possible through the unauthorized initiative of the American Consul in Bremen. He issued the necessary health certificates for the boat but – in violation of normal procedures – did not report the matter to the American Embassy in Berlin.[7]

Deutschland had been designed for cargo capacity. Its stocky, thick hull was a third shorter than conventional boats. It looked more like a submersible closed bathtub. The boat's short axis created an unstable situation when submerged, leading to dangerous diving situations. Bad weather in the Atlantic delayed travel. The boat rolled and pitched so violently in heavy seas that even die-hard sailors became seasick.

Rumors

In the United States, rumors mounted. As early as June 10, 1916, the *Baltimore News* reported on the imminent arrival of a German submarine. On June 30, the *New York Times* elaborated on the rumor in more detail.

Since the exchange rate against the US dollar was higher in Germany than it was in the United States, one US company offered to transport German paper currency to Germany on a cargo submarine that would shortly arrive in Baltimore. Currency translation rates on the New York Stock Exchange began to go wild. The US Securities and Exchange Commission intervened and issued a complaint for illegal stockmarket manipulation against the company involved.[8]

Heitmann records that speculation was rampant. Bookmakers on the east coast of America were taking bets on the merchant submarine. One newspaper compared the mysterious German underwater freighter to the legendary Flying Dutchman.[9]

By decryption of commercial telegrams Britain quickly got wind of the undertaking but was unable to obtain clarifying details. The Royal Navy increased its monitoring activities along the North American coast and ordered all German boats to be sunk without warning. London prepared sharp diplomatic protests should Wilson allow this merchant submarine to run into a US port. For the British, every German Uboat was a potential warship, and they believed that the neutral United States was duty-bound to immediately seize and detain any such vessel.

Arrival

In the early morning hours of July 9, 1916, following a journey of 4,250 nm in sixteen days, *U-Deutschland* reached American territorial waters on the eastern seaboard outside Baltimore.

The astonished pilot who received *U-Deutschland*'s request for safe navigation into port, blurted out, 'I'll be damned, here she is!' The next day, the port health officer authorized the submarine to moor in the harbor.

The British Ambassador to the United States called for *U-Deutschland* to be interned, but this demand fell on deaf American ears. Following a thorough inspection, US State Department officials acknowledged that *U-Deutschland* was a cargo ship.

American newspapers praised the deft performance of the boat and its captain in surmounting the hated British blockade with headlines like 'Hats Off to the *Germany* [*U-Deutschland*]' and 'His finest Victory'.[10]

Heitmann described Count Bernstorff's overwhelmingly positive reaction, 'that it seemed as though the last two years of hatred and resentment against the German Reich had been forgotten. The British Ambassador, on the other hand, had to acknowledge that this sensational reception had an enormously [positive] effect on public opinion in the USA.'[11]

Press furor and the attentiveness of the American public went on for weeks. A fifth of Baltimore's 500,000 residents were of German heritage and the crew of the boat went from one special event to the next. A delegation of the team visited

U-Deutschland arrives at Baltimore.

Unloading of *U-Deutschland*.

the official rooms of the White House in nearby Washington and was received by the Deputy Secretary of the Navy, Franklin D. Roosevelt, who was able to make conversation with them in German.

The enthusiasm of US citizens for the cunning circumvention of the British blockade knew no bounds. Countless requests were received for spots as passengers on the return trip, and some Americans offered up to $50,000 for a ticket.

The wildest rumors also began to circulate: a Zeppelin, the Z-*Germany*, would land in America as the harbinger of an entire fleet of airships.

The Sale of the Cargo

In the meantime, a dispute flared up over the price and distribution of the cargo. American authorities intervened in favor of the US federal printing office, which was heavily dependent on the dyes for the printing of bank notes.

Eventually the dyes were sold for six million dollars – twelve times their pre-war value – to the four leading chemical companies in the United States, all of which were subsidiaries of German industrial groups.[12] Revenues earned from subsequent processing ultimately ended up in the US accounts of German parent companies.

The *Deutschland*'s cargo had already been sold for more than five times the ship's construction costs. Impressed by the fantastic profit margins, an American businessman grandly announced that he would put together $100 million in capital and invest in a fleet of eighty American merchant submarines, each with a cargo capacity of 5,000 GRT.

Back home

At the end of June loading began for the boat's return trip to Europe. Cargo consisted of 327 tons of nickel and 79 tons of tin from Krupp's American inventory, and 349 tons of rubber.[13]

Because allied cruisers patrolled just beyond American territorial waters, Bernstorff urgently requested an American escort for the departure.

On the evening of August 1, under the eyes of countless onlookers, *U-Deutschland* sailed out, accompanied by several US Customs cutters which kept their station all the way to the three-mile territorial zone.

Captain König knew that several Allied warships lurked just beyond the limit, in international waters. By deceptive maneuvering and diving he delayed the boat's travel, remaining in shallow coastal waters until shortly after midnight when he broke into the open Atlantic. On August 25, following an incident-free crossing and a total journey of 8,450 nm, *U-Deutschland* arrived back in Bremerhaven.[14]

Deutschland Arrives back at Bremen.

Summary

For the German war economy the cargo came as a great relief. The nickel cargo represented one-seventh of 1913's annual consumption,[15] and the 349 tons of rubber were enough to provide tires for more than 11,000 trucks.[16] And better gasmasks.

In terms of foreign policy, *Deutschland*'s appearance in the United States was a turning point in strained German-American relations. By the summer of 1916, the average American probably would not have given a second thought to the reasons for the bloody conflict between the Europeans and their kings, emperors and tsars. What the citizens of the freest and most powerful nation in the world did take note of were the ongoing economic restrictions imposed by an overbearing British blockade, and occasional Uboat brutalities.

Now, in a brilliant coup, Germany had outmaneuvered the British by shipping urgently needed goods to America, bringing hard-hit economic sectors back to life. Any anger that was felt over the summary sinking of passenger steamers by German submarines was tempered. The German Empire was reinstated as an accepted trading partner in the world of American commerce, and a balance was once again struck between pro-British and pro-German sympathies.

For Ocean Rhederei, this first journey was also a resounding success. Raw rubber, declared upon departure from the US at a value of $560,000 was sold in Germany for 17.5 million RM, an 800% increase in value. Along with profits from sale of the dyes, this first trip had earned tenfold what had been spent on construction costs. Ocean Rhederei immediately ordered six new merchant submarines.

At the Admiralty in London, alarm bells were ringing. As predicted by professionals in the trade division, Germany would be able to circumvent the blockade of strategic raw materials by using a small fleet of submarine freighters. It was reckoned that a total of four annual trips by eight merchant boats could transport about 20,000 tons of cargo each way for export and import. In so doing, the Reich could meet the annual American demand for dyes and use the proceeds to purchase critical raw materials in the United States to take back home. Unsurprisingly, the British assessment was, 'Shortages in the rubber and metal sectors [in Germany would be] completely eliminated.'[17]

Construction of the merchant submarines had been done at the initiative of the Krupp Company. Once again, a private industrial concern provided alternatives to the uncoordinated activities of governmental authorities.

But the military was not accustomed to dealing with economic issues. The Imperial Navy, in compliance with Tirpitz's vision, continued to further expansion of the High Seas Fleet. For the hundreds of millions of Reichsmark that were spent on construction costs for surface ships, it would have been possible to knock out entire fleets of merchant submarines in short order. And, had a merchant war in accordance with prize rules been conducted in 1916, England could have been critically threatened and forced to make concessions – at least, in the area of the food blockade.

In the summer of 1916, the Reich with its civilian and military submarines held a singular trump card, one which could have decisively strengthened German economic resilience, might well have saved the German civilian population from a looming winter of starvation, and have forced significant concessions from England, perhaps even leading to peace talks.

But the leadership of the High Seas Fleet turned down any and every strategic alternative. In the shipyards, battle fleets continued to be built for the expected onset of German world domination. Submarines at their North Sea bases lay idle.

Chapter 27

Uboat Armament

At the outbreak of the war, the Imperial Navy consisted of some 250 units with one million tons of displacement and 55,000 crew members.

In the first twenty-four months of war, the Imperial Naval Office, under Grand Admiral von Tirpitz (until March, 1916) and Admiral von Capelle was responsible for equipping the fleet and had undertaken an ambitious shipbuilding program. In this time 600,000 tons of new warships were laid down – the equivalent to two-thirds of the total German fleet of 1914.

But if anyone had expected a massive Uboat building initiative he would have been disappointed. Eight super-dreadnoughts, along with 161 cruisers, destroyers, torpedo boats, minelayers, and minesweepers accounted for 500,000 tons of the program. By comparison, a mere 32 coastal Uboats and 173 ocean-going Uboats amounting to 106,000 tons made do for the submarines' participation in the war.

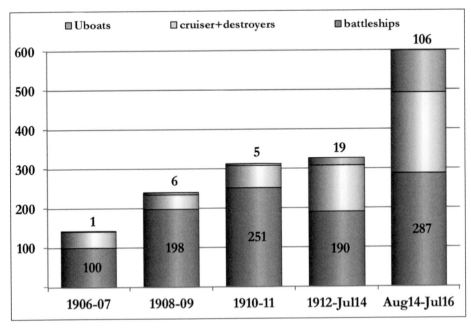

German Warships laid down from 1906 to 1916 (1,000 tons).[1]

The Kaiser, on the evidence of the failed battleship strategy, had already ordered in October 1914 'that no more dreadnoughts are to be built.'[2] And Bethmann was not fundamentally opposed to a submarine commerce war, if only the numbers promised a chance for success. In his opinion, the war would last years, and so he supported the idea 'of creating an increasingly stronger Uboat fleet – building, building, and building – and preparing for a very long war.'[3]

The government could only helplessly take note of the Navy's renewed lust for battleship construction at the beginning of 1915, as Riezler remarked: 'Fearful of the interest of the Navy for battle fleets. Submarines and raiders offer no jobs for admirals.'[4]

An ocean-going Uboat of the 1914 class had a displacement of 650 tons and a construction price of 3.3 million RM; a dreadnought of the latest class, around 70-80 million RM. In simple terms: for the eight modern battleships alone, the navy could have constructed some 160 additional Uboats.[5] From laying keel to commissioning took one to two years for submarines, while battleships took four to five years. Tirpitz's new, fast battleship squadron would not be able to put to sea before 1919 or 1920.

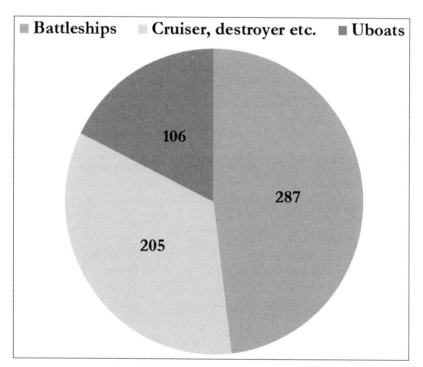

German Warships laid down between August 1914 and July 1916 (1,000 tons).[6]

Within the navy there were also voices that favored a massive Uboat construction program. The Admiralty Staff had demanded as early as April 1915 that an additional 200 submarines be ordered, and in January 1916 another 350. The strategic concept behind this was an exhaustive submarine commerce war in the Atlantic and Mediterranean to effectively block British trade.[7] Not just dozens, but hundreds of submarines would be required to create an iron curtain around England.

Adequate yard capacities were available. In the year 1914, Imperial Germany commissioned 380,000 GRT of merchant vessels and 192,000 tons of warships. Had it been a priority, it would have been an easy feat to build many more than the 300 submarines that the navy commissioned during the war. It was not a question of yard capacity or raw materials – there was plenty available for the eight dreadnoughts and fifteen cruisers that were laid down in the first two years of the war.

Budgetary constraints also did not affect the decision not to build submarines. By December 31, 1917, the Imperial Navy had spent seven billion RM for operations and new construction since the outbreak of the war.[8] Total war costs amounted to around two billion RM monthly, meaning that by the end of 1917 they totaled around 80-90 billion RM.[9]

Expenditures for the navy made up about seven or eight per cent of the total cost of the war. In total in the first two years of the war the Imperial Navy spent 25-30 per cent of its budget on submarines. A mere two per cent of the total war costs financed submarine construction by the end of 1917. In view of the gargantuan propaganda for this 'war-deciding miracle weapon', this was an astonishing discrepancy.

As early as January 1916, the Admiralty Staff too had requested, in addition to the 133 Uboats that had already been ordered, the construction of another 350 boats to enable them to efficiently conduct merchant warfare in the Atlantic and Mediterranean.

Tirpitz's successor was plagued by quite different worries. On November 8, 1916, Capelle complained to the Admiralty Staff about the exorbitant number of orders for Uboats. He wished, 'with regard to the continuing construction of large battleships and the development of the Navy after the war,'[10] to keep orders for new boats to a minimum. He declared that the war would soon be over – the large number of Uboats that would thereafter need to be maintained would have a negative impact on the Navy's postwar budget for battleship development.[11] His solution was a declaration to the Reichstag in January 1917 that: 'At the Imperial Naval Office, we are already considering the possibility of designating a particular port to serve as a Uboat graveyard after the war is ended.'[12]

In their opposition to increases in Uboat construction, the Imperial Naval Office resorted to any argument no matter how far-fetched – there were not enough officers, there were too few shipyards, worker shortages, materials were scarce, etc – but none of these challenges seemed to pose a problem to the intensive construction of large surface units.

Even bids from a number of shipyards that had not yet been involved in Uboat construction, who offered not to charge for the first boats contracted, were rejected because they were too 'inexperienced'.

The Imperial Navy preached the waters of Uboat warfare, but secretly enjoyed the wine of battle fleet construction.

The American naval historian Gary Weir explained this armament strategy: 'Tirpitz felt the political necessity of responding to foreign and domestic pressures and thus involved the RMA in enough U-boat development to satisfy most critics, departing as little as possible from his original plans for the High Seas Fleet.'[13]

Under a different naval armaments policy, a far greater number of Uboats would have been available during the third year of the war, and the Allies might have been convinced to negotiate a peace.

Naval historian Friedrich Forstmeier wrote, 'Had all of the competing extraneous activities been radically eliminated and had there been an early focus on the materials and personnel required for Uboat construction, such a large number of boats could have been built during the war that their deployment, even following prize rules, would have been a threat to England's existence.'[14]

Tirpitz biographer Raffael Scheck explains the situation for the German Imperial Navy: A victory over France would extort enormous financial reparations from France, which it could use for further naval armaments. Thus strengthened, Germany could then defeat England one day, in a 'Second Punic War'.[15]

It could thus never be said that Tirpitz gave priority to building Uboats. His armaments strategy consisted more of preparations for a future 'Second Punic War' against Great Britain once Germany had won the current wars with France and Russia.[16]

Chapter 28

Uboat Strike continues

Also in the summer of 1916, the High Seas Fleet once again insisted on an unrestricted merchant war, sinking all cargo ships, whether hostile or neutral.

In an argument with Scheer on June 24, Admiral Müller summed up his 'all or none' attitude. He asked to avoid a situation 'in which his Majesty would be confronted with the task of not just granting approval, but having to intervene by ordering Uboats into the Mediterranean.'[1] This threat of imperial intervention did not impress Scheer. He preferred to keep his steadily growing Uboat fleet safely at harbor rather than dispatch them out into the Atlantic to conduct restricted warfare.

On July 1, Kaiser Wilhelm, Commander in Chief of the Imperial Navy, commanded his subordinates to deliver a petition. 'It is to be communicated to the Chief of the High Seas Fleet that his Majesty does not at this time grant approval for ruthless Uboat merchant warfare, although he fully understands the purely military justification. He cannot, however, agree with the High Seas Chief in rejecting a more moderate form of Uboat merchant war like the consistently successful one conducted in the Mediterranean.'[2]

On July 18, Admiral Müller attempted to overcome the High Seas Fleet's blockade: 'The merchant war being carried out in the Mediterranean continues to be exemplary. Transferring the methods employed in the Mediterranean to the operations in the North Sea and the Atlantic, despite complete acknowledgment of the difficult conditions in those waters, holds the promise of success, which we may under no circumstances forego. This makes the resistance of the fleet command all the more regrettable. This resistance must be overcome, and if by no other means, then by imperial command. The insistence on proceeding ruthlessly is impractical.'[3]

Even Chief of the Admiralty Staff Holtzendorff, in a letter from August 10, pleaded with Scheer to – cautiously – resume Uboat warfare: 'I feel myself obliged, however, to strongly advise you not to completely neglect the western coast of England. The complete halt of the Uboat merchant war, precisely and solely on the western coast of England, where the main import traffic is found, greatly facilitates England's war situation, freeing up its naval guard and defense forces for the Mediterranean and the Channel. For psychological reasons, I would like to advise you to consider the Emperor's mood. He continually refers to the success in the Mediterranean and also finds the lack of activity around England all the more personally embarrassing since he, as the Commander in Chief, is accused by the Pan-Germans of rallying to "spare England." Could you not now and again dispatch a boat to make a foray on the western coast?'[4]

The Kaiser, Prussian King by the Grace of God, and Commander-in-Chief of the Navy, requested that a proxy petition one of his military subordinates who was refusing to use the weaponry available to him, to carry out a raid 'now and again'. There may be no more fitting example of the pitifully helpless role played by the Emperor.

In this post-feudal German empire, strategically-coordinated concepts for warfare were neither attainable nor enforceable. There was no central institution, no strong Chancellor who might have choreographed an effective foreign and domestic policy, finance, economy and military. It was all rather loosely held together according to the direct relationship of the acting players to the Emperor himself.

This late-feudal government style represented a social structure that was still pervaded by medieval thinking, and this was particularly prevalent within the Army and Navy.

The Army Officer Corps[5]

Prussia was the largest individual state within the Reich, accounting for two-thirds of both population and territory. Prussia's great size meant that the Reich was, in actuality, more or less an extended Prussia, or, as some conservatives occasionally described it, a Prussia-Germany.

In the Reich's standing army, made up of about 600,000 to 700,000 men, Prussia also had the largest number of soldiers. In peace time, the army consisted solely of aristocratic officers and peasant recruits.

In Prussia it was nearly exclusively the nobles who were allowed to become professional military officers. The regimental officers chose the officer recruits themselves, so that the officer corps of the standing Prussian army was chiefly recruited from among Prussia's 25,000 aristocratic families. These officers did not swear allegiance to the state or to the constitution but by personal oath to the German Emperor.

The typical Prussian officer, following a few years of instruction by a tutor at the paternal estate, began his career as a young boy at a cadet academy. The most intelligent went through General Staff training, which led to the formation of a type of 'Jesuit Order'. The Army General Staff also commanded the non-Prussian troops and its leadership was centered in Berlin. The Chief of the General Staff was the de-facto commander of the troops, someone with whom even the Kaiser dared not intervene.

The Prussian Army was a guaranteed career for the second and later-born sons of aristocrats who would have no claim to an inheritance. The size of the army was always determined by the number of aristocrats available for officer positions. Even in the final years before the war, Prussian Junkers blocked any measurable increase in the size of the army since it would have meant admitting bourgeois officers and proletarian recruits from large cities and industrial areas. The latter were used in the 'reserve units', which were only called up for exercises or in times of war.

This standing peacetime army under the command of the General Staff in Berlin was the guarantor for maintaining the Wilhelminian social order and Prussia's domination in the Imperial Reich.

Prussian officers were representatives of a closed military caste. They had never attended a public school, had not pursued any university studies, and interacted only among those of their own status. Outside their tight circle, they had no competence in economic, financial, domestic, or foreign policy issues. Riezler commented, referring to their intellectual level: 'The education of all these people stopped at hunting.'[6]

The Navy

In the Imperial Navy the aristocracy played only a subordinate role, the fleet was 'bourgeois' and 'national'. In the selection of the officer cadets, emphasis was placed on a solid bourgeois upbringing within an affluent family, including a strictly national-conservative political orientation. As in the army, liberal or socialist ideas had no place among the Kaiser's officers.

The marriages of all officers required the permission of the Kaiser, thereby precluding undesirable misalliances between unequal social classes. The naval officer corps – like its army counterpart, aristocrats – was also governed by a closed and socially-insular elite group whose members were sworn only to the monarch.

Any weakening of these class boundaries by means of social climbing was not desirable. On the contrary, what the members of the elite class promised themselves was a caste-like class distinction which would serve as a dam against the social dislocation and new currents that came on the heels of industrialization.

For conservative elites, the ideal was the firmly-established medieval feudal state in which every person at birth was permanently assigned a social niche. Kaiser Wilhelm concisely summarized the system in a speech he gave to a group of Krupp workers in September, 1918. 'All of us will be assigned our responsibilities from God. You will stand at your steam hammer, you at your lathe, and I will sit on my throne.'[7]

The army and the navy resembled two self-contained, competing chivalric orders from the times of the crusades, who, in representing their own interests, did not shy away from conflicts with the monarch. Junkers felt certain that they represented the 'true' interests of the fatherland, while naval officers saw themselves as standard-bearers of an emerging maritime realm that would oppose all internal and external resistance.

A Channel Offensive?

In early August, Holtzendorff, in an attempt to move a step closer to unrestricted Uboat warfare, tried to launch a submarine offensive in the English Channel. Accordingly, on August 2, 1916, Müller wrote, 'A new plan to wage unrestricted submarine warfare in the English Channel.'[8]

If Holtzendorff speculated that an offensive against munitions and troop transports to France would secure the support of the army, he was disappointed, given Army Commander Falkenhayn's reaction a few days later, on August 7. Falkenhayn concluded that it was not worth risking a breach with America by undertaking a ruthless Uboat war in the Channel. Bethmann concurred.[9]

At the same time, the Navy resumed a propaganda offensive. Riezler noted on August 10, 1916, that 'Pan-Germans continue to stir up the situation. It is an absolute madhouse. The wildest of rumors fly all about. The Kaiser – it is said that he is glum, too weak, and close to abdicating. This disastrous Tirpitz with his Uboats and his dishonest pronouncements. The Chancellor said last night that Uboats would follow him to his grave.'[10]

On August 20, Weizsäcker complained that 'The entire Uboat situation has been so deliberately put to use by the Pan-Germans and Prussian conservatives to incite against the Imperial Chancellor that this psychosis has also become quite widespread.'[11]

Riezler described the predicament in which the government found itself as a result of the general agitation. 'The Uboat war,' he predicted, 'is the sole, though weak, way to win the war but should it fail, there is a dramatic deterioration to its possible outcome, which we otherwise may still hope will be an impasse. It is the most difficult of all decisions. Should there be an unfavorable peace agreement, without deployment of the weapons in which the people now believe, Germany will be ruined for at least a century.'[12]

Holtzendorff was isolated.

Also, far-right press hostility was nothing new for the Chancellor. Admiral Müller went on the attack. On August 24 and 25, in discussions with the Chancellor he suggested 'resuming cruiser warfare with submarines against the western coast of England and in the Channel. We should first try to see how far we could proceed with this warfare without becoming involved with America.'[13] The Chancellor agreed with him.

The situation at the beginning of the third war year was grim. A victory, whether on land or sea, seemed impossible. Compounding difficulties was that the grain harvest had not been plentiful and the rainy summer promised another catastrophic potato harvest. Food imports from neutral sources no longer arrived and the specter of starvation loomed on the doorstep.

On August 25, Bethmann shared his assessment of the situation with Müller. 'Our situation is such that we must make peace soon, while we are still in the position of victors. A general status quo. The Kaiser agreed with his view that no chance of making peace must be rejected.'[14]

The Kaiser, the Chancellor and the Army formed a clear front against the Navy. At the end of August, however, events led to a reshuffling.

Chapter 29

New Leadership

Falkenhayn overthrown

The relationship between Bethmann and Chief of the General Staff Falkenhayn had been dysfunctional for a long time. The Chancellor's professional assessment of Falkenhayn in the face of the senseless battle of Verdun (which had raged since February, with 600,000 dead on both sides) was scathing: 'Where do we draw the line between incompetence and criminal behavior?'[1] he demanded to know. It was only Falkenhayn's favored status with the Kaiser that allowed him – non-political but completely unsuited for the position – to remain in office.

Romania's declaration of war on Germany and Austria-Hungary on August 27, 1916, caught the Chief of the General Staff completely off-guard, threatening the collapse of an essential ally. This strategic miscalculation was the final straw. Within 48 hours he was summarily dismissed.

On August 28, 1916, Müller noted: 'During the course of the day the idea gained ground that Hindenburg must replace Falkenhayn. This decision caused the Kaiser to shed tears.'[2] On the next day, 'Hindenburg was appointed Chief of the General Staff and Ludendorff First Quartermaster-General. Falkenhayn quietly left for Berlin.'[3]

Imperial Navy reaction was joyful. 'The announcement that Hindenburg has been named Chief of the General Staff, which had just been made public, unleashed wild speculation. Fleet staff sees this as a victory for the Uboat war.'[4]

Hindenburg and Ludendorff vs. Bethmann Hollweg

Hindenburg, at the age of 69, became the new Chief of the General Staff, the Commander-in-Chief of the Army. It was his Quartermaster-General, however, the 51-year-old brilliant tactician Erich Ludendorff, who made decisions. The first action taken by the two new military leaders was to bring a halt to the Battle of Verdun.

The change in leadership introduced significant shifts in domestic politics. Falkenhayn's position depended upon the goodwill of the Kaiser and Wilhelm had, when necessary, been able to assert himself as in the *Sussex* crisis. But this dynamic was impossible with Hindenburg and Ludendorff who brought with them their own power base: public opinion.

Above left and right: Field Marschal Paul von Hindenburg and General Erich Ludendorff.

At the very beginning, in September 1914 under the high command of Paul von Hindenburg, the Russian army which had broken through to eastern Prussia was crushed in battle. At that time, after the loss of the battle of the Marne on the Western front, this brilliant defensive victory was touted by the war propagandists as a veritable miracle.

By virtue of his 'destruction of invading Russian hordes', Hindenburg was elevated by the German press as an icon of the invincibility of the Reich, and the justification of its own interests. This mindset had broad appeal, embracing every social class. Hindenburg, in private, was a rather dull, deeply conservative aristocrat, stereotypical of the Prussian Junker caste. He had never expressed political ambitions but was able to rise above all others to become the guiding super-father of the nation.

Erich Ludendorff was actually too young to be a general. On his mother's side, he was the descendant of an East Prussian aristocratic family, but his father was bourgeois. Only the missing 'von' preceding his last name distinguished him from his aristocratic Prussian comrades. In contrast to Hindenburg, the 'young' Ludendorff embodied elements of the modern zeitgeist. When it came to achieving goals, he could radically ignore any social ramifications, and in contrast with the staid Hindenburg, he was a fire-spitting volcano, the embodiment of the *furor teutonicus*.

Each was dependent on the other. For Hindenburg, the efforts of his Quartermaster-General brought him public glorification. In turn, Ludendorff required Hindenburg's authority to carry out exceedingly ambitious plans.

Hindenburg, Kaiser Wilhelm, and Ludendorff.

With Hindenburg and Ludendorff appointed, the Kaiser's veto was effectively blocked. The most important decisions fell to the leaders of his army. They needed only to threaten their resignations – which they often did – to force Wilhelm to concede. The function of the supreme arbitrator transferred from the Kaiser to Hindenburg. Ludendorff hastened to transform Wilhelminian Imperial Germany into a military dictatorship.[5]

Ludendorff was determined to eliminate the chaos he saw in German domestic and foreign policy, the economy, and warfare, and transform the Supreme Army Command into a new center of power. But he needed time and proven military successes. For the moment, he was preoccupied with finding a solution to the Romanian crisis, and thus initially pursued a harmonious working relationship with Bethmann.

The Army Leaders and the Uboat War

On August 31, the issue of unrestricted submarine warfare was raised once again in a decisive meeting between the Chancellor, the Army and the Navy.

Holtzendorff attacked Bethmann. 'The Chancellor's objections to this [form of] warfare have nothing to do with defeating England, but are all concerned with the repercussion from America. America can hardly become more hostile than it already is. I do not see in this operation the downfall of Germany, but rather, an unwillingness to use the *one* weapon that would destroy England's ability to wage war.'[6]

Admiral Capelle, of the Imperial Naval Office, considered it 'impossible for us to emerge victorious without the deployment of Uboats. He did not in any way ignore the risk. Even if Uboat warfare did not lead to ultimate success, he would not regard this as a catastrophe, but merely as a war of attrition.'[7]

Capelle thus did not share Holtzendorff's certainty of victory. He was unwilling to guarantee success, and proposed, as Plan B, 'merely' a war of attrition between Germany and the rest of the world.

The Chancellor criticized the Navy's speculations. 'The Admiralty Staff is of the opinion that reducing the shipping capability [of the Allies] will lead to a catastrophe that would cause England to grow weary of war. That was an assumption, not evidence.'[8] 'He was prepared to support Uboat warfare immediately if convinced that it would bring about a positive outcome to the war. But this was a life or death battle. Pointless discussion was not an option.' [9]

Once again, the irreconcilable positions held by the Navy and the Reich leadership clashed, based as they were on fundamentally different strategies. For the Navy, peace through victory, and for the Chancellor, a negotiated peace.

Ludendorff up until this point had little involvement with the issue. In March 1916, he had admitted: 'My understanding of the Uboat situation is so limited that I am not able to judge it.'[10]

At the pivotal meeting on August 31, the Army ultimately prevailed. Ludendorff described the unpredictability of the Romanian campaign and the uncertainty of the position that would be taken by the Netherlands and Denmark in the event the US entered the war. 'If Uboat warfare would cause the neutrals to become our enemies, then we shall have to rethink our decision on this issue.'[11] Hindenburg underscored this point of view with a paternalistic, 'Look before you leap!'[12]

Army leadership had – for the moment – spoken out against unrestricted Uboat war. Ludendorff's immediate horizon consisted of victory over Romania, threat of the Netherlands or Denmark entering the war, and the disposition of a handful of divisions.[13] As soon as the situation on Germany's front lines was clarified, the army leaders could be expected to change their minds.

Müller neatly summarized the situation: 'The Navy in favor of immediate unrestricted Uboat warfare and the risk of offending America. The civilians against it. Hindenburg wants to review the progress of operations against Romania before making a decision. Postponed for some weeks.'[14]

Bethmann's First Peace Feeler

Appointing Ludendorff and Hindenburg briefly brought a measure of calm. Riezler noted on September 6, 1916: 'Feeling relieved by the appointment of Hindenburg along with involvement of the Chancellor. The Chancellor and Hindenburg enjoyed cordial relations. Opposition points of view wanted to approach the Army leadership but realized that as long as Hindenburg agreed with Bethmann they could not ramrod the Uboat issue.'[15]

In Holtzendorff's game of dare, the Chancellor once again prevailed, but the unified front that the government and the army currently presented against the navy could not hold indefinitely.

But Bethmann realized that time was running out. On September 2 he provided information about the situation to German Ambassador Bernstorff in Washington who was in constant communication with Edward House. President Wilson's chief advisor on European affairs urged Wilson to undertake a peace initiative: 'Otherwise, all-out submarine warfare would have to be seriously considered.'[16] The answer from Bernstorff was disheartening. He believed that as long as Wilson was in the middle of a presidential campaign, no assistance from him could be expected.[17]

For the Fleet, the issue of unrestricted Uboat warfare had progressed from an 'if' to a 'when' and it would no longer be the Kaiser who made the decision but the Army. Could the Imperial Navy assist in speeding up a 'showdown'?

War with the United States?

The Imperial Navy called for unrestricted merchant warfare against both the enemy and neutrals. Civilian leadership's respect for the concerns of the US was a hindrance. What could be done to remove the obstacle?

During its exit through the shallow coastal waters of Baltimore in August, *U-Deutschland* barely escaped the English cruisers lurking in wait at the boundaries of American territorial waters. A sister submarine, *U-Bremen*, departed on its first crossing from Heligoland to America on August 25, 1916, and was scheduled to leave again in early October.

On September 3, Holtzendorff visited the High Seas Fleet in Wilhelmshaven and instructed Scheer regarding the outcome of the August 31 meeting. 'At the end, he conveyed his most ardent desire that a Uboat be sent to American waters.'[18] The Chief of the Admiralty Staff tasked this Uboat with the protection of the *U-Bremen* as it departed from America. Scheer then ordered U-53, under the command of Lieutenant Hans Rose, to prepare for a long-distance operation.

The notion that a Uboat off the American coast would provide military cover for *U-Bremen*'s departure may have seemed plausible initially. Facts, however, stood in the way. U-53's fuel supply was barely sufficient for the outward and return journey. Shifting currents, storms, or technical problems could significantly delay their 4,000 nm crossing. That left a highly uncertain, shortened timeframe of only a few days for a rendezvous with *U-Bremen*. Even more significant, justification for protection of *U-Bremen* had been removed because the port designated for merchant submarines had been changed to New London, Connecticut.

The advantage was that New London is a deep-water port that allowed submarines to immediately dive while still within the American three-mile zone.[19]

The Kaiser's orders communicated by Holtzendorff were also extremely dubious. At the August 31 meeting, discussion centered on the development of major strategy and there had been no mention of a desire by the Kaiser to send a submarine to America. In face of the position taken by political leadership, i.e. not to risk any conflict with the US, such a deployment would also have been ill-founded.

On September 8, a preparatory meeting took place between the Admiralty Staff and the High Seas Fleet where astonished Fleet officers were informed by members of the Admiralty Staff about expansions to the orders for U-53's tasking. Following completion of the protective mission, the boat was to proceed to a US military port for a courtesy call and then to conduct merchant warfare in accordance with prize rules off the US coast. The aim was to demonstrate 'that the capability of German submarines is sufficient to prosecute underwater merchant warfare off the North American coast.'[20]

Visiting foreign fleet bases was a diplomatic act, one which even in peacetime required months of advance preparation. The unannounced arrival of a Uboat to a neutral naval base in the middle of a war could pose a serious diplomatic conflict for its host. The opposing side would be expected to demand immediate internship of the enemy warship. In addition, a Uboat war within sight of the American coast was also clearly a provocative act, one that would make a fool out of Wilson who had campaigned to be President under the slogan 'He Kept Us Out of War.'

Ernst von Weizsäcker noted, 'In response to the remark that [the visit] could lead to serious complications with America, representatives of the

U-53 in Harbour.

Admiralty Staff replied, "That is precisely what we want. We have to finally get the ball rolling."[21] U-53's original defensive mission had now been transformed into a deliberate provocation of the United States.

Admiral Scheer harbored serious concerns and, in a letter to Holtzendorff on September 10, warned that 'the U-53 mission may bring about war with America.'[22] He demanded a vote from the political leadership and the army. 'It is my conscientious conviction,' he insisted, 'that the mission may only be carried out if the responsible parties in the military and political leadership are instructed as to the potentially grave consequences of this undertaking and give their express consent to the plan – which, according to your Excellency, has not been granted.'[23]

On the same day, Holtzendorff sought support from army leadership for his aggressive course of action, which was meant to lead to unrestricted submarine warfare. He was coldly received. Ludendorff proposed that the notion of unrestricted warfare at the present time was a bluff. Not mincing his words, he had taken 'many risks during his battles, but always when he was firmly convinced of success. A bluff like this was not boldness, but recklessness, and he would not agree to it.'[24]

Holtzendorff replied to Scheer on September 11, 'I do not share your concerns regarding the consequences of the planned operation. I have thus also refrained from communicating with the political leadership of the Reich about this undertaking, as it is a military operation, which is in accordance with the highest biddings of His Majesty.'[25] Holtzendorff, it seems, made the prospect of war with the most powerful nation on the planet his own private affair.

Scheer continued to be mistrustful and on September 12 threatened to have the Kaiser intervene. 'The Commander of the Fleet once again requests the Chief of the Admiralty Staff to instruct the Chancellor and the Chief of the General Staff regarding the potentially grave consequences of this undertaking. Should this request be denied, he will consider himself obliged to approach His Majesty directly.'[26]

The next day, Holtzendorff informed Scheer that 'His Majesty has approved plans for the U-53 mission,' adding that 'The Chancellor has absolutely no concerns.'[27]

What led to the approval of Wilhelm and Bethmann Hollweg, as alleged by Holtzendorff, to an operation that was so dangerous that it raised apprehension even within the Navy?

First and foremost – the question was just *which* order had the Kaiser approved? There were two radically different orders in U-53's command log.[28] Both issued by Holtzendorff 'on highest command' – in other words, in the name of the Kaiser. Both were dated September 11. The first 'harmless' order commanded U-53 to provide protection for *U-Bremen*. The second order added commencement of the merchant war off the American coast: 'Following the arrival of *U-Bremen*, enemy naval forces are expected to guard the eastern approaches to Long Island Sound. You are to search out these forces and attack. After accomplishing this mission, you should proceed to Newport, Rhode Island to give US naval authorities an opportunity to visit the boat. *After accomplishing [these] missions, or should they need to be abandoned, merchant war in accordance with prize rules may be commenced.*'[29]

Almost certainly, Bethmann would not have agreed to a merchant war off the America coast. Such an act violated this cool-headed, straightforward statesman's entire political lineage. To ask Wilson to initiate peace talks while simultaneously waging submarine warfare right under his nose was absurd.

Either Holtzendorff had misled the Kaiser with the shorter 'harmless' orders for the fleet visit or he had simply made up the story of the Kaiser's approval and lied to Scheer. The only statement regarding approval by the Kaiser and Chancellor came directly from Holtzendorff.

Ernst von Weizsäcker candidly describes the prevailing situation in the Fleet in September 1916 in a letter to his father. 'The Naval Officer Corps sits around, eating, drinking, politicizing, and scheming, and considers itself thereby yet patriotic, because it is seeking by dishonest means to carry out [unrestricted] Uboat warfare. The Uboat war is intended to cover up the absurdities in the construction of the fleet and of its employment in the war. The propaganda for this reflects a guilty conscience.'[30]

For Chief of the Admiralty Staff Holtzendorff, any means of getting 'his' war were justified. Conflict with the United States eliminated all impediments to a ruthless Uboat war.

On September 17, 1916, U-53 departed Heligoland.

Bethmann's Second Peace Feeler

While U-53 was en route, Bethmann together with the Kaiser and Ludendorff drafted a note to Wilson requesting help with peace negotiations. The note was sent to Bernstorff on September 26.[31] The Navy was excluded from participation. Their oppositional stance would have made coordination futile.

The tone of the letter was balanced and realistic. Chancellor, Kaiser, and the top military commander described the situation from the German perspective, that the land war remained undecided and that the Imperial Navy contemplated turning the tide by waging an unrestricted Uboat war. They concluded that 'The overall situation would completely change if President Wilson were to offer to mediate peace between the powers. Such an action would, however, need to be taken soon.'[32]

In effect, the request to the US President asked him to reinforce their own opposition to the Navy's strategic mindset and to pave the way to peace talks.

Given the Navy's and Pan-German propaganda which so successfully pervaded in public opinion, only Wilson, with the magic word 'peace' on his lips, could reverse the situation and avoid surrender to bellicose public opinion.

But once again, Bernstorff's answer following discussions with Mr House was disheartening. During Wilson's presidential campaign, there could be no expectation of an initiative on the part of the President.[33]

Attack on Reason – Uboat Propaganda

Uboat propaganda in Germany was taking on increased irrational, even hysterical, proportions.

A comparable discussion about the strategic options of the army, for instance an attack on Russia or an offensive in the West, was unthinkable because the generals simply would not have permitted it. The army practised censorship of all army-related military issues in the press. It was unimaginable for the General Staff to allow public discussion of such an issue or permit the 'plebes' to referee.

The admirals, however, permitted all press articles favoring unrestricted Uboat warfare to circumvent censorship and, in collaboration with the chauvinistic Pan-Germans, continued to fan the flames of the Uboat issue.

The call for unrestricted submarine warfare even made its way to the Reichstag. A request from the Chairman of the National Liberal Party for the commencement of unrestricted warfare in the Channel led to an on-going debate that lasted from September 29 until October 7, 1916.

Experience showed that technical naval details presented in confidential meetings of the parliamentary group would sooner or later seep into German and neutral media, and eventually make their way to enemies abroad to the decided disadvantage of German military secrecy. Bethmann Hollweg stated to the representatives, 'Gentlemen, I am obliged to tell you that a large portion of the content of our negotiations between March and May [1916], which had been designated confidential, has appeared in the French press. Within such a large circle, it is very difficult to prevent information from trickling out.'[34] The parliamentary discussion of the Uboat issue, initiated by the Navy, was deliberate irresponsibility that bordered on treason.

Count Westarp, Chairman of the Conservative Party, first blamed the Chancellor for 'not waging [unrestricted] "diving boat war" against the Allied ammunition transports in the English Channel, which had cost the lives of "thousands and tens of thousands of our brothers".'[35]

Admiral Capelle, Tirpitz's successor in the Imperial Naval Office, objected immediately: 'He doubted whether ruthless warfare would achieve a better result [against troops and ammunition transporters in the Channel], since the military difficulties remained the same.'[36]

Capelle provided parliamentarians with precise information about the number of available Uboats and outlined deployment possibilities: 'We can expect to have 60 Uboats continuously ready for combat. We can interfere with supplies reaching England by sea, *but there is no question of hermetically sealing off England. The thought of starving out England has disappeared*, and has been replaced by a call for the sinking of cargo.'[37] He reiterated Holtzendorff's old magic formula from the spring which promised that in a ruthless Uboat war, 600,000 GRT per month would be sunk.[38]

Mantra-like, the right offered up all of the well-known arguments for unrestricted war. Impact on England from 600,000 GRT monthly losses as 'guaranteed' by the Navy, were calculated back and forth. For them it seemed even possible to determine the actual date when starvation would force Great Britain to surrender.

Westarp responded blindly to Holtzendorff's numbers. For Westarp, 'the number of available Uboats was not critical to the question of intensified warfare. The only thing that was important was the declaration from the naval authorities that 600,000 tons per month could be sunk.'[39]

The socialist parliamentarian Eduard David, one of the most brilliant minds in the SPD, had fundamental doubts about the tonnage calculations. 'In this situation, Pan-Germans who believed that Germany would be strong enough to compel the world to fall under German domination should finally desist from such fantasies. In particular, the 600,000 tons cannot be accurate. This number was determined in the spring. Meantime, the number of Uboats has doubled. The calculation of the same number of tons of destroyed cargo does not reconcile with the increased number of Uboats.'[40] And further: 'The question of whether or not this would cause such terror within the neutral countries that no ship would risk the journey to England is completely up in the air.'[41]

Addressing the members of Parliament, Bethmann left no doubt about the entry of America into the war, nor did Secretary of State Gottlieb von Jagow. 'There is no question that ruthless Uboat warfare will lead to a breach with America, and I personally am convinced that this breach will also lead to a war.' [42]

The Secretary of the Interior, Karl Theodor Helfferich, stressed the importance of the food imports that were shipped by the neutrals: 'If Uboat warfare results in these imports not making their way to us, what good does it do if England is finished off perhaps in six or eight months, but we ourselves are done in perhaps two or three months? We need to bear in mind: *once we play the card of unrestricted Uboat warfare and [a favorable outcome] is not victory, then we are lost.* In the event, America, too, would side with England. For instance, once in the war, America would no longer require collateral from its allies for loans. *Should the Uboat war eventually fail, no one should be able to say afterwards that he had known nothing about this thing or that.*'[43]

According to the liberal parliamentarian Friederich Payer: '*Indeed, the Uboat issue is only a tactical question.* The entire calculating of tonnage is wrong. Moreover, one must be clear that unrestricted Uboat warfare would mean not only war with America, but also with all of the neutral countries. This would be desperado politics.'[44]

Bethmann stated, 'There is no call for desperado politics, and I would never agree to it. I am not taking a principled position either for or against the Uboat war. I merely ask how would it help us? Would it bring us victory and peace? When I can answer that question in the affirmative, then we will pursue it, and until then, we will not!'[45]

He probably had other items that required his attention, but this debate forced him to remain at the Reichstag for many days. 'It is essential to finally bring clarity to the matter. Yes, Gentlemen, if I myself could obtain this finite, mathematical clarity I would thank the heavens. What can be made technically clear is the number of Uboats. But determining the impact of sinkings by these ships on England's ability to wage war, this, I believe, cannot be proven mathematically.'[46]

The right remained stiff-necked, unyielding. For them, Uboat war was a matter of faith, a crusade for a peace gained by victory.

Westarp summarized the history of Prussian conflicts. 'It may sound paradoxical [indeed!] when I say that, in our evaluation, the number of Uboats does not necessarily play a large role. Factually, of course, the number of Uboats available is decisive. The question of what success can be achieved must be technically assessed by the Navy. When, initially, destruction caused by Uboats in the designated war zones, in contrast to the present cruiser warfare, also leads to a loss of life, the terror will produce an entirely different effect than it has up until now. We estimate that the danger that would thereby threaten us from America and the other neutrals is by no means slight. But in taking our position, we are led by beliefs that have been instilled over the course of the entire history of Prussia and Germany. Prussia-Germany always had to prevail against the massive superiority of its enemies. When, in times at which it was outnumbered, it has acted timidly and with restraint, such a policy has always led to failure. When, however, Prussia has committed its entire strength, *its entire existence*, then it has sparked the developments that led to the founding of the German Reich.'[47]

Was it the spirit of a chivalrous medieval knight speaking here – 'many enemies, much honor' – or was it already that of a modern stockmarket speculator, 'in times of trouble, double?'

The right demanded deployment of uncertain military means, which, in the event of failure would mean the certain loss of the war and a threat to the very existence of the state, a high-risk gamble to preserve the *ancien régime* and its own social existence.

Attack on America: U-53 on the US East Coast

Early on the morning of October 7, 1916, after a stormy journey U-53 reached the coast of Long Island. Rose was unable to make out any enemy naval forces over the course of the morning, and there were no messages from *U-Bremen*, and never would be. The boat never arrived in America, and to this day remains an unsolved mystery.

After a few hours, Rose decided to embark upon the next part of his assignment and wrote, 'No enemy forces, therefore heading to Newport.'[48]

At around 3 pm, U-53 arrived unannounced at the Newport, Rhode Island, naval base. An American naval officer reported that he was 'more than surprised to see the German submarine as she came up the harbor, dropping anchor at about 2:30 p.m.'[49]

Rose paid courtesy calls on the Newport station chief, Admiral Knight, who 'was quite reserved.'[50] Back on board, Rose and his officers led curious visitors through the submarine. 'There were very many officers with their ladies, civilians, reporters, and a photographer who came aboard.'[51]

The American naval officer noted: 'Coming alongside at 3:15 p.m. we were invited on board and had the opportunity of seeing what a modern German naval submarine looks like, as her Captain and First Officer escorted us all over her. Her officers presented a very natty appearance in their naval uniforms. They looked as though they had just come out of a bandbox. Their linen was spick and span, white and starched. [Rose told us:] 'We are leaving at 5:30 and going to look out for enemy ships.' Weighing anchor at 5:17 p.m., she proceeded slowly to sea.'[52]

This strange short visit ended as surprisingly as it had begun after less than three hours.

Rose (2nd from left) welcomes US Officers on board U-53.

Merchant War

Followed by several US Navy destroyers, the Uboat proceeded overnight in the direction of the Nantucket Lightship, a crossroads of American coastal traffic. 'The waters around the Nantucket Lightship are the most promising. The trade routes from New York, Philadelphia, Baltimore, and Providence all run together just a few nautical miles south of here,'[53] Rose recorded.

As dawn broke the next morning, October 8, 1916, U-53 commenced the Uboat merchant war off the coast of the United States. The weather that entire day was clear and practically cloudless.

Observed at a distance by the attending US warships, Rose's first target was an American steamer. Rose halted the ship with a warning shot fired from the deck gun. He reviewed the cargo list and decided that there were no goods on board that were banned by German regulation and let the ship pass.

Over the course of the day, Rose stopped three steamers, two British and one Norwegian, carrying contraband. He sank the ships and towed the rescue boats in the direction of the Nantucket Lightship. American witnesses aboard the destroyers were deeply disturbed by what they saw.

The next target was the Dutch freighter *Blommersdyk*, carrying wheat destined for Rotterdam. Rose suspected the cargo was actually intended for an English port, but he hesitated to sink the ship 'since the regulations permit release as well as capture.'[54]

Suddenly, he sighted several fast-running American destroyers heading for U-53, while another ship, with 'passengers on board'[55] also entered the scene. The situation swiftly became unclear.

Using warning shots, Rose halted the passenger ship, the 3,449 GRT English *Stephano*. Some of the US destroyers stopped in the vicinity of the *Stephano* and began to evacuate the crew and passengers.

Rose noted, 'I now had to seriously create the impression to everyone involved that the presence of the American destroyers compelled me not to feebly comply and to renounce my rights. Meanwhile, in addition to the two steamships, sixteen American destroyers gathered in the narrow waters so that it was necessary to maneuver with care. Among the embarked civilian observers were representatives of the press. An American warship came so close to U-53 that the engines of both vessels had to be reversed in order to avoid a collision. We came within about 50 meters [half a boat length] of each other.'[56]

Rose gave the crew of the *Blommersdyk* twenty-five minutes to disembark. 'A destroyer, which was in close proximity to the steamer, was asked via Morse code to move further away so that the ship could be sunk. He immediately complied with this request.'[57] Rose fired two torpedoes to sink *Blommersdyk*.

Then, escorted by two American warships, he headed for the *Stephano* which had in the meantime been abandoned by passengers and crew. Rose wrote: 'Steamer sunk with the last torpedo on board. Proceeded outward in an easterly direction, the two destroyers moved away to the west. Commencing return journey.'[58]

Thus ended a tension-filled encounter between U-53 and the US Navy. The potential mayhem of close proximity between nineteen warships and merchant ships in a confined space made collision a constant threat. A misfired torpedo, a single misinterpreted signal, or the slightest misunderstanding on the part of anyone, any chain of unfortunate coincidences, could have led to an incident between German and American warships. What did occur was an inflamed account in national US media that riled the population and did incalculable damage to Germany's reputation in the United States.

On October 28, following a 42-day journey that covered 7,550 nm, U-53 arrived in Heligoland.

Wilsons non-reaction

The half-day merchant war waged by U-53 caused a brief stockmarket panic[59] as well as renewed anti-German uproar in the American press.

Wilson ignored this. He was in the middle of an election campaign – the next US President would be elected on November 7 – and had no desire for a public debate on this issue.

He also had no desire to injure German-American relations. The request that had come at the end of September from the German government, asking for peace negotiations, had left him hopeful that, following a re-election, he could once again take on an active role.

However, via diplomatic paths he intervened with German Ambassador Bernstorff, who, in a private conversation with Wilson, had to listen, as, 'in very serious words, I was told that the sinking of neutral ships off America's coast could not be made justifiable to the public and that a continuation of German submarine merchant warfare in this area could make the mood in his country 'very bitter.' For this reason, the President emphatically requested that such an operation not be repeated.'[60]

Conclusion

The same High Seas Fleet that for five months now refused to consider anything other than unrestricted Uboat warfare had sent U-53 across the Atlantic to spend twelve hours off the New England coast waging merchant warfare in accordance with prize rules, witnessed by a horrified American public.

To threaten the United States Navy, or demonstrate as a discreet display of power, it would have sufficed if Rose held operations off Canada's Atlantic coast. U-53's presence there might have served as a compelling deterrent.

In the end, the Imperial Navy was blithely unaware of America's mood and spirit and sought only to be openly provocative. Why Rose did not simply dive and withdraw when US warships appeared remains enigmatic, other than that he was over-eager to avoid an impression of 'feeble compliance', and insisted on his 'right' to sink a neutral vessel.[61]

After the war, Rose likened his situation to a 'proconsul in ancient Rome'[62] who was empowered in distant provinces to declare, on his own, war on enemies of the Empire.

Once again, the Imperial Navy brought about a situation in which the actions of an individual submarine commander could precipitate a decision by the United States to abandon peace and join the Allies.

On October 10, the Chancellor's hapless reply to a member of parliament was that 'the leadership of the Reich has still not had any news regarding the activities of Uboats off the American coast, nor have we received a statement in this regard from the government of the United States.'[63]

Only Wilson's restraint prevented conflict with Germany. And that restraint was growing ever weaker.

Chapter 30

Soft Uboat War

The Kaiser, along with Bethmann and Müller, emphatically rejected the demands of the High Seas Fleet for unrestricted Uboat war. Müller wrote on October 3, 'His Majesty confessed to me this evening that he had no intention of launching the [ruthless] U-boat campaign. I fully agreed with him that unrestricted U-boat warfare in the present political situation was absolute suicide.'[1] Again, on the next day, 'By and large His Majesty maintains there are so many aspects in our favor that we should not embark upon unrestricted U-boat warfare.'[2]

In early October, fifty Uboats of the High Seas Fleet were lying idle in port because the Navy refused to conduct a restricted submarine war on the Atlantic coast of England. Instead, a single Uboat was sent to the east coast of the US to spend twelve hours conducting merchant war following prize rules.

U-53's mission must have been the last straw for Kaiser Wilhelm. Finally, he accepted his role as Commander-in-Chief of the Navy and on October 6, 1916 – after prolonged urging from Müller and Bethmann Hollweg – issued an order. 'Uboats should, first and foremost, conduct merchant warfare following prize rules, and this merchant war, with the deployment of as many boats as possible, is to be commenced on October 15 with a great show of force.'[3]

Tactical restrictions were more severe than ever. Any torpedoing of merchant vessels was prohibited. Neutral ships, particularly American, could be sunk only if they transported clearly identifiable contraband.

With the absolute 'torpedo prohibition', any 'special policy' the Imperial Navy may have had in mind, as in the case of passenger liners, was excluded.

The imperial command insisted that 'the security of the crew is particularly to be ensured. A vessel may only be sunk after it has disembarked all aboard. If conditions make it improbable that these persons can reach safety, the sinking should not be carried out. Incidents that might lead to justifiable complaints from neutrals should be avoided at all costs. The commanders are to proceed with great care and diligence. In the event of doubt, the ship is to be allowed to pass.'[4]

All the restrictions bore the clear handwriting of Müller and the Imperial Chancellor. A complaint from the Navy as to why, in the north, they were not at least allowed to torpedo armed merchant ships, like Uboats in the Mediterranean, received the reply that 'Uboats operating in the Mediterranean are permitted to attack armed enemy steamers because, in the Mediterranean, the likelihood that armed vessels will be carrying Americans is extremely low, while this is not the case for America-England transport [in the Atlantic].'[5]

The political concern for Wilson's America could not have been more resolutely formulated.

From the Fleet's perspective, this was a major defeat. The commander of the Flanders Corps, Admiral von Schröder, summed up the prevailing bitterness in the Navy in a letter to Scheer: 'It is with a heavy heart that I have decided to grant provisional permission [for the Flanders Uboats] to conduct Uboat war following cruiser rules. I am well aware that this type of warfare will mean high losses with limited results. Above all, however, it is clear to me that even these limited results may mislead public opinion and may awaken the belief that this path, too, might achieve something important. If I have nevertheless decided to depart at this time from my previous opinion – either unrestricted Uboat war or none at all – the decision was founded on the emergence of new, hard-weighing aspects. The long-held hope that the leadership of our Reich would sooner or later approve a ruthless Uboat war proved to be futile. Attempts to use the boats purely for military reasons have remained ineffective, despite the utmost efforts of the commanders. I cannot, for the duration, permit the boats to lie idle. I believe, however, that it is strongly desirable, if your Excellency agrees that the successes of the current merchant war may not be used by the press to dig the grave, as it were, for unrestricted Uboat war.'[6]

The Navy felt that it was being forced against its better judgment to deploy Uboats, which they held to be useless in military operations in a scaled-down merchant war against the English merchant fleet. On the one hand, the Navy acted as though it did not believe in the success of this warfare. On the other hand, it also feared success because of public opinion. What sort of commitment could be expected from a Navy that held such a conflicted mindset?

On October 9, 1916, the Navy ordered the beginning of submarine merchant warfare in a W/T message to all Uboats at sea: 'War against merchant ships, according to prize regulations, is left to your discretion. American ships are not to be sunk.'[7]

Nineteen High Seas Fleet Uboats left their bases for the first time to enter the merchant war; four Flanders boats and six Mediterranean boats were already at sea. This was the strongest submarine offensive yet against the Allies.

Uboat Warfare in the Atlantic

Merchant warfare in the north quickly proved itself to be, contrary to all earlier claims, both feasible and efficient. The two most successful cruises were the raids carried out by U-49 and U-50.

Both boats were of the same class and had been put into service in the summer of 1916. Submerged, they displaced 940 tons with a cruising range of 9,400 nm. Each carried a crew of 35, and was able to remain submerged to a depth of 50 meters for several hours. They were armed with six torpedoes and an 8.8 cm (3.5 inch) deck gun.

U-49's commander, 33-year old Lieutenant Richard Hartmann, had thirteen years of service in the Imperial Navy and previously participated in two North Sea military operations with his boat.

On October 23, U-49 departed from Emden. Four days later, U-50, under the command of Lieutenant Gerhard Berger, began the same journey.

Following a trip around Scotland and then southwestward, the boats arrived at the end of October within a few days of each other in the Bay of Biscay. They both became caught up in the same North Atlantic gale. The category nine swells meant that for days they were unable to use either their torpedoes or their deck guns.

On October 29, U-49 halted a Danish fishing trawler carrying contraband. A boarding team took over command of the ship, which then was put into service as an auxiliary ship for holding crews from vessels about to be sunk. On November 6, Hartmann released the trawler and its prisoners, and replaced it with the confiscated Norwegian steamer, *Varig*. At night, these auxiliary vessels piloted their own courses and during the day rendezvoused with the submarine at prearranged meeting points.

On November 15 Hartmann, after having sunk fourteen freighters carrying 35,000 GRT, began his return journey without having been able to locate *Varig* in the previous four days. On November 26 he reached his home port of Emden.

What happened to *Varig*? On November 11 she lost contact with U-49, and the following day sighted a group of steamers that had been stopped, along with a German Uboat. It was U-50, under the command of Berger.

U-49's boarding team was taken over by U-50. Berger's captives were taken on board *Varig*, which he then released. Berger adopted Hartmann's idea and, beginning on November 13, took the Norwegian steamer *Older* into service as a prison ship.

The weather deteriorated and during the night of the 16th, U-50 and *Older* lost track of each other. At the next agreed-upon meeting point, south of St. Kilda, *Older* was unable to find U-50. It ran straight into the arms of a British cruiser. *Older's* boarding team was equipped with explosives and revolvers, but these were thrown overboard and surrender was without resistance.

After sinking eight ships with a total of 25,000 GRT, U-50 arrived in Emden on November 23.

Conclusion

Hartmann noted in U-49's command log: 'It was attempted, in keeping with preliminary considerations, to comply with the mission of conducting merchant warfare following prize rules, taking the greatest possible care, and with the aid of an auxiliary vessel to spare the lives of the crews. This method proved itself to be wholly effective.'[8]

During the capture and sinking of the twenty-two freighters, there had not been a single death. The imprisoned crews had been released again after being held for only a few days. The Imperial Navy lost nine prisoners of war aboard the *Older*.

In two instances, resistance from armed merchant ships had been defeated by superior artillery fire from the submarines. Uboat gunners had more experience than reservists on board merchant ships, with their armaments of outdated guns of every caliber. The captain of an armed English steamer noted, 'Shooting at the submarine was very difficult, because it provided too small a target and it was not easy to identify its course. The steamer was armed with a sixteen-pound deck gun (approximately 8 cm/3.15 inch caliber) with 80 rounds of ammunition on board; in addition, there were two Navy Reserve gunners.'[9]

Berger noted, 'With heavy artillery it is possible to quickly defeat the resistance of steamers equipped only with light guns and running at normal speed. The Italian and neutral steamers presented no difficulties at all. The crews proceeded with utmost haste into their life boats.'[10]

Assertions by German admirals that, faced with the armament of Allied merchant ships, the submarine surface war in Atlantic waters could not be conducted without large losses, turned out to a chimera. In the First World War, not a single German Uboat was lost to the guns of an armed merchant vessel.

Room 40 followed the cruises of U-49[11] and U-50[12] on the basis of decoded radio messages, but could not take advantage of this knowledge since there were no Royal Navy units in the enemy's operational area.

The elements proved to be an even stronger factor in the merchant war than were the enemy's defenses. Aboard U-50, Berger wrote: 'The determining factor for overall success is, above all else, the weather.'[13] During four days wind force was at Beaufort scale 10, making any use of weapons impossible. A single Atlantic storm could have a significant impact on the monthly results of the merchant war.

All boats up to U-70 were pre-war designs. They had proven themselves extraordinarily reliable and easy to manage. The 'Uboat weapons system' had been well-engineered even before the war. Had priority been given to Uboats rather than to further development of the battleship fleet, now, in the third year of the war, many times more submarines could have been available.

The assertion of the admirals after the war that there simply were not sufficient experienced naval officers to command more Uboats, is contradicted by the examples of Hartmann and Berger. As novice submarine commanders on their first missions they achieved above average results.

In their war diaries, the men developed ideas for enhancing the effectiveness of the submarine war. A merchant war far away from the coasts of England – such as in the Mediterranean – held greater promise of success, because virtually no organized resistance was to be expected. Hartmann had sighted only few hostile warships on his route from Scotland to the south, and he was able to easily escape them. His greatest successes were achieved in the unprotected Bay of Biscay.

In an effort to increase the number of successful sinkings, Hartmann recommended establishing hunting groups to cover a larger area. 'In keeping with overall results, the following is therefore proposed: in order to conduct more effective Uboat warfare in the future, individual Uboat groups should be established. These should consist of two Uboats and one merchant submarine, which will serve as a floating base station (and should preferably also be armed). The latter will have oil, water, and ammunition stores, as well as spare parts, so that Uboat cruises in the operational areas can be extended by up to four or five weeks. In addition, it will carry the crew for an auxiliary cruiser.'[14]

Using this method, the groups would be able to interfere for months at a time with trade at important, but unprotected, trade cross points, such as the north-western tip of Spain, the Canary Islands or the Azores, or at the outlet of the Mediterranean near Gibraltar.

As crews and officers of Uboats in the Atlantic successfully and imaginatively attempted to lead a submarine war in accordance with prize rules, one that would avoid bloodshed, proposing measures to increase its effectiveness the admirals were busily occupied with domestic and international politics. It seems they did not consider the development of tactical and strategic operational concepts to be their area of responsibility.

Chapter 31

England and the Uboats

Allied Warship with 'Dazzle' camouflage.

Submarine Defense

The use of Uboats as merchant war destroyers represented a new type of weapon, and the development of defenses against them was in its infancy. The Royal Navy resorted to any means, no matter how bizarre, that seemed to hold promise of any success. One of the many measures taken was the so-called 'dazzle' camouflaging of war and merchant ships, intended to disguise their contours, thus making them more difficult to target.

A captured Uboat captain seemed 'genuinely amused at the idea of the efficacy of dazzle painting, and did not consider that it assisted ships to escape submarine attacks.'[1]

Successes

Between the outbreak of war and the end of 1916, twenty-two ocean-going and twenty-seven coastal Uboats were lost.

Although W/T intelligence and decryption provided the British Admiralty with a precise picture of the Uboat situation, this advantage did not pay off on

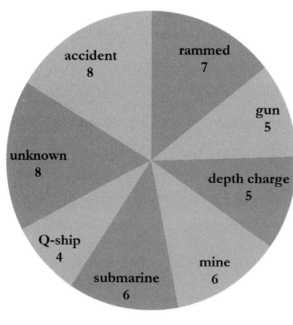

Uboat losses August 1914 – December 1916.[2]

the battlefield. As long as the Uboat hunters patrolled only their own sectors, it often took half a day before they arrived at a Uboat's last known position. By then, their quarry could be 100 nautical miles away, off somewhere within a circle covering 30,000 nm^2 – and perhaps submerged.[3]

Even if a German submarine was found, there were only limited means of destroying it, as seen in Room 40's assessment of the Allied submarine defense in 1916: 'Aeroplane bombs and depth-charges were likewise small and ineffective and, though irritating, did not constitute a very serious danger to a careful commander.'[4]

Hundreds of British warships, along with thousands of armed auxiliary ships, continued daily patrols of their sectors off the British coast, hoping to surprise a Uboat and sink it either with artillery or by ramming.

The arming of merchant ships and the mining of the North Sea also proved to be only minimally effective: 'Though more than half the British merchant ships were armed, their guns were many of them of too small calibre to be effective against the 4.1" weapon which was gradually mounted in all the larger submarines. The poor quality of British mines prevented their having their due effect. Submarine orders issued during January calmly announced that British mines generally do not explode and the German officers regarded them with mingled pity and derision. One commander who found himself caught in mined nets off the Flanders coast, when he had managed to clear himself, deliberately fished up two of the mines, carried them home as trophies and later had them converted into punch-bowls.'[5]

Q-ships

British submarine traps, known as 'Q-ships', were small steamers and sailing ships that carried hidden guns. To Uboat commanders, these small vessels were not worth torpedoing – they would, instead, surface to stop the seemingly harmless freighter, whereupon a well-rehearsed 'panic party' would visibly abandon the ship in lifeboats.

As the Uboat approached the apparently abandoned vessel, within seconds, camouflaged guns were uncovered, the British war flag was hoisted, and the Q-ship would open fire.

By the end of 1916, four Uboats had fallen victim to a Q-ship, some of them under brutal circumstances. In the case of U-27, for instance, once the submarine was sunk its entire surviving crew was murdered by the crew of the *Baralong*.

The Q-ships were not a decisive weapon but, because of their 'perfidy', they received special attention in the German propaganda.

For the Reich's admirals, armed merchant ships and the submarine traps presented the most persuasive arguments against restricted Uboat warfare – submarines operating on the surface were badly exposed to these dangers and the major losses that could be expected to the Uboat fleet would be completely unjustifiable. But experiences in the Mediterranean in 1916 had already proved quite the opposite.

Convoy

The use of convoys as a defense measure had been discussed as early as 1916. Warships accompanied the troop transporters in the Channel and at the end of that year the Royal Navy implemented convoys between England and Scandinavia as well as to the Netherlands.

However, the Royal Navy declared that it was unable to consolidate and protect thousands of ships per day in the waters surrounding the British Isles. Even the long, time-consuming process of gathering ships together in the ports to form an escort would have reduced the transport capacity of the merchant marine by fifteen to twenty per cent.

Moreover, if the Royal Navy were to deploy all of its smaller units – so robbing the battle fleet of its vital escort – this would still not be nearly enough to protect *all* ships, according to the British admiralty.

In a memorandum to the Cabinet on October 14, 1916, former battle fleet Commander-in-Chief and current First Sea Lord of the Admiralty, John Jellicoe, said of the British submarine defense: 'No conclusive answer has as yet been found to this form of warfare; perhaps no conclusive answer ever will be found.'[6]

The Uboat threat was new and the Admiralty attempted to combat it with everything within their grasp: minefields, patrols, airships and aircraft as reconnaissance units, dazzle camouflage, the redirection of merchant vessels away from known Uboat locations, night-time arrivals and departures of freighters, and, most importantly, the arming of merchant vessels. A radically divergent measure, such as the convoy, was rejected out of hand: without testing, or even the willingness to make an attempt, it was simply proclaimed to be impossible.

In the autumn of 1916, the British Navy seemed paralyzed in the face of German Uboats, and no response to the 'Uboat question' was expected. The best-armed fleet in the history of the world could only attempt to disguise its failure to defend Britain against the Uboats as being 'not wholly helpless'.[7]

Hierarchies kill imagination, curiosity, discussion, and the willingness to experiment. The entire Admiralty agreed with Jellicoe's assessment. British admirals – just like their German counterparts – were blinded by their fixation on battleships.

The World Merchant Fleet

The price that Great Britain paid for the twenty-two ocean-going Uboats destroyed was high: the destruction of 1,600 world trade fleet merchant ships, with a cargo capacity of 2.8 million GRT. For each Uboat destroyed, several dozen freighters of 125,000 GRT were sunk.

On the western front, the losses of the opposing armies, whether through offensive attacks or in defense, became more or less comparable. The trench warfare on land was a war of attrition, with hundreds of thousands of dead annually, and both sides losing equally in proverbial 'man to man' exchange.

At sea, however, Uboats could inflict an exponential degree of material damage on the enemy. A Uboat cost two to three million Reichsmark; 125,000 GRT of commercial tonnage was worth approximately ten times that amount, to which could be added the value of destroyed cargo, which amounted to several times the price of the ship.

The merchant war made a direct hit right at the opponent's most vulnerable assets. The contemporary British maritime expert Sir Arthur Salter remarked: 'The combined value of all the world's ocean-going ships prior to the war [8,000] amounted to no more than 300,000,000 GBP [6 billion Reichsmark, equivalent in 2018 to 120 billion USD]; this is less than the capital that would be invested in two English railway companies.'[8] This 6 billion Reichsmark represented the approximate monthly expenditures of all of the participants in the war.

As of October 1916, Allied new construction was no longer able to keep up with the losses, while the German Uboat fleet grew by eight to ten new boats per month. At the end of the year, it would consist of about 100 Uboats.

Decimation of the world merchant fleet seemed unstoppable and, from the British perspective, the prospects for 1917 were catastrophic.

It didn't matter how many millions of men the Allies brought to the field – how many aircraft, warships, machine guns, rifles, or munitions they manufactured – if international trade, the heartbeat of the world economy, came to a halt, the entire organism would be irreparably damaged. Salter stated: 'It would have been one of the most disproportionate things in history if for the want of application of so relatively small an amount of human energy to one part of their economic system the whole economic effort of the Allies had failed and the whole of their military effort been wasted.'[9]

The British Cabinet

In the spring of 1916, Wilson had been coldly rejected by the British on the issue of peace mediations. The Allied summer offensives had incurred huge losses while achieving only minor gains. Germany was still undefeated. And now, the Uboat threat loomed.

Outwardly, the British gave the appearance of confidence in their victory. At the end of September 1916, War Minister and future Prime Minister David Lloyd George stated in a striking interview with the American press that 'England would view any peace move by the United States, the Vatican or any neutral state as pro-German.'[10] And, 'The fight must be to the finish – to a knockout.'[11]

Behind the scenes, however, there was growing doubt about this strategy.

The British Board of Trade reported that in September 1916 foodstuff imports were at 83%, and total imports amounted to only 70% of the prewar level. The shipbuilding industry was no longer able to keep up with losses, the commercial fleet was shrinking. The only solution was to restrict the import of non-essential goods.[12]

In October 1916, Admiral Jellicoe warned the Admiralty of 'a serious danger that our losses in merchant ships, combined with the losses in neutral merchant ships, may by the early summer of 1917, have such a serious effect upon the import of food and other necessaries into the allied countries, as to force us into accepting peace terms which the military position on the Continent would not justify, and which would fall far short of our desires.'[13]

Along with the threat to imports posed by the Uboats, there lurked a still greater danger – bankruptcy. Forty per cent of Great Britain's economic resources were imported from the US. It was still possible to pay for American imports with gold or dollars, but foreign exchange reserves were dwindling, and very soon Great Britain would be dependent upon American loans for funding.

British Treasury Secretary John Maynard Keynes warned: 'A statement from the United States Executive deprecating or disapproving of such loans would render their flotation in sufficient volume a practical impossibility. It is hardly an exaggeration to say that in a few months' time the American executive and the American public will be in a position to dictate this country on matters that affect us more nearly than them.'[14]

At a Cabinet meeting on October 24, the British Chancellor of the Exchequer warned: 'We ought never to be so placed that only a public issue in America within a fortnight stands between us and insolvency. Yet we are quickly drifting in this direction. If things go on as at present, I venture to say with certainty that by next June or earlier, the President of the American Republic will be in a position, if he wishes, to dictate his own terms on us.'[15]

The influential secretary of the British Cabinet's War Committee, Maurice Hankey, summed up the situation on October 31: 'It is highly improbable that the enemy will be completely defeated as the result of a single great effort.'[16] Neither the army nor the blockade would be able to bring about a decisive victory, and the ship losses would weaken England's ability to defend itself.

In a few months' time, the purchases from the US would result in the depletion of the foreign exchange reserves – the Allies would 'become entirely dependent upon the goodwill of the President of the United States of America for their power to continue the war.'[17]

Hankey recommended reducing England and France's war objectives in the west to a minimum: restoration of Belgium and the return of 'at least the French portions'[18] of Alsace-Lorraine to France. Without the British realizing it, their minimal goals coincided precisely with Bethmann Hollweg's conditions for peace in the west.

Time was on Wilson's side when it came to peace negotiations. Germany sought out American aid, while Great Britain's dependence on the USA became ever greater.

At the beginning of December 1916, the new British Prime Minister David Lloyd George was confronted with a dramatic situation, as described by his biographer John Grigg: 'The war was in imminent danger of being lost.'[19]

I Get By with a Little Help from My Friends

Scheer's Uboat strike from May through October, 1916, spared the world's merchant fleet the loss of one-and-a-half million GRT in cargo space.[20]

For six months not a single Uboat operated along Great Britain's western supply routes. Only in response to the imperial command in mid-October did Scheer once again order his Uboats to the Atlantic. And the rapid success of the merchant war that followed prize rules refuted all of his previous arguments against restricted Uboat warfare.

The High Seas Fleet Uboats experienced neither devastating losses – as had been predicted by Scheer – nor were their results any less successful than those of the Mediterranean submarines.

In October 1916 in all theaters of the war an average of twenty of the seventy-five available Uboats were at sea. During the month they sank more than 300,000 GRT. Not a single Uboat was lost. The number of Uboats grew steadily, but the High Seas Fleet restricted their use to 22% of the available Uboat fleet – although, as indicated by the figures from Mediterranean operations, a ratio of at least 33% was standard.

Very soon then, monthly sinkings would exceed the magic number of 600,000 GRT that Holtzendorff had 'calculated' were necessary to defeat England. This, however, would have taken the air out of the last argument held by advocates of unrestricted Uboat warfare and prove that Uboat warfare following prize rules was every bit as successful as any ruthless merchant warfare.

Von Weizsäcker described the mood among the High Seas Fleet: 'Results of the Uboat war are currently at 300,000 to 400,000 tons. I would imagine that a switch to unrestricted Uboat war under these circumstances is unthinkable.'[21]

Riezler added, 'Oh, this Navy! From March to October everyone, from the Commander of the High Seas Fleet to the lowliest Lieutenant, was in an uproar about the absurdity of Uboat cruiser warfare, about conducting "underwater warfare above water." Now it appears that once it was finally ordered by Admiral Müller on October 10th, 4 – 500 000 [*sic*] tons have been sunk.'[22]

And what was Scheer's response to this situation? He recalled Admiral Schroeder's request, 'that the success of the current merchant war not be used to dig the grave as it were of unrestricted Uboat war' and, under the pretext of a 'lack of maintenance personnel on the yards'[23] drastically reduced the deployment of the Uboats.

The percentage of High Seas Fleet Uboats in operation dropped from an already lean 22% in October to 13% in December. Monthly sinking totals fell below 300,000 GRT.

Conclusion

In carrying out the merchant war that they had been ordered to conduct following prize rules, the High Seas Fleet went on a slowdown and, by the end of the year, spared Great Britain another half million in tonnage losses. In total, Scheer's 'strategy' saved the Allies a minimum of two million GRT in 1916.

The right-wing press accused the Kaiser and the Chancellor, through their refusal to authorize ruthless submarine war, of 'sparing England', and defamed them as 'secret allies of Great Britain'.

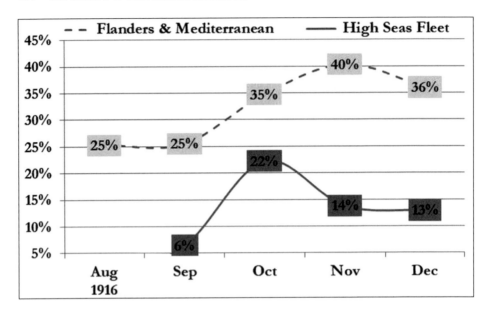

Percentage of Available Ocean-going Uboats Deployed in the Merchant War.[24]

In Britain, the Admiralty was already practicing defeatism, and the Cabinet saw the portent of Britain's downfall written on the wall.

What would the situation in Great Britain at the end of 1916 have been like if it had been forced to begin the new year with an additional two million GRT in losses? What if not a mere 100, but 170 or 250 Uboats had threatened England's trade routes in early 1917?

England's true secret allies were Tirpitz, with his battle fleet armament, and Scheer, with his reductions to Uboat operations.

Chapter 32

Famine, Peace, Uboats

Germany in the Face of the Turnip Winter

Before the war, the German Reich was able to supply its own grains and potatoes, but had to rely on imports for meats and fats as well as for livestock feeds and agricultural fertilizers.

Lack of imports during the war led to a reduction in food supply. In the 'Great Swine Murder' of 1915, one-third of the pig population had to be slaughtered due to a lack of feed leading, in the years that followed, to a reduction in the meat supply. At the same time, harvest yields declined due to a lack of workers, draft animals, and fertilizer.

By looking at agricultural nitrogen applications we can trace the decline in food production.[1] In 1913, 210,000 tons of nitrogen were used as agricultural fertilizer, 125,000 tons of which had been imported.

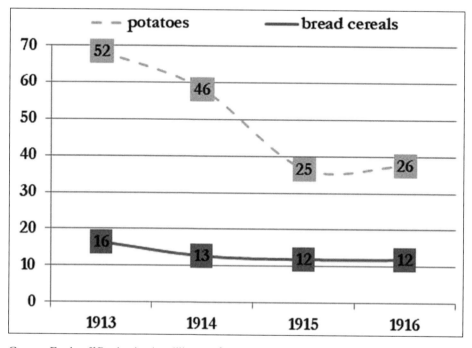

German Foodstuff Production in million tons[2]

In 1915, imports were reduced to zero, and only the new Haber-Bosch method for extracting nitrogen from the air ensured domestic production of 150,000 tons in 1916.

As seen above, the bulk of this nitrogen, however, was used for the production of explosives, and only about 80,000 tons, slightly more than one third of pre-war requirements, were allocated to the agricultural sector.

German food production literally went up in gunpowder smoke.

The Food Crisis

The grain harvest in the summer of 1916 was modest, but the potato harvest in autumn was, for the second time in a row, catastrophic amounting to only half the pre-war harvest. In the last six months of 1916, as a result of the intensified British blockade, indirect food imports from neutral countries came to a standstill.

Loss of imports and decline in self-production meant that the quantity of available food was cut in half. Even if scarce supplies were stretched to their maximum, famine threatened between the end of winter and the next harvest in the summer of 1917.[3] In the autumn of 1916, farmers were ordered to plant fast-growing turnips, which normally were used for animal fodder.

Normal daily nutritional needs before the war had been around 3,500 calories per person. In 1916, food supplies were extensively rationed. Food ration cards for the 'normal consumer' promised 2,432 calories daily but only half of that was actually available.[4]

Behind the Lines – One Woman's War

Ethel Cooper was a 43-year-old unmarried Australian singing and music teacher living in Leipzig when war broke out. She was to spend the entire war there. Intelligent, witty, and sociable she moved in artistic and intellectual circles, and occasionally had access to neutral and Allied newspapers.

Thus, she was able to make sense of many things that remained oblique to the average German citizen. In letters she wrote during the war she described daily life in the city.

In February 1915 bread was rationed and she was allotted two kilograms per week. This 'war bread' was 'a mixture of rye, white flour, and potato flour – it is very good indeed. There is a surplus of potatoes and sugar produced in the country, but the corn supply is limited.'[5] For Ethel, this 'organic bread' was, at first, a treat.

Ethel enjoyed regular financial support from her relatives, in British pounds. '50 British pounds in normal times is worth here M. 1030 [Reichsmark], on the 26th November [1915] it was worth 1184, and on the 26th December, 1266 marks!'[6]

However, price increases for foodstuffs that were still available quickly ate up any gain in currency exchange. A well-informed acquaintance explained to Ethel the reasons: 'He says that for each gold piece, in normal times it is legitimate to issue 3 pieces of paper money, that [Finance Minister] Helfferich began issuing five, and it is now [January, 1916] 20 times the allowed amount.'[7]

The revving up of currency printing presses and the sevenfold increase to currency in circulation during the war steadily led (until the end of 1918) to a 50% monetary devaluation. The way was being paved for hyperinflation which would lead to the collapse of the Reichsmark and the decimation of the middle class after the war.

In April 1916 meat was rationed to 600 grams per week[8] and new 'substitute' foodstuffs appeared on rationing cards: 'There are substitutes for everything – artificial honey, jam, meat, but I confess to avoid them and I really flourish on my 7 lbs. of potatoes and 3 lbs. of bread per week.'[9]

In May 1916 the potato ration was reduced to 2.5 kg per week and sugar reduced to half a kilo per month. Soap became scarce and textiles unaffordable.[10]

In the summer of 1916, the fields were drowning in rainwater: 'The rain pours down almost unceasingly, fruit and vegetables are just four times the price that I have ever known them at this season, and the crops are half under water. It can't be anything but a poor harvest in spite of the Kaiser's twaddle about 'our great Ally in Heaven'!'[11]

The urban bourgeoisie resorted to weekend looting in their districts. Ethel reported, 'We came back from a long tramp in the country, with our pockets and my blouse full of stolen apples and plums! I nearly stole a duck too, I am still regretting her.'[12]

In the autumn of 1916, the situation grew even more desperate. Ethel wrote in September, 'Nothing is coming in from Scandinavia or the Netherlands, and one can give up the daily hunt for milk with a good conscience. We have got an egg-card now, which entitles us [to] one egg a week, but I have not been able to find my one egg yet.'[13]

Tobacco became a scarce commodity – just one more torment for Ethel, a heavy smoker.[14]

Dark Future

In the autumn of 1916 the food supply was just enough to feed a member of the urban middle classes, but it was bland and monotonous. A great amount of energy was spent on the hunt for 'daily bread'.

The rural population was at the source of the food production. Sailors and soldiers were – for better or worse, but at least regularly – supplied by the military, but the workers in the industrial centers lived literally from hand to mouth.

Those who could afford it attempted to supplement their food supplies on the black market. Approximately one-third of the already scarce food supply could be purchased illegally. The more affluent classes were able to meet their needs at exorbitant prices.

Historian Avner Offer wrote, 'Imagine relegating one-third of the food supply to the status of narcoting [*sic*] drugs. Not all the excess price of black-market goods was super-profit: much of it covered the real costs of evading regulations, of concealing, transporting and selling goods in contravention to the law, and of making up for confiscations or fines.'[15]

The educated Wilhelminian classes were reduced to goose thieves and black market fences. The authoritarian state appeared unable or unwilling to organize even the supply of food to the lower classes of society.

Bethmann's Third Peace Feeler

In late October 1916 Bethmann issued a renewed appeal to Wilson. He had the Emperor compose a personal letter to the President which Bernstorff and House ultimately presented to Wilson on October 24, 1916.

The Kaiser referred to Wilson's earlier offer of peace mediation 'Meanwhile, the constellation of war has taken such a form that the German Government foresees the time at which it will be forced to regain the freedom of action that it has reserved itself in the note of May 4th last [the *Sussex* note]. The German government thinks its duty is to communicate this fact to Your Excellency in case you should find that the date of the intended action of the President should be far advanced towards the end of the year.'[16]

This note to the American President was not a threat, it was a warning from Bethmann to Wilson about the internal developments in Germany, which could force the Chancellor to pursue unrestricted Uboat warfare, thus breaching the agreement with the United States. It was a cry for help, an urgent request for Wilson to intervene.

Link commented, 'This, along with the 2 *Arabic* notes and the *Sussex* note, was the most important communication that the Washington government had received from Berlin since the outbreak of the war.'[17]

But Wilson's attention was completely directed to his political survival – his chance for re-election being very shaky. Also, as a harbinger of the debilitating illness that later overtook him, he simply lacked the energy now to deal with foreign policy.

Link wrote: 'But he had obviously been greatly excited by the German memorandum and was beginning to think very seriously about future action should the American people invest him with their sovereignty for another four years.'[18]

The Army Leadership

In October 1916, having taken inventory of the military situation, Ludendorff and Hindenburg came to the conclusion that the fronts would hold, but that a decisive victory on land was impossible.[19] They turned their attention to Uboat warfare. The honeymoon between the new Supreme Command and the political leadership was coming to an end.

Hindenburg's position was reflected in a letter to his daughter on October 23, 1916: 'When it comes to the Uboat war, I can only say this much here: I am wholeheartedly in favor of it, even though the Navy somewhat overestimates its effect but, at the present time, common sense still speaks against it.'[20]

The Kaiser's domestic policy adviser Rudolf Valentini wrote, 'Only a few weeks after they had taken control, [Hindenburg and Ludendorff] completely reversed themselves regarding Bethmann's assessment, in which, until that time, they had demonstrated the utmost confidence. On top of that, from the start they had willingly opened their ears to heavy industry interests and the conservative Pan-German movement.

'They were also united by their hatred of Bethmann, whom they considered the representative of a moderate war policy and domestic reorientation.'[21]

Army leadership was determined to centralize the persistently chaotic decision-making and policy-forming powers of Wilhelminian Germany and put them under a revamped structure.

They had already rejected Bethmann's authority over foreign policy decision-making with regard to Uboat warfare, and on this issue they swung slowly back and forth over the line held by the Navy and the Pan-Germans.

In a subsequent move, Ludendorff turned his attention to the war economy where he listened carefully to the concerns of the heavy industry sector. The army, the political right-wing, and the armament industry joined forces.

The Hindenburg Program

For Hindenburg and Ludendorff, a German offensive on the western front was, in view of Germany's inferiority of resources, illusory.

To attack, one needed to have decisive superiority in machine guns, artillery, and ammunition. Only if Uboats were able to disrupt Allied supply routes and Germany increased its weapons production would it be in a position to seek a decision on the western front in the coming year.

Before the war, German mines produced 190 million tons of coal annually. In 1916 their output was 159 million tons.[22] Steel production fell from 19 million tons (in 1913) to 13.2 million tons. It was the workforce deficit, above all, that led by 1916 to a two-thirds reduction in production of the pre-war level – and it was only with utmost effort that even this level could be sustained.[23]

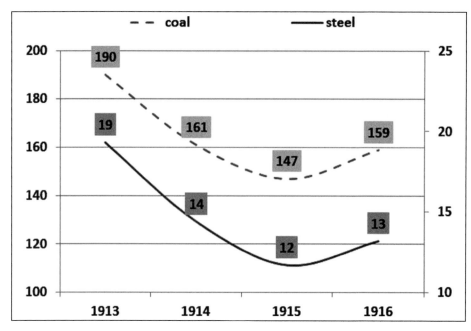

Steel and Coal Production in Germany in million tons.[24]

In September 1916 in the midst of this already extremely tense economic situation, army leadership (to the applause of heavy industry) cooked up plans for a 'Great leap forward', a program designed to increase production. In consultation with Gustav Krupp, Hindenburg and Ludendorff made plans to triple armament output.[25]

Hindenburg's biographer Wolfgang Pytha noted, 'In essence, Hindenburg demanded nothing less than the introduction of a command economy, based on the military model.'[26] Due to the scarcity of resources, an axis of military plus heavy industry, the 'military-industrial complex', was established at the expense of food.

Big industry received government funding to expand production. Krupp alone was given 55 million RM in start-up funding and received another 19 million RM annually. James wrote, 'The company had practically become a department of the German Reich.'[27] In other words, the government became big industry's banker.

The 'Great leap forward' only worsened the chaos that dominated the ailing economy. In Finance Minister Helfferich's judgement, 'The program was ordered by the military without first investigating whether or not it would be feasible.'[28]

Within only a few months it became clear that, simply due to the lack of workforce and raw materials, the Hindenburg program was not going to be able to be implemented.[29]

New Incidents on the Open Sea

The Imperial Navy was not even considering adherence to Bethmann's 'torpedo ban'. On October 24, they had issued a secret order to Uboats via W/T: 'Tank steamers which are undoubtedly armed may be sunk without warning.'[30] And a few days later, they were allowed to torpedo armed enemy steamers.[31]

On November 4, the Navy commenced unrestricted U-boat warfare in the middle of the Channel. 'Ships on a course between England & France may be sunk without warning in the English Channel between Beachy Head & the line St. Albans Head – Cap de la Hague.'[32]

The Navy had surreptitiously loosened battle conditions. The situation was now the same as it had been in the spring of 1916, before the torpedoing of the *Sussex*. It was only a question of time before the change would once again lead to diplomatic incidents with the United States.

Washington

On October 28, the armed British cargo ship *Marina* was sunk by a torpedo without warning. Eighteen sailors lost their lives, including six Americans.

Wilson's Foreign Secretary Lansing viewed this as a violation of Germany's assurances following the *Sussex* affair and urged the President to break off relations. But Wilson rebuffed him: 'I do not believe the American people would wish to go to war no matter how many Americans were lost at sea.'[33]

On November 6, Mediterranean Uboats sank the armed British passenger liner *Arabia*, killing fifty-seven people, including nine Americans.

Wilson intentionally did not react to these incidents. In April 1916, during the *Sussex* crisis, the US President had engaged in a confrontation with Germany, but now he consciously refrained from declaring an American position on the Uboat issue. It had become clear to Wilson that the German Navy and the political leadership in Germany were pursuing two opposing strategies.

He would not do the warmongers the favor of reacting to their provocations with counterclaims that would only serve to weaken Bethmann Hollweg.

The best means for taking the wind out of the sails of German aggression would be a public peace initiative. He had already received more than enough signals from Bethmann to know that the German Foreign Office expected this step.

Colonel House's diary entry of November 14 is apropos: 'The President desires to write a note to the belligerents, demanding that the war cease. His argument is that, unless we do this now, we must inevitably drift into war with Germany upon the submarine issue. He believes Germany has already violated her promise of May 4, and that in order to maintain our position we must break off diplomatic relations.

Before doing this he would like to make a move for peace, hoping there is sufficient peace sentiment in the Allied countries to make them consent.' [34]

House saw the weakness in the US's position: 'The Allies would regard a peace move as an unfriendly act and understand that Wilson was trying to avoid controversy with Germany.'[35]

Why should they do the US President this favor? England needed only to continue to maintain its stance of rejection, allowing the contradictions between the United States and Germany on the issue of the Uboat war to dangerously mount up, to inevitably bring America round to side with the Allies.

If, however, only the German Reich approved the peace initiative, House believed that there was a danger that the United States would 'inevitably drift into a sympathetic alliance with [Germany], and if this came about, England and France might, under provocation, declare war against us.'[36]

The United States thus ferried between Scylla and Charybdis. Sooner or later they would come to blows with one of the two warring parties.

In the short term, all Wilson could do was attempt to avoid conflict with Germany so as not to pull the rug out from under a possible peace initiative from the outset.

For this reason, House urged Lansing to 'soft-pedal' on U-boat activities and not press the President to action on the *Marina* [and *Arabia*] cases. We were unanimous in our belief that it would be stupendous folly to wage war against the Allies. If war must come, we thought it should be on their side and not against them.'[37]

Berlin

Bethmann, meanwhile, was battling on two fronts. He needed to rein in the Navy's use of torpedoes and also show himself receptive to the olive branch that Wilson was proffering.

The honeymoon was over between Bethmann and Ludendorff, as revealed in a diary entry of Riezler in late November 1916: 'The Kaiser has fled to the two soldiers and is floating passively in their water. Ludendorff is a brilliantly energetic man, perhaps a great strategist but politically clueless, completely uneducated, nervous, and abrupt. If he were let loose, Germany would rapidly find itself staring into the abyss. Whether just out of his own passion or perhaps even disloyalty – he incites the Kaiser. Ludendorff is too uneducated and, like all soldiers, has no respect for the difficulties of the politics.'[38]

The Supreme Command succeeded in replacing the standing Secretary of State Gottlieb von Jagow, who had objected to unrestricted Uboat warfare. His successor was the brash Arthur Zimmermann, a faithful devotee of the Supreme Command. Bethmann's ability to manage foreign policy became even further restricted.

On November 20, the High Seas Fleet urged Holtzendorff to intensify Uboat warfare.[39] Ludendorff agreed.[40] The Army increasingly distanced itself from the position held by the Chancellor and maneuvered itself ever more openly behind the demands of the Navy. The Kaiser could no longer be relied upon. Balance of power shifted inexorably to the Supreme Command.

On November 24, Bethmann therefore demanded in vain from Holtzendorff 'that, for the next few weeks, Uboat orders avoid any possibility of new conflict as the boats are only permitted to torpedo warships without warning.'[41]

On November 26, the Chancellor requested from the influential Müller: 'aid in obtaining from the All-Highest an order to confine U-boat warfare to strictly surface attacks against any vessel that cannot be considered a warship. In other words, a considerable alteration of the recent practise against transports and armed merchantmen.'[42]

On the same day, the Chancellor, via Bernstorff, urged the President to act as quickly as possible, since the military's preparations for new offensives were already underway, and thus, 'The carrying out of [military preparations for the spring offensive] would presumably strengthen existing military opposition to the peace move. Please urge these points cautiously and without empressment, as if representing your personal opinion in your talks with House, and keep me continuously informed.'[43]

Bethmann requested that the US President come to his aid against the 'existing military opposition' he faced at home. He urgently needed a peace initiative that would reinforce the Kaiser's position against the military.

A new imperial order to the Navy was also issued on November 26: 'His Majesty the Emperor, on the basis of incidents involving the *Marina* and the *Arabia*, commands that orders for Uboat operations be so altered that, for the foreseeable future, any entanglements with America be avoided at any cost.'[44]

This order is not found among the comprehensive file of German W/T messages to Uboats that were decrypted by Room 40. This likely means it was never sent. Fortunately, Uboat commanders, the majority of whom complied with prize rules, spared the Chancellor from any new conflict. Only a handful of the total of 122 ships that were sunk in the North Sea and the Atlantic during December were torpedoed without warning.

Washington

Wilson's greatest concern was Great Britain's open rejection of a peace initiative. His demarche therefore had to be delayed. Until adequate groundwork was laid, this step would be senseless. A unilateral agreement on the part of Germany would have placed the USA in the untenable position of being in opposition to the Allies.[45]

But should he exert economic pressure on the British Empire?

At this time, faced with the undecided situation in Europe and the ever-growing Allied debt in the USA, a Senate committee investigating American armaments shipments came to the following conclusion: 'The continuation of the war, therefore, appears madness, [and] as long as nobody knows how long this madness will last, there is no saying in what condition Europe will be when the war ceases. The feeling generally appears to be breaking through here at Washington that the end of this war will be a draw; that the sooner it ends the better; and that continuing the war means only a needless and fruitless sacrifice of life and treasure.'[46]

The American financial world feared 'that there was some danger of a creditor becoming so much involved with one debtor that finally, no matter whether the creditor wanted to or not, he would go in deeper and deeper.'[47]

The war in Europe was becoming economic hara-kiri, and the US feared being drawn into this maelstrom.

Allied demand had sparked an economic boom in America and the economy was overheating dangerously. No matter how the war ended, a sudden halt to orders would trigger a crash in America, and the greater the ruin in Europe, the deeper this crash would be.

To lay the groundwork for a 'soft landing' and to prevent an overly intertwined relationship at the end of November 1916, the Federal Reserve Board issued a warning to private financial institutions to take a more conservative approach to granting loans to the Allies. The tightening on credit caused panic in the British government. Their foreign exchange and gold reserves would be exhausted by, at the latest, April 1, 1917.[48]

Wilson was cracking the whip in front of the Allies. From his perspective, the situation at the end of 1916 offered hope of an end to the war. The German Reich, faced with famine, was willing to participate in talks. Great Britain was threatened with bankruptcy. Without American food and weapons imports, the British Empire would fall behind, and Uboats were already gnawing away at the Allied merchant fleet.

It was sooner rather than later that England would have to change course. A little pressure from the Germans by way of Uboats could only help in speeding up this process. Therefore certain minor incidents were better left unmentioned. A German merchant war fought in compliance with prize rules suited Wilson's purposes well.

Chapter 33

Uboat Peace?

The Holtzendorff Plan

In Berlin, Holtzendorff was at work on the Navy's 'peace solution': a Uboat-generated peace.

In two memoranda to the supreme military command on December 8 and 22, he explained his long-thought-out strategy: 'There is no convincing evidence with which to counter the Chancellor's assertion that a soft Uboat war would keep America and the neutrals out of the war. This is perhaps a more secure route to success than a ruthless Uboat war against the entire world.'[1]

Holtzendorff was forced to admit that the Chancellor's strategy – the pursuit of a 'legal' Uboat war in order to attain a negotiated peace – had promise. Restricted Uboat warfare could lead to concessions from England without the war expanding to involve the neutrals.

'It must be emphatically pointed out, however, that only ruthless Uboat warfare will succeed in interfering with England's import of supplies from the neutrals, which constitute 35% of total imports. This, therefore, is the only means to a quick success. Uboat cruiser warfare would indeed increase England's suffering, but it cannot force them within a sufficient period of time to pursue peace, while unrestricted Uboat warfare would assuredly, within no more than five months, bring about England's collapse. This leaves us with February 1 as the date upon which Uboat warfare must be commenced.'[2]

'I therefore conclude that unrestricted Uboat warfare, commenced promptly, will bring about peace before the summer harvest in 1917. That is, before August 1, and that even a potential breach with America must therefore be risked because we are left with no other choice. Despite the risk of a breach with America, the prompt onset of Uboat warfare is the proper approach to ending the war victoriously. It is also the only path to this goal.'[3]

The core element of his strategy was deterrence of the neutrals. This element was not predictable. Rather, it was psychological calculus. Simply, an unquantifiable *hope*. Would all the neutrals immediately and permanently break off trade with England? And what about the remaining two-thirds of supplies provided by Allied shipping? Wouldn't England always be able to import the essential minimum of foodstuffs?

The risk that the USA might enter the war was knowingly accepted. Should Holtzendorff's plan succeed within five months, it would not be a factor. Should the plan fail, then Germany would be at war with the rest of the world.

If military victory was the goal – and the Navy needed this to ensure its very survival – then the only remaining option was ruthless Uboat warfare.

Only warningless sinking of neutral ships in waters around the British Isles would bring about a signal reduction of supplies from the neutrals and bring England's trade economy to a collapse. At least this was Holtzendorff's hope.

Even within the Navy, the plan was controversial. Von Weizsäcker avowed, 'My estimates are conservative. Given the Navy's view on the current situation, I would not consider ruthless Uboat warfare against England alone as hopeless from the outset. It remains, however, a gamble with only moderate chances of success.'[4]

And: 'The decision on whether to take this step will be based, among other things, on a memorandum of the Admiralty staff that states that within five months 39% of English import tonnage will have been destroyed or halted, guaranteeing victory within this time frame. I personally have no faith in this guarantee. What it does not take into account are greater frugality in military shipping operations, stricter cargo control, limitations on the import of luxury items to only the absolute essentials, [and] new construction.'[5]

Holtzendorff was playing Russian roulette. To rescue the Imperial Navy, he was willing to put the very existence of the Wilhelminian Empire on the line. Von Weizsäcker remarked, '[This decision can only be made by someone] who sees our position as desperate and is compelled to play all of his cards at once.'[6]

Consequently, Uboat war was not undertaken on account of anticipated impending starvation that winter (as the admirals would contend after the war). Even defeating England in the summer of 1917 would not prevent a famine in Germany in the spring.

There was widespread longing for peace, but the Navy and political right used Uboat war and its promise of salvation as a Trojan horse in which they concealed their objectives – military victory, Germany's ascension to world power, and the preservation of the interior political status quo.

The propaganda did its job. Riezler remarked, 'For the public everything points to a sure victory within six months, and this should not be abandoned out of hand [in favor of] a dreadful peace conference.'[7]

The right-wingers hadn't even waited for an invitation to join in the Navy's lemming march, and now even the Army was going along with it.

Bethmann's Proposal for a Peace Conference

Back in November, Bethmann Hollweg, with the support of the Kaiser, prepared a 'peace offer', and in early December he discussed this with Ludendorff.

On December 4, 1916, Müller wrote, 'Conversation with Ludendorff on the Uboat war and the forthcoming peace negotiations. Ludendorff hopes to see clearly in a couple of days' time when we can reckon on the fall of Bucharest.'[8] The Rumanian capital fell two days later and the Army regained its freedom to negotiate.

On December 8, Ludendorff and Hindenburg gave approval for the peace proposal to be published on December 12. However, in the event of its rejection by the Allies, they insisted that unrestricted Uboat warfare commence.[9]

It is highly doubtful that Bethmann himself had faith in the success of the very vaguely worded German peace offer. Still, the wait for a reply from the enemy would postpone any decision on the Uboat issue and would pressure Wilson to finally take the initiative himself. Riezler noted on December 9, 1916, 'Preparing for the "big démarche". The peace proposal comes out on Tuesday the 12th. Sitting here working on the draft of a speech. It will be a long time before the word "no" is spoken, and the 'no' will even then be only half-hearted. Hopes and illusions will continue to prevail and will be used over and over again as arguments against Uboat operations.'[10]

The Army had no faith in success and was pursuing quite different objectives. Hindenburg's biographer, Wolfram Pytha, wrote, 'Hindenburg had endorsed the Chancellor's peace initiative primarily on the basis of its tactical appeal and, in fact, showed no genuine interest in initiating American-mediated peace talks.'

For him, Bethmann Hollweg's move primarily served to 'paint the opponent to the world as prolonging the war and to demonstrate to his own people an honest desire for peace.'[11]

The peace offer, first and foremost, was meant to have an internal effect, to show the German people that the enemy was unwilling to negotiate and was sworn to the annihilation the German Reich. In addition it was meant to prepare them for the deprivations that would be brought on by the continuation of the war. Abroad, an Allied rejection would support the German Reich's justification to the neutrals for the implementation of additional military measures, such as unrestricted Uboat warfare.

On December 12 Bethmann Hollweg, seemingly certain of victory, appeared before the Reichstag to announce the German offer to enter into peace negotiations with the enemy, with no preconditions.[12] Riezler noted: 'The Chancellor now very good. The démarche and the speech both made a strong impression. Indeed, every reasonable person was convinced that this is a worthy coup. I also believe that, with this one stone, he is killing many birds, both at home and abroad. Now we must reasonably and judiciously tackle the issue of the Uboats.'[13]

For once, the Navy was also pleased with Bethmann Hollweg as they were counting on the failure of the initiative and the subsequent commencement of unrestricted Uboat warfare. Scheer wrote on December 13, 'If the enemy were now to reject, we will be utterly ruthless.'[14] Holtzendorff noted on December 14: 'The overall situation so clearly meets with our resolutions that now even political obstacles are being toppled.'[15]

The harsh rejection from the Allies came swiftly. On December 17, 1916, Müller wrote, 'The Kaiser has lost his 'Hooray' mood chiefly because foreign statesmen have looked down their noses at our peace feelers.'[16]

Wilson's Peace Proposals

Wilson was caught off-guard by Bethmann's initiative. On December 13 a confidential message relayed via Bernstorff informed him of the Chancellor's intentions: 'The Chancellor wishes me to inform you that the steps he is taking today are intended to meet the wishes of the President, and that he therefore hopes for the President's cooperation.'[17]

Now – six long weeks after his re-election – Wilson took the initiative and on the evening of December 18 sent his proposal to the war leaders: each party should confidentially relate to him the conditions under which they would be prepared to cease combat and to work to restore peace.

Rather than calling for a peace conference, the US President thus steered the warring parties to initially call a halt to combat while he sounded out conditions for a ceasefire.[18]

Great Britain's reception to Wilson's proposal was severe: 'English press reaction on the whole was bitter, in spite of a warning from the Foreign Office that editors had to be discreet and avoid questioning the President's sincerity.'[19]

For Lloyd George, the new Prime Minister, the fact alone that Wilson had formally put the German and Allied war objectives on a par was an insult, as he expressed during a Cabinet meeting.[20] The Prime Minister reacted swiftly. On December 19 in a public speech he presented Great Britain's conditions: restoration of pre-war conditions, reparations, and future 'guarantees' on the part of Germany.[21]

In practical terms, the German Reich was to restore conditions to those that had existed on July 31, 1914, and make reparations for all that had happened since. Lloyd George was, in a way, calling on the German Reich to confess that it alone bore responsibility for the war. Everyone knew that these conditions would not be acceptable to an undefeated Germany. They could only be decided on the battlefield.

Britain administered the largest empire in history, stretching across five continents. She had to take into account not only the interests of her allies, but also those of Canada, India, and Australia.

She supplied weapons to Russia, money to France, and just about everything imaginable to Italy. Each of the Allies had their own territorial war objectives.

Russia had been promised the division of the Ottoman Empire and possession of Constantinople. Italy's territorial claims against Austria-Hungary were extraordinary and stood in no relation to its ineffective conduct of the war. France wanted the return of Alsace-Lorraine and a strategically 'safe' border with Germany at the Rhine, as in Napoleon's days.

All of these sprawling and partially-overlapping war objectives were irreconcilable, one with the other. There were already disputes over the distribution of the German colonies and the partitioning of the Ottoman Empire. Every vote on territorial war objectives posed more of a risk that the Coalition would implode rather than that it would lead to an acceptable result. A decision would have to be brought about by weapons alone.

Wilson's biographer Arthur Link described how stunned Wilson was by Great Britain's rejection, which in no way correlated to its stricken situation. England's war effort depended on American imports for which it would very soon no longer be able to pay.

Its merchant fleet had melted away under the German Uboat offensive. British generals were sending their volunteer army to be slaughtered, and without causing any reversals worthy of mention to Germany. France had been insolvent since October and only British subsidies rendered it capable of mounting an offensive. Despite epic quantities of Allied arms deliveries to Russia the Germans were, step-by-step, forcing the Czar's army back into the interior.

Great Britain's situation in late 1916 seemed better suited to providing material for the final chapter in a new history book à la Gibbon 'The Rise and Fall of the British Empire'.

So, what made England persevere?

Link wrote: 'Was it possible that the Allies proclaimed aims such as could be achieved only on the battlefield in the expectation that their announcement would compel the Germans to launch unrestricted submarine warfare, because this seemed to be the only way to obtain American belligerency? The available records do not answer the question.'[22]

Link finished his richly-sourced Wilson biography in the mid-1970s. It was not until a decade later, nearly three generations after the First World War, that the documents related to the decryption activities of Room 40 were released.

It's the Intelligence, stupid!

Thirty-year-old Nigel de Grey worked since 1915 as a cryptographer for Room 40's 'America Department' and, in 1916, had cracked the communications code between the German Foreign Office in Berlin and the German Embassy in Washington.[23] Room 40 also deciphered American telegrams. De Grey described his work in his memoirs: 'The American-German situation [was] our daily bread.

As I was daily decoding the messages, I knew the position between Wilson, Lansing, Bernstorff and Bethmann Hollweg pretty well.'[24]

An internal history of Room 40 describes the situation in late 1916: 'Germany was faced with an enemy acquainted with all her designs and ready to reveal them, if occasion arose, to the American Government.'[25]

The British government had the same level of knowledge regarding the situation in Germany as did the American President, and was aware of Bethmann's warnings to Wilson about the Navy's insistence on unrestricted Uboat warfare.[26]

In this high-stakes poker game in late 1916, Great Britain had an unparalleled view of the cards held by both America and Germany. Tellingly, Room 40 analyzed that 'The Entente, into whose hands the German military party had played so blindly, held stronger cards than anyone in Germany knew.'[27]

England needed only to quietly hold out and allow Wilson's peace initiative to come to nothing. The military in the German Reich would then turn to their last resort, unrestricted Uboat warfare, thus crossing the line that Wilson had drawn. America would then necessarily have to side with the Allies, and with their help Germany would be crushed in a war of attrition.

An undecided war, with a European post-war order that could only be maintained through American dominance, would be intolerable to the British Empire. Germany had to be wrestled to the ground.

Berlin at the turn of the year

The situation in Germany was utterly different. Riezler commented, 'Yes, if anyone were able to say today how much stronger we are, all told, than the enemy, how badly or how well they are faring, that person could easily answer the insoluble question of destiny: peace or submarines?'[28] And, 'Nine months ago supporters of total Uboat warfare were already saying that time was running out, that it was either Uboats immediately or we would perish. Now we hear that no bad peace is desired, but instead, Uboats and overwhelming victory.'[29]

For the victory-conscious German political right, Wilson's initiative was merely a maneuver to save England from what they believed was certain defeat. According to Arthur Link, 'The Navy, Pan-Germans, and Conservatives angrily rejected Wilson's interference and accused the President of wanting to protect the Allies from defeat and prevent the US from having to enter the war.'[30]

The liberal press cautiously welcomed the move. The social-democratic newspaper *Vorwärts* argued, 'Let us not forget that the chauvinist press of England rages against Wilson, just as the Pan-German papers among us do. The Pan-Germans brand the Wilson proposal as an English maneuver. English jingoism argues that the German attitude toward Wilson is nothing but a feint.'[31]

The Army, meanwhile, came to full agreement with the Navy's arguments. On December 22, 1916, Ludendorff told the Foreign Ministry 'that without ruthless submarine warfare [we] would lose. His impressions from the western front had reinforced his position.'[32] He continued: 'The time to begin Uboat warfare would be at the end of January. Field Marshal [Hindenburg] could no longer bear responsibility for the course of the campaign if the government did not approve this measure.'[33] Hindenburg put pressure on the Kaiser by threatening to resign.

What had swung Ludendorff to this change of opinion? After all, three months earlier he referred to Holtzendorff's call for unrestricted Uboat warfare as a bluff?

Before their appointments, the two commanders always blamed the lack of progress in the west on Falkenhayn's incompetence, but once they themselves had taken command, they were forced to quickly revise their assumption. Even Napoleon would have found it impossible to break through the frozen fronts. Only massive material superiority in guns and ammunition promised the certainty of success in this new, mechanized form of battle.

As a result of the tense economic situation, Ludendorff's hastily improvised 'Hindenburg' armaments program proved to be a crashing failure and that made impossible a German offensive on the western front in 1917. The sole, faint prospect of victory was perceived to be the Uboat arm.

Regardless of whether or not Ludendorff believed that Uboat warfare was decisive for victory, it would at least severely hamper the buildup of Allied armies for new major offensives in the coming year. And America was the least of his worries. How many divisions did the President have? The Navy grandly guaranteed resounding success. If it happened, all the better, and if not then *his* army could not be blamed, and the diplomats would simply have to try to make the best of a bad situation and get things back on track.

Should he position himself with the inflamed public opinion which believed that England could be destroyed virtually on command, bringing the war to a victorious end, or with the ever-hesitating Chancellor?

The feeble Kaiser would not dare to contradict Hindenburg's authority. All bridges to a negotiated peace would be burned, all doubters inside Germany silenced and a combined energetic war led by the Supreme Command would press the backs of the ever-lamenting politicians and Reichstag against the wall. From his perspective at least, Bethmann Hollweg's days were numbered . . .

Müller described the new cordial relations between the Army and the Navy: 'Holtzendorff was delighted with Hindenburg's resolution to start unrestricted U-boat warfare at the end of January if a few divisions are available for the Dutch and Danish frontiers. Hindenburg and Ludendorff are both of the opinion that our military situation – by the end of January – will warrant us risking a declaration of war by America.'[34]

On December 23 Hindenburg sent the Chancellor a letter informing him of the Army's ultimatum for unrestricted Uboat warfare: 'I believe that England called upon Wilson to make his offer in order to stop us. Your Excellency stated that the decision to intensify the Uboat war would be dependent upon a declaration from me. I believe the right moment has arrived. *That moment will be at the end of January* [author's italics].'[35]

Bethmann Hollweg argued against this view and disputed the military's decision-making power on the issue. According to the Constitution, as Chancellor he bore sole responsibility for Uboat warfare.[36]

On December 26, Ludendorff sent a blunt message via Hindenburg in which he insisted that 'military action will be taken in accordance with what I think is correct.'[37]

Riezler: 'Once again, Ludendorff is in a state and sending off wild telegrams – all because he again spent ten days with no supervision. The time of critical issues and greatest divergences between the military and the politicians has only just begun.'[38]

Renewed discussion on the Uboat war between Bethmann and Ludendorff on December 29 brought no agreement. In the war objectives to be communicated to Wilson, an agreement had been reached for a status quo ante in the west, i.e. the restoration of Belgium, minor concessions in the Alsace and, in the east, a free hand when it came to Russia.[39]

Faced with a stalemate between the Chancellor and the Navy, Holtzendorff called Ludendorff on December 30, 1916, for a clear position to be taken for unrestricted Uboat warfare. Namely, 'It will not be possible to win over the Chancellor [to prosecute all-out Uboat warfare]. He views the situation as not at all being the only path still open for ultimate victory over England but as a [certain] path to defeat.

'His tactic has been and remains to delay by holding prolonged negotiations over details. Success can only be expected with certainty if the chief of the General Staff takes up the issue so vehemently that the Kaiser is confronted with a decision of either "Bethmann or Hindenburg" and will by necessity have to vote against the Chancellor.'[40]

As 1916 came to an end, the fronts had hardened. The Navy and Army issued an ultimatum for unrestricted Uboat warfare, Chancellor Bethmann Hollweg was strictly opposed and the Kaiser wavered.

Wilhelm, who perennially avoided conflict and decision-making, would once again be compelled to take on the role he so hated: the role of mediator between the Reich's military and political leadership whose strategic differences over warfare had become irreconcilable. How would he decide?

And Washington?

In December 1916 more and more signs were coming from Berlin in the direction of unrestricted submarine warfare. House became impatient with Wilson: 'Those close to the President were troubled that there was not a more definite and active preparation for the crisis, in both a military and a diplomatic sense. We are on the verge of war, and not a move is being taken in the direction of immediate preparation. I believe the President will pull through without anything happening, but I could not sleep at night if I had this responsibility upon my shoulders. The State Department is worried sick over the President's *laissez-faire* policy. It is practically impossible to get the President to have a general consultation. I see him and then I see Lansing; and the result is, we get nowhere. What is needed is consultation between the three of us, and a definite program worked out and followed as consistently as circumstances will permit.'[41] Also in Washington there was no 'War Cabinet' or any kind of concerted action. Instead Wilson retired and sat down on his little typewriter, creating memorandums going to and fro…

5

1917 – ALL-OUT UBOAT OFFENSIVE AND WAR WITH AMERICA

Chapter 34

January – Final Decisions

Hindenburg and Ludendorff were determined to initiate all-out Uboat warfare and to this end at the beginning of January they 'worked on' the Kaiser by threatening to resign should the Chancellor stand in the way and the decision go against them. The Kaiser was now confronted with the unpleasant alternative of choosing between the Supreme Command and his Chancellor.

Holtzendorff was finally certain he had the support of the Supreme Command and pressed for an Imperial Council meeting and a decisive display of authority from the Kaiser. Müller, on January 6, 1917, recorded, 'Received a copy of a telegram from Holtzendorff to Hindenburg saying that unrestricted Uboat warfare was not making headway and that he must ask His Majesty for a decision.'[1] The conference was scheduled for January 9 in Pless.

Holtzendorff was prepared. In a letter to Ludendorff he pressed his opinion firmly: 'Your Excellency's unconditional approval of the position currently agreed upon will be decisive. I request a brief consultation on Monday the 8th, and will be available from the morning on. The Chancellor will not be able to arrive before Tuesday.'[2]

On January 8, the Navy and the emperor held a preliminary meeting. Müller wrote, 'Audience this evening at 7 o'clock with the Kaiser who has suddenly come round to the idea that unrestricted U-boat warfare is now called for, and is definitely in favor even if the Chancellor is opposed. He voiced the very curious viewpoint that Uboat war was a purely military affair that did not concern the Chancellor in any way. Moreover, there was no question of discussion with him. We (Holtzendorff and I) pointed out to him that it was absolutely essential that the Chancellor remain [in office], even in the event of unrestricted Uboat warfare, for in the eyes of the neutrals it would then appear to be the logical result of the political situation rather than a *desperate coup* [author's italics].'[3]

Meanwhile the Chancellor was on his way to the Imperial headquarters. Riezler noted, 'The Uboat question once again. The Chancellor set off yesterday. Uboat war a fetish for pure military energy. Outrageous, actually, that the [restricted] Uboat war, which is now going so well, has always been rejected and mocked as a non-military imposition.'[4]

Upon his arrival, Bethmann already suspected that the Kaiser would fold under pressure from the Army and Navy. Müller met him in Pless on January 9: 'From a telephone conversation with Bethmann, I felt that the Chancellor was very agitated and depressed. I went early this morning to meet him at the station, to pacify him and put him in the picture on the different decisions that lay before us.'[5]

Imperial counsellor Valentini reported on this critical conference, which was chaired by the Kaiser: 'From six to seven-fifteen in the evening, the Imperial Conference met with the Emperor. We all stood around a big table on which the Kaiser, pale and excited, rested his hand. Holtzendorff spoke first. From the Navy's point of view all was well, and he was confident of victory throughout. England would be stretched on the ground in six months at the most, in any case before an American had set foot on the mainland. The American danger did not frighten him. Hindenburg spoke very briefly, emphasizing only that we expect a shrinkage of American munitions shipments as a result of this measure. Bethmann, as last briefer, outlined in visibly excited temper the reasons which had impelled him to [be] a dissenting voice against the submarine war exceeding the limits of cruiser warfare until now, namely, his concern for all the consequences of America's going over suddenly to the camp of our enemy. Now, however, in view of the recent changed position of the Supreme Army Command and the Admiral's categorical declarations concerning the success of the measures, he had decided to abandon his opposition.'[6]

And Müller: 'The crux of the Chancellor's speech was that, in view of the opinions of the Chiefs of Staff of the Army and the Navy, he could not oppose unrestricted U-boat warfare. His was not so much approval as an acceptance of facts. Then His Majesty replied much in favor of unrestricted Uboat warfare, [and] signed the decree that was laid before him. He remarked in passing that he expected a declaration of war by America.'[7]

That same evening, the Imperial edict went to the Navy: 'I order that unrestricted submarine warfare begin with full vigor on February 1. You are to immediately make all necessary preparations, but in such a way that these plans are not prematurely revealed to the enemy or the neutrals. Basic operational plans are to be submitted to me. A copy of these are to be delivered to the Chancellor. Wilhelm.'[8]

The die had been cast.

The Blues

Following this meeting, Bethmann, Valentini and Müller had dinner together away from the court. Müller: 'The Chancellor made bitter remarks about the Kaiser, who at today's meeting had once again offended him with a gesture that said, 'My God, this man still has reservations.' He feels that over the past twenty years, the Kaiser has ruined the German people from the ground up and raised them to vanity and chauvinism. Only the lower classes of the population remained truly modest.'[9]

Valentini found Bethmann to be in a very depressed mood following his de-facto disempowerment. 'We were both convinced that this measure would result in a declaration of war from America and with it, the endless perpetuation of the war. We both considered Holtzendorff's promise of England's swift defeat to be utopian.'[10]

Why didn't the Chancellor simply resign? According to Valentini, 'The Chancellor emphasized that it was obvious and tempting for him to use this opportunity that his resignation was, in the opinions of many, both among the population and in the Reichstag, desirable. But that for the overall war situation it would doubtless be a mistake, since he would have to divulge to the public the dissonant opinions held by the leading military circles. At such a critical moment, there must be an outward portrayal of unity.'[11]

Riezler wrote, 'Paradoxically he would have been compelled to have gone along, even though he never wanted to believe in it. No way to prevent it once the Kaiser and Hindenburg made a decision. He could have left, but then no one – neither within Germany nor abroad – would have believed in the possibility of success. His departure would have encouraged the Social Democrats and the neutrals to resist and distrust, and the whole thing would have been ruined.'[12]

Riezler's summation was that 'Despite all of the Navy's vows this is a leap of faith. We all have the feeling that this issue hangs over us like a black cloud. If history followed the laws of tragedy, the fateful Uboat question that has embodied all of Germany's tragic miscalculations to date would be its downfall. Whatever happens, the German people will at least be freed in the future from the nightmarish question: how would things have turned out if we had pursued a ruthless Uboat war? Now no one can back out. The Chancellor must put a good face on it. He is the only one who can maintain calm among the population because everyone believes that he would never frivolously or without justifiable hope of success undertake Uboat warfare.'[13] And: 'Since the military has declared that, from now on, any offensive or progress [is impossible], the alternative can only be U-war or peace. May God grant that history not prove that the latter of these was possible and better. The fate of this war is making everything more and more terrible for everyone. If peace with the west is indeed attainable through Wilson, it would be tragic if comprehension of this and agreement to it once again came a week too late.'[14]

Berlin

In the Reich's capital, preparations were underway. Riezler's notes on January 17 include, 'Consultations over the manner in which the U-war is to be conducted against America. It is necessary to awaken the belief that in a relatively short period of time it is certain that England will be crushed, and an enormous amount of tonnage will be destroyed. Perhaps then, America will take a [fresh] look at the issue. If the U-war fails, Germany will end up in ruin, bankruptcy, and revolution. But if the Navy is only half correct, it will be successful. The political right will do anything to make it seem as though the U-war is their own cause and to say that their program is finally being achieved, in spite of the Chancellor. Perhaps they will cautiously try to shield themselves by saying that it may be too late. And Tirpitz, in keeping with his notorious manner, will surely say that it is now too late and that a 1916 U-war would have been better than one in 1917, despite the illegal idiocy of such a statement. The announcement will thus be made on the 27th and, on February 1, it begins.'[15]

The Foreign Ministry was still able to persuade the Navy to avoid sinking passenger liners without warning. In Riezler's estimation, 'The Navy, which placed its hopes on the initial shock, surrendered certain especially harsh and gruesome details that would make it impossible for the Americans not to immediately declare war. *Victory or obliteration*!'[16]

Washington

On January 4, 1917, House and Wilson discussed the steps that would be necessary if Germany declared an unrestricted submarine campaign: 'I took the occasion to express the feeling that we should not be so totally unprepared in the event of war. The President replied, "There will be no war. This country does not intend to become involved in this war. We are the only one of the great nations that is free from war to-day, and it would be a crime against civilization for us to go in."'[17]

But reality spoke another language. On January 19, Bernstorff received an encrypted telegram from the Chancellor. It contained the message that unrestricted Uboat warfare would soon begin and that he was to undertake all preparations in the event diplomatic relations were broken off. This message was read in Room 40 as well. England was forewarned.

The German Ambassador became noticeably more restrained in his dealings with House, leading House to the conclusion that the Germans were preparing for intensified Uboat warfare. On January 20, House urged the President to quickly call for a peace conference: 'If we can pin down Germany to a conference we will have made an enormous gain. Once negotiations begin, they can only lead to peace.'[18]

Wilson reacted. On January 22, 1917, in a speech to the United States Senate that received worldwide attention, he called upon Europe to reach a peace agreement, a 'peace without victory', as the only possible solution for a stable post-war world.

He asked, 'Is the current conflict a battle for a just and secure peace, or simply for a new balance of power? If it is merely a battle for a new balance of power, then who is willing to, who can guarantee the stable equilibrium of the new order? We must not strive for a balance of power, but only a community of powers. No organized rivalry but rather an organized peace.'[19]

The speech was addressed to the liberal and left-wing forces among Europe's warring nations, whom he wished to support in their struggle against the prevailing war chauvinism.

Wilson dictated a personal message for the German government to House and directed him to relay this via Bernstorff to Berlin.

When House met Bernstorff on January 26, he found Bernstorff in an exceptionally pessimistic mood. The German Ambassador indicated that Germany's military had taken over power. But the content of Wilson's message electrified him, as he cabled to Berlin: 'Wilson is confidentially offering to mediate for peace. House shared with me in detail the President's thoughts. Our enemies have apparently called for unacceptable conditions for peace, upon which the President has based his proposal. Wilson hopes that we will be able to stipulate conditions for peace that can, without risk, be presented to the public. If we will only place our trust in him, he is convinced that he will be able to arrange a peace conference. The President was of the opinion that the Entente's note was a bluff and therefore need not be taken into further consideration. He was certain that he could arrange for peace negotiations to be held, so that renewed bloodshed in the coming spring offensives could be avoided.'[20]

Arthur Link concludes: 'This was obviously the most important message passed between Washington and Berlin since the war had broken out. Wilson was extending the right hand of friendship and offering confidential collaboration on an absolutely irresistible move toward peace. It might have led to a peace where there was no victor, and a new chance for humanity. It was now up to the Germans to vote.'[21]

Bernstorff immediately forwarded this proposal to Berlin, urgently requesting that unrestricted submarine war be postponed, as it would otherwise be a slap in the face for the President and mean war with America. In his opinion, 'From another perspective, if we cooperate with Wilson and his plans then are shipwrecked by the intractability of our opponents, it would be very difficult for the President to start a war against us, even if we were then to commence unrestricted Uboat warfare. This means that we would now simply need to briefly delay, so that we can strengthen our diplomatic position.'[22]

At the very last minute, an alternative surfaced: one could postpone the new Uboat offensive for a few weeks and allow on-going restricted Uboat warfare to continue. During this interlude Wilson would propose negotiations. If the Allies rejected this, then unrestricted Uboat warfare could be justified as a means of forcing them into a willingness to negotiate.

Even Wilson would not be able to raise any objections.

The telegram reached Berlin on Sunday, January 28. Bethmann Hollweg forwarded it directly to Imperial headquarters and took the night train to Pless.

A Very Last Chance?

On January 28, 1917, Müller noted: 'The Kaiser told us that a telegram had come in from Washington asking for a few days postponement of the decision. Zimmermann replied by telegram: "Too late." The Kaiser thinks that Wilson only asked for a postponement in the interest of England.'[23]

On the morning of January 29, Bethmann Hollweg arrived at Imperial headquarters, according to Müller 'to discuss news from Washington with His Majesty. It concerns the handing of our peace terms to Wilson. The Kaiser is beside himself because once more he has to make a decision. I was summoned to His Majesty about 12 o'clock. The Chancellor, Zimmermann, Hindenburg, and Ludendorff were already there.'[24]

Wilson's proposal was met by the Kaiser, the Army, and the Navy with a cold shoulder. None of them were willing to sound out the opportunities and chances that were being presented. Holtzendorff cited dishonest statements about the technicalities of the situation – orders to the Uboats had already been issued and it would not be possible to rescind them in time.

This was objectively false. The nine Uboats that were deployed after January 20 received sealed orders that were to be opened only when they received a special W/T message. Until that time, all Uboats – including the five boats that had been deployed before January 9 – were to conduct merchant warfare following prize rules. In the absence of an activation W/T message (actually sent on January 31)[25] Uboats continued to pursue restricted merchant warfare.

Bethmann Hollweg tried to make the best of the situation. Müller wrote that 'instructions in the response which were read aloud by the Kaiser, still called for unrestricted warfare as of February 1, conceded to Wilson to continue his efforts for peace for the time when the Entente's frivolous will to wage war would be broken. At its conclusion, the war objectives were shared with Wilson in complete confidence and for his eyes only. The Chancellor cleverly defended the instructions which, without revealing the Uboat war, were designed to at least prevent the immediate entry of America into the war. Perhaps the effect of a Uboat war would be to completely deter America's desire. Hindenburg agreed. As did the Kaiser, though he didn't fail to enjoy praise-filled statements such as 'The German Kaiser hits back hard.' He demanded that the instructions clearly state that the Kaiser does not agree to Mr. Wilson serving as a peace mediator or to America's participation at the peace conference.'[26]

Bethmann Hollweg sent this message to Bernstorff that same evening. In it he laid out Germany's objectives in the war against England and France, which scarcely differed from the minimum requirements acceptable to Great Britain at the end of 1916: the restoration of Belgium and minor cessions to France in the Alsace.

He also indicated his willingness to participate in a peace conference and concluded with instructions that: 'Your Excellency will present this communication to the President together with the declaration of Uboat warfare.'[27]

It was another show of Wilhelminian Germany's disingenuous diplomacy. While breaking the promise made to Wilson in the wake of the *Sussex* affair, they simultaneously declared their willingness for peace negotiations!

All that Bethmann Hollweg could do was to hide behind Holtzendorff's fictitious statements and describe the unfortunate situation to Wilson as a tragic chain of technical events: 'If only this proposal had arrived a few days earlier we would still have been able to postpone the commencement of Uboat warfare. Inform him that, unfortunately and to our deepest regret, due to technical circumstances, it is too late.'[28]

Attack, Forward, Sink!

On January 31, 1917, with a single W/T message, unrestricted Uboat warfare commenced: 'Beginning on February 1st, Uboats that left base before January 20th are to attack all armed ships, including armed passenger ships, without warning. For Uboats that left base after January 20th, the sealed orders given them remain in effect.'[29]

At that moment there were fourteen High Seas Fleet Uboats in the North Sea and Atlantic who would, on the following day, torpedo without warning all enemy ships within the declared war zone.

The neutrals were given a grace period to leave British ports. Total merchant warfare against neutrals in the war zone was not to begin until February 10, as instructed in a W/T message to the Uboats on February 2. 'Within the war zone that has been announced today, all ships, with the exception of hospital ships, are to be attacked without warning. Restriction: neutral steamers and unarmed passenger ships are to be handled in accordance with prize rules until February 10th.'[30]

Even at the end of January, it would have been easy for the Navy to postpone all-out submarine warfare with a single radio message, or to extend the grace period for the neutrals so as to make time to consider Wilson's proposal. That this was not the case is due simply to a lack of willingness. The Navy would not tolerate any backing down and placed all of its bets on the Uboat offensive.

Riezler had already criticized this attitude in the spring of 1916. 'There are limits to violence. Everything hangs on whether the use of force will pay off in the end. No one wants to consider this. More moderate forms of Uboat warfare, such as excluding the neutrals, are rejected by the Navy always with new excuses.'[31]

Indeed, there were sufficient alternatives. Riezler, for example, had suggested a declaration to initiate unrestricted submarine warfare, 'as a three-month exception to the rules. This would be easier for the neutrals to swallow and once they've swallowed it, they will also swallow every extension of it. If not, then we will need the bridge [to America].'[32]

Müller passed on the idea presented by a German-American businessman who recommended an official statement 'if possible, in a Chancellor's speech, that we would give up our Uboat blockade as soon as the English abandoned theirs. We should at all events have made a very effective gesture to the United States.'[33]

It was not only in the US that the British blockade was condemned as an illegal act of violence; the view was shared even in England's liberal circles. Blockage of food imports to Germany was regarded as inhuman.

A demand from the Germans that the blockade be relaxed or called off would have placed England under international pressure. In terms of war economy it would have been a zero-sum game for Great Britain. Every Reichsmark, every ton of coal the Reich had to use to pay the neutrals in exchange for food imports, was extracted from the German armaments industry. With a little skill, this would even allow the City of London, with its monopoly on insurance and financing of maritime transportation, to turn a profit.

The USA, now the largest foodstuffs exporter in the world, who had defied Britain in 1915 by continuing to deliver American cotton to Germany, could be counted upon for support.

Making such a connection between Uboat warfare and the blockade would have been a skillful strategic move to gain the acceptance of the neutrals.

The Imperial Navy's post-war explanation, that unrestricted Uboat war had been a desperation move in the face of the unbearable British starvation blockade, is therefore just a myth.

But the simplest approach would have been to merely *announce* war against the neutrals, but not to pursue it. Neutral shipping was halted immediately following the *declaration* of the blockade zone, long before any neutral ship had been torpedoed.

But the diplomats' hands were tied by the military who rejected any political alternative. A violent course ensued, leaving the Allies with a choice solely between surrender or asserting themselves. It was an affront to European neutrals and it burned all bridges with America.

The Navy was blindly throwing punches. Did it perhaps find itself under pressure from its own propaganda to attack and prove the 'truth'? Those who live by populism will generally die by it.

The German Reich was left with a choice only between victory or obliteration. A game based rather more than less on 'heads or tails'.

Commencement of Unrestricted Uboat Warfare

On January 31 the Chancellor announced to the Reichstag and the rest of the world that unrestricted submarine warfare had commenced.

Admiral von Capelle downplayed the danger posed by America: 'When it comes to financial and economic factors, I have always emphasized the significance of an

American entry into the war. But from a military perspective, the effect of this would be precisely nothing. I repeat, from a military perspective, America means nothing.'[34] This turned out to be arguably the biggest miscalculation in German history.

Riezler remarked, 'Uboat message delivered today and discussed in the Reichstag. A terrible fate. The Navy is not to be believed but one cannot deny its conviction. The brazenness with which people in their memorandums still want to justify the U-war of 1915 and 1916, the superficial statistics regarding English starvation, based upon principles, which, if they were correct, would mean that we ourselves should have starved for the past two years. And yet, if the navy's promised sinking numbers are correct, all will be well. But if America joins the enemy, peace will certainly not be the better for it. No one thanked the Chancellor for his determination. If things go well, Tirpitz will be seen as the deliverer, and if things go badly the same man whom they accused of sparing the enemy will be cursed because he allowed it. May it go differently and may Uboats lead us to success. A signature has been affixed to a paper and no one knows if it holds our death verdict or notice of a million-dollar inheritance. Wilhelm the Great or Wilhelm the Last?'[35]

Wilson Breaks Off Diplomatic Relations

On the afternoon of January 31, Bernstorff delivered the German declaration of strategic Uboat warfare to Secretary of State Robert Lansing at the State Department in Washington. Lansing was 'as cordial as the circumstances allowed and remarked that as he saw the Ambassador's eyes fill with tears when he left, he felt deep sympathy for him.'[36]

That evening, Wilson and Lansing discussed the situation. The Secretary of State was in favor of an immediate break in diplomatic relations, but Wilson postponed a decision.

According to Link, Wilson 'had no desire for a decisive victory for either the Allies or the Germans. He was still convinced that the most important thing was to be able to quickly negotiate a cease-fire and bring about peace. This attitude may explain his extreme reticence to undertake any action that would put the nation on the path to war with Germany.'[37]

The next morning, news of the announcement of unrestricted submarine warfare appeared in the American press. Colonel House delivered Bethmann Hollweg's second message (that of January 28) to the President. It contained Germany's conditions for peace. House commented on this 'masterpiece' of German diplomacy: 'At the moment that the Berlin Government took the step which meant war with the United States, it asserted its friendship for America and begged the President to continue his efforts for a peace.'[38] Earlier he had remarked: '[The Germans] are slippery customers and it is difficult to pin them down to anything definite. With the English, one knows where one is. They may be stubborn and they may be stupid, but they are reliable.'[39]

House found the President 'sad and depressed, and I did not succeed at any time during the day in lifting him into a better frame of mind. He was deeply disappointed in the sudden and unwarranted action of the German Government. The President said he felt as if the world had suddenly reversed itself; that after going from east to west, it had begun to go from west to east, and that he could not get his balance.'[40] And: 'He had exaggerated the proximity of success in the matter of bringing the belligerents together, and his disappointment was intensified.'[41]

The Germans' heavy-handed manner put him in a hopeless situation: 'The essential and decisive aspect of the German decision was that it left no room for compromise or gradual retreat.'[42] The abruptness of the German approach excluded any chance for diplomacy.

The Cabinet met on the afternoon of February 2. Wilson queried them, 'Should I sever diplomatic relations with Germany?' In the evening he held discussions with key senators. There was consensus that relations should be broken off. Wilson had made threats often enough that were he now to take a passive stance, it could only be viewed as capitulation to the brutal methods of the Germans.

On the afternoon of February 3, the President announced to Congress that he was severing relations. 'I have therefore instructed the Secretary of State to advise the German Ambassador that all diplomatic relations between the United States and the German Reich are to be broken off immediately and that the American Ambassador in Berlin is to be called back without delay.'[43]

A declaration of war, however, as Lansing had proposed, was not an option for him. He left the decision in Germany's hands. He could not believe, he continued, that the Germans would destroy American ships or kill Americans: 'I will only be convinced if there is an open act [of war] on their part.'[44]

In that event, he would request Congress, which held the authority to declare war, to permit him to pursue every possible alternative means.

Wilson said, 'We do not desire hostile conflict with Imperial Germany. We will not believe that it harbors hostile intentions to us until we are forced to believe so. This is a foundation for peace and not for war. God forbid that we be challenged to defend it against willful acts of injustice on the part of the German government.[45]

The US President had drawn a line. Were Germany to sink American ships *without warning*, this would mean war. As long as US freighters were handled according to prize rules, a cold peace could be maintained after relations had broken off.

Seymour: 'Even now, however, Wilson refused to be convinced that the diplomatic rupture meant war. Perhaps he had in mind the arguments that merely by sending Bernstorff home, the United States would so impress Germany that she would see the hopelessness of her cause and the war would end. Colonel House did not agree. He had always believed that a diplomatic break would inevitably lead to war, and he was the more sure of this because the defeat of liberal elements in Berlin signified Germany's unalterable determination to push the submarine blockade to its most effective limits.'[46]

Berlin

On February 4, 1917, Müller wrote: 'This morning, a Reuters telegram came in announcing that diplomatic relations have been broken off between ourselves and America. This evening [the Kaiser] arrived in the drawing room with the words, 'America has broken with us.' Then he handed me the telegram in question, which announced the breaking-off of diplomatic relations. It is all very disturbing. I had to remember that we had all taken this eventuality into account.'[47]

The new German Foreign Secretary, Arthur Zimmermann, in his brusque Pan-German manner, commented to the Reichstag on the severing of diplomatic relations. 'As regretful as the breach with America may be, it at least means that we are finally rid of this man as a peace mediator. I shudder at the type of peace he would have granted us. It would have been a peace that could not be worse if the Entente [powers] themselves had dictated it.'[48]

Chapter 35

February – Prelude

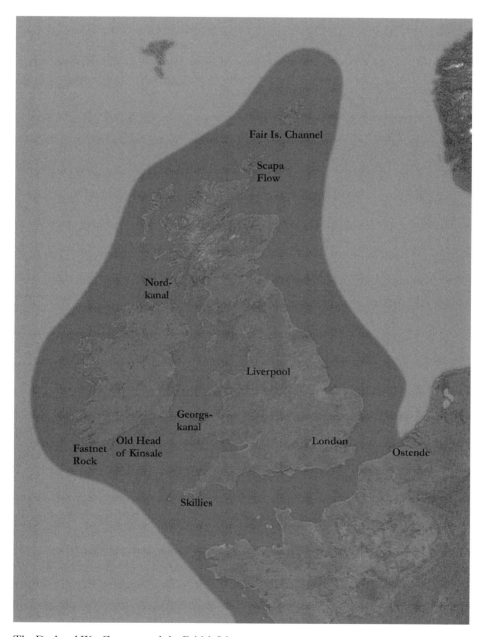

The Declared War Zone around the British Isles.

The Imperial Navy

Distribution of Ocean-going Uboats in February 1917.[1]

In February, on a daily average, 31 of 103 available Uboats, or about 30% of the submarine fleet, were deployed in merchant warfare operations. Fifteen High Seas Fleet units plus eight from Flanders and eight Mediterranean Uboats were at sea daily.

In that month they sank 257 ships comprising 470,000 GRT, half of them without warning. This included sixty-four neutral ships – six without warning – consisting of 125,000 GRT. The proportion of neutral ships sunk was relatively low, since the neutrals had largely halted trade with England in February.

Contrary to all previous announcements of all-out Uboat warfare around England, Germany entered into economic agreements with most of Europe's neutrals, chiefly in diplomatic response to their strong protests.

Room 40 noted, 'Germany's whole policy with regard to neutrals was a mixture of terrorism and sudden weakness, which produced concessions whenever relations threatened to become strained, especially in the case of Sweden and Spain whose good-will she was unwilling finally to forfeit.'[2]

On February 9, 1917, von Weizsäcker remarked, 'Negotiations with Denmark underway.'[3] Denmark provided the German Reich with a loan for purchase of horses and feed, and in return Germany granted permission for Denmark to ship foodstuffs to England.

On February 24 the Navy instructed the Uboats: 'Neutral ships exclusively laden with foodstuffs of Danish origin are to be allowed to pass until further notice from Danish harbors to [Norwegian] Bergen, outside the blockaded area.'[4] From Bergen, the cargo made its way to England.

On February 28, Scheer complained to Holtzendorff: 'The allowances granted the Danish government – and now the Dutch as well – are already creating difficulties by inhibiting the work of the Uboats. I urge Your Excellency to ensure that no further concessions are made.'[5]

Von Weizsäcker's pragmatic comment succinctly summed up the matter. 'This plan of action is not clear to me. If we wish the Uboat war to force England to starve to death, then we cannot make any concessions regarding foodstuffs. If we need concessions for Germany then we should not initiate a Uboat war that brings about a breach with America.'[6]

The deadline for neutrals to leave Great Britain was extended and the German Admiralty Staff promised safe conduct.

On February 22, on its return cruise from the Mediterranean, U-21 under Lieutenant Otto Hersing encountered a group of seven ships traveling together off the Isles of Scilly. Hersing had not received W/T messages for several days.

Initially Hersing attacked with two torpedoes while submerged. These either missed their marks or failed in some other way. U-21 then surfaced to identify the target as a Dutch ship. The crew was permitted to man lifeboats and finally all seven ships were sunk by gunfire or demolition charges places aboard.[7]

Because U-21 had not received radio instructions to spare neutral ships leaving Great Britain the German government admitted the mistake, apologized to the Netherlands, and compensated for the sunken freighters with German ships interned in the Dutch colonies.

The Navy was just as inconsistent in its concentration of forces as it was in its treatment of neutrals. A quarter of available Uboats were operating in the Mediterranean where they conducted general warfare against world trade. These boats were not available in the Atlantic for the direct blockade of England.

With forces stretched thin everywhere, two different strategies were pursued simultaneously: the starvation of England via Atlantic operations, and a common war against the world trade fleet in the Mediterranean.

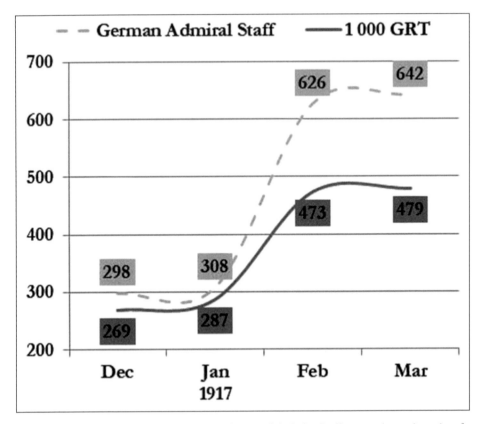

Alternative Facts: Sinkings announced by the German Admiralty Staff contrasting real numbers.[8]

In view of concessions to European neutrals and especially due to the shortage of boats, the Imperial Navy was simply in no position to carry out a systematic 'ruthless' Uboat war that would suddenly curb England's food imports.

In their propaganda the Imperial Navy touted unrestricted Uboat warfare as a sure means of increasing the number of sinkings in order to hasten the war's end. Uboats would destroy a minimum of 600,000 GRT monthly, it was predicted. And this result must now be achieved, if only on paper.

Numbers provided by the German Admiralty Staff on sinkings in 1916 were five to ten per cent higher than those which came from the Admiralty in London. But from February 1917 on, German statistics abruptly rose by a third, ultimately climbing to seventy per cent above British figures.

At the armistice in November 1918 the Imperial Navy had built up a 'surplus' of six million GRT in sinkings in contrast to the twelve million GRT that was confirmed by the British as having been destroyed by mines and Uboats, and which were required to be compensated by the German Reich following the Armistice. Even after the war the Imperial Navy unwaveringly insisted that it had sunk eighteen million GRT, a number that continues to appear even in modern history works.

How did this 'surplus' come about?

Entries in Uboat command logs and W/T transmissions deciphered by the British in which Uboat commanders reported their successes corresponded closely to British figures. These near-correct losses were collected within the Uboat flotillas and then passed on to the Admiralty Staff in Berlin.

Bestowing medals of honor to Uboat commanders, for instance, was determined precisely on this criteria. 'The first award, the House Order of the Hohenzollern, was given when a commander had sunk 75,000 tons, and was followed by the Order 'Pour le Mérite' when his total reached 150,000 tons [High Seas Fleet]. For other flotillas, the figures were, respectively, 100,000 [Flanders] and 250,000 tons [Mediterranean].'[9]

Berlin took the results reported from the flotillas and inflated them with notional sinkings from minefields and other operations. The revamped 'official' sinking numbers were used to justify unrestricted Uboat warfare, thus creating a false sense of confidence in victory among the German population, to which even the government, otherwise skeptical when it came to the Navy, fell victim.

Riezler, duped like the others, noted on February 18, 1917, 'Every day we all tally up the amount of tonnage sunk. Thank heavens, the Navy appears, at least partially, to be able to keep the promises it has made. The nightmarish atmosphere of distrust is slowly beginning to dissipate.'[10]

England - Where have all the Neutrals Gone?

Great Britain had been forewarned by Room 40 and was prepared. On the day unrestricted Uboat warfare was announced, the British War Cabinet ordered all 600 neutral ships docked in Allied ports to be interned.[11] There was a justifiable fear that the neutrals would halt their shipping to England, and Cabinet members wanted to ensure that the ships, with their 500,000 GRT, were held as hostages.[12]

One week after Uboat warfare began, almost no neutral freighters entered British ports.[13] The USA, for example, sent a W/T message at the beginning of February recalling its at-sea trade ships.[14] England began a 'ship-for-ship policy' by allowing only precisely the same number of interned neutral freighters to leave their ports as had entered Great Britain.

Diplomatic pressure and payment of premiums to the crews made it possible to resume trade with Norway, but ships' traffic to England from America, Sweden, Denmark and the Netherlands remained severely restricted.[15]

Lloyd George and the War Cabinet

Since taking office on December 6, 1916, two problems were given highest priority by the new British Prime Minister, 54-year-old David Lloyd George: shipping and food; in other words, maritime transport and food supply.[16]

David Lloyd George.

Biographer John Grigg described the situation thus: 'The war was in imminent danger of being lost. Lloyd George rightly dwelled upon the supreme importance of the maritime threat. The men he appointed, and the measures that he and they together took, can fairly be said to have saved the country. But it was a close run thing.'[17]

The first step was to concentrate war leadership in the 'War Cabinet', a five-member council chaired by the Prime Minister. The three major political parties, Conservatives, Liberals, and Socialists, were represented.

The Cabinet had its own Secretary, the influential Maurice Hankey, who organized and prioritized memoranda and other writings from the ministries, providing them in a form designed to facilitate decision-making, and invited experts to speak to the Cabinet.

On the basis of this almost scientifically-prepared decision-making process, the Cabinet determined measures to be taken, ranging from Uboat warfare to imports, from the position to be taken towards America and the European neutrals, to India's participation in the war, to the issue of a channel tunnel, the use of the Australian wheat harvest, all the way to pacifist activities and strikes in England and how to deal with conscientious objectors.

The scope embraced British fronts against the Turks in Palestine and Mesopotamia that needed to be strengthened, and the need to prevent English generals on the western front from throwing themselves into further suicidal offensives. Also within the Cabinet's brief was reining in the defeatist Admiralty which believed the submarine war to have been lost. Every cog in the Empire's machine, no matter how small, would be inspected.

In addition, Great Britain had to support allied France with money and raw materials, supply Russia with weapons, and provide Italy with essentially everything, all the while remaining vigilant in avoiding any possible conflict with the USA.

During the crisis in early 1917, the War Cabinet met twice daily. A stream of information flowed through the ministries in the motherland as well as to the British dominions in Canada, South Africa, Australia, and New Zealand, all the way to the outmost imperial outposts in Samoa, Hong Kong, or Jamaica. British diplomats in Paris, Rome, and Moscow received new instructions, and if necessary, inter-allied conferences on the most pressing topics were convened in Paris, London, or Rome. Secretary Hankey monitored the implementation of the measures and rigorously followed up.

In effect, the War Cabinet was a kind of a revolutionary Committee of Public Safety (Comité de salut public) of the British Empire, and – with the exception of the guillotine – did not shy away from any measure. If war interests required it, entire industry branches like the national railway were expropriated or, as with the Allied shipping industry, briefly placed under government administration.

Uprisings in the Empire were brutally crushed and all methods short of military force were used to break the resistance of European neutrals to the British blockade.

If we compare this British imperialist central committee – which, in a tireless attempt to square the circle, sought to bridge, resolve, or eliminate national and international problems – to the decision-making and enforcement activities taking place in Wilhelminian Germany, then the German Reich can only be viewed as pure anarchy.

There, semi-autonomous and competing institutions and single-minded interest groups paralyzed each other in their attempts to pursue selfish interests and opposing strategies. All of the responsibility for decisions closed in on the helpless and indolent Kaiser who attempted, as best he could, to avoid or postpone or seek weak compromises that he then could rescind the following day.

Initial Actions

As reported by the British Admiralty, active submarine defense held little promise of success. 'In February 1917, about two-thirds of our destroyer strength and all our submarines, minesweepers, and auxiliaries were engaged in some branch of submarine warfare. In home waters and the Mediterranean, about three thousand destroyers and auxiliary patrol vessels were engaged in combating the submarine menace either directly or indirectly, so that every German submarine was diverting some twenty-seven craft and their crews from other duties by pinning them to patrol areas and forcing them to spend their time in screening, searching and hunting operations which, in nine cases out of ten, gave no result. When an encounter took place, the Uboat captain's chances of escaping were about fourteen to one [in his favor].'[18]

Admiral Jellicoe informed the Cabinet that no existing method could prevent the Germans from continuously having more boats in service than could be destroyed. 'The position is exceedingly grave, and it is a matter for the consideration of those responsible for the import of food, munitions, etc., to this country, and for the supply of necessities to our allies for the prosecution of the war, to determine how long we can continue to carry on the war if the losses to merchant shipping continue at the present rate.'[19]

Faced with the Royal Navy's impotence, the War Cabinet's strategy against Uboats was purely defensive. There could only be an attempt to offset the losses in ships' tonnage by means of purchases and new construction and by limiting imports to an absolute minimum.[20]

The War Cabinet increased import restrictions and drastically reduced the import of paper, timber, luxury goods, and tropical fruits. Timber imports, for example, which had previously been at six million tons per year and accounted for fifteen per cent of all imports, was cut in half. The overall plan was to reduce imports by 500,000 tons per month, that is, by more than ten per cent.[21]

February 3, 1917: *Housatonic*

On the very same day that diplomatic relations were broken off, the first incident involving a Uboat and an American ship at sea took place.

The German freighter *Georgia*, 3,143 GRT, had fled to an American port when war broke out. In 1915 it was purchased by a US shipping company and forthwith sailed under the American flag as the *Housatonic*.

Capture of the *Housatonic* by U-53 (Claus Bergen).

The ship, carrying grain, departed America on January 16, 1917, headed to England. On February 3 at around 10.30 am it was stopped within the blockade zone by two warning shots fired from U-53 (Hans Rose commanding).

Housatonic's captain brought his cargo documents aboard the Uboat whose commander concluded, 'You are carrying foodstuffs to an enemy of my country, and though I am sorry, it is my duty to sink you.'[22]

Rose permitted the *Housatonic*'s crew to board lifeboats and then torpedoed the ship. He towed the lifeboats for two hours in the direction of the English coast until he spotted a British patrol boat. When the English warship failed to react to the appearance of this strange group of travelers, Rose called over to the captain of the *Housatonic*: 'That fellow is asleep, but I will wake him up for you.'[23] He then fired a shot from his deck gun in the direction of the 'watchman' and dove away. *Housatonic*'s crew was rescued and landed safely.

This was the first American merchant ship to be sunk since the beginning of unrestricted Uboat warfare.

The US State Department saw no cause for protest: the sinking had been pre-warned and the crew brought to safety, cruiser warfare rules within the blockade zone were complied with. Further, *Housatonic* had been 'Americanized' after the outbreak of war, so that, according to international maritime law, it was not entitled to the protection of the American flag: only a ship's nationality before the war counted.[24]

An Indecent Proposal?

American 'soft-pedalling' was in line with Wilson's intention to keep the door open for talks with Germany.

In the days before his departure, Count Bernstorff stayed in Washington. Switzerland had taken over diplomatic functions for the German Reich. Through the Swiss Ambassador, Bernstorff launched a proposal to Berlin for negotiations with the United States over the protection of American ships, hoping thereby to create the impression that the initiative came from the USA.[25]

On February 8, 1917, Müller noted, 'This evening, news from Switzerland that America wishes to negotiate on the blockade.'[26]

On February 12, Wilson and House received an ambiguous reply from Zimmermann via the Swiss ambassador. They replied the same day to Berlin. Wilson began by repeating his previously-stated position and demanded that the order for unrestricted submarine warfare be rescinded.

But he softened his position. Link wrote: 'Then, however, followed the startling statement that the United States could not negotiate with Germany "concerning the policy of submarine warfare against neutrals". Was the President saying in fact that the Washington government would not negotiate until Germany reaffirmed its pledges concerning *neutral shipping*?'[27]

Wilson appeared to be signaling that he would accept Germany's ruthless U-boat war against the Allies as long as cruiser warfare rules were followed for neutral ships, which was the reason why he also had not protested the sinking of the American-flagged *Housatonic*. He had also not protested the torpedoing of neutral ships.

Indeed, Wilson's entire attitude gave the impression that the destruction of any European merchant ship, whether Allied or neutral, would not drag America into the war. In the end, Wilson's only concern was that US ships be exempt from ruthless Uboat war.

In breaking off diplomatic relations on February 3, he had warned Germany against sinking American ships without warning. This was the line between cold peace or hot war with the German Reich.

Wilson was still determined to maintain America's neutrality, even at the price of tolerating unrestricted submarine warfare against the Allies and European neutrals. Reassurance from Germany that the American merchant fleet would be treated in accordance with cruiser warfare rules could have defused the German-American situation and reinstituted talks.

Zimmermann made no move in that direction. He did not dignify Wilson's note with a response. Instead, on February 5 he publicly announced that 'unrestricted war against all sea traffic in the announced barred zones is now in full swing and will under no circumstances be restricted.'[28]

As previously noted, the Imperial Navy did indeed scale back its Uboat war against certain European neutrals, but it was not prepared to do so with the United States.

Even in February 1917, a single radio message like the one sent in October before 'American ships are not to be sunk'[29] would have avoided the entry of the USA into the war. This was not a sin of omission, but rather a testimonial to the firm desire to bring on war with America.

February 12, 1917: *Lyman M. Law*

On February 12, 1917, off the coast of Sardinia the *Lyman M. Law*, a four-masted, 1,300 GRT American sailing ship carrying a cargo of timber crate ran straight into the sights of Arnauld de la Perière's deck gun. He allowed the crew to board lifeboats in calm seas and move off in the direction of the Sardinian coast, 25 km away, before setting the ship ablaze.

Once again, there was no protest from the State Department as the sinking had been carried out following prize rules, despite the fact that the classification of timber crate as 'contraband' by the Germans remained disputable. Americans sought to avoid confrontation and did not pursue the case.[30]

Riezler had the same impression. 'So far, the U-war is proceeding better than our opponents thought it would and America is indecisive. In its naive arrogance, it realizes that it cannot, in fact, protect Americans, even in war.'[31] He added on February 18, 'America vacillates. Bernstorff sent a message that the country is peaceful. Wilson will thus prolong the undecided situation.'[32]

Washington

Wilson felt compelled to react to the criticism of pro-Allied US opinion to his passive attitude towards Germany. He finally authorized the American merchant fleet to again sail to Europe. There were two options for protecting these ships: an American warship escort or arming freighters with deck guns.

Had American warships sailed into European waters, this would only have led to unforeseeable military entanglements. Ultimately, at the end of February the President chose the latter option calling it 'armed neutrality'. Deck guns might not be able to prevent warningless torpedoing, but at least his critics would be appeased.[33]

February 25, 1917: *Laconia*

On February 25, 1917, U-50 sank without warning the armed British passenger liner *Laconia*, 18,002 GRT, with 75 passengers and a crew of 217 on board, 160 nautical miles off the south-western coast of Ireland There were twelve casualties, including three Americans. This was a new incident of the same magnitude as the *Lusitania* and the *Sussex*. On February 27, the news reached America.

Wilson was caught up in violent debates over the arming of American ships. To avoid providing impetus to pro-English factions in the USA he made a decision not to discuss the *Laconia* incident.

As his biographer Rodney Carlisle described it, 'The United States would not go to war over the violation of the *Sussex* pledge in the sinking of a British liner. Germany would have to take a direct, overt act against the United States before Wilson would be forced to abandon neutrality.'[34]

In the wake of the *Sussex* incident a year before, Wilson had indirectly threatened Germany with war, but now, faced with the open battle-thirstiness of the Imperial Navy, he retreated. It was no longer an issue of Americans being injured or killed on Allied ships, as had been the case in 1915 and 1916.

Now, the line would only be crossed if there were a German attack on the American flag, specifically, the warningless sinking of a US merchant vessel.[35]

The situation remained unresolved. Carlisle wrote, 'However, as the end of February approached, the United States appeared to be no closer to war than it had been on February 1.'[36]

Chapter 36

March – High Noon

The Uboats

In March, on average, 37 of 110 available German Uboats were at sea, sinking 306 ships comprising 479,000 GRT.

The percentage of tonnage torpedoed without warning rose to two-thirds (39 – 28 – 54 – 67%), although there had been no increase in the sinking results per submarine and sea days. Quite the contrary – the results per boat and day in March were the worst in four months (436 – 447 – 549 – 423 GRT).

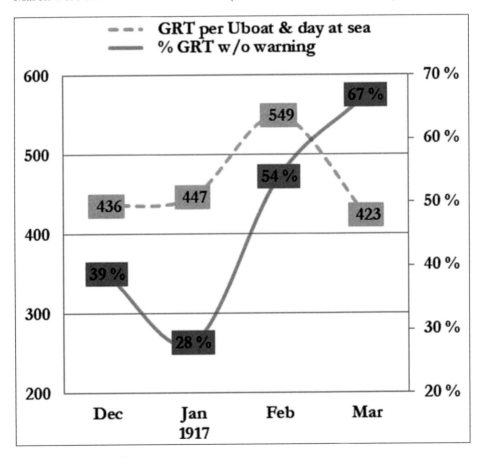

Uboat Sinking Results.[1]

The daily sinking ratio could vary wildly, more dependent upon the weather than the tactical type of sinking – using deck guns in accordance with prize rules or by torpedo without warning. A single North Atlantic storm could protect the overseas freighters from attacks by the Uboats for days, since neither deck guns nor torpedoes could be used in rough waters. Weather conditions alone led to extreme fluctuations in results.

Two windstorms with force ten winds and swells of eight to nine at the beginning and end of the month literally 'swamped' the March results.

The second-most critical factor for achieving a high level of sinking results was the number of Uboats deployed.

In March 1917, the Uboat fleet expanded to 110 boats, while at the same time the percentage of deployed units increased to 33%, i.e. from 31 to 37 Uboats at sea daily. The slowdown on the part of the High Seas Fleet was finally a thing of the past.

Within the Imperial Navy, the results of the Uboat war met with disappointment – they bore no semblance to the promised increase that ruthless torpedoing was meant to ensure. In the face of this apparent failure, some voices called for milder treatment of the neutrals – most notably the USA – while others called for further intensification.

In a diary entry on March 10, 1917, Weizsäcker described discussions among staff officers about the 'question of whether or not it might today be appropriate to deter America by completely abandoning [unrestricted] Uboat warfare. In view of the various parties responsible – including the Supreme Command – I can imagine hardly such a reversal is still possible.'[2]

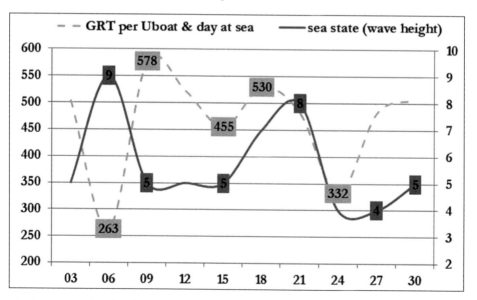

Sinking Rates of the High Seas Fleet Uboats per Day at Sea (3 days average) and Weather Conditions in the Atlantic in March 1917.[3]

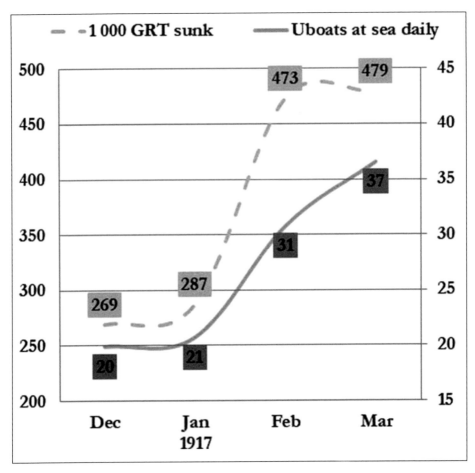

1,000 GRT of Merchant Ships Sunk and Number of Uboats at Sea (daily average).[4]

The admirals pressed for drastic measures against the neutrals. On March 13, Holtzendorff complained to Scheer about certain all-too-compassionate Uboat commanders: 'The commanders [have] in some cases stopped ships in the restricted area with warning shots before sinking, and in other cases, have towed the life boats closer to land or to other vessels, facilitating the rescue of the crews of the sunken ships. As understandable as such an approach may be from a purely humanitarian viewpoint, it is equally detrimental to the intended effect of the Uboat war. For the purposes of the effectiveness of the Uboat war, it is therefore ordered that any measures taken to rescue crews of sinking ships be left to themselves. Should injuries or deaths be inevitable in such an approach, this is outweighed by the fact that an effective deterrent will save far more lives from being lost.'[5]

On March 27, Scheer retaliated with a complaint to Holtzendorff about the numerous exceptions that had been granted for the neutrals: 'I quite agree with

Your Excellency's statement that it is critical for us to deter the neutrals from the resumption of crossings to England. It is thus all the more disconcerting for us to be undermining the effects of Uboat terror ourselves, as is doubtless happening now with the concessions that have been made to the Danes.'[6]

Even within the Navy itself, there was not yet a coherent Uboat strategy, let alone any agreement with the civilian leadership. Faced with irreconcilable incongruities, the admirals passed the buck back and forth, engaging in mutual accusations of blame while practicing the fine art of squaring the circle.

The entire pursuit of the Uboat war was reduced to a single rampage.

March 12, 1917: *Algonquin*

On February 20, 1917, the American ship *Algonquin* departed New York for England. As an inducement for making this perilous journey, a 50% pay bonus had been promised to the ship's officers, with the crew receiving a bonus of 25%.

Because of its contraband cargo, the ship was sunk by U-62 on March 12 within the blockade zone, in accordance with prize rules. The crew was not harmed.

The fact that the ship had been carrying contraband meant that this 'orderly' sinking within the declared blockade zone did not constitute an 'overt act' against the USA.

The American State Department elected not to pursue the case.[7]

The Neutrals

Eighty of the 306 ships destroyed in March 1916 were neutral freighters, of which sixteen were sunk without warning. Neutral tonnage made up approximately 25% of total sinkings.

Over the course of February, the neutrals had largely halted their shipping to England. For instance, after January 31, 1917, only seven American ships sailed out towards England.

The dangers that the neutrals faced from all sides is illustrated by the case of the 4,489 GRT American oil tanker *Healdton*. The vessel left Philadelphia on January 26 heading for the Dutch port of Rotterdam. It had reached the middle of the Atlantic when, on February 1, a W/T message was received, ordering its return to port due to the commencement of Uboat warfare. In early March, the *Healdton* once again started out from the United States, sailing via Norway, i.e. outside the blockade zone, when on March 21 off the Dutch coast it ran into a freshly-laid British minefield. Two explosions ripped the *Healdton* apart, causing the ship to immediately sink and killing twenty-one crew members.[8]

The Zimmermann Telegram

The Germans had made the decision to pursue unrestricted Uboat warfare on January 9, 1917. On January 16, even before the public announcement scheduled for the end of the month could be made, Zimmermann sent the following confidential telegram via the German-friendly Swedish Ministry of Foreign Affairs in Stockholm to the German Embassy in Mexico:

'It is our purpose on the 1st of February to commence the unrestricted U-boat war. The attempt will be made to keep America neutral in spite of it all. In case we should not be successful in this, we propose Mexico an alliance upon the following terms: Joint conduct of war. Joint conclusion of peace. Ample financial support and an agreement on our part that Mexico shall gain back by conquest the territory lost by her at a prior period in Texas, New Mexico, and Arizona. Arrangement as to details is entrusted to your Excellency. Your Excellency will make the above known to the [Mexican] President in strict confidence at the moment that war breaks out with the United States, and you will add the suggestion that Japan be requested to take part at once and that he simultaneously mediate between ourselves and Japan. Please inform the [Mexican] President that the unrestricted use of our U-boats now offers the prospect of forcing England to sue for peace in the course of a few months.'[9]

This telegram was cabled by the German Foreign Ministry in parallel via the American Embassy in Berlin via London – where it attracted the attention of Room 40 – to Bernstorff in Washington. This use of American diplomatic cables by the Germans had been personally approved by Wilson as a means of speeding up message exchanges regarding peace negotiations.

The British Deciphering of the Telegram

Looking back at this message, Nigel de Grey remembered: 'We could at once read enough groups to see that the telegram was important. Together he and I worked solidly all the morning upon it. By about mid-day we had got a skeleton version, sweating with excitement as we went on because neither of us doubted the importance of what we had in our hands.'[10]

Within the course of a single morning, Grey was able to present the decrypted text to his superior, Admiral Sir William Reginald Hall: 'As soon as I felt sufficiently secure in our version, even with all its gaps, I took it down to Admiral ['Blinker'] Hall. I was young and excited and I ran all the way to his room. I burst out breathlessly 'Do you want America in the war, Sir?' 'Yes, why?' said Blinker. 'I've got a telegram that will bring them in if you give it to them.' As may be seen I had all the confidence of my years. Then came the job of convincing a man who knew no German with a half readable text. And Blinker was no sort of a fool. But he was patient with me and was convinced. Then the three of us talked out all the implications and as I was daily decoding the messages I knew the position between Wilson, Lansing, Bernstorff and Bethmann Hollweg pretty well.

I think it must have been the next day that he sent for me. He then discussed with me again the pros and cons. By far the greatest [fear] was that we should 'blow' Room 40 – a crazy risk to run when it is remembered that we read the German Naval codes operationally and always currently, unrestricted submarine warfare to be declared at once and the shipping position already hazardous.'[11]

Admiral Hall decided to meet with the American Ambassador in London and to ask him to bring along a copy of the encrypted telegram that had arrived in Washington. On February 24, 1917, Grey deciphered the telegram before the eyes of the astonished US ambassador.

Washington

On the evening of February 25, Wilson was informed by his Secretary of State about the telegram. Lansing noted: 'The President two or three times during the recital of the foregoing reclaimed 'Good Lord!'. He showed much resentment at the German Government for having imposed upon our kindness in this way and for having made us the innocent agents to advance a conspiracy against this country.'[12]

Wilson was shocked and angry: the Germans had transmitted this treacherous telegram over the cables of the US Embassy in Berlin! His trust in the Germans had been so great that he had never asked them, as was customary in such cases, to submit a decoding key so that the contents of messages could be monitored. He had given them *carte blanche* and had then been deceived in the most ignominious manner! Obviously the German Foreign Ministry could also no longer be considered a trustworthy negotiating partner – it had been usurped by the German military and the Chancellor had been sidelined.

Link wrote: 'The Zimmermann telegramm did not convert Wilson to war. It simply caused him to lose all faith in the German government.'[13]

London

The British could rest content – the scene was now set for a political disaster.

All that remained was to make the news public – but how could the telegram be published without revealing the source? Nigel De Grey: 'The only thing therefore was to steal a copy in Mexico City in the form delivered to the German Legation. How we succeeded in stealing the copy I never knew but money goes a long way in Mexico and steal it we did.'[14]

This last claim is highly dubious. A stolen document would have had no greater authenticity than would a forgery. In reality, Admiral Hall had an entirely different problem. He needed to keep news of the decryption not only from the Germans, but also from the Americans, since Nigel de Grey deciphered *all* messages transmitted between Wilson, Lansing, Bernstorff and Bethmann Hollweg, including the American telegrams.

Since Washington officials had already been alerted to the decryption of the *German* diplomatic cable, the cover-up story of an apparent break-in at the German embassy in Mexico was enough for the public. There was no need to draw further attention to Room 40 – it sufficed to simply *declare* that an original German document had been obtained. Who could say – perhaps the reaction of the Germans to this flap would provide further capital?

Washington

On March 1, 1917, the Zimmermann note was published in every American newspaper.

What impression did it make on the Americans? Rather than communicating conditions for peace, the Germans were inciting Mexico and Japan against the United States and were already redistributing large areas of American territory to the enemies.

EXPLODING IN HIS HANDS.
—Kirby in the New York *World.*

Exploding in his hands.[15]

Link described the reaction of the American public: 'It was as if a gigantic bolt had struck from the blue across the American continent. No other event of the war to this point, not even the sinking of the *Lusitania*, so stunned the American people. They were speechless, a bit incredulous, and generally voiceless.'[16]

It was *the* ruinous final straw for Germany's reputation in the USA.

Berlin

To paraphrase Mark Twain – there are three kinds of lies: simple lies, damned lies, and diplomacy.

Normally, to save face in the wake of such a humiliating revelation, a professional diplomat would deny any participation in the event. Zimmermann would only have had to publicly dispute the authenticity of the telegram and portray it as a heavy-handed British forgery – Admiral Hall would then have been under pressure to provide evidence.

But what he did instead was to begin justifying his actions, thereby personally confirming to the world the authenticity of the telegram.

On March 3, 1917, in a statement to the Reichstag, he declared: 'By way of an unexplained means still unknown to him, the instructions that he had sent on January 16th to the German Ambassador in Mexico had become public knowledge. In America, there were actually no grounds to take exception to these instructions; he had no idea what the reaction there had been. In any case, Mexico should not be underestimated as an Ally. I do not believe this indiscretion will bring about any significant problems.'[17]

Why would the United States *not* see anything amiss in a conspiracy against them? Why was he the Secretary of State if he could not even anticipate the effect of the telegram on America? And why was Mexico suddenly a major player in world politics?

The old Roman advice word for such a situation was *tacuisset* (you should have kept your silence), but the brusque Foreign Affairs Minister palavered Germany's position into the ground. Riezler, on another occasion, had already made snide comments about Zimmermann's notorious inability to hold his tongue: 'In the Reichstag, Zimmermann blabbered everyone to death; he sounds like a chauvinist student and a peasant. *This* is our statesman.'[18]

The assessment of the Room 40 cryptographers, who had already long been following Zimmermann's war activities on the basis of other diplomatic telegrams was: 'His knavery was sufficient to cloak a certain degree of folly, but at each step we are left wondering whether behind his apparent folly some deeper knavery did not lurk.'[19]

If it is true that in politics stupidity is a worse offense than crime, then Zimmermann held first place among the foreign policy figures in Wilhelminian

Germany. However, before he finally and forever disappeared into the sinkhole of history as the perfect example of personal and professional reckless stupidity in the autumn of 1917, there remained sufficient opportunity for him to prove his 'bravado'.

Foreign policy leaders like Zimmermann are rarely islands unto themselves – his uni-dimensional thinking only reflected that of the Army leadership, who were far more concerned about Dutch or Danish infantry divisions than they were about the economic power of the US, or the Imperial Navy admirals, who were taking a mild approach to the Netherlands, Denmark and Spain, but not to America.

These were the actors who made up the Wilhelminian elite who anticipated elevation to world power: militarists from the materially and intellectually decaying lesser nobility, or diplomats and politicians from the – drowning in chauvinism – 'educated bourgeoisie'.

Riezler commented: 'Just too sad. This is the insane attitude of the Prussians. People just cannot see beyond the small military state and its allure.'[20]

Great Britain – Under Pressure

British shipping was now being controlled by the newly-established 'Ministry of Shipping'. It was headed by Joseph Maclay, a shipping magnate who could save the British shipping lines from nationalization only by taking on the post as 'shipping controller'.

Very soon ninety per cent of British shipping was put under the control of this ministry, and management of the ships was placed in the hands of the government. Officially the freighters remained in the possession of their owners, who had to content themselves with extremely modest profits.

In the face of the threat posed by the Uboats, British shipowners were left powerless: they could only grit their teeth and accept that an entire branch of capitalist industry was now state-controlled[21] and being realigned from profit maximization to performance optimization – war socialism trumped ownership. Ultimately, in 1917, all Allied shipping came under the control of the British Ministry of Shipping.

Before the war, the core of the world merchant fleet consisted of about 8,000 large ships of at least 1,600 GRT used to transport cargo across the oceans, while another 14,000 freighters were used in continental coastal shipping to distribute goods locally.[22]

During peacetime, England imported nearly 50 million tons of goods annually, one-third of them on non-British ships. To provide this transport, four thousand 3,000 GRT freighters with a total cargo capacity of 12.5 million GRT were needed; these would, on average, make four trips across the Atlantic per year.[23]

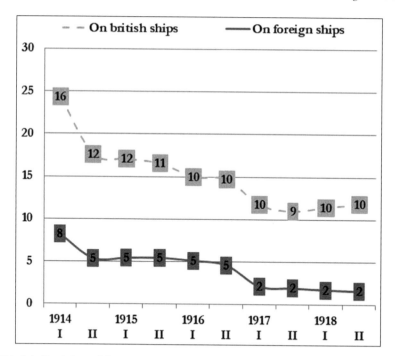

Great Britain's Semi-Annual Imports in millions of tons.[24]

The first decline in world transport capacity had been seen at the beginning of the war with the stoppage of the approximately five-million-GRT German merchant fleet, which had led within days to a 5-10% reduction in transport capacity. England then began to requisition merchant ships for troop and supply transport, new construction was reduced by 50% during the first two years of the war, and on top of this came the losses incurred as a result of submarine attacks. By the beginning of 1917, the transport situation was already strained to its limits.

In 1916, imports had fallen to sixty per cent of pre-war levels. One hundred and forty ships from overseas sailed into British ports every week, bringing with them an annual total of thirty million tons of imports.[25]

After February 1, when Uboat warfare started, apart from losses of British ships, most neutral shipping companies halted trade with England. In February and March only eighty-four ships per week arrived in England, and in the first six months of 1917 British imports would drop to fifty per cent of pre-war levels.

This was partly a consequence of the restrictions that had been ordered on imports, limiting them to essentials – food, raw materials, weapons, and ammunition – and also partly the result of the shrinking amount of available cargo space.

To make more efficient use of the dwindling shipping capacity, only loaded freighters were permitted to sail – to avoid 'in ballast' voyages of empty ships. Imports were rerouted over the shortest possible routes – grain was now shipped across the Atlantic from the USA, rather than from far-distant Australia. This was more expensive and required payment in foreign currency (US dollars), but the grain was able to be acquired more quickly and helped to replenish the rapidly-diminishing food supply.

According to Grigg, these emergency measures 'helped to avert total disaster in the early part of 1917,'[26] but if losses continued at the same high rate, this head-to-head race between fleet reductions and more efficient use of the remaining resources would very quickly become detrimental to the import situation. The world merchant fleet was now shrinking by an alarming one to two per cent per month!

The Admiralty helplessly asked itself: 'Can the Army win the war before the Navy loses it?'[27]

Convoy

Lloyd George knew all of the British Admiralty's arguments against the use of convoys: the ships' captains would not be able to comply with the established navigation rules for escorts; the convoys would merely provide ideal targets for the submarines; and there were not enough armed escort ships to provide *every* steamer with a guard. Even the success of the first convoys between England and Scandinavia, which were in operation since December 1916, could not inject any doubt into their preconceived opinion.

Grigg wrote: 'In January it was still the collective opinion of the Board of Admiralty that convoys would make merchant ships more, rather than less, vulnerable to U-boats, quite apart from other objections.'[28]

The Admiralty fought against yielding their precious destroyers to convoy duties – without them the Grand Fleet would no longer be capable of mounting an offensive against the German High Seas Fleet in the North Sea. British admirals too were thinking in terms of naval battles like in Nelson's time, not in economic wars.

But statistics from the Ministry of Shipping indicated that there were at least enough resources available for the escort of *incoming overseas freighters*. Their protection *alone* was critical for the continued delivery of imports; losses to coastal shipping were of secondary importance and could be offset by inland transport.

By early February, Lloyd George was able to convince the nay-saying Admiralty at least to give 'scientifically-organized convoys'[29] a chance, and in March, for the first time, coal transports from England to France sailed together, escorted by warships.

But still a dozen ships were lost daily and the situation was chaotic. J.S. Salter, then an employee at the Ministry of Shipping, remembered: 'The position in the spring of 1917 was indeed more serious than at any time of the war before or after.

The losses were at their maximum, the new system of defence, the convoy, had not yet demonstrated its efficacy, building in the Allied countries was at its minimum. So grave was the situation that at this moment there were many who thought that it was hopeless and that the Government ought to take the shortage of shipping into account in considering their policy with regard to continuing the war.'[30]

With Our Backs to the Wall Street

If the shipping situation was devastating in the medium term, the financial situation was threatened with immediate disaster.

Until the end of 1916, US war exports to the Allies had accumulated to seven billion dollars (700 billion USD equivalent in 2018), contributing to an unprecedented economic boom in America, with full employment and rising per capita income.[31] The positive US trade balance had increased sevenfold since 1914.[32] This American surplus stood in contrast to a corresponding drop in the British trade balance, where foreign exchange and gold reserves were melting away like snow in the spring sun: England's ability to pay for foreign purchases was threatened.

In March 1917, the British Chancellor of the Exchequer was forced to give the war Cabinet a shocking overview of the financial situation: at the end of the month, only 219 million US dollars in foreign exchange reserves and 114 million pounds from the emergency gold reserve would be available. Purchases from the United States alone devoured 300 million dollars monthly – by early May or June England would be bankrupt.[33] The American ambassador in London was already warning Washington of a 'collapse of world trade and of the whole of European finance.'[34]

Hope on Deliverance

Everything, simply everything, would change for England if America were to enter the war on its side, but Wilson's behavior was still disappointingly passive. Link described the Allied view of the US President: 'The image of [Wilson in] early 1917 was that of a man who was indecisive, [and] eager to avoid trouble with Germany.'[35]

The torpedoing of a single US merchant ship was all that stood between the fall of either the British Empire or the German Reich.

Give Peace a Chance?

In late February 1917, Wilson had begun a confidential exchange of messages with the Austro-Hungarian Foreign Minister, Count Czernin, on the topic of peace negotiations for the Habsburg Empire. Diplomatic relations between the two countries still existed, and the American ambassador to Vienna was Wilson's direct line to the central powers.

After a conversation on March 13 in Vienna with the US Ambassador, Czernin related his version of the conversation to the German Foreign Office: 'On the 13th instant, the American Ambassassador expressed the wish, quite spontaneously, that the next American ships which were en route for England might be 'overlooked' and not torpedoed. This would satisfy President Wilson in the light of the public opinion of the United States; that, as things stood, the United States must determine whether it was to be war or peace. [I have got] the impression, that the American Ambassador, in addressing [me], was following instructions.'[36]

The Foreign Office in Berlin sent this message to Admiral Holtzendorff for evaluation; he drafted a memorandum to be delivered to the Kaiser. Once again, the Admiral denied the possibility of being able to reach the Uboats at sea by radio; it would take at least six weeks to provide new written instructions to all outgoing boats. And further: 'But, moreover, this would mean a possible taking up of negotiations which would make impossible demands on us, both from the military and political standpoints.'[37]

Kaiser Wilhelm agreed with Holtzendorff's rejection of any measures to spare the United States and, on March 18th, returned Holtzendorff's statement, with the following comment, to the Foreign Ministry: 'Now, once and for all, an end to negotiations with America. If Wilson wants war, let him make it, and let him have it.'[38]

The Foreign Ministry allowed this official statement to be published. On March 22, 1917, the *Lokal-Anzeiger*, a Berlin newspaper, printed: 'If Wilson wants war, let him bring it on, and he then can have it too. For our part there remains only to give assurance that we have once and for all put an end to negotiations regarding the submarine war. The colossal guilt for a German-American war, if it comes, would fall wholly and exclusively on President Wilson and his government.'[39]

Ironically, there had never been such an initiative from Wilson: it was Czernin, seeking a peace settlement for Austria-Hungary, who had in his report to Berlin put these words in the mouth of the American ambassador in Vienna!

This incident once again clearly revealed the determination of the Germans, not only to break off relations – in other words, to refuse any discussion of a negotiated peace – but also to go to war with America.

In mid-March 1917, a single W/T message to spare US ships could still have prevented America's entry into the war. By the end of that month however, it was irrevocably too late: the die had already been cast.

Friday, March 16: *Vigilancia*

On February 28, 1917, the 4,115 GRT American merchant vessel *Vigilancia* left New York for France. The departure had been delayed by a three-day strike by the crew – only the inducement of a fifty per cent increase in pay convinced them to resume their responsibilities.

On the clear, cold morning of March 16, 1917, 150 miles south of the Irish coast, the *Vigilancia* steamed its way through force 5 winds and rough swells. The ship flew a large US flag and both the flag and the name of the ship had also been conspicuously painted on each side of the hull.

The commander of U-70, Lieutenant Otto Wünsche, was a cold-blooded Uboat veteran with a bag of fifty ships sunk. He was a man of few words: 'Steamer with two slender smokestacks sighted, course 60 degrees. Bow shot. Hit.'[40]

His torpedo hit the *Vigilancia* mid-ship – the vessel sank within ten minutes. The surviving crew had to climb in the rough seas into the five lifeboats: three capsized and fifteen crew members drowned, including six Americans. Thirty survivors in two boats rowed off in the direction of the Irish coast.

Wünsche remained submerged and did not come to the aid of the crew as they fought for their lives in the freezing Atlantic waters. Only after the lifeboats were off at a distance did he surface. He rescued one remaining survivor clinging to a floating piece of wreckage.

This was the first American ship to be sunk *without warning* by the Germans, and there had been casualties.[41]

Saturday, March 17: *City of Memphis*

On January 23, 1917, the American *City of Memphis*, 5,225 GRT, set off for Europe carrying a load of cotton. On January 30, two days before unrestricted Uboat warfare began, she was stopped by a German Uboat – and released. The ship safely reached its port of destination in France.

She began the return voyage to America on March 16 with no cargo ('in ballast'). On that afternoon, 35 nm south of Ireland, the ship was halted by warning shots fired from UC-66 under the command of Herbert Pustkuchen (who had one year previously attacked the *Sussex*.) He gave the signal to abandon ship, the crew boarded the lifeboats, and only then did UC-66 sink the ship with its deck gun.

The sinking took place following a warning and there were no crew casualties. But prize rules stipulated that empty neutral ships were to be permitted passage through the blockade zone.

As will be remembered, cruiser warfare was not about the ships themselves, but about the cargo and whether or not it was contraband.

Sunday, March 18: *Illinois*

On February 17, the *Illinois*, a 5,225 GRT tanker, had departed Texas for London. Following its safe arrival in England, the ship left London on March 16 'in ballast' heading back to its home port. The next day, in the Channel, it encountered UC-21 from the Flanders flotilla. The Uboat opened fire by its deck gun on the *Illinois*. The crew boarded the lifeboats and reached land a few hours later.

Here too the sinking of a neutral ship in ballast was a clear signal that prize rules no longer applied to US ships.

This was the third blatant violation of international maritime law involving US ships in the space of forty-eight hours.

On Monday, March 19, 1917, the US press published the news of these sinkings. Three American ships had been 'illegally' destroyed in one fell swoop!

Along with rumors that circulated about the still unknown whereabouts of some of the crew members of these ships, the brutal sinking of the *Vigilancia* and the casualties thereby incurred touched a particularly raw nerve with the American public.

American blood had been spilled. Wilson was now *forced* to act.

Chapter 37

April – Mr Wilson Goes to War

House described Wilson's predicament: 'He had continued to hope to the very end that the Germans would yield the single thing that he commanded, oberservance of the rules of cruiser warfare in dealing with American merchantmen.'[1]

On Monday morning, March 19, the President spoke with Lansing and the Secretary of the Navy, initially preserving his neutral stance. That afternoon he spoke with the editor-in-chief of an influential newspaper: '[Wilson] said he couldn't see any alternative, that he had tried every way he knew to avoid war. Is there anything else I can do?'[2]

American entry into the war was still not a viable option for Wilson: 'Germany would be beaten and so badly beaten, that there would be a dictated peace, a victorious peace. It means an attempt to reconstruct a peace-time civilization with

Wilson delivers his War Message to a Special Session of Congress on the Evening of April 2, 1917.

war standards, and at the end of the war there will be no bystanders with sufficient power to influence the terms. There won't be any peace standards left to work with. There will be only war standards.'[3]

Wilson called for a Cabinet meeting to be convened at the White House on the afternoon of March 20. The President explained to the ten Cabinet members that now 'overt acts' had taken place – the very type of open hostilities that he had warned Germany against. He asked them to consider whether or not he should convene Congress, which had the power to declare war, and requested that their decision be submitted to him.

For two hours, one member after another spoke. Lansing, who had long believed that American entry into the war was inevitable, was surprised to find that all of his colleagues who had previously held out for neutrality were now calling for war. 'When at last every Cabinet officer had spoken and all had expressed the opinion that war was inevitable and that Congress ought to be called in extraordinary session as soon as possible, the President said in his cool, unemotional way: 'Well, gentlemen, I think that there is no doubt as to what your advice is. I thank you.'[4]

The following day he called on Congress to convene on April 2. Wilson's decision had been made – war.

Doeneke wrote: 'Even when Germany declared unrestricted submarine warfare in January 1917, Wilson exercised caution. He severed diplomatic relations but would have accepted a limited form of submarine warfare if American ships had remained relatively immune. He decided for war only after US ships were sunk.'[5]

And Link assessed: 'He chose war over a risky and ambigious armed neutrality in part, certainly, because he had lost all confidence in the Imperial German Government on account of its assault upon American shipping and the Zimmermann telegram. He was not indiscriminate in his indictment, but events had convinced him that militarists and extreme nationalists were now in the saddle in Berlin, and that he simply could not do business with them or hope for any lasting peace so long as they were in control of Germany.'[6]

The American Declaration of War

The US Congress (i.e. the joint assembly of the House of Representatives and the Senate) convened on April 2, 1917. Wilson delivered his message at around 8.30 pm that evening.

He did not mention the attacks on the *Lusitania* and the *Sussex* or the Zimmermann telegram, but restricted himself to the most recent incidents, the sinking of American freighters without warning: 'With a profound sense of the solemn and even tragical character of the step I am taking, and of the grave responsibilities which it involves, I advise that the congress declare the recent course of the Imperial German Government to be in fact nothing less than war against the government and the people of the United States.'[7]

The President then cast America's inevitable entry into the war as a type of crusade: 'We are glad to fight thus for the ultimate peace of the world and for the liberation of its peoples, the German peoples included: for the rights of nations great and small and the privilege of men everywhere to choose their way of life and of obedience. The world must be made safe for democracy.'[8]

And in an appeal to American values: 'It is a fearful thing to lead this great peaceful people into war, into the most terrible and disastrous of all wars, civilization itself seeming to be in the balance. But the right is more precious than peace. The day has come when America is privileged to spend her blood and her might for principles that gave her birth and happiness and the peace she has treasured. God helping her, she can do no other.'[9]

The Decision

Debates dragged on for several days. In the middle of them, news broke that two more American ships had been torpedoed, with another twelve casualties.[10]

On April 4, the House finally voted 82 to 6 for war. The Senate followed suit on April 6, with a vote of 373 to 50. It was the only declaration during the war that was not decided upon by Cabinets, ministers or monarchs, but rather by representatives of the people – in an overwhelming majority.

American historian Rodney Carlisle summarized the situation at the beginning of April 1917: 'The war began for the United States because the public, Congress, and the president concluded that the rights of Americans to use the seas of the world had been sorely infringed by Germany. German espionage, sabotage, the leaked Zimmerman telegram offering a German-Mexican alliance, all contributed to the anger at Germany, but none of these developments had been acts of war. The sinking of the *Vigilancia* and two other merchant ships on the same weekend stood out as a clear an undeniable casus belli.'[11]

The Great War between the European empires had now become a World War.

England

On April 1, Lloyd George had already impatiently queried: 'I wonder if America will come in this week? It would be the best piece of luck we have had for some time.'[12]

But even after the American declaration of war on Germany, the British Empire was still far from being out of danger; every day was still a life and death battle.

J.A. Salter described the situation during the first half of April as the German Uboat war reached its terrible apex: 'In a single fortnight in April, 122 ocean-going vessels were lost. The rate of British loss in ocean-going tonnage during this fortnight was equivalent to an average round-voyage loss of 25 percent – one out of every four ships leaving the United Kingdom for an overseas voyage was lost before its return. The continuance [at] this rate would have brought disaster upon all Allied campaigns, and might well have involved an unconditional surrender.'[13]

Only the hope of the timely arrival of massive US aid gave England the strength to carry on the fight.

Facing a drastically shrinking merchant fleet and the collapse of its allies, how could the British Empire have survived the early months of 1917 on its own, without the aid of the United States, without the loans that made food and weapons purchases possible?

From the distance of almost a century, US historian Justus Doeneke wrote: 'Ironically, Germany was introducing submarines to sever the Allied lifeline when the sorry shape of British and French finances was poised to accomplish the same result. A breakdown of the Anglo-American exchange system would have practically terminated American war exports. To plunge into unrestricted warfare at this point was snatching defeat from the jaws of history.'[14]

Without the Imperial Navy's ruthless Uboat war and its triggering of the American entry into the war, Great Britain would have been forced to request an armistice in 1917.

Germany

Admiral Müller noted on April 6, 1917: 'News from America that Wilson has carried his proclamation of a state of war through the Congress. So we are actually at war with the United States. No one can say where this will lead, but we hope that the U-boat campaign will bring about the end of the war in Europe before America can take a serious hand.'[15]

Ludendorff was unimpressed. In light of the invented Uboat successes being reported by the Navy, along with Russia's current faltering, he was convinced that within two or three months England would have to be begging for peace. A negotiated peace – which, to his way of thinking, would be a 'peace of abdication' – was out of the question for him: 'The German people do not want peace to be attained by abdication and I do not want to end up being stoned by them.'[16]

The ill-fated Zimmermann proclaimed to the Reichstag on April 28, 1917: 'Since America has not officially communicated this declaration [of war], according to the provisions of the Hague Land Warfare Convention, it may be regarded as an American domestic affair. We do not expect any active intervention of troops and ships that would benefit the Entente.'[17]

His contemporary, Riezler, summarized this insane combination of unwillingness to face reality, stubbornness, and illusion in his diary: 'If there should ever be a history of this Uboat war, the ultimate lie, it must reveal the lack of education, the military stupidity, and the rottenness of the entire chauvinist ruling class. We are on the verge of internal catastrophe – I simply do not believe that with people like the Kaiser, Hindenburg, or Ludendorff (and Zimmermann) things can end well for us.'[18]

Chapter 38

The Epochal Year

The Great War was *the* dividing line between the 'long' nineteenth century, from 1815 to 1914 (Hobsbawm), which had been the (relatively) most peaceful European epoch in over a millennium, and the 'short' twentieth century, between 1917 and 1989, with its revolutions, civil wars, mass murders, and international wars, both cold and hot.

How did it come to this?

German Submarine Warfare

Although the Imperial Navy had propagated Uboat war at the end of 1914 and had pursued it in early 1915 with completely inadequate resources, it failed to give priority to Uboat construction, laying keel on new battle fleets for a distant imperial future instead. In 1916 the High Seas Fleet had refused and/or delayed the use of their Uboats, thereby providing Great Britain a reprieve. The Navy's insistence on ruthless Uboat warfare was meant to 'torpedo' any possibility of a negotiated peace that would have proven fatal to its own existence.

The Chancellor did not tire of denouncing the speculative character of this 'heads or tails' strategy that would decide the fate of the Reich. No matter how reasonable or how well-founded all of his arguments against unrestricted Uboat warfare were – the deafening roar of Pan-German chauvinistic propaganda drowned out all else. For neither the first nor the last time in history, volume trumped reason.

In early 1917, the Imperial Navy began a Uboat offensive aimed at *forcing* war with America. The staff working in Room 40 at that time wrote: 'Had the warfare from the beginning been conducted as a whole with a reasonable regard for principles of humanity and chivalrous behaviour at sea [*à la* Arnauld de la Perière], the civilised world would have been much more likely to condone the irregularity of the methods employed and might have accepted, though under protest, Germany's plea of necessity, very much as it accepted certain highhanded methods of blockade and general interference in neutral rights practised by Great Britain. As it was, her disregard of all laws governing war at sea was as great a blunder as a crime.'[1]

Had the Navy not pursued its 'visionary' armaments strategy over the course of many years, there could have been many more submarines available at the beginning of 1917. Even with an American declaration of war in 1917, this would have forced the English to capitulate and brought the war to an end.

More Uboats *and/or* Uboat warfare following prize rules – *either one of these two options* could have forced the Allies to the negotiating table in 1917.

However, simultaneously making both 'mistakes' – building too few Uboats *and* not deploying them following prize rules – intensified the effect of these errors, ultimately leading to Germany's collapse in 1918.

Was it truly a 'mistake' or was there a hidden agenda at work? If one had wanted, *at any cost*, to strategically build up a battle fleet that would rival that of the Royal Navy, with the aim of taking control of world politics, then war had to be used – indeed, it practically had to be craved and set into motion – to finally make a 'giant leap' forward, unfettered by Parliament, who held control of the budget. This meant that during this short window of time, Uboat construction *would have to be* neglected for the benefit of the surface fleet and to prevent, *using all available means*, an undecided end to the war, as this would have also brought all dreams of world domination to an end.

In 1917, in response to sharp criticism from some parliamentarians regarding the Uboat war, Admiral von Capelle remarked to the Reichstag: 'We were practically accused by you – let's just say it – of committing treason against the German Reich.'[2]

Since Capelle himself first brought up the word: the interference with or hindrance of the deployment of armed forces does indeed constitute military treason. Whether or not this term is applicable to Scheer's Uboat strike, to Tirpitz's armament policy, or to Holtzendorff's attack strategy is left to the reader's judgment.

The Economic Blockades

Following the outbreak of war, England's control over ocean waters allowed them to implement a long-planned economic blockade of Germany. With its Uboats, the Imperial Navy attempted to mount a counter-blockade of England.

Salter wrote: 'If an adequate history of the war is ever written it will probably give as much space to the economic as to the purely military struggle. It was as much a war of competing blockades, the surface and the submarine, as of competing armies. Behind these two blockades the economic systems of the two opposing groups of countries were engaged in a deadly struggle for existence, and at several periods of the war the pressure of starvation seemed likely to achieve an issue beyond the settlement of either the entrenched armies or the immobilized navies.'[3]

The British blockade had a far more detrimental effect on Germany's economy than the Uboat blockade ever managed to have on that of Great Britain. In late 1916, England found itself in the same situation that the German Reich had itself suffered two years earlier: dwindling importation and the threat of reductions to the food supply.

No food rationing had yet been instituted in Great Britain and industrial production there could still be sustained. England was still further removed from a 'surrender' – approximately those eighteen months that Weizsäcker had calculated – than was the German Reich, whose Kaiser, even in the face of looming starvation, gave not the remotest thought to laying down his arms.

Neither the British blockade nor the German Uboat war would be able to force the opponent to set down their weapons and put themselves at the mercy of their enemy's whims. These measures could only serve to break the enemy's determination to continue the war *at any cost* until victory could be assured.

The goal of economic blockades is not to achieve the unconditional surrender of the enemy, but rather to coerce a willingness to negotiate. However, when enacted upon irrational opponents – fanatics fighting for their own survival, whether religious groups, political parties, or societal classes, the influence of whom is permitted to trickle down to the dominated classes with no fear of rebellion – they cannot be effective.

In actuality, it was on the high seas that the war was strategically decided. The British blockade succeeded in restricting Germany's import of raw materials, to paralyze its industry, while Great Britain, with great effort, managed to sustain its overseas imports and, after 1917, profited from unrestricted American economic aid. It was a war of economic numbers – finances, manufacturing, and control over the Atlantic supply routes decided the war.

The manner in which the British surmounted the challenges posed by the German Uboat blockade is, in any event, a prime example of highly-efficient management. Though Lloyd George's War Cabinet could also be characterized as a collection of unscrupulous imperialists and war hawks, their work was structured, goal-oriented, and – successful.

We need only to compare this to the German war economy. The historian Albrecht Ritschl wrote: 'The economic history of Germany's Great War appears intellectually unexciting. It is the story of a failed *blitz* campaign and a subsequent war of attrition. It is the chronicle of dissappointed expectations, painful adjustment, and of quixotic efforts to ignore reality. It is the account of an insufficient ressource base, and probably of misallocation and disingenuous economic planning. And, last, it is the story of a half-constitutional yet undemocratic system in denial of defeat, unable to compromise, unable to make peace, finally drawing the whole of society into the abyss of its own political and military collapse.'[4]

Wilson's America

From the distance of a century, American historian Justus Doeneke assessed: 'Consider the outcome of the president's three major aims: to keep the United

States out of War, to uphold the right to sell American goods without hindrance, and to negotiate a conflict that he realized was becoming increasingly fratricidal. At certain crucial junctures, his policies proved counterproductive to these goals.'[5]

By 1915 the United States had become the main supplier for the Allies. Would not their economic and financial connections therefore automatically draw them to side with the Entente?

After the sinking of the *Lusitania* in May 1915, Secretary of State William Jennings Bryan had warned Wilson against a one-sided reaction. But the President elected to put severe diplomatic pressure on the Germans only, including threatening to break off relations. In protest of this policy, Bryan resigned.

What could Wilson have done about American sailors on Allied merchant ships or American civilians who found themselves in London or Paris just as German air raids were being carried out by zeppelins and bombers? How could he have protected any US citizens outside America?

In early 1916, Wilson attempted to do so through cooperation. He negotiated with the German government and convinced them to scale back their planned Uboat offensive to meet his conditions. In exchange, he relented – in the face of sharp British protest – on the issue of the sinking of armed merchant ships.

Tirpitz undermined this collaboration between Bethmann and the US President by unilaterally ordering the Flanders Uboats to wage unrestricted Uboat warfare, which eventually led to the torpedoing of the *Sussex*.

Wilson now reversed course and explicitly threatened to sever diplomatic relations. He forced the German government into a 'showdown' with its own Navy, which was eventually compelled to abandon its Uboat war.

Wilson had meddled deeply in Germany's domestic affairs and this had nearly led to war with the German Reich. He was not about to make the same mistake again. If he hoped to preserve America's neutrality, he had to make a move. In early 1916 he began his first peace initiatives, to no effect.

The summer of 1916 passed with no further crises, and when, in autumn, the first serious requests from the German government for peace negotiations reached Washington, Wilson was embroiled in a presidential campaign and no longer receptive. Even following his re-election in early November he remained conspicuously restrained.

He tolerated the renewal of Uboat war in October 1916, even when isolated incidents crossed the red line he had set. According to Doeneke: 'During the fall of 1916, when Germany flagrantly violated the *Sussex* pledge, he did not protest.'[6]

Wilson remained passive. He exerted no pressure on Germany regarding the Uboat war, nor did he involve himself further with the question of peace. Had he perhaps been compelled to recognize that, given the irreconcilable war aims of the two opposing sides, it would be futile to take action, or that Secretary of State Lansing and Colonel House had been correct in saying that sooner or later it would come to conflict with the German Reich, and that he would then be *forced* to side with the Allies? His last energetic push in late January 1917 came too late.

In the wake of the *Sussex* affair, Wilson made up his mind. The continuation of unrestricted Uboat warfare on the part of the Imperial Navy would force him to break off diplomatic relations with Germany.

This was precisely what the Imperial Navy was counting on, exactly what they *wanted* to bring about, and the British, who were convinced that America would enter the war on the side of the Allies, had also pinned their hopes on this. Wilson was predictable and had, indirectly, put himself at the mercy of the two warring European camps. Great Britain's ruling elite as well as Germany's had no desire for the war to end indecisively: both camps were committed to a life-or-death battle to the finish.

Faced with this situation at the beginning of 1917, the Imperial Navy's determination to incite conflict with America left the US President with no alternative – Germany's recalcitrant behavior imposed its will upon him.

Doeneke wrote: 'Certainly, without Germany's submarine activity, it would have been most difficult for [Wilson] to have taken America into the conflict. Even had he so desired (a proposition that remains highly dubious), he would have experienced extreme difficulty had not the Germans kept sinking US merchant ships while making no provisions for their crews. If, by many indications, the public in early 1917 was not anxious to enter the conflict, it was the continued U-boat warfare that brought American participation.'[7] He continues: 'In the end, it was Germany that forced the administration's hand, doing so at a moment when [American] relations with Berlin were improving and those with London were growing worse. When U-boats began sinking American vessels without rescuing their crews, Wilson had run out of options.'[8]

Why did he fail?

Wilson did everything to prevent America's entry into the European war. But in March, 1917, German military obduracy – most especially the Zimmermann telegram and the sinking of American ships – led to an increasingly restive citizenry, effectively neutralizing his ability to negotiate an end to hostilities. He could not act against American public opinion.

British imperialists and German militarists were ready to pay any price to resist Wilson's ideas of a new world order. Both sides of the ruling oligarchies preferred to play heads or tails rather than subordinate themselves to Wilson's ideas.

US industry and finance were profiteering handsomely from the war in Europe. If the Britsh blockade hadn't existed, would America have provided both warring sides with ammunition? Wilson in 1917 could not act against major national economic interests, it was much too late for that.

Like most neutrals, America held restricted in port, or recalled, shipping destined for Britain on February 1, 1917. By the end of the month US ships set out again to navigate the Uboat cordon around the British Isles. Why weren't they restricted to stop only at neutral ports in Norway, Sweden, Denmark or in the Netherlands, leaving it to the Allies to risk transshipping US-origin goods to their own ports? An interesting question: who was responsible for setting American shipping on a collision course with an aggressor?

Wilson was the last man standing for neutrality in the US administration. He was the President of the most powerful nation in the world, but the American army was smaller than Belgium's. At this time its arsenal had the capacity only for a fifteen minute fire barrage on the Western Front. Its most impressive weapons were economic and financial, over which Wilson had no decisive control. Radical liberal democrats like Lloyd George in Britain or Georges Clemencau in France were able to 'nationalize' whole industries. At the end of 1914 Wilson toyed with the notion of nationalizing American arms manufacturing, but nothing came of it.

On March 27, 1917, House had met Wilson who had just been forced to go to war: 'I said that it was [a situation] for which he was not well fitted. He admitted this and said he did not believe he was fitted for the Presidency under such conditions. I thought he was too refined, too civilized, too intellectual, too cultivated not to see the incongruity and absurdity of war. It needs a man of coarser fibre and one less a philosopher than the President, to conduct a brutal, vigorous, and successful war. I felt that he had taken a gamble that there would be no war, and had lost.'[9]

House in 1926 about Wilson: 'He had his shortcomings, even as other men, and having them but gives him the more character and virility. As I saw him at the time and as I see him in retrospect, his chief defect was temperamental. His prejudices were strong and oftentimes clouded his judgments. But, by and large, he was what the head of a state should be – intelligent, honest, and courageous.'[10]

Wilson didn't play *Realpolitik*, but *Idealpolitik*. His aims – or better said, ideals – were neutrality, free American trade and peace in Europe. They were contradictory ideas that cancelled out one another. He handled crises badly. When America went to war, it was completely unprepared to do so.

His visions of a new world peace were revolutionary. In any case, he was not able to enforce them in Versailles on the Europeans.

'Speak softly, but carry a big stick' is the motto of *Realpolitik*, but this was not Wilson's language. Wilson was a product of university studies, an idealist, a dreamer. By education, instinct and training he was unsuited for *Realpolitik*.

Wilson – like Bethmann Hollweg – had failed. Common sense, reason, and rationality had been eradicated, in their place reigned chauvinism, imperialism, greed, and ruthless revenge-seeking. Nineteenth century liberalism had come to an end.

It was not only in Europe that the lights went out – a new, dark century had begun.

Wilhelminian Germany

The United Forces of Post-feudalism: the German and the Austrian Kaiser, Ottoman Sultan, and Bulgarian Czar united.

While nineteenth-century rationalist liberals like Bethmann – and Wilson – set their hopes on the enlightened citizenry, Germany's domestic opposition unhesitatingly conducted a campaign of slander, intrigue, and character assassination. The poison worked its evil on the generation that followed. Preaching visions of salvation and conjuring up apocalyptic horror scenarios, they, with the help of the mass media, enflamed public opinion, specifically the conservative majority of the population. Throughout history, irrational phases such as this seem to arise epidemically.

In Germany it was the prospect of a negotiated peace and restoration of a European power balance, as well as of threatening internal landslides – necessarily leading to repression of the old elite classes – that were the critical factors generating panic among the military, the aristocracy, and the bourgeois upper classes, and which drove them to take this risky gamble. The very survival of the Wilhelminian social order was at stake. By spreading 'Uboat war' propaganda, the chauvinistic right-wing was able to enforce their desired course of action.

In this Prussia-Germany there was no longer a Bismarck, who in his own personal regiment prevailed over king or emperor and subordinated the military to the rule of politics. In the face of the internal paralysis, Kaiser Wilhelm II, vacillating and unwilling to engage in conflict, and Chancellor Bethmann Hollweg, acting with no political power of his own, were unable to fill the power vacuum left by Bismarck – as they might have done through the establishment of new institutions that achieved a better balance of interests or had they been able to develop a unified overall strategy for the war effort.

It was this vacuum that had drawn the popular generals Hindenburg and Ludendorff into the nucleus of power. The Army seized power, and, in 1917, the German Reich ultimately became a military dictatorship.

These rigid tin soldiers – like most 'specialists' – were neither able nor willing to evaluate factors that lay outside their own fields of knowledge and to include them in their decision-making. Riezler noted: 'The primary threat to the Reich [is] the *miles furiosus* who has made his way into politics. But it is precisely this type of mad warrior who is the idol of public opinion – not of the lower classes, which would be fathomable, but of the educated, which is incomprehensible. The few visionaries left in Germany have a secret war aim: the annihilation of Prussian (political) militarism. It cannot be uttered aloud, because this is also the English war aim.'[11]

In Germany, the military had been able to prevail, and now dictated domestic, economic, and foreign policy.

The relieved middle-class victors – Journalists, Lawyers, and History Professors: Lloyd George (Great Britain), Vittorio Emanuele Orlando (Italy), Georges Clemenceau (France), Woodrow Wilson (USA).

Even contemporaries characterized the First World War as 'a chain of errors', expressing the idea that although it is not always the better party which wins, the one which has made the most mistakes will most definitely lose. And in this case, that party was the German Reich.

It was the obvious functional weakness of post-feudal Prussian Germany (like Tsarist Russia) that led to its defeat. It *also* simply boiled down to a war of political systems – the American and French republics and parliamentary England were to survive the overthrow of the Russian Czar as well as the Habsburg and German emperors.

Ultimately, Wilhelminian society, with its rigid corporative state thinking, its rejection of reforms, its unwillingness to adapt, and in fear for its very survival, brought about its own demise.

The Sorcerer's Apprentices

In the First World War the British fought their dragon, Prussian Junker militarism and imperialism, by any and all means. To stiffen the will to fight on, their secret service – MI5 – 'sponsored' allied politicians and journalists with large sums of money. Beneficiaries included an influential journalist in Italy, Benito Mussolini.

The German General Staff under Ludendorff financed Russian revolutionaries, specially Vladimir Lenin and his gang. Equipped with German gold, Bolshevists overthrew the liberal Russian government in October, 1917, and erected a mass-murder dictatorship.

In beaten Germany, anti-democratic, racist, and imperialist ideas went into hibernation for a while, only to make an explosive re-entry on the world stage in the follow-up to the Great Depression. The still important Junkers, in desperate fear of a communist revolution in Germany, helped to install a radical right-wing dictator, Adolf Hitler. Riezler's 1916 prediction came true: 'Germany seems to be condemned to undergo a Pan-German dictature one day.'[12]

Fifteen years after the end of the Great War, the 'War to end all Wars', the dragon's seed sprouted anew. The scene for the next global conflict had been set.

Would a realization of Wilson's ideas not have prevented this?

APPENDIX

Chapter 39

History and History Writing

The following is an attempt to explain the obvious national differences in the historiography of the Uboat war.

The British Version

In 1926, as the official English naval history was nearing its completion, the British Admiralty felt that the depiction of the submarine war was far too realistic: 'These chapters provide gloomy reading from the British point of view and there is much in them to encourage potential enemies who may consider that it is in their competence to subjugate the Empire by a large submarine-building program. The encouragement of these ideas by means of an official publication is very much to be deprecated, particularly at a time when we are advocating the abolition of the submarine.'[1]

Significant amendments to the draft were required. The threat that the Uboats posed to maritime trade was the British Empire's strategic Achilles heel: it was in their best interests to downplay the danger.

A typical example of the preferred official approach can be found in Winston Churchill's *World Crisis*, written in 1931: 'It is commonly said that unrestricted Uboat warfare "nearly succeeded." [There] was never any chance of it. The seafaring resources of Great Britain were, in fact and in the circumstances, always superior to the Uboat attack.'[2] Churchill, speaking for the British elite, was deliberately revising history.

The Germans had an even more difficult time accepting the historical facts.

The German Version

Following Germany's defeat in the war, the reputation of its navy sank to its lowest point: its battle fleet armament before 1914 had led to England's siding with the 'enemies' – especially France. In 1917 it was the navy's Uboat war that had resulted in America's entry into the war. After the Armistice, the fleet's capital ships were delivered to the Allies, deliberately sunk, or scrapped. It was a wretched ending for a military force that had been built up with such high expectations.

The primary decision-makers all vanished in late 1918 – the Kaiser ran off to the Netherlands, Ludendorff fled to Sweden, and Tirpitz, fearing that 'his' rebellious sailors would lynch him, hid out for several months in deep forests, staying in hunting cabins that belonged to friends.

In the summer of 1919, the Grand Admiral published his apologia, in which he accused the Kaiser and his Chancellor of having prevented him, immediately after the outbreak of the war, from deploying the High Seas Fleet against the British, instead waiting until it was 'too late'. Scheer's memoirs were also published around this time, and were quite in keeping with Tirpitz's view.

All the elements for this naval post-war interpretation had already existed during the war. Riezler, a contemporary, made a remark in early October 1914 about the non-deployment of the battle fleet and Tirpitz's consent to this: 'The father of the lie is making sure that he is not blamed for the idiotic battle fleet politics. He seemingly apologizes, but continues, however, with his bald-faced lies. Tirpitz shields himself behind the Chancellor, because at first he had wanted to save the fleet. If the Chancellor were to say "deploy", he would backtrack at once.'[3] On the issue of unrestricted Uboat war, he wrote on January 17, 1917: 'The [Pan-German] fringe will do anything to portray the Uboat war as their cause and to declare that their program is finally going to be achieved – against the wishes of the Chancellor. It may be that they will already begin to cautiously remark that it might be too late. Tirpitz, in his well-known manner, will certainly say that it now is too late and that a Uboat war in 1916 would have fared much better than the one in 1917 – despite the insane unlawfulness of such a claim.'[4]

It was precisely this line of argument that the Navy would take up after the war – everything had always happened 'too late': the feeble Kaiser, a government sympathetic to England, and the cowardly diplomats had trammeled the powerful fleet and betrayed Germany's opportunity for victory. A stab in the back from above.

In 1925, Admiral Andreas Michelsen, commander of the Uboats in 1917, published a book intended to excuse their failures. He made the following remarks regarding suspension of the Uboat war in 1915, when, compared with more than 20,000 vessels belonging to the world merchant fleet, a dozen ocean-going Uboats had been available: 'The German Uboat war in the meantime, hog-tied by our diplomacy, continued its uncreative existence.'[5] And, in commenting upon the interruption of the second Uboat war in April 1916, he remarked: 'In any event, the Chancellor's fear of America and his England-friendly policies are what won. At that moment, the last sure opportunity to rescue the Reich was passed up.'[6]

In his view, America's entry into the war in 1917 had been inevitable long before the war: 'Even at that time [1912], there existed unwritten agreements between the two Anglo-Saxon powers [England and the United States] in the event of war; Wilson's choice was determined by English-Jewish financial considerations.'[7]

Ludendorff and Hindenburg, as well, in an effort to whitewash their activities, spread the myth: ever since the outbreak of the war, President Wilson had pursued a course hostile to the Germans, therefore American entry into the war had been unavoidable – regardless of when or what type of Uboat war anyone had started. Michelsen wrote: '[It was] not the Uboat war, but rather Wilson's policies, that ultimately convinced Americans to go to war against Germany.'[8]

Germany against the rest of the world – this was not the result of an error on the part of the military leadership, but, rather, a tragic fate predetermined by the angry gods on Mount Olympus. It was to be endured, preferably silently – and, above all, without criticism.

The Kaiser's Navy and the 'Official' History of the Uboat War

Official history books on the land war were already being written in the mid-1920s, as were those on the Navy's surface vessels, covering battleships right down to the smallest minelayer. But there was a deafening silence when it came to the Uboats.

It was not until 1933 that the first three volumes of the Navy's official history of the Uboats were published: *Merchant War with Uboats*, written by Rear Admiral Arno Spindler. They covered the period from the outbreak of war to the end of January 1917.

Based on the commanders' logs, Spindler lists every Uboat operation and its sinkings, as well as citing information from important naval files. He appears to be presenting 'facts', but the information is often manipulated.

A brief command log entry such as 'Steamer determined to be hospital ship. Attacked nevertheless,'[9] would be rewritten by Spindler to reflect quite the opposite: 'In the belief that he was confronted by a transporter, Lieutenant Schwieger obeyed orders and fired a torpedo. Too late, he noticed that the vessel had been painted white and bore the insignia of a hospital ship.'[10] Once again, a 'too late.'

The night-time, warningless sinking on March 16 of the 13,911 GRT neutral Dutch passenger steamship *Tubantia*, brightly-lit and at anchor, by UB-13, he briefly describes as 'Unknown steamer of about 2000 T [sunk by UB-13].'[11] He does not mention the name of the vessel, he cites misleading tonnage, and he fails to report that the ship was sunk by a torpedo.

Naturally then, for Spindler, the *Lusitania*, with over 2,000 civilians on board, was not a passenger liner, but rather a munitions transport, and its sinking was justified.

He lists the number of Uboats built, but does not compare them to the statistics for other newly-constructed naval vessels – Spindler assures us that 'enough' Uboats had been built.

His entire book is a biased and either fact-disregarding or a falsified justification of the Uboat war from the Navy's perspective.

As he continued working on the Uboat offensive during 1917 and 1918, Spindler ran into a problem. He was only able to list the sinkings he found in the deck logs: just under eleven million GRT by the Uboats, plus one million GRT from the mines. The resulting total of twelve million GRT corresponded to the figures arrived at by the British. However, this would stand in contradiction to the eighteen million GRT that, even long after the First World War, the Imperial Navy swore it had destroyed. This would make it clear that unrestricted Uboat warfare had been no more efficient than that conducted following prize rules, and would thereby expose a propaganda lie.

Volume IV, covering 1917, was printed in 1941, but was only circulated among the Admiralty Staff. Volume V, the final volume of the work, was not even printed.

It was not until 1964 and 1966 that these two volumes would be published, two generations after the First World War.

Only then could historians prove that attack strategy – whether sinking according to prize rules or by torpedo attacks – had been irrelevant to the efficiency of the merchant war.[12]

Conclusion

Because submarine warfare had been so successful and because of the danger that it would be used again, the British Admiralty downplayed the topic in the interwar years. At the same time, it was tacitly ignored by the German Navy, because, contrary to all of its communications and assurances, it had not been successful enough – and, once America entered the war, it had led to Germany's defeat.

For half a century, no official German history of Uboat war was published: instead, German naval propaganda was promulgated. This propaganda dug itself so deeply into the German psyche that even a century later, a fallacy like Tirpitz's 1915 lie that the *Lusitania* was an 'auxiliary cruiser' still finds journalistic support in respected German journals.[13]

Chapter 40

Sources Used

Selected sources from the German Navy's archives by Gerhard Granier: 'Die Deutsche Seekriegsleitung im Ersten Weltkrieg'

This document collection, taken from the German Imperial Navy archives in Freiburg and published between 1999 and 2004 by Gerhard Granier, was a veritable treasure trove. Granier presents the most important files for every critical phase of the war – information that could only be unearthed by years of searching through the complete disorder of the naval archives.

Diaries of Admiral Müller

The diaries of Admiral Georg Alexander von Müller, Naval Representative at the German Imperial Court from 1906 to 1918, were published in 1959 and have also already been cited by Arthur Link in his biography of Woodrow Wilson (see below). They provide extremely detailed insight into Kaiser Wilhelm's reactions to the individual phases of discussions regarding Uboat warfare. The handwritten original can now be viewed as a facsimile on the German Federal Archives intranet.

Diaries of Kurt Riezler

The publication of the diaries of Kurt Riezler, who worked closely with the Chancellor from 1909 to 1917, developed into quite a political issue during the late 1960s.

Like almost every member of the contemporary elite class, Riezler regularly maintained a diary. On his death in 1955, his brother inherited these documents, which contained the stipulation that it was the last will of the deceased that they be destroyed. He nevertheless gave them to a German historian, Karl-Dietrich Erdmann, who, after ten years of solitary editing, finally published them in 1972.

The published version begins in early 1910 but breaks off in August 1911. The next section of the diary begins in the middle of the 1914 July crisis, but there is a gap during the early weeks of August. From August 14, 1914, until

Bethmann's downfall in the summer of 1917, the diary provides a compact picture of government policy; it is an absolutely invaluable source of information on the political situation and discourse in wartime Imperial Germany.

It remains unknown whether the Riezler diaries were incomplete or were simply not published in their entirety.

During the time of the Third Reich, Riezler emigrated with his family to the USA and maintained a close relationship there with the OSS intelligence agency.[1]

If a complete edition of his diaries were to still exist, in the possession of his family or in a US archive, then the question of exactly what took place at the Reich Chancellery in Berlin during those critical days at the outbreak of war could be conclusively answered. Maybe that's the reason why they don't exist anymore?

The saga of the Riezler diaries continues to be a mystery.

Innocents Abroad? – The monumental Wilson biography by Arthur S. Link

Arthur S. Link, in his decades of work leading up to the publication of his 'Wilson Papers' and the five-volume, several-thousand-pages-long biography of Wilson, set new historical research standards.

The three volumes that cover the war years were published between 1960 and 1965, and – a further stroke of luck for my research – for the most part provide a detailed, richly-referenced discussion of the British blockade and the German Uboat war.

Link's view of Wilson is subjugated to the primacy of foreign policy; domestic and economic aspects hardly play a role.

I personally find that the picture of Wilson painted by Link is 'too smooth', lacking the contradictions that one expects to find in a politician of his rank. Even someone like Bethmann had his dark, Machiavellian side. Was Wilson truly the lonely decision-maker and 'philanthropist' on the presidential seat, and if yes, what role was played by his staff, the Cabinet members, the administration, and the corporate elite?

Wilson's strategy of neutrality is undisputed, but his initial interference in German domestic affairs, which he justified on human rights and moral grounds, became a trap that he had laid for himself. By 1917 the provocative confrontation course taken by the German right and the passive reaction of the British imperialists to the proposed peace negotiations left Wilson with no alternative but to enter the war. Certain circles in the US – including the members of the financial industry, who feared that England, to whom they had loaned enormous sums of money, might be defeated in the submarine war and who, therefore, also *had* to fear its imminent bankruptcy – were able to exploit the situation to their own benefit: entering the war on the side of the Allies would mean that both the British Empire and they themselves would be saved from financial ruin.

In the end it was Wilson alone who defended American neutrality, against the interests of his administration and the economy.

Anyone with an interest in rearranging or adding to the puzzle pieces of the reasons why the US entered the war would find themselves enmeshed in a massive undertaking involving many, many years of research.

If, even after a century, it is still possible to reinterpret the history of the Uboat war on the basis of sources that have been accessible for decades, the Sisyphean task of the historian – and the limits of historiography – can perhaps begin to be somewhat appreciated.

Secondary Literature

It was only against the background of the common standard literature that it was possible to classify and interpret all of these documents and eyewitness accounts. Even if the works listed below are not quoted in detail in this book, the writings herein nonetheless stand on their shoulders.

Otto Pflanze's extensive Bismarck biography and John C.G. Röhl's three-volume biography of Kaiser Wilhelm are indispensable sources for gaining an understanding of the Wilhelminian Reich.

Hobsbawm describes the industrialization process and its social impact. Jürgen Kocka, Wolfgang J. Mommsen, Hans-Ulrich Wehler and Wilhelm Deist describe its specific influence on the German Reich.

Christopher Clark and Niall Ferguson are modern classicists on the topic of the lead-up to and history of the First World War.

Volker Berghahn and Michael Epkenhans have both written important works on the maritime arms race. In 2003, Joachim Schröder published the very first modern German history of the Uboat war from 1914 to 1918.

Sebastian Haffner's brilliant essays summarize Germany's historical development from the Bismarck era through the Third Reich.

Fritz Fischer deserves a special place of honor: in 1968, after fifty years of silence on the subject, he was the first to rekindle discussion about the origins of the First World War in Germany.

This book draws on the spirit of all of these works.

Desiderata – Still Missing

Within German society, there reigns a notorious lack of interest in the country's history before 1933.

German historians also share a portion of the blame for the lack of pertinent information. It is an absolute scandal that *no modern historical researcher has written*

a comprehensive, research-based biography of Theobald von Bethmann Hollweg –
one of the three most influential German Chancellors of the twentieth century![2]

There remains, thus, work enough for the current generation of historians in
providing a new understanding of the First World War.

Who knows which of the private writings and diaries of the former elite class
still slumber in the attics or cellars of their family members?

Ad fontes!

Hans Joachim Koerver, December 2018

Chapter 41

Statistics – My Numbers

German Warships Under Construction and in Service

All of the statistics regarding the construction and inventory of the Imperial Navy's ships cited herein were taken from Erich Gröner's standard work, which lists all of the German warships built between 1815 and 1945, along with their size, cost, crew strength, time needed for construction, shipyard, and commissioning and decommissioning dates.

Between 1900 and the end of 1918, 1,604 German warships were ordered, laid on keel, or commissioned.[1]

The Uboat Cruises

The primary source regarding operational Uboat maneuvers in the First World War is Spindler's history of submarine merchant war,[2] supplemented by Bendert's[3] data on the UB and UC boats, as well as the British archives in Kew.[4]

Documentation was able to be located for 3,101 Uboat patrols. Many of the cruises undertaken by the small UB-I and UC-I coastal Uboats could not be identified. With the ocean-going Uboats, it was sometimes difficult to distinguish whether their deployment was for purely military or merchant war purposes. The information provided in this book with regard to Uboat patrols represents *at least* an estimated 95% of the wartime reality.

Merchant Ships Sunk

Information on ships that had been sunk was obtained from the National Archives in Kew.[5] These English sources provided the name, tonnage, and type of sinking of a ship, but not the name of the submarine responsible for the sinking. This information was obtained from Bendert's writings on the UB and UC boats as well as Spindler's writings on the merchant war.

Documentation could be found for the sinking of 5,408 Allied and neutral merchant vessels that were listed *not only* in the 1919 British loss register but in Spindler's writings *as well*. According to calculations by the author, these vessels comprised 10,874,287 GRT, corresponding to 97.5% of the 11,153,506 tons that the British reported had been destroyed by Uboats 1914-18.

	High Seas Fleet		Flanders		Mediterranean		Total	
	coastal subs	ocean-going Uboats	coastal subs	ocean-going Uboats	coastal subs	ocean-going Uboats	coastal subs	ocean-going Uboats
1915 Jan	9	15					9	15
Feb	8	16					8	16
Mar	6	18					6	18
Apr	6	18	3			1	9	19
May	6	18	10		3	1	19	19
Jun	5	19	14		4	1	23	20
Jul	5	17	15		6	1	25	18
Aug	5	14	14		7	3	26	17
Sep	4	11	15		7	5	25	16
Oct	3	10	14		7	5	24	16
Nov	2	11	13		7	6	22	17
Dec	2	12	14		6	7	22	19
1916 Jan	2	12	14		6	7	22	19
Feb	1	13	15	1	6	7	22	20
Mar	2	15	14	3	6	7	22	26
Apr	2	20	14	4	5	7	21	30
May	2	26	12	4	4	8	18	39
Jun	3	31	10	5	4	9	17	45
Jul	3	37	9	7	4	11	16	55
Aug	3	41	9	7	4	13	16	60
Sep	3	45	8	9	3	15	14	69
Oct	2	46	8	12	3	17	13	75
Nov	1	46	9	15	2	21	12	81
Dec		50	9	14	2	24	11	88
1917 Jan		56	9	14	2	25	11	95
Feb		60	9	19	2	24	11	104
Mar		58	9	27	1	26	10	110
Apr		60	9	27	1	27	10	114
May		63	9	25	1	28	10	116
Jun		66	9	23	1	29	10	119
Jul		62	9	25	1	29	10	116
Aug		59	8	26	1	29	9	114
Sep		65	8	27	1	32	9	124
Oct		62	6	27	1	35	7	123
Nov		63	6	26	1	35	7	124
Dec		62	6	23	1	35	7	120
1918 Jan		63	6	23	1	35	7	121
Feb		60	6	22	1	35	7	117
Mar		61	5	22	1	35	6	118
Apr		60	5	20	1	36	6	116
May		58	4	17	1	33	5	108
Jun		57	4	17	1	31	5	105
Jul		66	3	17	1	29	4	113
Aug		70	3	16	1	30	4	116
Sep		74	1	14	1	31	2	119
Oct		76		8	1	30	1	113

Uboats in Service (Monthly Average, rounded).[6]

	Flanders				High Seas Fleet				North Sea + Atlantic			
	Uboats on merchant war daily	BRT sunk	%BRT w/o warning	BRT per Uboat daily	Uboats on merchant war daily	BRT sunk	%BRT w/o warning	BRT per Uboat daily	Uboats on merchant war daily	BRT sunk	%BRT w/o warning	BRT per Uboat daily
1915 Jan					1	17 126	70%	778	1	17 126	70%	778
Feb					3	22 784	94%	259	2	22 784	94%	495
Mar					5	71 004	44%	447	4	71 004	44%	573
Apr		11 753	100%		4	27 879	14%	227	3	39 632	39%	404
May		222			5	107 002	62%	728	4	107 224	61%	858
Jun		18 082	98%		6	95 722	27%	515	5	113 804	38%	744
Jul		6 274	85%		3	84 855	5%	816	3	91 129	10%	1 072
Aug		8 064	84%		4	142 578	17%	1 033	4	150 642	21%	1 345
Sep		595			2	61 488	38%	1 098	1	62 083	37%	1 725
Oct												
Nov												
Dec		1 669	100%		1	14 001		500	1	15 670	11%	560
1916 Jan		389			1				1	389		24
Feb		1 730	100%	346						1 730	100%	346
Mar	1	53 170	99%	1611	4	64 124	18%	562	5	117 294	55%	798
Apr	1	22 408	82%	606	5	91 983	21%	617	6	114 391	33%	615
May	1	476		24	1	26 503	50%	914	2	26 979	50%	551
Jun						1 972				1 972		
Jul	1	6 570		168		5 139	56%		1	11 709	25%	300
Aug	1	19 525		651		9 514	48%	3 171	1	29 039	16%	880
Sep	3	79 826		928	3	24 288	14%	279	6	104 114	3%	602
Oct	4	51 864		387	10	131 380	7%	414	15	183 244	5%	406
Nov	6	79 496	6%	418	6	67 814	7%	361	13	147 310	7%	390
Dec	5	91 185	10%	563	6	50 138	6%	249	12	141 323	9%	389
1917 Jan	5	69 057	3%	470	12	140 233	22%	368	17	209 290	16%	396
Feb	8	111 586	35%	526	15	256 350	58%	593	23	367 936	51%	571
Mar	10	160 330	63%	511	18	259 382	67%	456	28	419 712	65%	475
Apr	9	132 107	65%	504	22	445 101	72%	669	31	577 208	70%	623
May	10	162 032	49%	538	20	222 623	75%	368	29	384 655	64%	425
Jun	9	130 904	76%	494	27	334 408	77%	418	36	465 312	77%	437
Jul	9	109 190	68%	400	22	284 767	79%	415	31	393 957	76%	411
Aug	10	109 075	86%	350	20	259 285	84%	414	30	368 360	85%	393
Sep	11	106 155	78%	331	24	110 760	75%	151	35	216 915	76%	206
Oct	11	85 273	94%	256	21	170 629	77%	267	31	255 902	82%	263
Nov	9	82 708	98%	303	15	81 205	79%	178	24	163 913	88%	225
Dec	9	90 198	92%	337	22	124 494	91%	181	31	214 692	91%	225
1918 Jan	9	47 478	98%	164	19	111 677	85%	190	28	159 155	89%	181
Feb	8	52 111	96%	242	27	171 988	78%	225	35	224 099	82%	229
Mar	10	71 511	97%	231	23	139 280	69%	198	33	210 791	78%	208
Apr	8	74 289	99%	320	23	110 690	89%	159	31	184 979	93%	200
May	7	27 326	99%	135	24	134 905	96%	183	30	162 231	96%	172
Jun	7	56 585	100%	264	16	132 673	69%	271	23	189 258	78%	269
Jul	6	47 009	84%	246	28	142 785	93%	163	34	189 794	91%	178
Aug	7	48 300	97%	234	24	164 948	72%	219	31	213 248	78%	222
Sep	6	31 643	99%	184	28	112 141	89%	136	33	143 784	91%	144
Oct	3	8 022	100%	100	22	66 942	94%	99	24	74 964	94%	99

Uboat Cruises and Merchant Ship Sinkings, North Sea + Atlantic.[7]

	North Sea + Atlantic				Mediterranian				Total			
	Uboats on merchant war daily	BRT sunk	%BRT w/o warning	BRT per Uboat daily	Uboats on merchant war daily	BRT sunk	%BRT w/o warning	BRT per Uboat daily	Uboats on merchant war daily	BRT sunk	%BRT w/o warning	BRT per Uboat daily
1915 Jan	1	17 126	70%	778					1	17 126	70%	778
Feb	2	22 784	94%	495					3	22 784	94%	259
Mar	4	71 004	44%	573					5	71 004	44%	447
Apr	3	39 632	39%	404					4	39 632	39%	307
May	4	107 224	61%	858					6	107 224	61%	627
Jun	5	113 804	38%	744					6	113 804	38%	612
Jul	3	91 129	10%	1 072		5 601	100%	800	4	96 730	16%	871
Aug	4	150 642	21%	1 345	2	14 840	75%	280	6	165 482	26%	866
Sep	1	62 083	37%	1 725	3	50 240		577	5	112 323	21%	785
Oct					2	63 004	27%	1 068	2	63 004	27%	1 033
Nov					2	140 842	13%	2 428	2	140 842	13%	2 428
Dec	1	15 670	11%	560	2	82 925	43%	1 536	3	98 595	38%	1 202
1916 Jan	1	389		24	2	27 974	34%	451	3	28 363	33%	364
Feb		1 730	100%	346	2	33 040	36%	688	2	34 770	39%	656
Mar	5	117 294	55%	798	1	20 045	68%	514	6	137 339	57%	738
Apr	6	114 391	33%	615	2	51 205	51%	813	8	165 596	39%	665
May	2	26 979	50%	551	2	71 922	2%	959	4	98 901	15%	798
Jun		1 972			3	66 929	10%	712	3	68 901	9%	733
Jul	1	11 709	25%	300	3	86 341	12%	919	4	98 050	14%	737
Aug	1	29 039	16%	880	4	128 391	16%	1 044	5	157 430	16%	1 009
Sep	6	104 114	3%	602	3	98 007	27%	1 032	9	202 121	15%	754
Oct	15	183 244	5%	406	6	120 293	61%	665	20	303 537	27%	480
Nov	13	147 310	7%	390	8	91 101	62%	378	21	238 411	28%	385
Dec	12	141 323	9%	389	8	127 859	72%	501	20	269 182	39%	436
1917 Jan	17	209 290	16%	396	4	78 149	61%	680	21	287 439	28%	447
Feb	23	367 936	51%	571	8	105 233	64%	483	31	473 169	54%	549
Mar	28	419 712	65%	475	8	59 856	76%	239	37	479 568	67%	423
Apr	31	577 208	70%	623	11	220 295	68%	697	41	797 503	69%	642
May	29	384 655	64%	425	11	148 320	68%	432	40	532 975	65%	427
Jun	36	465 312	77%	437	12	148 745	55%	417	47	614 057	72%	432
Jul	31	393 957	76%	411	8	82 061	86%	332	39	476 018	78%	395
Aug	30	368 360	85%	393	10	71 922	66%	244	40	440 282	82%	357
Sep	35	216 915	76%	206	12	104 087	75%	298	47	321 002	76%	229
Oct	31	255 902	82%	263	12	143 164	87%	397	43	399 066	84%	299
Nov	24	163 913	88%	225	10	81 970	98%	286	34	245 883	91%	242
Dec	31	214 692	91%	225	12	124 973	93%	338	43	339 665	92%	256
1918 Jan	28	159 155	89%	181	10	112 109	97%	364	38	271 264	92%	229
Feb	35	224 099	82%	229	10	79 156	94%	272	45	303 255	85%	239
Mar	33	210 791	78%	208	11	102 434	95%	310	43	313 225	84%	234
Apr	31	184 979	93%	200	12	74 744	96%	214	43	259 723	94%	204
May	30	162 231	96%	172	12	118 173	98%	320	42	280 404	97%	214
Jun	23	189 258	78%	269	7	49 934	98%	230	31	239 192	83%	260
Jul	34	189 794	91%	178	8	69 709	99%	282	42	259 503	93%	197
Aug	31	213 248	78%	222	8	60 001	95%	229	39	273 249	82%	224
Sep	33	143 784	91%	144	8	36 035	98%	142	42	179 819	93%	144
Oct	24	74 964	94%	99	8	34 267	96%	147	32	109 231	95%	110

Uboat cruises and merchant ship sinkings, total.[8]

Chapter 42

Documents

Room 40: the Magdeburg Code Book (Signalbuch der Kaiserlichen Marine) (TNA, ADM 137/4156).

Front Page.

Supplement — 304 —

Zahlen-Signal	Buchstaben-Signal	Bedeutung
625 55	N L Z	Meßübung
56	N L α	Meßübung abbrechen
57	N L γ	Meßübung zu Anker auf das zu bezeichnende Schiff
58	N M A	Meßübung fällt aus
59	N M Ä	Meßübung findet statt (um)
625 60	N M B	Meßübung für laufendes Gefecht
61	N M C	Meßübung vorbereiten
62	N M D	Metall =isch
63	N M E	Metazentrum =zentrisch
64	N M F	Meteor
65	N M G	Meteorologe -isch
66	N M H	Meter (m)
67	N M Î	(n) Meter breit
68	N M J	wieviel Meter breit?
69	N M K	(n) Meter dick
625 70	N M L	wieviel Meter dick?
71	N M O	(n) Meter hoch (hohe)
72	N M Ö	wieviel Meter hoch?
73	N M P	(n) Meter lang
74	N M Q	wieviel Meter lang?
75	N M R	(n) Meter tief
76	N M S	wieviel Meter tief?
77	N M T	wieviel Meter?
78	N M U	Methode =isch
79	N M ü	Meuchelmord -er
625 80	N M V	Meuterei
81	N M W	Meuterei an Bord (der, des, von)
82	N M X	Meuterei an Land
83	N M Y	Meuterer =isch
84	N M Z	meutern
85	N M α	Mexikaner =isch
625 86	N M γ	mich
573 81	H O Ö	für mich (mein)
625 87	N O A	Miene
88	N O Ä	Miete, mieten
89	N O B	Mikrometer
625 90	N O C	Mikrophon
91	N O D	Mikroskop =isch
92	N O E	Milch =ig (n)
93	N O F	mild, Milde
94	N O G	mildern -ung
95	N O H	Militär =isch, Militär=
96	N O Î	Militärattaché (in)
97	N O J	Militärbeamter
98	N O K	Militärbehörde
99	N O L	Militärbevollmächtigter (von)
626 00	N O M	Militärkabinett [s. Chef]
01	N O Ö	militärpolitisch
02	N O P	Militärstrafgerichtsordnung (§ n)
03	N O Q	Militärstrafgesetzbuch (§ n)
04	N O R	Militärstrafvollstreckungsvorschrift (§ n)
05	N O S	Miliz
06	N O T	Milliarde
07	N O U	Millimeter
08	N O ü	Million
09	N O V	
626 10	N O W	
11	N O X	
626 12	N O Y	
626 13	N O Z	Milreis
14	N O α	Milzbrand
15	N O γ	minder
16	N Ö A	minderwertig =keit
17	N Ö Ä	Minderzahl
18	N Ö B	mindest, mindestens
19	N Ö C	Mindestabstand
626 20	N Ö D	Mine [s. Ankerplatz, Beobachtungs-, Einfahrt, Fahrwasser, Feind usw. (s. auch Signale für Minendienst S. 90 ff.)], Minen=
21	N Ö E	(n) Minen abgeben
22	N Ö F	Mine abschießen
23	N Ö G	nach Minen absuchen [s. Ankerplatz, Defilee. Fahrwasser]
626 24	N Ö H	nach Minen abgesucht
45 13	P K	Achtung Minen! Gerät ist ausgeschlippt
508 34	A α U	Ankerplatz des Feindes mit (n) Minen verseuchen
626 25	N Ö Î	zum Auffüllen der Minen einlaufen
26	N Ö J	Minen aufnehmen
27	N Ö K	beim Auftreffen auf Minen [vgl. Minengefahr]
28	N Ö L	mit (n) Minen ausrüsten [s. Torpedoboot]
29	N Ö M	habe (-n, hat) (n) Minen an Bord
626 30	N Ö O	(n) Minen an Bord nehmen
31	N Ö P	Minen einstellen auf (n) Meter
32	N Ö Q	Minen sind eingestellt auf (n) Meter
626 33	N Ö R	(n) Minen ergänzen
41 20	D G	Fahrwasser nach Minen absuchen
45 14	P L	(n) Mine gefunden (bei, in)
626 34	N Ö S	Minen klarmachen zum Werfen
45 16	P N	Minen legen (bei, in) [s. Minenlegen, Torpedoboot]
626 35	N Ö T	habe Minen gelegt (bei, in)
45 17	P O	es liegen Minen im Fahrwasser (bei, in)
626 36	N Ö U	Minen lichten (Stunder entfernen)
37	N Ö ü	klar zum Minen lichten
38	N Ö V	scharfe Mine
39	N Ö W	schnellsteigende M.
626 40	N Ö X	schußsichere Mine
45 18	P Ö	Mine (-n) in Sicht
626 41	N Ö Y	Minen sprengen
626 42	N Ö Z	Minen steigen nach (n) Minuten
45 15	P M	bin (ist, sind) auf Minen gestoßen (bei)
45 19	P Q	Minen suchen [s. Boot, Fahrt, Minensuchen]
626 43	N Ö α	treibende Mine
44	N Ö γ	Minen übernehmen (an, in, bei)
45	N P A	Mine (n) unschädlich machen
46	N P Ä	Minen unschädlich machen und über Bord werfen
47	N P B	Minen sind unwirksam nach (n) ...tagen
48	N P C	
49	N P D	
626 50	N P E	
51	N P F	
625 52	N P G	

304

Mine ('Miene') corresponds to chiffre 625 87 or code NOA.

Room 40: known position of U–20 (TNA, ADM 137/4152).

	Register No.		Minute Sheet No. 4.	
1915				
Apr. 0914	Firing practice Varel Tief.			
20 Apr.	Wilhelmshaven, ready April 21st.			
Apr.	" to Emden.			
23 Apr.	Ems ready for German Bight.			
Apr.	Ems to advance into German Bight.			
8pm.	U.20 and U.27 going to Irish Sea and Bristol Channel.			
29 Apr.	Emden.			
Apr. 1130	Left Ems to N.W.		(1 gun aft).	
1400	In 64E area 7 (53.45 N 5.55 E).			
1600	" 38E " (54.03 N 5.25 E).			
1700	" 32E " (54.09 N 5.15 E).			
1800	" 14E " (54.21 N 4.55 E).			
1905	" 161G " (54.27 N 4.45 E).			
2000	" 143G " (54.33 N 4.25 E).			
2100	" 114G " (54.45 N 4.15 E).			
2200	" 108G " (54.51 N 4.05 E).			
2300	" 75G " (54.57 N 3.45 E).			
2400	" 54G " (55.03 N 3.35 E).			
May 0200	" 25D " (55.21 N 3.15 E).			
0400	" 157A area 5(55.39 N 2.45 E).			
0600	" 124A " (55.51 N 2.15 E).			
0800	" 59A " (56.15 N 1.18 E).			
5 May night	Missed British s.s.CAYO ROMANO by torpedo off Fastnet. (F.6/2)			
May 1730	Sank British s.v.EARL OF LATHOM by gunfire 8'S.by W.of Old Head of Kinsale. (F.6/3).			
evening	Position:- 51.32 N 8.22 W.			
2130	Reported 12'S. of Daunt's Rock. (F.6/1).			
May 1100	Stopped British s.s.CANDIDATE by gunfire and sank her by torpedo 13'S.by E.½E. of Coningbeg Light Vessel. (F.7/1).			
1300	Sank British s.s.CENTURION by torpedo without warning 20'S. of Coningbeg Light Vessel. (F.7/3).			
May 1430	Sank British s.s.LUSITANIA by torpedo without warning 15'S. of Old Head of Kinsale. (F.7/6).			
1600	Missed American s.s.NARRAGANSETT by torpedo 16'S.350W.(true) of Old Head of Kinsale. (F.7/11).			

Minute Sheet No. 4.

U.20.

(3180) 24338/P610 30m. 4/13 M. & B., Ltd.

Register No.

Minute Sheet No. 5.

1915		
May	1100	Sighted 60'N.W. of Blaskets, steering N.R.E. (F.9/1).
May	0100	Sighted and chased by armed trawler STANLEY WEYMAN 2' off Butt of Lewis. (D.10/2).
May	0900	Position 28/57E (57.06 N 6.20 E). Has sunk 1 sailing vessel, 2 steamers and LUSITANIA.
	0915	3rd S/m Half Flotilla asks that U.20 may be warned of the numerous mines and enemy s/ms in the German Bight.
	1300	In 70E area 4 (56.33 N 6.45 E).
	1434	Requests mine free way. Horns Reef - Ems.
	1530	Told that mouth of Ems, if entered from the North is free of mines.
	1455	C.in C. to Norddeich for U.20. To Captain and crew my warmest appreciation of success achieved of which H.S.F. is proud and my best wishes for return.
	1600	Reports having sunk on May 5th in the afternoon, the small vessel EARL OF LATHOM. Wreck is in 51.32 N 8.22 W.
	1643	Told to come direct to Wilhelmshaven. In approaches to List and fairway E.of Amrum Bank, apparently no danger of mines. Enemy s/ms so far reported West of Norderney.
	1740	Reports having sunk LUSITANIA on May 7th at 3.10 p.m. in 51.23 N 8.31 W by one torpedo.
	1815	Reports that on May 6th she sank s.s.CANDIDATE from Liverpool and an unknown steamer, both of about 5,000 tons. Wrecks are in 51.51 N 6.31 W and 51.36 N 6.28 W.
May	0535	At Amrum Bank. Going to Wilhelmshaven in accordance with orders from O.C. s/ms.
		Arrived Wilhelmshaven.
31 May		At Wilhelmshaven ready June 5th.
June		" " " " "
4 June		" " " " 20th.
June		" " " " " Air chamber, to be sent to Heligoland.
18 June		" " " " "
June		" " " " 21st.
23 June		" " " " 24th.
June	1041	Left Wilhelmshaven for Ems.
	2000	Entered Ems.
	2130	Emden ready.
June		" " for German Bight only. until July 3rd.
June		" " " " "

Minute Sheet No.5.

Room 40: deciphered Uboat W/T (TNA ADM 137/4594).

'Mein Standort ist 8 pm mit Uboat U-B 105 Quadrat 229 E [60.50N, 3.18W]. Morgen Vormittag 10 am Quadrat 1138 E [61.45N, 0.20W].' – My position at 20:00 with UB 105: 60.50N, 3.18W. Tomorrow morning 10:00: 61.45N, 0.20W.

Room 40: deciphered German W/T to the Uboats (TNA, ADM 137/4069).

[178] 20775/P1165 10m 9/19? 4151 G & S 110   89

| 1915 | Register No. | NORDDEICH to ALL SHIPS. | Minute Sheet No. 22 . |

No	Feb.		
33	" 19	On the 20th or 21st Feb., there will probably enter the Irish Sea, American steamers named 'Philadelphia' and 'West Haverford' bound for Liverpool. Spare both steamers. (sgd) Chief of N.S.Forces.	
34	" 20	Before English harbours there are in many cases steel wire nets, 8 metres under water, so that ships can pass above them. (sgd) C-in-C of H.S.Formations.	
35	" 21	In square 076 epsilon area 7, there may be mines. (where the American steamer was wrecked) (sgd) C-in-C H.S.Formations.	
36	" 21	Steamers declare they have passed mines E & W of N.Hinder Lightship, and 13 miles E. of Maas Lightship. (sgd) C-in-C H.S.Formations.	
37	" 21	Our own mines are laid from 51° 23' Lat.N. 3° 16' E. Long., to Lat.N. 51° 27' N. E.Long. 3° 18'. (sgd) C-in-C H.S.Formations.	
38	" 21	Steamers report continuous lines of mines, from Galloper Lighthouse to the coast. Our own mines in 51° 23' N. 3° 16 E., & 51° 27'N., 3° 18'E. (sgd) C-in-C H.S.Formations.	
39	" 21	Fourth Boat of 2nd S/m ½ Flot., (U.16) reports an extensive minefield on the position of the Ruytinger Lightship. Mines at low water on the surface, are 50 metres apart and less.	
40	" 21	On Feb.23rd, the English steamer Argo, from Rotterdam to Bristol. On Feb.24th, the English steamer Arabia leaves Liverpool.	
41	" 23	The restrictions ordered for the specially designated regions of the North Sea, are abolished. (sgd) O.C.S/ms.	
42	" 23	Reliable agent reports drifting mines off Sandettie Lightship, and between N.Hinder Lightship and Schouwen Lightship, some sixty mines. (sgd) C-in-C Formations.	
-	" 23	(Made "en clair" in German - a rough English translation was also made). - Notice. When approaching the German Bight, there is considerable danger unless Lister Tief is approached from west or north, from afar off. Long. 6° 30' E., should not in any circumstances be crossed South of the latitude of List on an easterly course.	
43	" 25	On Feb. 20th, 14 black mines with crooked arms, were sighted about 15 miles to the east of Nord Hinder Lightship.	
44	" 25	For U.34. - In the region bounded by the line - Faro Island - Lindesnäs Lighthouse, and the line - English coast on 55° Lat., as far as 0° Long., and from this point to Hanstholm Lighthouse - ships under neutral flags, are for the present under no circumstances to be attacked.	
45	" 25	(2214) (For) Norddeich: Please send the following message again:- Mines sighted (near) N.Hinder Lightship and between Maas Lightship and Schouwen Bank Lightship. (sgd) H.S.Formations.	

February 19, 1915: Spare American passenger liners *Philadelphia* and *West Haverford*.

20775/P1165 10m 9/19r 415! G & S 110

90

| Register No. | NORDDEICH to ALL SHIPS. | Minute Sheet No. 23 |

No.	Feb.	
46	" 25	According to reliable news; mines are at Sandettie Lightship, and Ruytingen Lightship, also on the line Galloper Lightship, North Hinder Lightship, Schouwen Bank Lightship, Maas Lightship, and east of Maas Lightship.
47	" 26	English ship MERCAVA or MANOVA (R), 8,000 to 10,000 tons, laden with Automobiles, passes the English Channel on 26th or 27th of Feb. Destination, London. Funnels painted black with 2 thin white rings. High upper works. (sgd) C-in-C High Sea Formations.
48	" 26	Great mine area in angular form W of N.Hinder Lightship. Apex - about the south point of Fairy Bank. From there the northern wing, in the direction N.W.½.N magnetic, the southern wing in the direction S.S.W. magnetic. Indicator of barrier is always a light buoy about ¼ of a mile E. of the apex, or the peace position of Ruytingen Lightship. The area is only to be traver--send in good weather and at low water.
49	" 26	Information from Paris states that the Compagnie du Nord, has resumed the interrupted Paris - London service via Boulogne and Calais. Evidently this is one to orders from above. (sgd) Formations. "CRUGSIDE"
50	" 26	On Feb. 20th, the English steamer Craigride left Las Palmas for London. (sgd) Formations.
51	" 27	The English Admiralty have from Feb.23rd, forbidden the northern entrance into the Irish Sea, for all lone ships, except by Channel, S.W. of Rathlin Is., by daylight. It is a forbidden area between :- . Lat. 55° 22' 5 W,Long. 6° 17'. " 55° 31' " " 6° 2' " 55° 10' 5 " " 5° 24" 5. " 55° 2 " " " 2° 40' 5. (sgd) C-in-C H.S.Formations
52	" 27	Press Telegram from Rotterdam :- The Swedish steamer SVARTON struck a mine on Feb.25th in Lat.54o 3' Long 5° 2' E.
53	" —	According to the observation of the 4th Boat of the 4th Submarine half Flotilla, the course of merchant ships, bound for the Irish Sea, is by Dubh- Artagh Lighthouse, and through Islay Sound, According to American (or another) source of information, English ships bound for Liverpool, only go through the North Channel by night, without lights. (sgd) O.C. S/Ms.
54	March 3	On 25th Feb., the English steamer "Thorpe Grange", left Las Palmas with horses for Havre, then to London under Italian flag. Funnel marks of the Navigazione Generale Italiana. On 26th Feb., the steamer Paul Woermann,left Las Palmas under English flag, and under the guidance of Naval Officers, for Liverpool.
55	" 3	The fast steamer Lusitania coming from New York, is expected in Liverpool on March 4th, or 5th.
56	" 3	1st. - During this week, 4 steamers arrive at London with horses. 2nd.- Several neutral steamers are are proceeding from Lisbon to Falmouth, because there is no mine- barrier there, (Falmouth). (Continued over.)

March 3, 1915: Arrival times of *Lusitania*.

90776/P1165 10m 9/19v 4151 G & S 110

91

| | Register No. | | NORDDEICH   to   ALL SHIPS. | Minute Sheet No. 24 |

No.	March		
56	"	3	(Continued).- 3rd. - From Southampton and Harwich every night troop transports, the steamers painted in grey or green. (sgd) C-in-C Formations.
59	"	6	Intercepted English Telegram : 3 mines, 10 miles true north of Hook of Holland, fairway-vessel buoy some 400 metres apart, in a triangle. In same bearing from the buoy, there is one more mine.
60	"	6	Le Havre harbour Lightship has been withdrawn. (sgd) C-in-C H.S.Formations. (continuation) On the South coast of England, numerous mine-layers are said to have been sighted.
61	"	6	English merchant shipping is directed round the north coast of Ireland until further notice.
62	"	8	The steamship Baltic of the White Star line, with 18.000 tons of war material for Liverpool, has left New York on March 3rd. Two steamers formerly Woermann Line and German-Australian steamship Company, are due to leave London on the 7th or 8th of March, with war material for France.
63	"	8	I herewith revoke the limitation as to neutrals, in the region from the Tyne to the Skagerak, for submarines.
64	"	8	Transport from Folkestone to Calais, commenced embarkation on March 7th.
65	"	9	On the 9th and 10th March, English grain ships, from South Atlantic Ocean, are to be expected, bound for London, Hull, Liverpool, Leith.
66	"	10	Large English S.S.Khuri and Omrah, leave London March 12th, for India. Fast steamer Lusitania leaves Liverpool, March 13.
67	"	11	Consul at Rotterdam reports : On evening of March 10th, Belgian steamers "Hainault"(?), "Prasident Bunge", "Leopold II", convoyed and under Dutch flag with over 1,000 Belgians bound for the English army, leave Hook of Holland. On Thursday they go on to Hull.
68	"	11	Canadian transports leave some harbour in S.E. of England for N.France, on the 13th.
69	"	11	On March 12th and 13th, several transports with provisions & munitions, leave Glasgow, probably for Gibraltar.
70	"	12	Area between 2o 30' E., 5° E., and 54° 30', 56° to be avoided as suspect of mines.
?71	"	13	Fast steamer Lusitania, leaves Liverpool March 13th.
71	"	14	For the transport of troops Southampton - Le Havre, former pleasure steamers are being used of 600 - 800 tons.
72	"	14	Same as 1115 of 13th, Antwerp to Bruges.
73	"	14	From the 16th traffic to Flushing will be resumed from Folkestone.

March 1915: Arrival and departure times of *Lusitania* and other passenger liners.

173] 20775/P1165 10m 9/19v 415: G & S 110

95

1915	Register No.	NORDDEICH to ALL SHIPS.	Minute Sheet No. 28

No.	April.		
26	" 12	For 1st Boat 5th Sub.½ (U.23).- Enemy forces in--cluding submarines near Terschelling Bank, on an E. course, have been seen. Keep your positions until dark on 15th.
27	" 12	English S.S. Zena with shells, leaves Gothenburg on evening of April 14th, at the latest.
29	" 16	10 destroyers near Schouwen Bank.
30	" 16	On 17th.April, S.S.LUSITANIA leaves Liverpool; on 24th S.S. TRANSYLVANIA, 15,000 tons, both for New York.
31	" 17	English W/T : Line of nets from Lizard L.V. to Black H. L.V., in Gerraus Bay, and S.W. of Trewavas (? Trevose) Head. Numerous English drifting mines.
32	" 18	For 1st Boat, 1st Sub.½ Fl. : On sighting our own aircraft, make recognition signals frequently. - Count on enemy submarines in German Bight.
33	" 21	English S.S. TRANSYLVANIA, 15,000 tons, leaves Liverpool on April 24th, for New York; about the same time, large English S.S. Orduna, arrives Liverpool.
34	" 27	English mines found N.W. of mouth of Ems in 81 epsilon.
35	" 27	Entrance to Ostend suspected of mines. Submarines if necessary to go to Zeebrugge.
36	" 27	For 4th Boat of 4th Sub.½ (U.30): S.S.ADRIATIC, 24,000 tons, arrives Liverpool, April 29th.
37) 38)	" 28	Following area dangerous for submarines: Area between 2 points, 30 miles S and E magnetic, Sector from Beachy Head Light buoy. Reliable news: - Folkestone barrier extends as far as Gris Nez. Barrier S. of Varna L.V. consists of mines. - Passage is said to be near coast.
39	" 29	Between Caloo and Deurlo Channel, off Westkapelle Lighthouse, new Dutch mine-field.
40	" 30	English warning to shipping S. of Goodwin L.V., moved 4 cables S.W. by W from it's old position.
41	" 30	Reliable. In Firth of Forth, on April 27th, 16 Dreadnoughts coaling.

April 1915: Arrival and departure times of *Lusitania* and other passenger liners.

Scns/9/18—[6393] 41211 P34 20m 1/19v 415: G & S 110

| 1915. | Register No. | NORDEICH N.I.C. | Minute Sheet No. | 96 |

1/5 NORDEICH to All Ships No.42, English W/T: A submarine
and a steamer are 20 miles S S W of Isle of Man.

2/5 NORDEICH to All Ships No.17. Following area to be avoided on account of danger from mines.
1st. Between 54°40' and 56°, 2°.30' E - 5° E.
2nd. Between 53°40', 2° E and 3°36' E.

3/5 NORDEICH to All Ships No.43.   Caution. Enemy submarine
in German Bight.

5/5 NORDEICH to All Ships No.44. Reliable: On May 4th
troop transports with troops on board leave Liverpool.

5/5 NORDEICH to All Ships No.45. An English cruiser is
doing patrol off entrance to Bukdem.

5/5 NORDEICH to All Ships No.46. Reliable: On May 3rd
there was a light cruiser in 75 Gamma area IV.
(ENEMY FORCES).

6/5 NORDEICH to All Ships No.47. On May 5th dreadnought
and light cruisers left Firth of Forth.

6/5 NORDEICH to All Ships No.48. S.S. LUSITANIA leaves
Liverpool for New York on May 15th. S.S. TUSCANIA leaves
Glasgow on May 7th for New York via Liverpool,
S.S. CAMERONIA 11,000 tons leaves on May 11th for
New York.   (SHIPPING I & III).

7/5 NORDEICH to All Ships No.50. Reliable: On May 5th
near North Hinder 2 cruisers with 3 funnels, 4 destroyers.   (ENEMY FORCES).

7/5 NORDEICH to All Ships No.49. Dutch Mine-field begins
Demloo Outer Buoy and lies in a S W direction.
(2). Mine-field between Nolleplaat and Ellsborg opposit
Swunenburg in W direction. Passage only between Green
Buoy at Torengroe.

7/5 NORDEICH to All Ships No.51. Following area to be avoid
ed at all cost on account of danger from mines. Between
54°40'.56° - 2°30' E 5° E.

8/5 NORDEICH to All Ships No.52. A Norwegian steamer near
Dover ran into a strong steel net slung by buoys over
part of the channel. She had to be towed off.
(ENEMY NET-BARRIER).

10/5 NORDEICH to All Ships No.53.   There are apparently
Mines and Net-Barriers between Lynus Point Lighthouse
and Isle of Man, also numerous armed trawlers there.
There is a constant torpedo boat patrol near New Brighto
near Liverpool.

10/5 NORDEICH to All Ships No.54. Reliable: On May 9th
8 or 9 ships of H S class (? aux. cruiser) 5 miles off
Schevenigen Lt. House, according to another report 7
English cruisers and torpedo boats are on N course there.
(ENEMY FORCES).

10/5 NORDEICH to All Ships No.55. 4th boat 4th U ½ Flot.
met in the channel E of Scilly Is. 2 striking looking
tankers, steering the same course in sight of each other,
under the lee of the second steamer was a torpedo boat.
Apparently this is a submarine trap.

May 1915: Arrival and departure times of *Lusitania* and other passenger liners.

4151 G.&S. 110

99

1915.	Register No.	NORDEICH. (cont).	Minute Sheet No.

11/5   NORDEICH to All Ships, No.56.   In the passage from
the Irish Sea to North Channel, there is probably a
Net-barrier in the latitude - Port Patrick, to bar the
way of submarines round Scotland.

11/5   NORDEICH to All Ships No.57.   New Mine-field is said
to lie off the Tyne between 55° - 1°6' W, 55°3.5 -1°7' W
54°50' - 0°19' W, 55°25.5' - 0°30' W. A kind of section
with broad side to the East.   (ENEMY MINES).

12/5   NORDEICH to All Ships No.58.   On May 15th S.S. CAMERONI
11,000 tons leaves Liverpool for New York.
(SHIPPING III).

13/5   NORDEICH to All Ships No.59.   Colliers and supply
vessels are going to Firth of Cromartie.

14/5   NORDEICH to All Ships No.60.   On May 10th in Firth of
Forth 1 Dreadnought, 3 older Battleships or Battle
Cruisers. On May 17th troop transports from Firth of
Forth to North and West.

15/5   NORDEICH to All Ships No 61, Reliable: Steamer near
S. Shields ran into a net.

15/5   NORDEICH to All Ships No. 62. Norwegian S.S. MARGIT
is said to be taking munitions from Newcastle to
Archangel.

16/5   NORDEICH to All Ships No. 63. S.S. CARMANIA leaves
Glasgow May 17th , S.S. TRANSYLVANIA leaves Liverpool
May 22nd, 2.30 p.m. ,S.S. MAURETANIA on May 29th.

16/5   NORDEICH to All Ships. No. 64. Probable: Ships of
Dreadnought class and light cruisers in Humber,
Little Minch and Firth of Lorn. Destroyers coal
in Morecambe Bay.

16/5   NORDEICH to All Ships. No. 65.   It has frequently
been reported of late that between Galloper L.V.
and Ruytingen L.V. or Sandettie L.V. a net barrier
has been, or is going to be, laid. Accuracy not yet
certain.

18/5   NORDEICH to All Ships No.66.   Square 112 Beta area VII
and vicinity suspected of Mines.

19/5   NORDEICH to All Ships No.67.   Reliable: On May 15th
18 warships coaling in Firth of Forth.

19/5   NORDEICH to All Ships No.68.   On May 16th between
Kentish Knock and Gallopen L.V. 2 trawlers, each with
about 60 mines on board, escorted by 2 trawlers with 2
funnels. Course S S E .

19/5   NORDEICH to All Ships No.69.   Between Christiania and
Hull regular weekly traffic by 3 Wilson line steamers
AARO, OSTO, ESKIMO. Mostly with cargo for Petrograd.

19/5   NORDEICH to All Ships No.70.   On evening of May 20th
a steamer with Belgians liable for military service
leaves Rotterdam for France.

20/5   NORDEICH to All Ships No.71.   On May 17th in Firth of
Forth 8 large cruisers and 14 destroyers.

May 1915: Arrival and departure times of *Lusitania* and other passenger liners.

[3898] 23200/h 50m 9/18 415: G & S 110

| 1915. | Register No. | NORDDEICH. (cont). | Minute Sheet No. | ·103 |

21/7 NORDDEICH to All Ships No.50. English S.S. ARABIA of P & O Line, 8000 tons, is sailing on 24th July from London for Asia.
SHIPPING III.

22/7 NORDDEICH to All Ships No.52. Swedish sailing vessel PALPNEER (sic) and Danish sailing ship PHILIPP were loading pit props on 20th July in Halmstadt for Granton near Edinburgh.

22/7 NORDDEICH to All Ships No.51. Reliable. Norwegian S.S. HEKLA with pine logs for Ireland was to sail from Copenhagen on the evening of 21st July. Carries the usual neutral marks.

22/7 Same as NORDDEICH to All Ships No.51 with additional details.

22/7 NORDDEICH to All Ships No.55. On 24th July following English steamers will leave Rotterdam: GRENADIER for Leith, KIRKHAM ABBEY for Hull, CITY OF DORTMUND for Belfast.
SHIPPING III.

23/7 NORDDEICH to All Ships No.56. Look out. An 800 ton steamer painted black and under the neutral flag fires, when approached, from two 10.2 quick firing guns. She was encountered on a course from Horns Riff to Fair Is.

24/7 NORDDEICH to All Ships No.57. On 21st July English S.S. CYMRIC, 13,200 tons, White Star Line left New York for Liverpool.
SHIPPING III.

25/7 NORDDEICH to All Ships No.59. Look out for S.S. MAY which sailed on 24th July from Gothenburg to Hull and Firth of Forth with contraband, further 4 steamers on 24th, 25th, 26th and 27th July.
SHIPPING III.

26/7 NORDDEICH to All Ships No.60. Beware! Enemy submarines off Horns Riff.

27/7 NORDDEICH TO All Ships No.61. Swedish S.S. PALLAST, Norwegian S.S. BRODE, S.S. NEDENAES and S.S. HALMSTADT are sailing with contraband from Gothenburg to Hull and the Firth of Forth on 25th, 26th and 27th July.
SHIPPING III.

27/7. NORDDEICH to All Ships No.62. In 74 Epsilon, 67 Epsilon VII a second mine-barrier has been located running approximately W by S.
ENEMY MINES.

27/7 NORDDEICH to All Ships No.63. Reliable. English s.s. CROMER sails from Rotterdam to Harwich on 27th July, S.S. ARGO to Bristol on 28th, S.S. ROTTERDAM to Leith on the 30th, S.S. KIRKHAM ABBEY to Hull on the 31st.
SHIPPING III.

27/7 NORDDEICH to All Ships No.65. Reliable. Danish S.S. KETSERINE DAGMAR which has been held up several times by our submarines is to be accompanied on her next voyage by an English warship, possibly a submarine.
SHIPPING III.

28/7 NORDDEICH to All Ships No.66. Norweigian steamers CORREKT, GRILLO, AIDELO, DASSIE, PROGRESS all of about 1500 to 1600 tons register are leaving Gothenburg for England with pit props to-morrow and in the next few days.
SHIPPING III.

August 1915: Arrival and departure times of passenger liners.

73] 20775/P1165 10m 9/19v 4151 G & S 110   *105*

Register No. 1915	NORDDEICH N.I.C.	Minute Sheet No.1.

KAV 74 — 1/8 — Norddeich to all ships: Reliable information. S.S. OLAF KYRRIE and ?ACHAESLAWD both of about 3,000 tons, leave Gothenburg for Hull and Hartlepool on August 3rd with a cargo of pit props.

KAV 75 — 1/8 — Reliable information: On July 31st 85? and on August 3rd, 4th, and 6th three other steamers leave Gothenburg for Hartlepool and Hull with contraband.

KAV 76 — 2/8 — In the next few days the following English steamers will probably arrive at Liverpool from New York; S.S. ARABIC 10,600 tons White Star Line. S.S. SAXONIA 10,400 tons.

KAV 77 — 3/8 — Beware of armed merchant cruiser with neutral markings; also of armed trawlers which are working with enemy submarines on the trade route between Lendeonds Lighthouse and the Firth of Forth.

KAV 78 — 3/8 — An E Class submarine (4 HI) has been seen between Haustholm Light and Homs Riff.

KAV 79 — 3/8 — Reliable information: Dutch steam dredger KAWI.II is shortly leaving Rotterdam for Dutch Indies. Description as follows:- 2 screws, 1 black funnel hull grey, name in white on both sides, painted with Dutch colours. She is to be permitted to pass.

KAV 80 — 4/8 — On July 26th the English S.S. ARDGAIR of 5000 tons with munitions will arrive at le Havre from New York about August 8th, also on July 27th the Russian steamer DWINSK 8,000 tons to Archangel.

KAV 81 — 4/8 — Seven Battleships and several Destroyers off Plymouth during the night of August 3rd-4th.

KAV 82 — 4/8 — The English North Sea Fishing Fleet is at present in 54° 23' N   3° 0' E.

KAV 83 — 4/8 — Six neutral steamers are leaving Gothenburg for England on August 4th and 5th with cargoes of timber-course via Skagen and Spurn Lighthouse.

1253 — 5/8 — C-in-C. informs HSF that in KAV 82 the position of English fishing fleet should read 54°25'N 3°30'E.

KAV 84 — 4/8 — Oiltank steamer DAMUBRYAN is proceeding from Dover to Texas through the Channel on August 5th.

August 1915: Arrival and departure times of passenger liners.

4151 G & S 110

156

| Register No. | NORDDEICH N.I.C. | Minute Sheet No. 2 |
| 1915 | | |

KAV
85   5/8   Reliable information. The number of English ships
             sailing under neutral flags includes all those
             between Hull and Rouen; also the steamers of
             8000 tons painted with Norwegian colours, TASKA
             of Bergen and BISTA of Bergen.

KAV
86   6/8   Communication from American Embassy: The
             American s.s.PHILADELPHIA, 11,000 tons, left New
             York on July 31st and will probably arrive in
             Liverpool on August 7th.

KAV
87   6/8   Very strong patrol to be expected off Fair Is.

KAV
88   6/8   English oil steamer DANOMA is due to arrive in
             the Thames on August 8th from the Mediterranean
             steaming 10½ knots, probably convoyed.

KAV
89   8/8   English S.S. IDAHO, Wilson Line left New York on
             31st July for Hull. S.S. ADRIATIC? White Star
             Line 24,000 tons left 4th August for Liverpool.

       8/8   Nordeich sends to Flag C-in-C. (Signature and
             calls missing) Southern minefield laid accord-
             ing to plan. Northern not possible because of
             patrol therefore sowed middle of Bay and
             steamer track favourably with mines.

KAV
91   9/8   Beware. All over the North Sea there are trawlers
             which tow nets or mines, and often work with a
             submerged s/m, also a number of small armed
             trawlers bulit like freight steamers. There are
             often enemy s/ms. in the neighbourhood of Homs
             Riff.

KAV
92   10/8   The English fishing fleet is at present in 54°
             25' N 3° 10' E.

KAV
93   11/8   Norwegian S S NORDPOL, left Malmö Sound for England
             probably Hartlepool on August 10th with a cargo of
             pit props.

KAV
94   11/8   Regular sailing of English steamers KIRKHAM ABBEY
             and JERVAULX ABBEY every Saturday and Tuesday between
             7 p.m. and midnight from Rotterdam to Hull. ditto
             SS MASCOTTE between 3 p.m. and midnight from
             Rotterdam to Leith. Return journey of the same
             steamers from Hull every Tuesday and Saturday at high
             water(night) from Leith ditto at high water (in the
             evening.)

KAV
95   12/8   Norwegian SS NIDELVENY left Copenhagen on August 10th
             with a cargo of butter casks staves and coal for
             Archangel.

August 1915: Arrival and departure times of passenger liners.

60m/9/18—[4603] 29334/P2365 60m 10/18 415: G & S 110

108

Register No.   NORDDEICH N.I.C.   Minute Sheet No. 4.
1915

KAV
10   21/8   Swedish diesel motor ship KRONPRINZESSIN MARGARETA
                with three masts,with Swedish signs on the ships side
                and captain's bridge, from Costa Rica to Christiania
                Gothenburg with a cargo of barley and coffee. Let
                her pass.

KAV
11   21/8   English steamer DEN OF OGIL,5700 tons, will arrive
                off Liverpool in the next few days from Dundee with
                heavy cargo of armour plates; also the steamer
                GRENOBLE from New Jersey with cargo unknown.

KAV
12   22/8   KAV to All Ships. Trustworthy: Eight (?battleships)
                or large cruisers in the Skagerak in the afternoon
                of August 21st.

KAV
13   22/8   KAV to All Ships. Beware ! Submarines off Horns Riff.

KAV
14   23/8   KAV to All Ships. English steamer ADRIATIC,24,000
                tons, sails on August 25th from Liverpool to New York
                Similarly CAMERONIA of 11,000 tons, on August 28th.
                On August 25th MAGDALENE,5,000 tons,to London and
                CORINTHIA, 7,000 tons to Canada.

KAV
15   24/8   KAV to All Ships. The provisions of the prize
                regulations No 8 as to treatment of mails are to be
                accurately observed.

0921   24/8   C-in-C. informs Norddeich N.I.C.: Transmit until
                further orders in the Great Programme: B% 2nd boat
                of 4th U ½ Fl.: Remember the limitations ordered by
                the All Highest.

KAV
16   24/8   KAV to All Ships: B% 2nd boat of 4th U.½ Fl.(?U.32)
                Remember the limitations ordered by the All Highest.

KAV
17   25/8   KAV to All ships. On August 27th sailing from Liverpool
                English steamer CITY OF LAHORE 17,000 tons for Asia
                On August 28th steamer DARRO,11,500 tons for Brazil;
                and CAMERONIA,11,500 tons, for New York.

KAV
18   26/8   KAV to All Ships. Swedish steamer GÖTEBORG leaves
                Gothenburg on August 27th or 28th for Hull. Cargo
                consists of iron,unfinished shells and machinery in
                cases.

No.
~~2350~~ ~~27/8~~ ~~Norddeich to Madrid.No 2350 of August 23rd. BARMOUTH~~
                ~~(?CASTLE) passed Eastwards and English armed steamer~~
                ~~flying naval flag. Returned from the Boat a floating~~
                ~~deck badly damaged.............British Warship 536~~
                ~~is completing repairs at Malta.(Original not kept)~~

KAV
19   26/8   KAV to all ships. Norwegian steamer SPICA with Norweg-
                ian Flag painted on her side and one funnel with white
                band and the letter A leaves Gravesens for Archangel
                with ammunition on the evening of August 27th or the
                morning of August 28th.

August 1915: Arrival and departure times of passenger liners.

50m/9/18—[4609] 29334/P2365 60m 10/18 4151 G & S 110

109

Register No.
1915

NORDDEICH N.I.C.

Minute Sheet No. 5.

KAV
20

26/8

KAV to All Ships. Two transports including LAKE
MICHIGAN leave Liverpool for Le Havre with 4,000 m
men on August 28th.

27/8

Norddeich to Madrid No.2350 of August 26th.Algéciras
August 23rd. BARMOUTH (?CASTLE) passed Eastwards and
English armed steamer flying naval flag. Returned
from the East a floatinf dock badly damaged........
British Warship 536 is completing repairs at Malta
(Original not kept)

KAV
22

28/8

KAV to All Ships. Danish steamer JOLANTGA laden with
iron and pitprops leaves Malmö Is. on the 28th or 29th
for England.

KAV
23

28/8

KAV to All Ships. Norwegian steamer Leander with a
cargo of 4000 tons of iron ore briquets for German
iron works sailed on 20th August from Kirkenaes
Varanger Fjord for Rotterdam.

KAV
24

29/8

KAV to all ships. Swedish steamer SYDLAND with cargo
of iron leaves Lutea for Rotterdam on 28th. Let her
pass.

29/8

Norddeich to Madrid.(1st group undecipherable.) U34
and U35 reached Cattaro on August 23rd.U39 left
Heligoland at noon on 27th August,U33 left Emden on
morning of August 28th,both bound for the Mediterranean. (Original not kept.)

KAV
25

30/8

KAV to All Ships. Norwegian steamers MUNCK,ANDAX,OLAF
and BLENDA left Gothenburg for England on 28th August
with pitprops.

KAV
26

30/8

KAV to All Ships. Swedish steamer SÜDLAND sailed on
28th from Lutea to Rotterdam, steamer NORDLAND on 29th
from Uarvik for Rotterdam.Cargo consists of ore. Let
them pass.

KAV
27

30/8

KAV to All Ships. Henceforth passenger steamers may
only be sunk after warning has been given and the
passengers and crew have been saved.

KAV
28

30/8

KAV to All Ships. Swedish steamer SKANDIA with iron
ore for Germany,left Lutea for Rotterdam on 27th.

August 30, 1916: Passenger steamers may only be sunk after warning has been given and the passengers and crew have been saved.

```
30m 9/13—[458] 2593/P563 20m 4/19c 4151 G&S 110
                                                                    10
```

1916.	Register No.	K B U.	Minute Sheet No.

26976 A Nº 21 1/10
KBU to ALL SHIPS: S.S.GRETCHEN MÜLLER, with cargo of value for Germany, left Aalesund for ? on Sept.27th. Protect the steamer as much as possible.

26998 A " 22. 1/10
KBU to ALL SHIPS: The English S.S. BRIERLEY, carrying contraband, left Gothenburg for Hull, on Sept.30th.

27209 A " 24 5/10
KBU to ALL SHIPS: Protection to be afforded, if possible, to the S.S. GRETCHEN MÜLLER, & BUSSARD, proceeding from Norway to Hamburg.

27240 A 1615 6/10
BRUGES to ALL SHIPS: Storm warning. Deep depression approaching from the Channel. Danger of storm shortly, with S.W. wind. Hoist signal for S.W. storm.

27241 A No.25. 6/10
KBU to ALL SHIPS: Norwegian S.S. RENEN, with cargo of pit props, will leave Gothenburg for England, on Oct.7th.

27242 A " 26 6/10
KBU to ALL SHIPS: Swedish S.S.AGNES, leaves Gothenburg for England, with cargo of pit props on Oct.6th. JANE & OTHALIA, with same cargo, on Oct.7th.

27254 A " 27 7/10
KBU to ALL SHIPS: The Norwegian S.S.LUPUS, leaves Rotterdam for Bergen on the evening of Oct.7th, with Russians on board.

27272 A " 28 7/10
KBU to All Ships: German S.S.VESTA, with valua--ble cargo for German authorities, left Bodo for Geestemunde, on Oct.4th. Steamer to be protected as far as possible.

27293 A " 29 8/10
KBU to ALL SHIPS : Look out for nets in 95 delta V, right lower.   (Net-barrier.)

27335 A " 30 9/10
KBU to ALL SHIPS : GLASENAPP has proceeded out.

27336 A " 31 9/10
KBU to ALL SHIPS : Norwegian S.S. CEDARBAN, with valuable cargo for the enemy, is on the way, probably to Archangel.

27338 A " 32 9/10
KBU to ALL SHIPS : For U.80: War against mer--chant ships, according to prize regulations, is left to your discretion. Spanish and American ships, are not to be sunk.   (Political)

27365 A " 33 10/10
KBU to ALL SHIPS : Norwegian S.S. RUDOLPH, chartered by the Wilson Line, will probably leave Christiania, with cargo of contraband for Hull, on the evening of Oct.11th, or morning of 12th.

27381 A " (?) 10/10
KBU to ALL SHIPS : Storm warning. Minimun (? barometer reading) 740. Danger in northern North Sea. Stormy S.W. winds.

Su-oppaite for 34

27406 A " 35 11/10
KBU to ALL SHIPS : Norwegian S.S. SANTIAGO, leaves Fredrikstrald, probably on the 12th or 13th Oct., with cargo of iron for England.

27429 A " 36 12/10
KBU to ALL SHIPS : Look out for S/m trap off the Scilly Islands.

October 10, 1916: American ships are not to be sunk.

4151 G & S 110

Register No.	K.B. U. (Cont.)	Minute Sheet No. 26

31/1	K.B.U. No: 30	S/Ms which left the Bight before 20th Jan, are to attack from 1st Feb: all armed merchant ships including armed passenger steamers without warning. For S/Ms which left the Bight subsequent to 20th Jan: the sealed orders which they took with them remain in full force.
31/1	K.B.U. No: 31	Danish S.S. George FORENEDE shipping Co., and S.S. HARRILDSBORG, Hansen shipping Co., are leaving Copenhagen for Newcastle and Leith respectively at 9 pm on 1st Feb: Cargo entirely of foodstuffs. Their capture is of urgent military importance.
1/2	K.B.U. No: 32	For the present Plymouth is the centre for the dispatch of troops. Three divisions are said to be waiting embarcation there. In Falmouth there are Greek Steamers, with war material for Salonica.
1/2	K.B.U. No: 33	On Feb 2nd or 3rd: two Steamers of the Old Dominion line are to leave Liverpool for Havre with war material: Steamers have 1 funnel and 4 masts, and are painted grey. Sailors from warships are on board.
3/2	K.B.U. No: 34	Tomorrow, Feb 4th, the English Steamers MALLARD, WOODCOCK and STARLING are to arrive at Rotterdam escorted by about 20 destroyers.
6/2	K.B.U. No: 36	A large number of French, Norwegian & Spanish ships are lying at Newcastle which brought ore, and will take coal back.
6/2	K.B.U. No: 37	Reliable information. Early on 6th Feb: the former British Minister at the Hague will leave Hook of Holland on a British Steamer.
6/2	K.B.U. No: 38	English S.S SERULA is probably leaving Rotterdam for England on 6th Feb:
6/2	K.B.U. No: 39	English Steamer, possibly the GLASGOW is to sail to-night with foodstuffs from Hook of Holland to LEITH.
7/2	K.B.U. No: 40	Norwegian S.S. GUS..... leaves Fredricks hold on 7th Feb: with iron for England. S.S. NYTAR & RENEN are ready to sail from Gothenburg with pit-props.
7/2	K.B.U. No: 41	English S.S. CROMER is probably leaving Hook of Holland with food for London to-night.

January 31, 1917, W/T instructions for All-Out-Uboat War: Attack all [also neutral] merchant ships.

Room 40: the deciphered Zimmermann–Telegram (TNA HW 7/8).

First Draft.

FROM:- Washington

TO:- Mexico   No. 3

The Foreign Office telegraphs on Jan. 16.

We intend to begin on the first of February unrestricted submarine warfare. We shall endeavour in spite of this to keep the U.S.A. neutral. In the event of this not succeeding we make Mexico a proposal of alliance on the following basis:-

MAKE WAR TOGETHER

MAKE PEACE TOGETHER

Generous financial support and an understanding on our part that Mexico is to reconquer the lost territory in Texas, New Mexico and Arizona. The settlement in detail is left to you. You will inform the President of the above most secretly, as soon as the outbreak of war with the U.S.A. is certain and add the suggestion that he should on his own initiative invite Japan to immediate adherence and at the same time mediate between Japan and ourselves.

Please call the President's attention to the fact that the ruthless employment of our submarines now offersthe prospect of compelling England in a few months to make peace.

Acknowledge receipt.

ZIMMERMANN.

Final Version.

Bibliography

Sources
TNA, The National Archives, Kew, London

ADM	1/8509/1	List of British vessels captured or destroyed by the enemy Aug 1914 - July 1917. Includes neutral vessels.
ADM	116/3421	History of the First World War: various aspects of the unrestricted submarine warfare campaign
ADM	137/3060	Interrogations of survivors of captured and sunk German submarines.
ADM	137/3897	German submarines UC 16 - UC 44: interrogation of survivors, translations of German officer's diary, and letters of prisoners of war.
ADM	137/3902	Papers concerning German submarines U 44 – U 59: activities and encounters, photographs and prisoner's statements.
ADM	137/3912	Original history sheets of U type German submarines, UA-U40.
ADM	137/3913	Original history sheets of U type German submarines: U41-U80.
ADM	137/4069	Intercepted German messages broadcast by W/T stations Nordeich, Nauen, Bruges, etc. relating to movements of British and Allied naval and merchant ships.
ADM	137/4151	U-boat history sheets compiled by Lt. Cdr. Tiarks in chartroom of Room 40. 1914-17. U-1 to U-80.
ADM	137/4152	U-boat history sheets compiled by Lt. Cdr. Tiarks in chartroom of Room 40. 1914-18. U-14 to U-23.
ADM	137/4153	U-boat history sheets compiled by Lt. Cdr. Tiarks in chartroom of Room 40. 1916.
ADM	137/4814	British vessels captured or destroyed by enemy causes.
ADM	137/4817	Foreign vessels sunk or damaged by enemy 1914-18.

| ADM | 186/603 | The Economic Blockade 1914–19. |
| ADM | 223/773 | Memo on 'Political' Branch of Room 40 by George Young |

| CAB | 23 | War Cabinet and Cabinet: Minutes |
| CAB | 24 | War Cabinet and Cabinet: Minutes |

HW	3/177	Nigel de Grey's account of how he worked on Zimmerman telegram in Room 40, Jan 1917 and then later decyphered it before Edward Bell of the US Embassy.
HW	7/1[1]	Contribution to the History of German Naval Warfare, 1914–18: volume one, The Fleet in Action, written by Birch and Clarke, chapters I –X.
HW	7/2	Contribution to the History of German Naval Warfare, 1914–18: chapters XI –XX.
HW	7/3	Contribution to the History of German Naval Warfare, 1914–18: volume two, The Fleet in Being.
HW	7/7	Room 40 German decrypts: diplomatic telegrams between Berlin and Mexico routed via Swedish diplomatic channels.

BA-MA, Bundesarchiv/Militärarchiv Freiburg

N	Nachlässe
Msg. 1	Militärgeschichtliche Sammlungen
RM 1	Kaiserliche Admiralität
RM 2	Kaiserliches Marinekabinett
RM 3	Reichsmarineamt
RM 5	Kaiserliches Oberkommando der Marine
RM 8	Kriegswissenschaftliche Abteilung der Marine
RM 47	Kommando der Hochseestreitkräfte
RM 86	Befehlshaber der Unterseeboote der Kaiserlichen Marine
RM 97	Unterseeboote der Kaiserlichen Marine

Guildhall Library, London

Lloyd's Shipping Index 1913.
Lloyd's List 1915 (of shipping, daily).
Lloyd's Daily Index 1915 (of ships, alphabetical).

NARA – United States National Archives

Uboat log books (KTB):

Uboat	Cruise(s)	NARA	BA-MA
U 20	1. Jan. - 17. March 1915	PG 61533	RM 97/577
	18. March - 31. Aug. 1915	PG 61534	RM 97/578
	29. Aug. 1915 - 15. Aug. 1916	PG 61535	RM 97/579
U 21	Feb. 1914 – Feb. 1915	PG 61537	RM 97/582
	5. Feb. - 3. March 1917	PG 61539	RM 97/591
U 24	1. Aug. 1914 - 31. Jan. 1915	PG 61548	RM 97/640
	12. March - 9. Apr. 1917	PG 61551	RM 97/643
U 27	31. July 1914 - 4. Aug. 1915	PG 61556	RM 97/680
U-35	26. July - 20. Aug. 1916	PG 61579	RM 97/766
U 69	4. Sep. - 15. Dec. 1915	PG 61642	RM 97/939
U 44	24. Feb. - 24. March 1917	PG 61596	RM 97/819
U-49	23.Oct. - 26. Nov. 1916	PG 61606	RM 97/828
U-50	27. Oct. - 23. Nov. 1916	PG 61607	RM 97/830
U-53	15. Sep. - 28. Oct. 1916	PG 61612	RM 97/855
U 70	29. Sep. 1915 - 31. Mai 1916	PG 61644	RM 97/942
UB 13	19. Nov. 1915 - 23. Apr. 1916	PG 61746	RM 97/1331
UB 18	12. Feb. 1916 - 9. Jan. 1917	PG 61758	RM 97/1373
UB 19	17. Dec. 1915 - 30. Nov. 1916	PG 61760	RM 97/1379
UB 29	18. Jan. - 27. Nov. 1916	PG 61776	RM 97/1453

Ubootarchiv Cuxhaven

Uboat log books (photographic copies from NARA).

Printed Sources

Der Hauptausschuss des Deutschen Reichstags 1915-1918. Eingeleitet von Reinhard
   Schiffers. Bearbeitet von Reinhard Schiffers und Manfred Koch in Verbindung
   mit Hans Bold. Volume I, 1915, Düsseldorf, 1981. Volume II, 1916, Düsseldorf,
   1981. Volume III, 1917, Düsseldorf, 1981. Volume IV, 1918, Düsseldorf, 1981.
Die Ursachen des Deutschen Zusammenbruches im Jahre 1918. Das Werk des
   Untersuchungsausschusses der Verfassungsgebenden Deutschen
   Nationalversammlung und des Deutschen Reichstages 1919-1928. Zweite
   Abteilung. *Der Innere Zusammenbruch.* Zehnter Band, Berlin, 1928.

Erdmann, K.D. (Hg.), *Kurt Riezler: Tagebücher, Aufsätze, Dokumente*, Göttingen, Vandenhoeck & Ruprecht, 1972.

Görlitz, Walter (Ed.), *Regierte der Kaiser? Kriegstagebücher, Auf- zeichnungen und Briefe des Chefs des Marine-Kabinetts Admiral Georg Alexander von Müller 1914-1918*, Göttingen, Musterschmidt-Verlag, 1959. *The Kaiser and his Court. The Diaries, Note Books and Letters of Admiral Georg Alexander von Müller, Chief of the Naval Cabinett 1914-1918*, London, Macdonald, 1961.

Granier, Gerhard, *Die deutsche Seekriegsleitung im Ersten Weltkrieg*, Volume 1, Bundesarchiv, Koblenz, 1999. Volume 2, Bundesarchiv, Koblenz, 2000. Volume 3, Bundesarchiv, Koblenz, 2000. Volume 4, Bundesarchiv, Koblenz, 2004.

Hill, Leonidas E., *Die Weizsäcker Papiere 1900-1932*, Berlin, Propyläen Verlag, 1982.

Koerver, Hans Joachim (Ed.), *Room 40. German Naval Warfare 1914-1918*. Vol. 1: *The Fleet in Action,* Steinbach, LIS Reinisch, 2008. Vol. 2: *The Fleet in Being,* Steinbach, LIS Reinisch, 2009. *German Submarine Warfare 1914-1918 in the Eyes of British Intelligence.* Steinbach, LIS Reinisch, 2010.

Schwertfeger, Bernhard, *Kaiser und Kabinettschef: Nach eigenen Aufzeichnungen und dem Briefwechsel des Wirklich Geheimen Rats Rudolf von Valentini*, Oldenburg, Gerhard Stalling, 1931.

Seymour, Charles, *The Intimate Papers Of Colonel House. Behind the Political Curtain 1912-1915*, Boston and New York, Houghton Mifflin Company, 1926. *From Neutrality To War 1915-1917*, Boston and New York, Houghton Mifflin Company, 1926.

Memoirs

Bethmann Hollweg, Theobald von, *Betrachtungen zum Weltkriege*. 2. Teil: *Während des Krieges*, Berlin, Reimar Hobbing, 1921.

Churchill, Winston S., *The World Crisis 1911-1918*, New York, London: F r e e Press, 1931.

Secondary Literature

Afflerbach, Holger, *Falkenhayn: Politisches Denken und Handeln im Kaiserreich*, 2nd edition, Munich, R. Oldenbourg Verlag, 1996.

Beesley, Patrick, *Room 40: British Naval Intelligence 1914-1918*, Oxford, Oxford University Press, 1984.

Bendert, Harald, *Die UB-Boote der Kaiserlichen Marine 1914-1918*, Hamburg, E.S. Mittler &Sohn, 2000. *Die UC-Boote der Kaiserlichen Marine 1914-1918*, Hamburg, E.S. Mittler &Sohn, 2001.

Berghahn, Volker R., *Der Tirpitz-Plan: Genesis und Verfall einer innenpolitischen Krisenstrategie unter Wilhelm II*. Düsseldorf, Droste Verlag, 1971.

Birnbaum, Karl E., *Peace Moves and U-Boat Warfare: A Study of Imperial Germany's Policy towards the United States April 18, 1916 – January 9, 1917,* Stockholm, Almquist & Wiksell, 1958.

Broadberry, Stephen, and Harrison, Mark, *The Economics of World War I,* Cambridge, Cambridge University Press, 2005.

Burhop, Carsten, *Wirtschaftsgeschichte des Kaiserreichs 1871-1918,* Göttingen, Vandenhoeck & Rupprecht, 2011.

Carlisle, Rodney, *U.S. Merchant Ships and American Entry into World War I,* Gainesville, University Press of Florida, 2009.

Clark, Christopher, *The Sleepwalkers: How Europe Went to War in 1914,* London and New York, Harper, 2013. *Wilhelm II: Die Herrschaft des letzten deutschen Kaisers,* Munich, Pantheon, 2009.

Cummins, Lyle, *Diesels for the First Stealth Weapon: Submarine Power 1902-1945,* Wilsonville, Carnot Press, 2007.

Deist, Wilhelm, *Militär, Staat und Gesellschaft: Studien zur preussisch- deutschen Militaergeschichte,* Munich, R. Oldenbourg Verlag, 1991. *Flottenpolitik und Propaganda: Das Nachrichtenbureau des Reichsmarineamtes 1897-1914,* Stuttgart, Deutsche Verlags-Anstalt, 1976.

Denholm, Decie, *Behind the lines: One Woman's War 1914-18,* London, Jill Norman & Hobhouse, 1982.

Doeneke, Justus D., *Nothing less than war: A new history of America's entry into World War I,* Lexington, The University Press of Kentucky, 2011.

Epkenhans, Michael, *Die wilhelminische Flottenrüstung 1908-1914: Weltmachtstreben, industrieller Fortschritt, soziale Integration,* Munich, R. Oldenbourg Verlag, 1991.

Fayle, Ernest C., *Seaborne Trade. Vol. III, The Period of Unrestricted Submarine Warfare,* London, Imperial War Museum, Department of Printed Books, 1924.

Fehr, Sandro, *Die Stickstoffrage in der deutschen Kriegswirtschaft des Ersten Weltkrieges und die Rolle der neutralen Schweiz,* Nordhausen, Verlag Traugott Bautz, 2009.

Feldmann, Gerald D., *Army, Industry and Labor in Germany 1914-1918,* Oxford, Berg Publishers, 1992.

Ferguson, Niall, *The Pity of War: Explaining World War I,* New York, Basic Books, 1999.

Fischer, Fritz, *Germany's Aims in the First World War,* New York, W.W. Norton, 1968.

Forstmeier, Friedrich, *Deutsche Grosskampfschiffe 1915-1918. Die Entwicklung der Typenfrage im Ersten Weltkrieg* Bonn, Bernard & Graefe, 2002.

Franken, Klaus, *Vizeadmiral Karl Galster: Ein Kritiker des Schlacht- flottenbaus der Kaiserlichen Marine,* Bochum, Dr. Dieter Winkler, 2011.

French, David, *British Strategy & War Aims 1914-1916,* London, New York, Routledge, 2014. *The Strategy of the Lloyd George Coalition 1916-1918,* Oxford, Clarendon Press, 2002.

Grigg, John, *Lloyd George: War Leader 1916-1918*, London, Penguin Books, 2002.

Gröner, Erich, *Die deutschen Kriegsschiffe 1815-1945*. Volume 1: *Panzerschiffe, Linienschiffe, Schlachtschiffe, Flugzeugträger, Kreuzer, Kanonenboote*, Bonn, Bernard & Graefe, 1985. Volume 2: *Torpedoboote, Zerstörer, Schnellboote, Minensuchboote, Minenräumboote*, Bonn, Bernard & Graefe, 1985. Volume 3: *U-Boote, Hilfskreuzer, Minenschiffe, Netzleger und Sperrbrecher*, Bonn, Bernard & Graefe, 1985.

Guichard, Louis, *The Naval Blockade 1914-1918*, New York, D. Appleton & Company, 1930.

Haffner, Sebastian, *The Ailing Empire: Germany from Bismarck to Hitler*, New York, Fromm International Publishing, 1987.

Halpern, Paul G., *A Naval History of World War I*, London and New York, Naval Institute Press, 1994.

Heitmann, Jan, *Unter Wasser in die Neue Welt. Handelsunterseeboote und kaiserliche Unterseekreuzer im Spannungsfeld von Politik und Kriegsführung*, Berlin, Berlin Verlag, 1996.

Herwig, Holger, *Das Elitekorps des Kaisers: Die Marineoffiziere im Wilhelminischen Deutschland*, Hamburg, Hans Christian Verlag, 1977.

Hobsbawm, Eric J., *The Age of Empire 1875-1914* London, Weidenfeld and Nicolson, 1987.

Hügel, Arnulf, *Kriegsernährungswirtschaft Deutschlands während des Ersten und Zeiten Weltkriegs im Vergleich*, Konstanz, Hartung-Gorre Verlag, 2003.

James, Harold, Krupp. *Deutsche Legende und globales Unternehmen*, Munich, C.H. Beck, 2011.

Jarausch, Konrad H., *The Enigmatic Chancellor: Bethmann Hollweg and the Hubris of Imperial Germany*, London, Yale University Press, 1973.

Johnston, Ian, and Buxton, Ian, *The Battleship Builders: Constructing and Arming British Capital Ships*, Barnsley, Seaforth Publishing, 2013.

Kelly, Patrick J., *Tirpitz and the Imperial German Navy*, Bloomington, Indiana University Press, 2011.

Kennedy, Paul, *Aufstieg und Fall der großen Mächte: Ökonomischer Wandel und militärischer Konflikt von 1500 bis 2000*, Frankfurt/Main, Fischer TaschenbuchVerlag, 1991.

Kitchen, Martin, *The German Officer Corps 1890-1914*, Oxford, Clarendon Press, 1968.

Kocka, Jürgen, *Industrial Culture and Bourgeois Society: Business, Labor, and Bureaucracy in Modern Germany*, Oxford, New York, Berghahn Books, 1999.

Lambert, Nicholas A., *Sir John Fisher's Naval Revolution*, Columbia, S.C., University of South Carolina Press, 1999. *Planning Armageddon: British Economic Warfare and the First World War*, London, Harvard University Press, 2012.

Leicht, Johannes, *Heinrich Claß 1868-1953: Die politische Biographie eines Alldeutschen*, Paderborn, Ferdinand Schöning, 2012.

Link, Arthur S., Wilson. *The Struggle for Neutrality 1914-1915,* Princeton, Princeton University Press, 1960. *Confusions and Crises 1915-1916,* Princeton, Princeton University Press, 1964. *Campaigns for Progressivism and Peace 1916-1917,* Princeton, Princeton University Press, 1965.

McKay, C.G., and Beckmann, Bengt, *Swedish Signal Intelligence 1900- 1945,* London, Frank Cass, 2003.

Michelsen, Andreas, *Der U-Bootskrieg 1914-1918,* Leipzig, von Hase und Koehler Verlag, 1925.

Mombauer, Anika, *Helmuth von Moltke and the Origins of the First World War,* Cambridge, Cambridge University Press, 2001.

Mommsen, Wolfgang J., *Imperial Germany 1867-1918: Politics, Culture, and Society in an Authoritarian State,* New York, Hodder Arnold Publication, Bloomsbury Academic, 2009.

Nebelin, Manfred, *Ludendorff: Diktator in Ersten Weltkrieg,* Munich, Siedler Verlag, 2010.

Nonn, Christoph: *Bismarck. Ein Preusse und sein Jahrhundert,* München, C.H. Beck, 2015.

Offer, Avner, *The First World War: An Agrarian Interpretation,* Oxford, Oxford University Press, 1989.

Pflanze, Otto, *Bismarck and the Development of Germany,* Princeton, Princeton University Press, 1990. *Der Reichsgründer,* Munich, C.H. Beck, 1997. *Der Reichskanzler,* Munich, C.H. Beck, 1998.

Pytha, Wolfram, *Hindenburg: Herrscher zwischen Hohenzollern und Hitler,* Munich, Siedler Verlag, 2007.

Randel, Jonathan Clay, *Information for economic warfare: British intelligence and the blockade, 1914-1918,* Diss, Chapel Hill 1993.

Ritschl, Albrecht, *The pity of peace: Germany's economy at war 1914-1918, and after,* published in: Broadberry, Stepen, and Harrison, Mark, *The Economics of World War I,* Cambridge, Cambridge University Press, 2005.

Röhl, John C.G., *The Kaiser and his Court: Wilhelm II and the Government of Germany,* Cambridge, Cambridge University Press, 1995. *Wilhelm II: Into the Abyss of War and Exile, 1900-1941,* Cambridge, Cambridge University Press, 2014.

Rössler, Eberhard, *Geschichte des deutschen U-Bootbaus.* Vol. 1: *Entwicklung, Bau und Eigenschaften der deutschen U-Boote von den Anfängen bis 1943,* Bonn, Bernard & Graefe, 1996. *Deutsche U-Kreuzer und Transport-U-Boote,* Bonn, Bernard & Graefe, 2003. *Die Torpedos der deutschen Uboote. Entwicklung, Herstellung und Eigenschaften der deutschen Marine-Torpedos,* Herford, Koehler, 1984.

Salter, J.A., *Allied Shipping Control: An Experiment in International Administration,* London, Clarendon Press, 1921.

Scheck, Raffael, *Alfred von Tirpitz and German Right-Wing Politics, 1914-1930,* Boston, Humanities Press, 1998.

Seligmann, Mathew S., Nägler, Frank, Epkenhans, Michael (Eds.), *The Naval Route to the Abyss: The Anglo-German Race 1895-1914*, Farnham, The Navy Records Society, 2015.

Schröder, Joachim, *Die Uboote des Kaisers: Die Geschichte des deutschen U-Boot-Krieges gegen Großbritannien im Ersten Weltkrieg*, Bonn, Bernard & Graefe, 2003.

Spindler, Arno, *Der Handelskrieg mit U-Booten*. 5 Vols. First Volume, Berlin, E.S. Mittler & Sohn, 1932. Second Volume, Berlin, E.S. Mittler & Sohn, 1933. Third Volume, Berlin, E.S. Mittler & Sohn, 1934. Fourth Volume, Hamburg, E.S. Mittler & Sohn, 1964. Fifth Volume, Frankfurt/Main, E.S. Mittler & Sohn, 1966. *Wie es zu dem Entschluß zum uneingeschränkten U-Boots-Krieg 1917 gekommen ist*, Göttingen, Musterschmidt Verlag, 1956.

Standage, Tom, *Das Viktorianische Internet: Die erstaunliche Geschichte des Telegraphen und der Online-Pioniere des 19. Jahrhunderts*, St. Gallen, Midas Management Verlag, 1998.

Stegemann, Bernd, *Der U-Bootkrieg im Jahre 1918*. In: *Marine- Rundschau* 65, Vol. 5, October 1968, pp. 333-45. *Die Deutsche Marinepolitik 1916-1918*, Berlin, Duncker & Humblot, 1970.

Still, William N. Jr., *Crisis at Sea: The United States Navy in European Waters in World War I*, Gainesville, FL, University Press of Florida, 2006.

Techel, H., *Der Bau von Unterseebooten auf der Germaniawerft*, Berlin, J.H. Lehmans Verlag, 1922.

Thompson, Wayne C., *In the Eye of the Storm: Kurt Riezler und the Crises of modern Germany*, Iowa, University of Iowa Press, 1980.

Tooze, Adam, *The Deluge. The Great War and the Remaking of Global Order, 1916-1931*, London, Penguin, 2015.

Valentiner, Max, *U38: Wikingerfahrten eines deutschen Ubootes*, Berlin, Ullstein, 1934.

Wehler, Hans-Ulrich, *The German Empire, 1871-1918*, New York and London, Bloomsbury Academic, 1997.

Weir, Gary E., *Building the Kaiser's Navy: The Imperial Navy Office and German Industry in the von Tirpitz Era 1890-1919*, Annapolis, Naval Institute Press, 1992.

Zuber, Terence, *The Real German War Plan 1904-1914*, Stroud, The History Press, 2011.

Journals

Cryptologia, Oct. 2000.

Frankfurter Allgemeine Zeitung (FAZ), May 7t, 2015

Marine-Rundschau 65, Vol. 5, October 1968.

Nauticus, Jahrbuch für Deutschlands Seeinteressen 1914, Berlin 1914.

Endnotes

Pre-War
Chapter 1: World Economy

1. Paul Kennedy, *Aufstieg und Fall der großen Mächte: Ökonomischer Wandel und militärischer Konflikt von 1500 bis 2000* (Frankfurt/Main: Fischer Taschenbuch Verlag, 1991), p. 370; *Nauticus, Zeitschrift für Deutschlands Seeinteressen*, 1914, p. 704-11, exports and imports for 1912/13, population in millions.
2. Nicholas A. Lambert, *Sir John Fisher's Revolution* (Columbia, S.C.: University of South Carolina Press, 1999), p. 88.
3. J. A. Salter, *Allied Shipping Control: An Experiment in International Administration* (London: Clarendon Press, 1921), p. 102.
4. Kennedy, *Aufstieg and Fall*, p. 310.
5. *Nauticus*, 1914, p. 712ff.
6. Lloyd's Shipping Index, 1913. Excluding Russia (0.8 Mio. GRT) and excluding American shipping on the Great Lakes (2.3 Mio. GRT).
7. *Nauticus*, 1914, p. 695, 712ff.
8. *Nauticus*, 1914, p. 695, 712ff.
9. *Nauticus*, 1914, p. 695.
10. Jonathan Clay Randel, *Information for economic warfare: British intelligence and the blockade, 1914-1918* (Diss.: Chapel Hill 1993), p. 149.
11. Tom Standage, *Das Viktorianische Internet: Die erstaunliche Geschichte des Telegraphen und der Online-Pioniere des 19. Jahrhunderts* (St. Gallen: Midas Management Verlag, 1998), p. 82 ff., 113ff., 120ff.
12. Nicholas A. Lambert, *Planning Armageddon: British Economic Warfare and the First World War* (London: Harvard University Press, 2012), p. 111f.
13. Lambert, *Armageddon*, p. 270ff.

Chapter 2: Anglo-German Naval Arms Race

1. Volker R. Berghahn, *Der Tirpitz-Plan: Genesis und Verfall einer innenpolitischen Krisenstrategie unter Wilhelm II.* (Düsseldorf: Droste Verlag, 1971).
   Mathew S. Seligmann, Frank Nägler, Michael Epkenhans (Eds.), *The Naval Route to the Abyss: The Anglo-German Race 1895-1914* (Farnham: The Navy Records Society, 2015).
2. John C.G. Röhl, *Wilhelm II.: Der Weg in den Abgrund 1900-1941* (Munich: C.H. Beck, 2008).
3. Author's calculation based on Erich Gröner, *Die deutschen Kriegsschiffe 1815-1945*.
4. Winston S. Churchill, *The World Crisis 1911-1918* (London: Free Press, 1931), p. 23.

5. Ibid., p. 61.

6. *Nauticus*, 1914, p. 712ff.

7. Klaus Franken, *Vizeadmiral Karl Galster: Ein Kritiker des Schlachtflottenbaus der Kaiserlichen Marine* (Bochum: Dr. Dieter Winkler, 2011).

8. Lambert, *Fisher's Revolution*.

9. Wilhelm Deist, *Flottenpolitik und Propaganda: Das Nachrichtenbureau des Reichsmarineamtes 1897-1914* (Stuttgart: Deutsche Verlags-Anstalt, 1976).

10. Wayne C. Thompson, *In the Eye of the Storm: Kurt Riezler und the Crises of modern Germany* (Iowa: University of Iowa Press, 1980).

11. Karl Dietrich Erdmann (Ed.), *Kurt Riezler, Tagebücher, Aufsätze, Dokumente* (Göttingen: Vandenhoeck & Ruprecht, 1972), July 20th, 1914, p. 188.

12. Erdmann, *Riezler diaries*, July 20th, 1914, p. 187-8.

13. Lambert, *Armageddon*, p. 89 and 91.

14. Ibid., p. 65.

15. Ibid., p. 71, 73, 77.

16. Ibid., p. 80.

17. Ibid., p. 116ff.

18. Spindler, *Handelskrieg*, Vol. I, p. 155.

19. Ibid., p. 99.

20. Lambert, *Fisher's Revolution*, p. 281.

21. Arno Spindler: *Der Handelskrieg mit U-Booten*. 5 Vols., Vol. I, p. 153f.

22. Image courtesy of the Department of History, U.S. Military Academy, West Point, New York.

23. Raffael Scheck, *Alfred von Tirpitz and German Right-Wing Politics, 1914-1930* (Boston: Humanities Press, 1998), p. 23.

24. Erdmann, *Riezler diaries*, May 25th, 1915, p. 274.

25. Terence Zuber, *The Real German War Plan 1904-1914* (Stroud: The History Press, 2011).
Anika Mombauer, *Helmuth von Moltke and the Origins of the First World War* (Cambridge: Cambridge University Press, 2001).

26. Charles Seymour, *The Intimate Papers Of Colonel House.. Behind The Political Curtain 1912-1915*, (Boston and New York: Houghton Mifflin Company, 1926), p. 114.

27. Ibid., p. 250.

28. Ibid., p. 255ff.

29. Ibid., p. 249.

30. Ibid.

31. Ibid., p. 260f.

August 1914 – Meltdown
Chapter 3: Great Britain

1. Lambert, *Armageddon*, p. 185-205.

2. Ibid., p. 193.

3. Ibid., p. 199.
4. Ibid.
5. William N. Still Jr., *Crisis at Sea: The United States Navy in European Waters in World War I* (Gainesville, FL: University Press of Florida, 2006), p. 77.
6. Lambert, *Armageddon*, p. 204.
7. TNA, ADM 186/603, p. 6, footnote 6.
8. Lambert, *Armageddon*, p. 216-31.

Chapter 4: Imperial Germany
1. Author's calculation based on Gröner, *Kriegsschiffe*.
2. BA MA, RM 2/1957, sheet 52-53, Admiral Pohl August 2nd, 1918 to Emperor Wilhelm [Granier, Vol. I, No. 6, p. 61].
3. Röhl, *Wilhelm 1900-1941*, p. 1158ff.
4. Erdmann, *Riezler diaries*, November 22nd, 1914, p. 228.
5. Christopher Clark, *Wilhelm II: Die Herrschaft des letzten deutschen Kaisers* (Munich: Pantheon, 2009), p. 291.
6. Granier, Vol. I, p. 21.
7. Clark, *Wilhelm*, p. 290.
8. Granier, Vol. I, p. 22.
9. Ibid., p. 13.
10. Ibid., p. 181, footnote 1.
11. Ibid.
12. Patrick J. Kelly, *Tirpitz and the Imperial German Navy* (Bloomington: Indiana University Press, 2011), p. 378.
13. Granier, Vol. I, p. 13ff.
14. BA MA, RM 47/1, sheet 6, Pohl to Ingenohl, June 30th, 1914 [Granier, Vol. I, No. 8, p. 67].
15. Erdmann, *Riezler diaries*, August 22nd, 1914, p. 201.
16. BA-MA, RM 2/1124, sheet 31, Pohl August 2nd, 1914.
17. BA-MA, RM 2/1957, sheet 65, Pohl August 3rd, 1914.
18. BA-MA, RM 2/1957, sheet 47, Pohl August 2nd, 1914, to Baltic command [Granier, Vol. I, No. 4, p. 59.
19. Walter Görlitz (Ed.), *Regierte der Kaiser? Kriegstagebücher, Aufzeichnungen und Briefe des Chefs des Marine-Kabinetts Admiral Georg Alexander von Müller 1914-1918* (Göttingen: Musterschmidt, 1959), August 11th, 1914, p. 46.
20. Lambert, *Armageddon*, p. 212.
21. Erdmann, *Riezler diaries*, August 22nd, 1914, p. 203.
22. Ibid., September 13th, 1914, p. 207.
23. Ibid., October 11th, 1914, p. 216.
24. Görlitz, *Müller diaries*, September 12th and 13th, 1914, p. 57.
25. Erdmann, *Riezler diaries*, May 25th, 1915, p. 275.

26. Ibid., February 20th, 1915, p. 251.
27. Ibid., October 1st, 1914, p. 211.
28. Ibid., October 6th, 1914, p. 212-13.
29. Scheck, *Tirpitz*, p. 24., Kelly, *Tirpitz*, p. 380.
30. Scheck, *Tirpitz*, p. 24.
31. Görlitz, *Müller diaries*, September 23rd, 1914, p. 61.

Chapter 5: Communication .

1. C.G. McKay and Bengt Beckmann, *Swedish Signal Intelligence 1900-1945* (London, Frank Cass, 2003); Randel, *Economic Intelligence*, p. 158ff.; Link, *Wilson 1915-1916*, p. 187, footnote.
2. Thomas R. Hammant, *Russian and Soviet cryptology – the Magdeburg incident: The Russian view*. Cryptologia, Oct. 2000.
3. Randel, *Economic Intelligence*, p. 132ff., 139ff., 146ff.
4. TNA, ADM 116/3421, p. 298.
5. TNA, ADM 116/3421, p. 297- 8.
6. Paul G. Halpern, *A Naval History of World War I*, (London and New York: Naval Institute Press, 1994), p. 367.
7. TNA, HW 7/3 [Koerver, Room 40, Vol. I, p. 285.]

Chapter 6: Neutral Countries.

1. Lambert, *Armageddon*, p. 272-8.
2. Ibid., p. 410 and 475.
3. Ibid., p. 423.
4. Arthur S. Link: *Wilson, The Struggle for Neutrality 1914-1915* (Princeton: Princeton University Press, 1960), p. 76-8.
5. Ibid., p. 14-15, 81ff.
6. Ibid., p. 14-15.
7. Seymour, House Papers 1912-1915, p. 303f.
8. Ibid., p. 251ff.
9. Link, *Wilson 1914-15*, p. 131.
10. Seymour, House Papers 1912-1915, p. 337.
11. Ibid., p. 105.
12. Lambert, *Armageddon*, p. 374.
13. Link, *Wilson 1914-15*, p. 56.
14. Ibid., p. 136.
15. Ibid., p. 133, 136.
16. Lambert, *Armageddon*, p. 423.
17. Link, *Wilson 1914-15*, p. 14-15, p. 53ff.
18. Ibid., p. 63.
19. Adam Tooze, *The Deluge*, 2015, p.15f.

20. Charles Seymour, *The Intimate Papers Of Colonel House. From Neutrality To War 1915-1917*, (Boston and New York: Houghton Mifflin Company, 1926), p. 52.

21. Seymour, House Papers 1912-1915, p. 355.

22. Ibid.

Chapter 7: British Blockade and German Uboats

1. Ibid., p. 236.

2. Louis Guichard, *The Naval Blockade 1914-1918* (New York: D. Appleton & Company, 1930), p. XV.

3. As quoted in Lambert, *Armageddon*, p. 322.

4. TNA, ADM 186/603, p. 7.

5. Ibid.

6. TNA, ADM 186/603, p. 5ff.

7. Lambert, *Armageddon*, p. 297ff.

8. Ibid., p. 342.

9. Ibid., p. 355.

10. Ibid., p. 272-78, 353ff., 360.

11. As quoted in Lambert, *Armageddon*, p. 358.

12. Lambert, *Armageddon*, p. 333ff.

13. Ibid., p. 335.

14. Ibid., p. 333ff.

15. BA-MA, RM 2/1124, sheet 154, Ingenohl August 30th, 1914 [Granier, Vol. I, No. 42, p. 147].

16. Author's calculation based on Gröner, *Kriegsschiffe*.

17. BA-MA, RM 8/522, Bl. 64-71, Ingenohl to Pohl 8. November 1914 [Granier, Bd. I, Nr. 297, S. 38f.].

18. BA-MA, RM 8/522, sheet 98, Pohl to Ingenohl November 10th, 1914 [Granier, Vol. III, No. 298, p. 42f.].

19. BA-MA, RM 8/523, sheet 125-127, Admiral's staff to Ingenohl January 26th, 1915 [Granier, Vol. III, No. 309, p. 63f.].

20. BA-MA, RM 1/1981, sheet 154, Tirpitz-Interview December 21st, 1914 [Granier, Vol. III, No. 301, p. 50ff.].

21. Görlitz, *Müller diaries*, December 22nd, 1914, p. 76.

22. BA-MA, RM 5/2972, sheet 148, Pohl December 26th, 1914 [Granier, Vol. III, No. 302, p. 53, footnote 2].

23. BA-MA, RM 3/2620, sheet 39, Kriegstagebuch Tirpitz [Granier, Vol. III, No. 302, p. 53].

24. Erdmann, *Riezler diaries*, December 23rd, 1914, p. 235-6.

25. Scheck, *Tirpitz*, p. 26f.

26. Theobald von Bethmann Hollweg, *Betrachtungen zum Weltkriege: Während des Krieges* (Berlin: Reimar Hobbing, 1921), p. 121.

1915 – Trial and Error
Chapter 8: Step by Step to the Uboat War

1. BA-MA, RM 8/522, sheet 202, Pohl to Ingenohl December 19th, 1914 [Granier, Vol. III, No. 300, p. 47, footnote 3].
2. Görlitz, *Müller diaries*, January 9th, 1915, p. 80.
3. BA-MA, RM 8/522, sheet 202, Pohl to Ingenohl December 19th, 1914 [Granier, Vol. III, No. 300, p. 47, footnote 3].
4. BA-MA, RM 8/523, sheet 75, Pohl to Ingenohl January 11th, 1915 [Granier, Vol. I, No. 75, p. 204].
5. Görlitz, *Müller diaries*, January 27th, 1915, p. 84f.
6. Erdmann, *Riezler diaries*, January 17th, 1915, p. 242.
7. BA-MA, RM 8/523, sheets 109-10, Ingenohl to Pohl and Müller [Granier, Vol. III, No. 307, p. 60f., see also footnote 9 on page 61].
8. Hans Joachim Koerver (Ed.), *Room 40: German Naval Warfare 1914-1918*, Vol. 2: *The Fleet in Being* (Steinbach: LIS Reinisch, 2009), p. 110.
9. BA-MA, RM 97/582, KTB U-21.
10. Koerver, *Room 40*, Vol. II, p. 112.
11. BA-MA, RM 5/2872, sheet 286, Pohl to Ingenohl January 26th, 1915 [Granier, Vol. III, No. 308, p. 62].
12. TNA, HW 7/1, p. 143 [Koerver, *Room 40*, Vol. I, p. 72]. See also BA-MA RM 8/523, sheets 77-110 [Granier, Vol. III, No. 303, 305, 307], where the 'war zone' declaration is discussed. Spindler doesn't mention the 'war zone' declaration.
13. BA MA, RM 97/577, sheets 13-14.
14. BA-MA, RM 97/577, sheet 8.
15. TNA, HW 7/1, p. 120f. [Koerver, *Room 40*, Vol. I, p. 60].
16. Spindler, *Handelskrieg*, Vol. I, p. 64.
17. BA-MA, RM 8/527, sheet 21 [Granier, Vol. III, p. 35, footnote 19].
18. BA-MA, RM 2/1990, sheets 182-6, Müller March 8th, 1915 [Granier, Vol. III, No. 323, p. 88f].
19. Görlitz, *Müller diaries*, February 18th, 1915, p. 91.
20. BA-MA, RM 5/2973, sheet 39, Pohl February 4th, 1915 [Granier, Vol. III, No. 312, p. 68f.].
21. Lambert, *Armageddon*, p. 361ff.
22. Link, *Wilson 1914-15*, p. 335.
23. Ibid., p. 323f.
24. Erdmann, *Riezler diaries*, February 27th, 1915, p. 252-3.
25. Görlitz, *Müller diaries*, February 15th, 1915, p. 90.
26. TNA, ADM 137/4069, p. 88, No. 29 and 30.
27. BA-MA, RM 86/223, sheets 318-20, February 13th, 1915.
28. BA-MA, RM 86/223, sheet 99, telegram February 22nd, 1915, 11:45 p.m.
29. Görlitz, *Müller diaries*, February 17th, 1915, p. 90-1.

30. BA-MA, RM 5/2975, sheets 46-7, Bachmann to High Seas Fleet February 17th, 1915 [Granier, Vol. III, No. 318, p. 80].
31. BA-MA, RM 5/2974, sheets 385-8, Bachmann to Pohl February 12th, 1915 [Granier, Vol. III, No. 314, p. 74], see also RM 86/223, sheet 317, Bachmann to Pohl February 13th, 1915.
32. Seymour, House Papers 1912-1915, p. 370.
33. Link, *Wilson 1914-15*, p. 325ff.
34. Ibid., p. 332f.
35. Görlitz, *Müller diaries*, February 28th, 1915, p. 93.

Chapter 9: First Submarine War

1. TNA, ADM 137/4069, p. 88, No. 33.
2. TNA, ADM 137/4069, p. 89, No. 40.
3. BA-MA, RM 97/680, sheets 94-104.
4. TNA, ADM 137/3912, p. 48, U 27, February 23th, 1915.
5. TNA, ADM 137/4151, U 20, U 27.
6. TNA, ADM 137/4069, p. 90, No. 51 and 53, February 27th, 1915.
7. BA-MA, RM 97/680, KTB U 27, p. 94ff. See also BA-MA, RM 5/4821, p. 187-8. Spindler, *Handelskrieg*, Vol. II, p. 32, describes this as follows: 'From the 1st until the night of the 4th, in waiting position outside the North Channel to watch the traffic going into the Irish Sea.'
8. Patrick Beesley: *Room 40, British Naval Intelligence 1914-1918*, (Oxford: Oxford University Press, 1984), p. 95.
9. TNA, ADM 137/4069, p. 91 No. 62, March 8th, 1915.
10. BA-MA, RM 97/577, p. 42.
11. BA-MA, RM 97/577, p. 43. Spindler, *Handelskrieg*, Vol. II, p. 32, doesn't mention this passenger liner.
12. TNA, ADM 137/4069, p. 91 No. 66, March 10th, 1915
13. TNA, ADM 137/1059, p. 82f. [Koerver, *Submarine Warfare*, p. 252.]
14. TNA, ADM 137/4069, p. 91 No. 71, March 13th, 1915.
15. BA-MA, RM 86/224, Naval Staff to High Seas Fleet March 28th, 1915, p. 54; the same in RM 8/528, sheet 129 [Granier, Vol. III, No. 326, p. 96].
16. BA-MA, RM 97/683, p. 87f.
17. Link, *Wilson 1914-15*, p. 358ff.
18. Eberhard Rössler, *Die Torpedos der deutschen Uboote: Entwicklung, Herstellung und Eigenschaften der deutschen Marine-Torpedos* (Herford: Koehler, 1984).

Chapter 10: British Blockade in Spring

1. Quoted in Lambert, *Armageddon*, p. 369.
2. Lambert, *Armageddon*, p. 369.
3. TNA, ADM 186/603, p. 8.

4. Ibid.

5. Ibid.

6. Link, *Wilson 1914-15*, p. 343-8.

7. Ibid., p. 348.

8. Lambert, *Armageddon*, p. 394.

9. Ibid., p. 398.

Chapter 11: Kaiser, Reich and Tirpitz

1. Erdmann, *Riezler diaries*, February 17th, 1915, p. 250.

2. Erdmann, *Riezler diaries*, October 22nd, 1914, p. 219.

3. Konrad H. Jarausch, *The Enigmatic Chancellor: Bethmann Hollweg and the Hubris of Imperial Germany* (London: Yale University Press, 1973).

4. Details in Johannes Leicht, *Heinrich Claß 1868-1953: Die politische Biographie eines Alldeutschen* (Paderborn: Ferdinand Schöning, 2012).

5. Erdmann, *Riezler diaries*, July 23rd, 1914, p. 190.

6. Details in Otto Pflanze, *Bismarck: Der Reichsgründer* (Munich: C.H. Beck, 1997), and *Bismarck: Der Reichskanzler* (Munich: C.H. Beck, 1998).

7. Scheck, *Tirpitz*, p. 36.

8. Erdmann, *Riezler diaries*, March 20th, 1915, p. 261.

9. Kelly, *Tirpitz*, p. 396.

10. Ex-chancellor von Bülow mentioned this in his scandalous post-war autobiography, *Denkwürdigkeiten*, a dozen times.

11. Scheck, *Tirpitz*, p. 37.

12. Görlitz, *Müller diaries*, April 18th, 1915, p. 97.

13. TNA, ADM 137/4069, p. 95, Nos. 30, 33, 36.

Chapter 12: Lusitania

1. TNA, ADM 137/4151, U 22, U 34, U 32.

2. BA-MA, RM 97/702, p. 3ff.

3. TNA, ADM 137/4151, U 30.

4. BA-MA, RM 97/578.

5. TNA, ADM 137/4069, p. 95, No. 30, April 16th, 1915.

6. TNA, ADM 137/4069, p. 95, No. 36, April 27th, 1915.

7. TNA, ADM 137/4152, U 20, minute sheet No. 4.

8. BA-MA, RM 97/578, p. 6.

9. TNA, ADM 137/4152, U 20, minute sheet No. 4.

10. BA-MA, RM 97/578, p. 8.

11. TNA, ADM 137/4152, U 20, minute sheet No. 4.

12. TNA, ADM 137/4069, p. 96, 6/5 1915.

13. Beesley, *Room 40*, p. 103.

14. TNA, ADM 137/4069, p. 96, Norddeich to all Ships No. 96, 6/5 1915.

15. Beesley, *Room 40*, p. 108.
16. BA-MA, RM 97/578, p. 11f.
17. TNA, ADM 137/4152, U 20, minute sheet No. 5.
18. Ibid..
19. TNA, ADM 116/1513 [Koerver, *Submarine Warfare*, p. 274]. Also Beesley, *Room 40*, mentions this statement, unfortunately without a footnote to the source.
20. BA-MA, RM 97/683, p. 101.
21. Max Valentiner: *U38. Wikingerfahrten eines deutschen Ubootes*, (Berlin: Ullstein, 1934), p. 70.
22. Beesley, *Room 40*, p. 122.
23. Seymour, House Papers 1912-1915, p. 432.
24. Ibid..
25. Erdmann, *Riezler diaries*, December 25th, 1915, p. 319.

Chapter 13: War of Words

1. Link, *Wilson 1914-1915*, p. 377ff.
2. Ibid.
3. Görlitz, *Müller diaries*, May 9th, 1915, p. 101.
4. BA-MA, RM 2/1164 sheet 112, Tirpitz to Müller May 9th, 1915 12:54.
5. *Frankfurter Allgemeine Zeitung* (FAZ), 7. May 2015, in 'commemoration' of the 100th anniversary of the *Lusitania* sinking, article Die Stahlhaie des Kaisers: 'The *Lusitania* was a secret auxiliary cruiser of the Royal Navy, transporting ammunition, and therefore, its sinking was in accordance with international maritime law.'
6. TNA, ADM 137/4069, p. 97, 12th May: 'On May 15th S.S. *Cameronia* 11 000 tons leaves Liverpool for New York.'; p. 97, 16th May: 'S.S. *Carmania* leaves Glasgow May 17th, S.S. *Transylvania* leaves Liverpool 22 nd 2:30 pm, S.S. *Mauretania* on May 29th'.
7. Link, *Wilson 1914-15*, p. 384f.
8. Ibid., p. 386.
9. Ibid., p. 392.
10. Ibid., p. 392-6.
11. Seymour, House Papers 1912-1915, p. 452.
12. Ibid.
13. Ibid., p. 453.
14. Erdmann, *Riezler diaries*, May 31th, 1915, p. 276; details also in Görlitz, *Müller-Tage-bücher*, May 30th, 1915, p. 105.
15. Görlitz, *Müller diaries*, May 27th, 1915, p. 104.
16. BA-MA, Msg. 1/764, sheets 126-131, Bachmann diary June 1st, 1915 [Granier, Vol. III, No. 335, p. 112ff.].
17. BA-MA, Msg. 1/764, sheets 149-152, Bachmann diary June 17th, 1915 [Granier, Vol. III, No. 344, p. 133].

18. BA-MA, Msg. 1/764, sheets 126-131, Bachmann diary June 1st, 1915 [Granier, Vol. III, No. 335, p. 112ff.].

19. BA-MA, RM 2/1982, sheet 144, Bachmann to Müller June 1st, 1915 [Granier, Vol. III, No. 336, p. 117].

20. TNA, ADM 137/4069, p. 99, No. 88, June 1st, 1915

21. Link, *Wilson 1914-1915*, p. 407, Bethmann to Treutler, June 1st, 1915.

22. Görlitz, *Müller diaries*, June 5th, 1915, p. 106.

23. BA-MA, Msg. 1/764, sheets 132-133, Bachmann diary June 2nd, 1915[Granier, Vol. III, No. 337, p. 119f.]; RM 2/1982, sheet 155, Müller to Bachmann June 5th, 1915 [Granier, Vol. III, No. 337, p. 121]; RM 2/1982, sheet 158, Bachmann to Müller June 6th, 1915 [Granier, Vol. III, No. 339, p. 122f.]

24. Erdmann, *Riezler diaries*, June 10th, 1915, p. 278.

25. Granier, *Seekriegsleitung*, Vol. I, p. 81, footnote 3.

26. BA-MA, RM 2/1982, sheet 158, Bachmann to Müller June 6th, 1915 [Granier, Vol. III, No. 339, p. 122].

27. BA-MA, RM 8/676, sheet 10 [Granier, Vol. III, p. 122 footnote 5].

28. BA-MA, RM 8/525, sheet 184 [Granier, Vol. III, p. 123, footnote 6].

29. TNA, ADM 137/4069, p. 99-108; TNA, ADM 137/4069, p. 108, Nos. 0921 and 16.

30. BA-MA, RM 5/6458, sheets 39-41, Naval Staff to Bachmann July 30th, 1915 [Granier, Vol. III, No. 351, p. 152].

31. Link, *Wilson 1914-1915*, p. 412.

32. Ibid., p. 410-32.

33. Erdmann, *Riezler diaries*, June 10th, 1915, p. 278.

34. Görlitz, *Müller diaries*, June 15th, 1915, p. 108.

35. Ibid., June 23rd, 1915, p. 110.

36. Link, *Wilson 1914-1915*, p. 433: *Tägliche Rundschau*, Berlin, morning edition June 13th, 1915.

37. Seymour, House Papers 1912-1915, p. 469.

38. Erdmann, *Riezler diaries*, June 23rd, 1915, p. 279-80.

39. Görlitz, *Müller diaries*, June 25th, 1915, p. 111.

40. BA-MA, RM 5/921, sheets 52-56, Bachmann June 25th, 1915 [Granier, Vol. III, No. 348, p. 141ff.].

41. Görlitz, *Müller diaries*, June 12th, p. 108-14.

42. Ibid., July 4th, 1915, p. 114.

43. Link, *Wilson 1914-1915*, p. 433.

44. Görlitz, *Müller diaries*, July 4th, 1915, p. 114.

45. Ibid., July 10th, 1915, p. 115.

46. Ibid., July 6th, 1915, p. 115.

47. BA-MA, RM 97/578, KTB U 20, Schwieger, July 3rd-16th, 1915, sheets 29-30, also RM 5/2991, sheets 307-9.

48. Ibid.

49. Ibid.
50. Link, *Wilson 1914-1915*, p. 445-8.
51. Erdmann, *Riezler diaries*, June 28th, 1915, p. 288.
52. Link, *Wilson 1914-1915*, p. 450f.
53. Görlitz, *Müller diaries*, July 19th, 1915, p. 117.
54. Ibid., July 20th, 1915, p. 118.
55. BA-MA, RM 5/6458, sheets 42-3, Naval Staff to Bachmann July 31th, 1915 [Granier, Vol. III, No. 352, p. 156].
56. TNA, ADM 137/4069, p. 103, July 21st, 1915.
57. Ibid., p. 105, August 2nd, 1915.

Chapter 14: Arabic

1. TNA, ADM 137/1131, p. 332ff. [Koerver, *Submarine Warfare*, p. 285ff.].
2. BA-MA, RM 97/642, KTB U 24, Schneider, August 5th – 26th, 1915.
3. BA-MA, Msg. 1/764, sheets 261-267, Bachmann diary August 31th and September 1st, 1915 [Granier, Vol. III, No. 361 and 362, p. 177-9].
4. Link, *Wilson 1914-1915*, p. 566.
5. Ibid., p. 567.
6. Ibid., p. 569.
7. Ibid., p. 567.
8. Görlitz, *Müller diaries*, August 24th, 1915, p. 125.
9. TNA, ADM 137/4069, p. 108, August 24th.
10. Ibid., p. 108, August 23rd and 25th, 1915.
11. Link, *Wilson 1914-1915*, p. 572.
12. Ibid., p. 572.
13. Ibid., p. 577.
14. Görlitz, *Müller diaries*, August 26th, 1915, p. 125.
15. Erdmann, *Riezler diaries*, August 29th, 1915, p. 296-7.
16. BA-MA, RM 2/1992, sheet 117 [Granier, Vol. III, p. 172f.].
17. Görlitz, *Müller diaries*, August 28th, 1915, p. 125.
18. BA-MA, RM 2/1991, sheets 91-92, Müller to Bethmann Hollweg March 18th, 1916 [Granier, Vol. I, No. 20, p. 98].
19. Link, *Wilson 1914-1915*, p. 580f.
20. TNA, ADM 137/4069, p. 109, KAV 27, August 30th, 1915.
21. BA-MA, Msg. 1/764, sheet 261-267, Bachmann diary August 31th and September 1st, 1915 [Granier, Vol. III, No. 361 and 362, p. 177-9].
22. Spindler, *Handelskrieg*, Vol. II, p. 270.
23. Erdmann, *Riezler diaries*, September 10th, 1915, p. 299.
24. Seymour, *House-Papers 1915-1917*, p. 37.
25. Görlitz, *Müller diaries*, September 4th, 1915, p. 126.
26. Görlitz, *Müller diaries*, September 10th, 1915, p. 128.

27. Ibid., September 13th, 1915, p. 129.
28. TNA, ADM 137/3192, sheet 28.
29. BA-MA, RM 97/579, KTB U 20, Schwieger, August 9th – September 15th, 1915
30. TNA, ADM 137/3912, U 20 August 31st, 1915.
31. BA-MA, RM 97/579, KTB U 20, Schwieger, August 9th – September 15th, 1915.
32. Ibid.
33. Seymour, *House-Papers 1915-1917*, p. 37.
34. Ibid., p. 42.
35. Görlitz, *Müller diaries*, September 10th, 1915, p. 128.
36. Link, *Wilson 1914-1915*, p. 653.
37. Ibid., p. 655f.
38. Ibid., p. 652.
39. Ibid., p. 658.
40. BA-MA, RM 2/1992, sheet 220, Holtzendorff to Pohl and Flanders September 18th, 1915 [Granier, Vol. III, p. 193].
41. Link, *Wilson 1914-1915*, p. 676.
42. Ibid., p. 659.

Chapter 15: Tirpitz's Uboat War

1. For details, see Appendix: Uboat War Statistics.
2. BA-MA, RM 8/1160, p. 456.

Chapter 16: British Blockade in Autumn

1. Lambert, *Armageddon*, p. 479.
2. Randel, *Economic Intelligence*, p. 215ff.
3. Lambert, *Armageddon*, p. 358.
4. Randel, *Economic Intelligence*, p. 148.
5. Ibid., p. 155.
6. TNA, ADM 186/603, p. 9.
7. Seymour, *House-Papers 1915-1917*, p. 69.
8. Ibid., p. 58.
9. Ibid., p. 51.
10. Ibid., p. 98.
11. Ibid., p. 79f.

Chapter 17: America and Germany

1. Link, *Wilson 1914-1915*, p. 55ff.
2. Ibid., p. 561.
3. Ibid., p. 563.
4. Ibid., p. 564.
5. Ibid., p. 36.

6. Seymour, *House-Papers 1915-1917*, p. 100f.

7. Link, *Wilson 1914-1915*, p. 66.

8. Arthur S. Link, *Wilson: Confusions and Crises 1915-1916* (Princeton: Princeton University Press, 1964), p. 15-18.

9. Ibid., p. 73ff.

10. Seymour, *House-Papers 1915-1917*, p. 80f.

1916 – All Options on the Table
Chapter 18: Storm warning.

1. Holger Afflerbach, *Falkenhayn: Politisches Denken und Handeln im Kaiserreich* (Munich: 2nd edition, Oldenbourg, 1996), p. 352, letter to Bethmann Hollweg, November 29th, 1915.

2. Ibid., p. 369, mid-December 1915.

3. Ibid., p. 379.

4. Ibid., p. 357.

5. Ibid., p. 359.

6. BA-MA, RM 2/1992, sheet 2-6, meeting of Falkenhayn, Holtzendorff, and Tirpitz, December 30th, 1915. [Granier, Vol. III, No. 373, p. 204ff.].

7. Karl E. Birnbaum, *Peace Moves and Uboat Warfare: A Study of Imperial Germany's Policy towards the United States April 18, 1916 - January 9, 1917* (Stockholm: Almquist & Wiksell, 1958), p. 56, memorandum from Holtzendorff to Bethmann Hollweg, January 4th, 1916.

8. Görlitz, *Müller diaries*, January 6th, 1916, p. 146.

9. Details in Appendix: Uboat Inventory Statistics.

10. Harald Bendert, *Die UB-Boote der Kaiserlichen Marine 1914-1918*, (Hamburg: E.S. Mittler & Sohn, 2000), p. 51, UB-10.

11. Erdmann, *Riezler diaries*, January 11th, 1916, p. 321-2.

12. BA-MA, RM 5/3002, sheets 27-28, meeting of Holtzendorff and Bethmann Hollweg, January 8th, 1916 [Granier, Vol. III, No. 375, p. 210].

13. Kelly, *Tirpitz*, p. 407.

14. Görlitz, *Müller diaries*, January 11th, 1916, p. 146-7.

15. Ibid., January 12th, 1916, p. 147.

16. BA-MA, RM 5/902, sheets 1-11, Holtzendorff January 13th, 1916 [Granier, Vol. III, No. 377, p. 213ff.].

17. Afflerbach, *Falkenhayn*, p. 386.

18. Görlitz, *Müller diaries*, January 15th, 1916, p. 147.

19. Erdmann, *Riezler diaries*, January 18th, 1916, p. 324-5.

20. Link, *Wilson 1915-1916*, p. 142-5.

21. Ibid., p. 83.

22. Görlitz, *Müller diaries*, January 31st, 1916, p. 151.

23. Ibid., February 1st, 1916, p. 151.
24. Link, *Wilson 1915-1916*, p. 92.
25. Ibid., p. 97.
26. Ibid., p. 155-6.
27. BA-MA, RM 2/1993, sheets 54-5, Holtzendorff to Müller, February 9th, 1916 [Granier, Vol. III, No. 386, p. 242f.].
28. Link, *Wilson 1915-1916*, p. 156.
29. BA-MA, RM 2/1993, sheets 54-5, Holtzendorff to Müller, February 9th, 1916 [Granier, Vol. III, No. 386, p. 242], details in footnote 4; see also Spindler, *Handelskrieg*, Vol. III, p. 87.
30. Link, *Wilson 1915-1916*, p. 160.
31. Ibid., p. 161-3.
32. Ibid., p. 165.
33. Görlitz, *Müller diaries*, February 19th, 1916, p. 157.
34. Erdmann, *Riezler diaries*, February 1st, 1916, p. 328.
35. BA-MA, RM 5/902, sheets 1-11, Holtzendorff, January 13th, 1916 [Granier, Vol. III, No. 377, p. 213ff.].
36. Erdmann, *Riezler diaries*, February 6th, 1916, p. 330.
37. BA-MA, RM 2/1983, sheet 107, Bethmann Hollweg to Tirpitz, February 9th, 1916 [Granier, Vol. III, No. 385, p. 241].
38. BA-MA, RM 3/47, sheets 173-6, Tirpitz to Bethmann, January 31st, 1916, [Granier, Vol. III, No. 384, p. 238].
39. Erdmann, *Riezler diaries*, February 11th, 1916, p. 331-2.
40. Scheck, *Tirpitz*, p. 48.
41. BA-MA, RM 2/993, sheets 65-7, Müller, February 11th, 1916 [Granier, Vol. III, No. 387 p. 246].
42. Görlitz, *Müller diaries*, February 9th, 1916, p. 154.
43. BA-MA, RM 5/902, sheets 49-51, Holtzendorff February 16th, 1916 [Granier, Vol. III, No. 387, p. 255].
44. BA-MA, RM 47/5, Bl. 293-7, Holtzendorff to High Seas Fleet, February 19th, 1916 [Granier, Vol. III, No. 390, p. 257].
45. Görlitz, *Müller diaries*, February 18th, 1916, p. 156.
46. Link, *Wilson 1915-1916*, p. 186.
47. Afflerbach, *Falkenhayn*, p. 369, 373.
48. BA-MA, RM 3/3014, sheet 6, Holtzendorff, February 22nd, 1916 [Granier, Vol. III, No. 392, p. 262].
49. BA-MA, RM 47/5, sheet 301, Scheer's order to Bauer, February 23rd, 1916 [Granier, Vol. III, No. 393, p. 263f.].
50. Erdmann, *Riezler diaries*, February 22nd, 1916, p. 334f.
51. Görlitz, *Müller diaries*, February 22nd, 1916, p. 158.

52. Ibid., February 25th, 1916, p. 159.

53. Bethmann Hollweg, *Betrachtungen*, p. 260ff.: Bethmann memorandum, February 29th, 1916.

54. Birnbaum, *Peace Moves*, p. 58.

55. BA-MA, RM 3/3014, sheet 180, Bethmann Hollweg to Holtzendorff, February 29th, 1916 [Granier, Vol. III, No. 396, p. 268].

Chapter 19: Conflicting Decisions

1. Erdmann, *Riezler diaries*, February 29th, 1916, p. 336.

2. Görlitz, *Müller diaries*, March 2nd, 1916, p. 159-60.

3. Ibid.

4. Ibid., March 2nd, 1916, p. 160.

5. Erdmann, *Riezler diaries*, March 7th, 1916, p. 337.

6. Röhl, *Wilhelm 1900-1941*, p. 1212.

7. Görlitz, *Müller diaries*, March 3rd, 1916, p. 161.

8. Ibid., March 4th, 1916, p. 161.

9. Ibid.

10. Ibid., March 4th, 1916, p. 162.

11. Erdmann, *Riezler diaries*, March 7th, 1916, p. 338.

12. Granier, *Seekriegsleitung*, Vol. III, p. 278, footnote 2.

13. Birnbaum, *Peace Moves*, p. 62.

14. Görlitz, *Müller diaries*, March 4th, 1916, p. 162.

15. Erdmann, *Riezler diaries*, March 7th, 1916, p. 337-8.

16. BA-MA, RM 5/902, sheet 67, discussions between Müller and Holtzendorff. March 5-7, 1916 [Granier, Vol. III, No. 398, p. 275].

17. BA-MA, RM 47/5, sheets 312-14, Holtzendorff, between March 4 and 7, 1916 [Granier, Vol. III, No. 397, p. 270f.].

18. BA-MA, RM 5/902, sheet 67, discussions between Müller and Holtzendorff, March 5-7, 1916 [Granier, Vol. III, No. 398, p. 275].

19. Birnbaum, *Peace Moves*, p. 65-6.

20. Afflerbach, *Falkenhayn*, p. 390.

21. Ibid., p. 391, Falkenhayn, March 11th, 1916.

22. Görlitz, *Müller diaries*, March 2nd, 1916, p. 160.

23. Ibid., March 4th, 1916, p. 163.

24. Erdmann, *Riezler diaries*, March 7th, 1916, p. 338ff.

25. Ibid., March 7th, 1916, p. 338ff.

26. Ibid., p. 339, footnote 12.

27. Details in Appendix: Uboat Inventory Statistics.

28. Erdmann, *Riezler diaries*, March 7th, 1916, p. 339.

29. Görlitz, *Müller diaries*, March 5th, 1916, p. 163.

30. Afflerbach, *Falkenhayn*, p. 403.

31. Görlitz, *Müller diaries*, March 9th, 1916, p. 163-164.
32. BA-MA, RM 2/1991, sheets 72-73, Müller to Holtzendorff, March 11th, 1916 [Granier, Vol. I, No. 18, p. 92f.].
33. Görlitz, *Müller diaries*, March 10th, 1916, p. 163.
34. Erdmann, *Riezler diaries*, March 10th, 1916, p. 339; 'regret' is meant sarcastically.
35. Görlitz, *Müller diaries*, March 13th, 1916, p. 166.
36. Erdmann, *Riezler diaries*, March 26th, 1916, p. 345.
37. BA-MA, RM 2/191, sheets 87-90, Müller, March 17th, 1916 [Granier, Vol. I, No. 19, p. 94f.].
38. Scheck, *Tirpitz*, p. 43.

Chapter 20: Hurricane

1. TNA, ADM 137/4069, February 6th, 1916, p. 119.
2. TNA, ADM 137/4069, February 23rd, 1916, p. 120.
3. Image courtesy of Princeton Univ Press.
4. BA-MA, RM 97/1331. KTB UB-13.
5. Spindler, *Handelskrieg*, Vol. III, p. 121, UB 13.
6. Bendert, *UB-Boote*, p. 57, mentions the sinking of the *Tubantia*.
7. BA-MA, RM 97/1373, KTB UB 18; RM 97/1379, KTB UB 19.
8. Spindler, *Handelskrieg*, Vol. III, p. 120.
9. Details in Appendix: Statistics on Ships Sunk.
10. BA-MA, RM 97/942, KTB U 70; RM 97/939, U 69.
11. Erdmann, *Riezler diaries*, March 15th, 1916, p. 341.
12. Ibid., March 22nd, 1916, p. 342.
13. Ibid., March 26th, 1916, p. 344.
14. *Reichstagshauptausschuss*, 2nd Vol., March 28th, 1916 p. 365-407.
15. Ibid., p. 386.
16. Ibid., p. 387.
17. Ibid., p. 389.
18. Ibid., p. 390.
19. Erdmann, *Riezler diaries*, April 15th, 1916, p. 347.
20. Afflerbach, *Falkenhayn*, p. 374.

Chapter 21: *Sussex*

1. Link, *Wilson 1915-1916*, p. 228.
2. BA-MA, RM 97/1453, KTB UB 29.
3. Link, *Wilson 1915-1916*, p. 228-9.
4. Ibid., p. 230.
5. Ibid., p. 231.
6. Ibid., p. 238.
7. Ibid., p. 240.

8. Ibid., p. 241.
9. Ibid., p. 242.
10. Ibid., p. 242.
11. Ibid., p. 243.
12. Birnbaum, *Peace Moves*, p. 71.
13. Görlitz, *Müller diaries*, April 21st, 1916, p. 170.
14. Ibid., p. 170.
15. Afflerbach, *Falkenhayn*, April 22nd, 1915, p. 393.
16. Link, *Wilson 1915-1916*, p. 263.
17. Ibid., p. 259.
18. Birnbaum, *Peace Moves*, p. 78-9.
19. Erdmann, *Riezler diaries*, April 24th, 1916, p. 348-9.
20. Birnbaum, *Peace Moves*, p. 79-81; Link, *Wilson 1915-1916*, p. 265.
21. Link, *Wilson 1915-1916*, p. 265.
22. Görlitz, *Müller diaries*, April 27th, 1916, p. 172.
23. BA-MA, RM 47/771, sheet 9, Scheer to Holtzendorff, April 27th, 1916 [Granier, Vol. III, No. 405, p. 290].
24. Erdmann, *Riezler diaries*, April 28th, 1916, p. 349.
25. Link, *Wilson 1915-1916*, p. 265.
26. Görlitz, *Müller diaries*, April 28th, 1916, p. 172.
27. Erdmann, *Riezler diaries*, April 30th, 1916, p. 350-1.
28. Erdmann, *Riezler diaries*, April 30th, 1916, p. 351-3.
29. Görlitz, *Müller diaries*, April 30th, 1916, p. 172-3.
30. Erdmann, *Riezler diaries*, April 30th, 1916, p. 351-3.
31. Görlitz, *Müller diaries*, May 1st, 1916, p. 173.
32. Link, *Wilson 1915-1916*, p. 269-70.
33. Görlitz, *Müller diaries*, May 1st, 1916, p. 173.
34. Birnbaum, *Peace Moves*, p. 89.
35. Görlitz, *Müller diaries*, May 3rd, 1916, p. 174.
36. Birnbaum, *Peace Moves*, p. 91-2.
37. Ibid., p. 99.
38. Erdmann, *Riezler diaries*, April 30th, 1916, p. 353-5.
39. Görlitz, *Müller diaries*, May 9th, 1916, p. 175.
40. Link, *Wilson 1915-1916*, p. 276.
41. Ibid., p. 277-8.

Chapter 22: British Blockade in Spring

1. Randel, *Economic Intelligence*, p. 228.
2. TNA, ADM 186/603, p. 11.
3. Randel, *Economic Intelligence*, p. 234.
4. TNA, ADM 186/603, p. 3ff.
5. Randel, *Economic Intelligence*, p. 240.

6. Ibid., p. 241.
7. Ibid., p. 236.
8. Avner Offer, *The First World War: An Agrarian Interpretation* (Oxford: Oxford University Press, 1989), p. 33.
9. Ibid., p. 24-68.

Chapter 23: Peace Wanted?
1. Arthur S. Link, *Wilson: Campaigns for Progressivism and Peace, 1916-1917* (Princeton, Princeton University Press, 1965), p. 10ff.
2. Ibid., p. 13.
3. Ibid., p. 15.
4. Ibid., p. 15-17.
5. Ibid., p. 17.
6. Ibid., p. 19.
7. Ibid., p. 19.
8. Ibid., p. 12.
9. Ibid., p. 26.
10. Ibid., p. 26.
11. Ibid.
12. Justus D. Doeneke, *Nothing less than war: A new history of America's entry into World War I,* (Lexington, The University Press of Kentucky), 2011, p. 178 and 182ff.
13. Seymour, *House-Papers 1915-1917*, p. 283.
14. David French, *The Strategy of the Lloyd George Coalition 1916-1918*, Oxford, (Clarendon Press), 2002. p. 11.
15. Leonidas E. Hill (Ed.), *Die Weizsäcker Papiere 1900-1932 (*Berlin, Propyläen Verlag, 1982), February 20th, 1916, p. 186.
16. Holger Herwig, *Das Elitekorps des Kaisers: Die Marineoffiziere im Wilhelminischen Deutschland* (Hamburg, Hans Christian Verlag 1977), p. 153.
17. Hill, Weizsäcker diaries, February 20th, 1916, p. 185, 187.
18. Erdmann, *Riezler diaries*, November 3rd, 1916, p. 378.
19. Ibid., July 4th, 1916, p. 363.
20. Ibid., June 14th, 1916, p. 359.
21. Ibid., November 22nd, 1916, p. 383f.

Chapter 24: Uboat Warfare
1. Author's calculation based on Gröner, *Kriegsschiffe*.
2. Author's calculations based on: TNA, HW 7/1, 2 and 3; Spindler, *Handelskrieg*; Bendert, *UB-* and UC-Boote, and TNA, ADM 1/8509/1, ADM 137/3921, 4814, 4817.
3. Author's calculations based on: TNA, HW 7/1, 2 and 3; Spindler, *Handelskrieg*; Bendert, *UB-* and UC-Boote, and TNA, ADM 1/8509/1, ADM 137/3921, 4814, 4817.
4. Chapter based on TNA, HW 7/1 and 2, Chapter XIV, p. 515ff. [Koerver, *Room 40*, Vol. I, p. 260ff.].

5. BA-MA, RM 5/6266 p. 40-1, December 4th, 1915 [Granier, Vol. IV, no. 605, p. 54f.].

6. Author's calculations based on: TNA, HW 7/1, 2 and 3; Spindler, *Handelskrieg*; Bendert, *UB-* and UC-Boote, and TNA, ADM 1/8509/1, ADM 137/3921, 4814, 4817.

7. TNA, HW 7/1 and 7/2, Chapter XIV [Koerver, *Submarine Warfare*, p. 218f.].

8. Based on KTB (war diary) U-35, NARA PG 61579 (BA-MA, RM 97/766).

9. KTB (war diary) U-35, NARA, PG 61579 (BA-MA, RM 97/766).

10. TNA, ADM 137/3897, Examination of the Crew of UC-61, sunk 26 July 1917.

11. Ibid.

12. KTB (war diary) U-35, NARA, PG 61579 (BA-MA, RM 97/766).

13. Author's calculations based on: TNA, HW 7/1, 2 and 3; Spindler, *Handelskrieg*; Bendert, *UB-* and UC-Boote, and TNA, ADM 1/8509/1, ADM 137/3921, 4814, 4817.

14. Arno Spindler, *Wie es zu dem Entschluß zum uneingeschränkten U-Boots-Krieg 1917 gekommen ist*, (Göttingen, Musterschmidt Verlag, 1956), p. 16.

15. Ibid., p. 17.

16. TNA, HW 7/1, Chapter IX [Koerver, *Room 40*, Vol. 1, p. 159ff.].

17. Author's calculation based on Gröner, *Kriegsschiffe*.

18. TNA, HW 7/1, Chapter VII [Koerver, *Room 40*, Vol. 1, p. 106ff.].

19. BA-MA, RM 5/5073.

20. BA-MA, RM 5/5091.

21. BA-MA, RM 5/921, p. 172-173, Holtzendorff to Müller, April 27th, 1916 [Granier, Vol. III, no. 406, p. 290].

22. Hill, *Weizsäcker diaries*, April 7th, 1916, p. 200.

23. Ibid., p. 203.

24. BA-MA RM 47/771 p. 39-40, /6378 p. 171-4, May 7th, 1916, von Trotha. [Granier, Vol. III, no. 410, p. 302ff.].

25. Walter Görlitz (Ed.): *The Kaiser and his Court: The Diaries, Note Books and Letters of Admiral Georg Alexander von Müller, Chief of the Naval Cabinet 1914-1918* (London: Macdonald, 1961), May 17th, 1916, p. 161.

26. BA-MA RM 47/771 p. 39-40, /6378 p. 171-4, May 7th, 1916, von Trotha. [Granier, Vol. III, no. 410, p. 302ff.].

27. Görlitz, *The Kaiser and his Court*, May 21st, 1916, p. 164.

28. Spindler, *Entschluß 1917*, p. 16.

29. Ibid., p. 18.

Chapter 25: Krupp and the Uboats

1. Harold James, *Krupp: Deutsche Legende und globales Unternehmen* (Munich: C.H.Beck, 2011), p. 104 and 149.

2. Ibid., p. 112.

3. Ian Johnston and Ian Buxton, *The Battleship Builders: Constructing and Arming British Capital Ships* (Barnsley: Seaforth Publishing, 2013), p. 235ff.

4. James, *Krupp*, p. 103ff.
5. Ibid., p. 77ff.
6. Ibid., p. 151.
7. Ibid.
8. James, *Krupp*, p. 103ff.
9. Michael Epkenhans, Die *wilhelminische Flottenrüstung 1908-1914: Weltmachtstreben, industrieller Fortschritt, soziale Integration* (Munich: R. Oldenbourg Verlag, 1991), p. 202ff.
10. Lambert, *Fisher's Revolution*, p. 38ff.
11. H. Techel, *Der Bau von Unterseebooten auf der Germaniawerft* (Berlin: J.H. Lehmans Verlag, 1922), p. 5.
12. Ibid.
13. Ibid., p. 78.
14. Ibid., p. 5 and 76ff.
15. Gröner, *Kriegsschiffe*.
16. Ibid.
17. Lyle Cummins, *Diesels for the First Stealth Weapon: Submarine Power 1902-1945* (Wilsonville: Carnot Press, 2007) p. ix.
18. Ibid., p. 35ff.
19. Ibid., p. 84f.
20. Ibid., p. 87ff.
21. Gröner, *Kriegsschiffe*.

Chapter 26: Merchant Submarines

1. Jan Heitmann, *Unter Wasser in die Neue Welt: Handelsunterseeboote und kaiserliche Unterseekreuzer im Spannungsfeld von Politik und Kriegsführung* (Berlin: Berlin Verlag, 1996), p. 70ff.; Eberhard Rössler, *Deutsche U-Kreuzer und Transport-U-Boote* (Bonn: Bernard & Graefe, 2003), p. 34ff.
2. Ibid., p. 128.
3. Ibid., p. 131.
4. Ibid., p. 130ff.
5. Rössler, *U-Kreuzer*, p. 39.
6. Heitmann, *Unter Wasser*, p. 95ff.
7. Ibid., p. 127ff.
8. Ibid., p. 105ff.
9. Ibid., p. 111.
10. Ibid., p. 112ff.
11. Ibid., p. 121.
12. Hoechst, BASF, Bayer and Casella.
13. Heitmann, *Unter Wasser*, p. 159f.
14. Ibid., p. 189f.

15. Louis Guichard, *The Naval Blockade 1914-1918* (New York: D. Appleton & Company, 1930), p. 273.
16. Heitmann, *Unter Wasser*, p. 207, calculates 30 kg of <u>rubber</u> needed to produce the tires for a complete motor truck.
17. Ibid., p. 207.

Chapter 27: Uboat Armament

1. Author's calculation based on Gröner, *Kriegsschiffe*.
2. Erdmann, *Riezler diaries*, October 22nd, 1914, p. 220.
3. Ibid., January 13th, 1916, p. 323-4.
4. Ibid., February 17th, 1915, p. 250.
5. Lambert, *Fisher's Revolution*, mentions examples for identical calculations on British side.
6. Ibid.
7. Eberhard Rössler, *Geschichte des deutschen Ubootbaus: Entwicklung, Bau und Eigenschaften der deutschen Uboote von den Anfängen bis 1943* (Bonn: Bernard & Graefe, 1996), p. 96-9.
8. BA-MA, RM 3/11676, sheet 17, Rüstung.
9. *Hauptausschuss*, Vol. I, December 16th, 1915, Helfferich, p. 309.
10. Rössler, *U-Kreuzer*, p. 67.
11. Eberhard Rössler, *Entwicklung, Bau und Eigenschaften der deutschen U-Boote von den An-fängen bis 1943*, Bonn, (Bernard & Graefe), 1996, p. 107.
12. *Die Ursachen des Deutschen Zusammenbruches im Jahre 1918. Das Werk des Untersuchungs-Ausschusses der Verfassungsgebenden Deutschen Nationalversammlung und des Deutschen Reichstages 1919-1928. Zweite Abteilung. Der Innere Zusammenbruch. Zehnter Band. Berlin 1928*, p. 128.
13. Gary E. Weir, *Building the Kaiser's Navy: The Imperial Navy Office and German Industry in the von Tirpitz Era 1890-1919* (Annapolis: Naval Institute Press, 1992), p. 198.
14. Friedrich Forstmeier, *Deutsche Grosskampfschiffe 1915-1918: Die Entwicklung der Typenfrage im Ersten Weltkrieg* (Bonn: Bernard & Graefe, 2002), p. 56.
15. Scheck, *Tirpitz*, p. 23.
16. Ibid.

Chapter 28: Uboat Strike Continues

1. Görlitz, *Müller diaries*, June 24th, 1916, p. 194.
2. BA-MA, RM 5/992 p. 9-10, Memorandum Holtzendorff July 1st, 1916 [Granier, Vol. III, no. 422, p. 332ff.].
3. BA-MA, RM 8/545 Folio 87-9, memorandum Müller July 18th, 1916 [Granier, Vol. III, no. 426, p. 339ff.].
4. BA-MA, RM 47/771 Folio 109-10, August 10th, 1916, Holtzendorff to Scheer [Granier, Vol. III, no. 433, p. 360].
5. Herwig, *Elitekorps*, and Martin Kitchen, *The German Officer Corps 1890-1914* (Oxford: Clarendon Press, 1968).

6. Erdmann, *Riezler diaries*, July 11th, 1915, p. 284.

7. James, *Krupp*, p. 152.

8. Görlitz, *The Kaiser and his Court*, August 2nd, 1916, p. 189.

9. BA-MA, RM 2/1993 Folio 283-5, August 7th, 1916, Bethmann to Holtzendorff [Granier, Vol. III, no. 431, p. 354ff.].

10. Erdmann, *Riezler diaries*, August 10th, 1916, p. 370f.

11. Hill, *Weizsäcker diaries*, August 20th, 1916, p. 206.

12. Erdmann, *Riezler diaries*, August 30th, 1916, p. 372f.

13. Görlitz, *The Kaiser and his Court*, August 24th and 25th, 1916, p. 196.

14. Ibid.

Chapter 29: New Leadership

1. Cited from: Manfred Nebelin, *Ludendorff: Diktator in Ersten Weltkrieg* (Munich: Siedler Verlag, 2010), p. 200.

2. Görlitz, *The Kaiser and his Court*, August 28th, 1916, p. 198.

3. Ibid., August 29th, 1916, p. 198.

4. Hill, *Weizsäcker diaries*, August 30th, 1916, p. 209.

5. Wolfram Pytha, *Hindenburg: Herrscher zwischen Hohenzollern und Hitler* (Munich: Siedler Verlag, 2007), p. 227ff.

6. BA-MA, RM 2/1993 Folio 300-305, September 1st, 1916 [Granier, Vol. III, no. 439, p. 372f.].

7. Ibid., p. 374.

8. Ibid., p. 375.

9. Ibid., p. 377.

10. Nebelin, *Ludendorff*, p. 287.

11. BA-MA, RM 2/1993 Folio 300-305, September 1st, 1916 [Granier, Vol. III, no. 439, p. 378f.].

12. Ibid., p. 379.

13. See also: BA-MA, RM 5/3028 Folio 251-4, September 10th/11th, 1916 [Granier, Vol. III, no. 440, p. 383ff.].

14. Görlitz, *The Kaiser and his Court*, August [not July, as on p. 199!] 31st, 1916, p. 199f.

15. Erdmann, *Riezler diaries*, September 21st, 1916, p. 375.

16. Link, *Wilson 1916-1917*, p. 169f.

17. Ibid., p. 170.

18. BA-MA, RM 47/771 Folio 221, September 3rd, 1916.

19. Heitmann, *Unter Wasser*, p. 252f.

20. Ibid., p. 228.

21. Hill, *Weizsäcker diaries*, September 9th, 1916, p. 211.

22. BA-MA, RM 5/6360 Folio 42-3, September 10th, 1916 [Granier, Vol. III, No. 441, p. 388].

23. Ibid., p. 388f.

24. BA-MA, RM 5/3028 Folio 251-254, September 10th/11th, 1916 [Granier, Vol. III, No. 440, p. 384].

25. BA-MA, RM 47/771 Folio 188, September 11th, 1916.

26. BA-MA, RM 47/771 Folio 222, September 12th, 1916.

27. BA-MA, RM 47/771 Folio 201f., September 13th, 1916 [Granier, Vol. III, No. 442, p. 390, footnote 5].

28. KTB U-35, NARA, PG 61579 (BA-MA, RM 97/766). See also BA-MA, RM 3/771, p. 189f. and p. 192.

29. KTB U-35, NARA, PG 61579 (BA-MA, RM 97/766).

30. Herwig, *Elitekorps*, letter from Weizsäcker to his father, September 27th, 1916, p. 149.

31. Birnbaum, *Peace Moves*, p. 354-8; see also Link, *Wilson 1916-1917*, p. 170.

32. Birnbaum, *Peace Moves*, p. 357; Link, *Wilson 1916-1917*, p. 171f.

33. Link, *Wilson 1916-1917*, p. 172.

34. *Der Hauptausschuss des Deutschen Reichstags 1915-1918*, second volume, session on September 29, 1916, p. 715.

35. *Reichstagshauptausschuss*, second volume, session on September 30, 1916, p. 737.

36. Ibid., p. 752.

37. Ibid., session on October 3, 1916, p. 769.

38. Ibid., session on September 29, 1916, p. 727.

39. Ibid., session on October 3, 1916, p. 769f.

40. Ibid., session on September 29, 1916, p. 729, 731.

41. Ibid., session on October 7, 1916, p. 844.

42. Ibid., session on October 5, 1916, p. 782.

43. Ibid., session September 30, 1916, pp. 746, 748, 754.

44. Ibid., session on October 5, 1916, pp. 786, 792, 794.

45. Ibid., session on September 30, 1916, p. 758.

46. Ibid., session on September 29, 1916, p. 715.

47. Ibid., p. 741f.

48. KTB U-53, NARA, PG 61612 (BA-MA, RM 97/855), October 7th, 1916.

49. TNA, ADM 137/3902, p. 145ff.

50. KTB U-53, NARA, PG 61612 (BA-MA, RM 97/855), October 7th, 1916.

51. Ibid.

52. TNA, ADM 137/3902, p. 145ff.

53. KTB U-53, NARA, PG 61612 (BA-MA, RM 97/855), October 7, 1916.

54. KTB U-53, NARA, PG 61612 (BA-MA, RM 97/855), October 8, 1916.

55. Ibid.

56. Ibid.

57. Ibid.

58. Ibid.

59. Doeneke, *Nothing less than war*, p. 45.

60. Heitmann, *Unter Wassser*, p. 245.

61. The sinking of the *Blommersdyk* was subsequently determined by a German prize court to be illegitimate and the Dutch owners were compensated.

62. Cited from Heitmann, *Unter Wassser*, p. 249.
63. *Reichstagshauptausschuss*, second volume, session on October 10, 1916, p. 873.

Chapter 30: Soft Uboat War
1. Görlitz, *The Kaiser and his Court*, October 3rd, 1916, p. 208.
2. Ibid., October 4th, 1916, p. 209.
3. BA-MA, RM 47/771 Folio 221-3, October 6, 1916 [Granier, Vol. III, No. 451, p. 408ff.].
4. Ibid., p. 410ff.
5. BA-MA, RM 47/771 Folio 187, September 25, 1916 [Granier, Vol. III, No. 448, p. 400].
6. BA-MA, RM 47/771 Folio 217f., October 1, 1916.
7. TNA, ADM 137/4069, No. 32, 9/10/1916, p. 10.
8. KTB U-49, NARA, PG 61606 (BA-MA, RM 97/828), p. 35.
9. KTB U-50, NARA, PG 61607 (BA-MA, RM 97/830), p. 243.
10. Ibid., p. 242.
11. TNA, ADM 137/4153, p. 108f.; ADM 137/3913, p. 31f.
12. TNA, ADM 137/3913, p. 36f.
13. KTB U-50, NARA, PG 61607 (BA-MA, RM 97/830), p. 244.
14. KTB U-49, NARA, PG 61606 (BA-MA, RM 97/828), p. 35f.

Chapter 31: England and the Uboats
1. TNA, ADM 137/3060, U-64, Folio 15 [Koerver, *German Submarine Warfare*, p. 583.].
2. TNA, ADM 137/3060, [Koerver, *German Submarine Warfare*, p. 583.].
3. TNA ADM 116/3421, p. 297-298.
4. TNA, HW 7/1 [Koerver, *Room 40*, Vol. 1, p. 224.].
5. TNA, HW 7/1 [Koerver, *Room 40*, Vol. 1, p. 224.].
6. TNA, ADM 116/3421, p. 281, see also TNA, CAB-24-2-40, p. 4, October 14th, 1916.
7. TNA, CAB-24-2-40, p. 4, October 14th, 1916.
8. Salter, *Allied Shipping Control*, p. 7.
9. Ibid.
10. Link, *Wilson 1916-1917*, p. 176.
11. Ibid.
12. TNA, CAB-24-2-42, Memorandum by the President of the Board of Trade, October 24th, 1916.
13. TNA, ADM 116/3421, p. 280.
14. Link, *Wilson 1916-1917*, p. 179f.
15. Ibid., p. 184.
16. TNA, CAB-24-2-46, The General Review of the War, October 31st, 1916.
17. Ibid.
18. Ibid.

19. John Grigg, *Lloyd George: War Leader 1916-1918* (London 2002), p. 45.
20. Halpern, *Naval History*, p. 309, quotes 1.6 million GRT for these 6 months.
21. Hill, *Weizsäcker diaries*, November 13th, 1916, p. 220.
22. Erdmann, *Riezler diaries*, December 23rd, 1916, p. 387f.
23. Hill, *Weizsäcker diaries*, January 8th, 1917, p. 228.
24. Author's calculations based on: TNA, HW 7/1, 2 and 3; Spindler, *Handelskrieg*; Bendert, *UB-* and *UC-Boote*, and TNA, ADM 1/8509/1, ADM 137/3921, 4814, 4817.

Chapter 32: Famine, Peace, Uboats

1. Sandro Fehr, *Die Stickstofffrage in der deutschen Kriegswirtschaft des Ersten Weltkrieges und die Rolle der neutralen Schweiz* (Nordhausen: Verlag Traugott Bautz, 2009), p. 148-52; Guichard, *Blockade*, p. 282.
2. Guichard, *Blockade*, p. 285.
3. Albrecht Ritschl, *The pity of peace: Germany's economy at war 1914-1918, and after*, published in: Stephen Broadberry and Mark Harrison, *The Economics of World War I* (Cambridge: Cambridge University Press, 2005), Table 2.2.
4. Carsten Burhop, *Wirtschaftsgeschichte des Kaiserreichs 1871-1918* (Göttingen: Vandenhoeck & Rupprecht, 2011), p. 201ff.
5. Decie Denholm, *Behind the lines: One Woman's War 1914-18* (London, Jill Norman & Hobhouse, 1982), February 1st, 1915, p. 55.
6. Ibid., p. 119.
7. Ibid., January 4th, 1916, p. 119.
8. Ibid., April 2nd, 1916, p. 134.
9. Ibid., April 16th, 1916, p. 136.
10. Ibid., May 14th, 1916, p. 140.
11. Ibid., July 9th, 1916, p. 147.
12. Ibid., August 20th, 1916, p. 155.
13. Ibid., September 3rd, 1916, p. 158.
14. Ibid., November 19th, 1916, p. 168.
15. Offer, *Agrarian Interpretation*, p. 57.
16. Link, *Wilson 1916-1917*, p. 165.
17. Ibid., p. 165.
18. Ibid., p. 175.
19. Nebelin, *Ludendorff*, p. 231ff.
20. Pytha, *Hindenburg*, p. 235.
21. Bernhard Schwertfeger, *Kaiser und Kabinettschef: Nach eigenen Aufzeichnungen und dem Briefwechsel des Wirklich Geheimen Rats Rudolf von Valentini* (Oldenburg: Gerhard Stalling, 1931), p. 140ff.
22. Ibid.
23. Ritschl, *The pity of peace*, p. 46, Table 2.2.

24. Guichard, *Blockade*, p. 270f.
25. James, *Krupp*, p. 147.
26. Pytha, *Hindenburg*, p. 248.
27. James, *Krupp*, p. 147.
28. Gerald D. Feldmann, *Army, Industry and Labor in Germany 1914-1918* (Oxford: Berg Publishers, 1992), p. 273.
29. Nebelin, *Ludendorff*, p. 261ff.
30. TNA, ADM 137/4069, No. 54, 24/10/1916, p. 12.
31. KTB U-50, NARA, PG 61607 (BA-MA, RM 97/830), Folio without page no. after page 248.
32. TNA, ADM 137/4069, No. 6, 4/11/1916, p. 12.
33. Link, *Wilson 1916-1917*, p. 187.
34. Seymour, *House-Papers 1915-1917*, p. 390f.
35. Link, *Wilson 1916-1917*, p. 188.
36. Ibid., p. 189.
37. Ibid.
38. Erdmann, *Riezler diaries*, November 22nd, 1916, p. 383f.
39. BA-MA, RM 47/771 Folio 291-2, November 20th, 1916 [Granier, Vol. III, No. 462, p. 428.].
40. BA-MA, RM 5/904 Folio 171-4, November 20th, 1916 [Granier, Vol. III, No. 463, p. 430ff.].
41. BA-MA, RM 5/921 Folio 461, November 24th, 1916 [Granier, Vol. III, No. 466, p. 436f.].
42. Görlitz, *The Kaiser and his Court*, November 26th, 1916, p. 219.
43. Link, *Wilson 1916-1917*, p. 192.
44. BA-MA, RM 5/921 Folio 461, November 24th, 1916 [Granier, Vol. III, No. 466, p. 436f.].
45. Link, *Wilson 1916-1917*, p. 193.
46. Ibid., p. 201.
47. Ibid., p. 200.
48. Ibid., p. 202f.

Chapter 33: Uboat Peace?

1. BA-MA, RM 5/6466 Folio 234-6, December 8th/9th, 1916 [Granier, Vol. III, No. 473, p. 449].
2. BA-MA, RM 5/6466 Folio 234-6, December 8th/9th, 1916 [Granier, Vol. III, No. 473f, p. 448].
3. BA-MA, RM 47/72 Folio 15-16, December 22nd, 1916 [Granier, Vol. III, No. 477, p. 456ff.].
4. Hill, *Weizsäcker diaries*, December 29th, 1916, p. 226.
5. Ibid., January 13th, 1917, p. 229.

6. Ibid., January 15th, 1917, p. 230.
7. Erdmann, *Riezler diaries*, December 23rd, 1916, p. 387f.
8. Görlitz, *The Kaiser and his Court*, December 4th, 1916, p. 221f.
9. Birnbaum, *Peace Moves*, p. 237-42.
10. Erdmann, *Riezler diaries*, December 9th, 1916, p. 387.
11. Pytha, *Hindenburg*, p. 238.
12. Birnbaum, *Peace Moves*, p. 247f.
13. Erdmann, *Riezler diaries*, December 13th, 1916, p. 387.
14. BA-MA, N 239/15 Folio 123, December 13th, 1916 [Granier, Vol. III, No. 475, p. 452.].
15. BA-MA, N 239/15 Folio 123-4, December 14th, 1916 [Granier, Vol. III, No. 476, p. 454.].
16. Görlitz, *The Kaiser and his Court*, December 9th, 1916, p. 224.
17. Link, *Wilson 1916-1917*, p. 215.
18. Ibid., p. 218.
19. Ibid., p. 229.
20. Ibid., p. 231.
21. Grigg, *Lloyd George 1916-1918*, p. 19.
22. Link, *Wilson 1916-1917*, p. 239.
23. TNA, ADM 223/773, Memo on Political Branch of Room 40 by George Young 1914-1918 [Koerver, *German Submarine Warfare*, p. 669.]
24. TNA, HW 3/177, Nigel de Grey's account of how he worked on Zimmerman telegram in Room 40, Jan 1917 [Koerver, *German Submarine Warfare*, p. 340ff.]
25. TNA, HW 7/1 [Koerver, *Room 40*, Vol. 1, p. 195].
26. TNA, HW 7/1, Bethmann Hollweg telegrams [Koerver, *Room 40*, Vol. 1, p. 209ff.].
27. TNA, HW 7/1 [Koerver, *Room 40*, Vol. 1, p. 214.].
28. Erdmann, *Riezler diaries*, December 29th, 1916, p. 389f.
29. Ibid., December 23rd, 1916, p. 387f.
30. Link, *Wilson 1916-1917*, p. 233.
31. Ibid., p. 233.
32. Nebelin, *Ludendorff*, p. 298.
33. Ibid.
34. Görlitz, *The Kaiser and his Court*, December 24th, 1916, p. 225f.
35. Nebelin, *Ludendorff*, p. 298.
36. Ibid., p. 299.
37. Ibid., p. 298f.
38. Erdmann, *Riezler diaries*, December 29th, 1916, p. 389f.
39. Link, *Wilson 1916-1917*, p. 243.
40. BA-MA, RM 5/6467 Folio 36, December 30th, 1916 [Granier, Vol. III, No. 481, p. 467ff.].
41. Seymour, *House-Papers 1915-1917*, p. 412f.

1917 – All-out Uboat Offensive and War with America
Chapter 34: January – Final Decisions

1. Görlitz, *The Kaiser and his Court*, January 6th, 1917, p. 246f.
2. BA-MA, RM 5/992 Folio 70, January 6th, 1917 [Granier, Vol. III, No. 485, p. 474].
3. Görlitz, *The Kaiser and his Court*, January 8th, 1917, p. 229.
4. Erdmann, *Riezler diaries*, January 9th, 1917, p. 393ff.
5. Görlitz, *The Kaiser and his Court*, January 9th, 1917, p. 229f.
6. Schwertfeger, *Valentini*, p. 145f.
7. Görlitz, *The Kaiser and his Court*, January 9th, 1917, p. 230.
8. BA-MA, RM 47/772 Folio 37, January 9th, 1917 [Granier, Vol. III, No. 488, p. 481].
9. Görlitz, *Müller diaries*, January 9th, 1917, p. 248f.
10. Schwertfeger, *Valentini*, p. 146.
11. Ibid.
12. Erdmann, *Riezler diaries*, February 14th, 1917, p. 404f.
13. Ibid., January 10th, 1917, p. 395f.
14. Ibid., January 12th, 1917, p. 397.
15. Ibid., January 17th, 1917, p. 398ff.
16. Ibid., January 25th, 1917, p. 401f.
17. Seymour, *House-Papers 1915-1917*, p. 411f.
18. Link, *Wilson 1916-1917*, p. 261.
19. Ibid., p. 265.
20. Ibid., p. 278f.
21. Ibid., p. 280.
22. Ibid., p. 279.
23. Görlitz, *The Kaiser and his Court*, January 28th, 1917, p. 234f.
24. Ibid., p. 235.
25. TNA, ADM 137/4069, 31/1/1917, p. 26.
26. Görlitz, *Müller diaries*, January 29th, 1917, p. 254.
27. Link, *Wilson 1916-1917*, p. 288.
28. Ibid., p. 288.
29. TNA, ADM 137/4069, 31/1/1917, p. 26.
30. Ibid., 2/2/1917, p. 148.
31. Erdmann, *Riezler diaries*, February 22nd, 1916, p. 334f.
32. Ibid., January 17th, 1917, p. 398ff.
33. Görlitz, *The Kaiser and his Court*, February 15th, 1917, p. 242.
34. Link, *Wilson 1916-1917*, p. 289.
35. Erdmann, *Riezler diaries*, January 13th, 1917, p. 402ff.
36. Link, *Wilson 1916-1917*, p. 290.
37. Ibid., p. 294.
38. Seymour, *House-Papers 1915-1917*, p. 431.
39. Seymour, *House-Papers 1915-1917*, p. 427.

40. Seymour, *House-Papers 1915-1917*, p. 439.
41. Ibid.
42. Link, *Wilson 1916-1917*, p. 294.
43. Ibid., p. 300.
44. Ibid.
45. Ibid., p. 301.
46. Seymour, *House-Papers 1915-1917*, p. 440.
47. Görlitz, *The Kaiser and his Court*, February 4, 1917, p. 239.
48. *Reichstagshauptausschuss*, Volume III, 122nd session, February 21st, 1917, p. 1109.

Chapter 35: February – Prelude

1. Author's calculations based on: TNA, HW 7/1, 2 and 3; Spindler, *Handelskrieg*; Bendert, *UB-* and *UC-Boote*, and TNA, ADM 1/8509/1, ADM 137/3921, 4814, 4817.
2. TNA, HW 7/1 [Koerver, *Room 40*, Vol. 1, p. 222f.].
3. Hill, *Weizsäcker diaries*, February 9th, 1917, p. 233f.
4. TNA, ADM 137/4069, 24/2/1917, p. 29.
5. BA-MA, RM 5/922 Folio 147, February 28th, 1917 [Granier, Vol. III, No. 495, p. 513].
6. Hill, Weizsäcker diaries, February 9th, 1917, p. 233f.
7. KTB U-21, NARA, PG 61539 (BA-MA, RM 97/591), March 3rd, 1917.
8. Author's calculations based on: TNA, HW 7/1, 2 and 3; Spindler, *Handelskrieg*; Bendert, *UB-* and *UC-Boote*, and TNA, ADM 1/8509/1, ADM 137/3921, 4814, 4817.
9. TNA, HW 7/1 [Koerver, *German Submarine Warfare*, p. 168].
10. Erdmann, *Riezler diaries*, February 18th, 1917, p. 405f.
11. TNA, CAB-23-1-51, War Cabinet, February 1st, 1917.
12. TNA, CAB-23-1-53, War Cabinet, February 3rd, 1917.
13. TNA, CAB-23-1-57, War Cabinet, February 8th, 1917.
14. Link, *Wilson 1916-1917*, p. 311, 313.
15. TNA, CAB-23-1-82, War Cabinet, February 28th, 1917.
16. Grigg, *Lloyd George 1916-1918*, p. 31ff.
17. Ibid., p. 45.
18. TNA ADM 116/3421, p. 322-3.
19. TNA, CAB-24-6-40, CAB-24-3-29, War Cabinet, February 21st, 1917.
20. TNA, CAB-23-1-57, War Cabinet, February 8th, 1917.
21. TNA, CAB-24-3-29, War Cabinet, February 14th, 1917.
22. Roger Carlisle, *U.S. Merchant Ships and American Entry into World War I* (Gainesville: University Press of Florida, 2009), p. 77.
23. Ibid.
24. Ibid., p. 75ff.

25. Link, *Wilson 1916-1917*, p. 318ff.

26. Görlitz, *The Kaiser and his Court*, February 8th, 1917, p. 240.

27. Link, *Wilson 1916-1917*, p. 323.

28. Ibid., p. 325.

29. TNA, ADM 137/4069, No. 32, 9/10/1916, p. 10.

30. Carlisle, *American Entry*, p. 81ff.

31. Erdmann, *Riezler diaries*, February 14th, 1917, p. 404f.

32. Ibid., February 18th, 1917, p. 405f.

33. Link, *Wilson 1916-1917*, p. 340ff.

34. Carlisle, *American Entry*, p. 95.

35. Ibid., p. 94ff.

36. Ibid., p. 87.

Chapter 36: March – High Noon

1. Author's calculations based on: TNA, HW 7/1, 2 and 3; Spindler, *Handelskrieg*; Bendert, *UB-* and *UC-Boote*, and TNA, ADM 1/8509/1, ADM 137/3921, 4814, 4817.

2. Hill, *Weizsäcker diaries*, March 10th, 1917, p. 237.

3. Author's calculations based on: TNA, HW 7/1, 2 and 3; Spindler, *Handelskrieg*; Bendert, *UB-* and *UC-Boote*, and TNA, ADM 1/8509/1, ADM 137/3921, 4814, 4817. Weather data: KTB U24, NARA, PG 61551 (BA-MA, RM 97/643), and KTB U-44, NARA, PG 61596 (BA-MA, RM 97/643).

4. Author's calculations based on: TNA, HW 7/1, 2 and 3; Spindler, *Handelskrieg*; Bendert, *UB-* and *UC-Boote*, and TNA, ADM 1/8509/1, ADM 137/3921, 4814, 4817.

5. BA-MA, RM 5/922 Folio 170f., March 13th, 1917 [Granier, Vol. III, No. 510, p. 521].

6. BA-MA, RM 5/922 Folio 179f., April 7th, 1917 [Granier, Vol. III, No. 518, p. 537].

7. Carlisle, *American Entry*, p. 100ff.

8. Ibid., S.128.

9. *Reichstagshauptausschuss*, Volume III, 122nd session, March 3rd, 1917, p. 1149, see also Link, *Wilson 1916-1917*, p. 343.

10. TNA, HW 3/177, Nigel de Grey's account of how he worked on Zimmerman telegram in Room 40, Jan 1917 [Koerver, *German Submarine Warfare*, p. 340ff.]

11. Ibid.

12. Link, *Wilson 1916-1917*, p. 350.

13. Ibid., p. 346.

14. TNA, HW 3/177, [Koerver, *German Submarine Warfare*, p. 342.]

15. Image courtesy of Princeton University Press.

16. Link, *Wilson 1916-1917*, p. 350.

17. *Reichstagshauptausschuss*, Volume III, 122nd session, March 3rd, 1917, p. 1149.

18. Erdmann, *Riezler diaries*, February 21st, 1917, p. 1109f.
19. TNA, HW 7/2, p. 415 [Koerver, *Room 40*, Vol. I, p. 208].
20. Erdmann, *Riezler diaries*, February 28th, 1917, p. 411.
21. Grigg, *Lloyd George 1916-1918*, p. 45ff.
22. Salter, *Shipping Control*, p. 7.
23. Ibid., p. 65.
24. Ernest C Fayle, *Seaborne Trade. Vol. III: The Period of Unrestricted Submarine Warfare* (London: Imperial War Museum, Department of Printed Books, 1924), p. 479.
25. Salter, *Shipping Control*, p. 123ff.
26. Grigg, *Lloyd George 1916-1918*, p. 48.
27. Churchill, *World Crisis*, p. 719.
28. Grigg, *Lloyd George 1916-1918*, p. 50.
29. Ibid., p. 51.
30. Salter, *Shipping Control*, p. 69f.
31. Doeneke, *Nothing less than war*, p. 187.
32. Ibid., p. 45.
33. Link, *Wilson 1916-1917*, p. 379.
34. Ibid., p. 381.
35. Ibid., p. 383.
36. Link, *Wilson 1916-1917*, p. 387.
37. Ibid., p. 388.
38. Ibid., p. 389.
39. Ibid.
40. KTB U-70, NARA, PG 61645 (BA-MA, RM 97/961).
41. Carlisle, *American Entry*, p. 9f., p. 106ff.; KTB U-70, NARA, PG 61645 (BA-MA, RM 97/961), March 16th, 1917.

Chapter 37: April – Mr Wilson Goes to War

1. Link, *Wilson 1916-1917*, p. 415.
2. Ibid., p. 398.
3. Ibid., p. 398f.
4. Ibid., p. 407f.
5. Doeneke, *Nothing less than war*, p. 301.
6. Link, *Wilson 1916-1917*, p. 413.
7. Ibid., p. 423f.
8. Ibid., p. 425.
9. Ibid., p. 425f.
10. Carlisle, *American Entry* at Sea, p. 141ff.
11. Ibid., p. 14f.
12. Grigg, *Lloyd George 1916-1918*, p. 72.
13. Salter, *Shipping Control*, p. 122.

14. Doeneke, *Nothing less than war*, p. 240.
15. Görlitz, *The Kaiser and his Court*, April 6th, 1917, p. 272.
16. Nebelin, *Ludendorff*, p. 316.
17. *Reichstagshauptausschuss*, Volume III, 148th session, April 28th, 1917, p. 1361.
18. Erdmann, *Riezler diaries*, April 13th, 1917, p. 426f.

Chapter 38: The Epochal Year
 1. TNA, HW 7/2, [Koerver, *Room 40*, Vol. 1, p. 174].
 2. *Hauptausschuss*, May 8, 1917, p. 1440.
 3. Salter, *Shipping Control*, p. 7.
 4. Ritschl, *Germany's economy*, p. 41.
 5. Doeneke, *Nothing less than war*, p. 301.
 6. Ibid.
 7. Ibid.
 8. Ibid.
 9. Seymour, *House-Papers 1915-1917*, p. 464f.
10. Ibid., p. 469.
11. Erdmann, *Riezler diaries*, January 12th, 1917, p. 397.
12. Erdmann, *Riezler diaries*, February 22nd, 1916, p. 334f.

Appendix
Chapter 39: History and History Writing
 1. TNA, ADM 116/3421, p. 11. See also Newbolt, *Naval Operations*, Vol. IV, chapter IX, *Unrestricted Submarine Warfare*, p. 323ff.
 2. Churchill, *World Crisis*, p. 736.
 3. Erdmann, *Riezler diaries*, October 6th, 1914, p. 212-13.
 4. Ibid., January 17th, 1917, p. 398ff.
 5. Andreas Michelsen, *Der U-Bootskrieg 1914-1918* (Leipzig: von Hase und Koehler Verlag 1925), p. 17.
 6. Ibid.
 7. Ibid., p. 162.
 8. Ibid., p. 163.
 9. KTB U-20, NARA, PG 61533 (BA-MA, RM 97/577), Folio 8, February 1st, 1915.
10. Spindler, *Handelskrieg*, Vol. I, p. 64.
11. Spindler, *Handelskrieg*, Vol. III, p. 121, UB-13.
12. Bernd Stegemann, *Der U-Bootkrieg im Jahre 1918*, Marine-Rundschau 65, Heft 5, October 1968, p. 333-45.
13. *Frankfurter Allgemeine Zeitung*, May 7th, 2015, article on the 100th anniversary of the sinking, *The Kaiser's Steel Sharks*: 'The *Lusitania* was a Royal Navy's secret auxiliary cruiser and munitions transport. Even as the ship sank, it had munitions on board. The sinking of the '*Lusitania*' was thus in compliance with maritime law.'

Chapter 40: Sources Used

1. NARA, OSS Records RG 226, Box 468, folder 42: Plan to subvert anti-Nazi German generals through Vatican contacts, by Prof. Kurt Riezler, 1943.
2. The most recent work is from 1973(!): Konrad H. Jarausch, *The Enigmatic Chancellor: Bethmann Hollweg and the Hubris of Imperial Germany* (London: Yale University Press, 1973).

Chapter 41: Statistics – My Numbers

1. Gröner, *Kriegsschiffe*.
2. Spindler, *Handelskrieg*.
3. Bendert, *UB-* and *UC-Boote*.
4. TNA, HW 7/3.
5. TNA, ADM 1/8509/1, ADM 137/3921, 4814, and 4817.
6. Author's calculation based on Gröner, *Kriegsschiffe*.
7. Author's calculations based on: TNA, HW 7/1, 2 and 3; Spindler, *Handelskrieg*; Bendert, *UB-* and *UC-Boote*, and TNA, ADM 1/8509/1, ADM 137/3921, 4814, 4817.
8. Author's calculations based on: TNA, HW 7/1, 2 and 3; Spindler, *Handelskrieg*; Bendert, *UB-* and *UC-Boote*, and TNA, ADM 1/8509/1, ADM 137/3921, 4814, 4817.

Bibliography

1. HW 7/1, HW 7/2 and HW 7/3 were published as: Koerver, Hans Joachim (Ed.), *Room 40: German Naval Warfare 1914-1918*, 2 Vols.

Index